CW00921317

The Life of the Longhouse
An Archaeology of Ethnicity

For two centuries, travellers were amazed at the massive buildings found along the rivers that flow from the mountainous interior of Borneo. They concentrated hundreds of people under one roof, in the middle of empty rainforests. There was no practical necessity for this arrangement, and it remains a mystery. Peter Metcalf provides an answer by showing the historical context, using both oral histories and colonial records. The key factor was a premodern trading system that funnelled rare and exotic jungle products to China via the ancient coastal city of Brunei. Meanwhile, the elite manufactured goods traded upriver shaped the political and religious institutions of longhouse society. However, the apparent permanence of longhouses was an illusion. In historical terms, longhouse communities were both mobile and labile, and the patterns of ethnicity they created more closely resemble the contemporary world than any stereotype of "tribal" societies.

Peter Metcalf is Professor of Anthropology at the University of Virginia. His research in Borneo spans thirty years, and he is the author of many books and articles.

The Life of the Longhouse

An Archaeology of Ethnicity

Peter Metcalf
University of Virginia

CAMBRIDGE
UNIVERSITY PRESS

CAMBRIDGE UNIVERSITY PRESS

Cambridge, New York, Melbourne, Madrid, Cape Town, Singapore,
São Paulo, Delhi, Dubai, Tokyo

Cambridge University Press
32 Avenue of the Americas, New York, NY 10013-2473, USA

www.cambridge.org
Information on this title: www.cambridge.org/9780521110983

© Peter Metcalf 2010

This publication is in copyright. Subject to statutory exception
and to the provisions of relevant collective licensing agreements,
no reproduction of any part may take place without the written
permission of Cambridge University Press.

First published 2010

Printed in the United States of America

A catalog record for this publication is available from the British Library.

Library of Congress Cataloging in Publication data

Metcalf, Peter.
The life of the longhouse : an archaeology of ethnicity / Peter Metcalf.
p.   cm.
ISBN 978-0-521-11098-3 (hbk.)
1. Borneo – Social life and customs.   2. Borneo – Antiquities.   3. Longhouses –
Borneo – History.   4. Ethnicity – Borneo – History.   5. Community life – Borneo –
History.   6. Borneo – Politics and government.   7. Borneo – Commerce – Social
aspects – History.   8. Borneo – Commerce – China.   9. China – Commerce – Borneo.
10. Brunei – Commerce – History.   I. Title.
DS646.3.M47   2010
305.89009598'3–dc22   2009037297

ISBN   978-0-521-11098-3 Hardback

Cambridge University Press has no responsibility for the persistence or
accuracy of URLs for external or third-party Internet Web sites referred to in
this publication and does not guarantee that any content on such Web sites is,
or will remain, accurate or appropriate.

There where your Indies have sprinkled their tribes
like ocean rains . . .

Allen Curnow,
Landfall in Unknown Seas

Contents

Contents

Contents

Figures

The Problem: Ethnicity
and Community

In the nineteenth and twentieth centuries, no one travelled along the fast-flowing rivers that snake toward the mountainous centre of Borneo without remarking on the stupendous buildings that were to be found along their banks. They were massive structures, accommodating hundreds of residents under one high-pitched roof, their floors raised well above ground level on sturdy pilings, their roomy interiors shady and inviting after the tropical brightness outside. To travel at all in the region was to travel between longhouses, and every arrival was a surprise. After hours of seeing nothing along the riverbanks but mangroves and palms and behind them the great trees of the rainforest, the first indication was a clump of canoes drawn up around an impromptu dock made of floating logs. On the bank above was a screen of fruit trees, and behind that the looming bulk of the longhouse. From apparently empty forest, the visitor was abruptly immersed in the social density of a city.

Why Longhouses?

No simple feature of ecology or geography requires this peculiar mode of residence. In other parts of Southeast Asia, populations with similar forest environments and technologies of swidden agriculture live dispersed more evenly across the terrain. Throughout large areas of the Philippines and

1

Indonesia, relatively insubstantial single-family houses are typically sited in small clusters directly adjacent to current farm sites. Indeed, there are obvious advantages to this arrangement, as compared to travelling back and forth between longhouses and jungle farms that have to be cleared anew every year. Even within Borneo, many people do not build longhouses, and evidently do perfectly well without them. So why do people in central Borneo live in longhouses? It is a perfectly reasonable question, but it will come as no surprise that ethnography has produced no direct answer. If you were to ask the longhouse residents, they would simply say that there was no other civilized way to live. I sympathise with their response, but it will not satisfy those who have never tried it. Consequently, my goal is to put longhouse communities in a broader context, using both ethnographic and historical data, and examining in turn the key issues of leadership, trade, and ritual.

The Larger Question

Despite their impressive size, however, longhouses are not as permanent as they appear. On the contrary, viewed over the century and a half for which we have historical records, and the longer period covered by oral history, they are amazingly volatile. This, too, requires explanation, but the point for now is that there is no neat fit between longhouse communities and "tribes." Elements of any one ethnic population are never neatly bounded. Instead, there are some here, some there, scattered among peoples of other ethnicities. Moreover, multiple ethnicities are represented even *within* longhouse communities, so that any discussion of community invariably becomes entangled in the complexities of ethnicity. Consequently, I am drawn into an issue that goes well beyond the shores of Borneo, one that bears on the whole practice of anthropology in the post-everything era.

The issue is this: most details reported in ethnographies are things characteristic of particular cultures or societies. How could it be otherwise? Is that not the whole *raison d'être* of ethnography, of "writing ethnicity"? Yet, we have become suspicious of all ethnic labels, seeing in them a reification of something invoked but unreal, without definite form or boundaries. It would be as if biologists suddenly discovered that any and all creatures could cross-breed without regard to species. Where then would be comparative zoology? The amazing achievements of generations of natural scientists in expanding and correcting the Linnean classification, a task still far from complete, would be reduced to nothing.

This is not going to happen, of course. Nor would it be reasonable to equate such an unthinkable crisis in the modern worldview with a mere change of fashion in what were once called the "social sciences" – a phrase that no longer carries any conviction. Nevertheless, the scepticism that now surrounds the notion of "a culture," if taken seriously, must surely bring the enterprise of ethnography to a halt. So pervasive is the critique that it would be laborious to enumerate even its major sources. As a summary of it, however, Robert Brightman's (1995) article, "Forget Culture: Replacement, Transcendence, Relexification," serves well to identify its main thrust. Fundamentally, we know that the world is not paved with neatly bounded cultures that we can set about describing in orderly fashion, one after another. Meanwhile, what is true of cultures is, *a fortiori*, true of ethnicities. This assertion has now become a platitude, and it amazes me to find that, having announced it, most of my colleagues then simply carry on as usual (Brumann 1999). This book is an attempt to confront the issue in one particular corner of the globe.

Sometimes the cultural indeterminacy that we see around us is taken to be a modern phenomenon, a recent product of the ever-increasing mobility of people and ideas in the contemporary world. Arjun Appadurai argues that each person is now the locus of intersection of global cultural influences in technology, economics, the media, and ideology, all pulling in different directions, so that our worlds are, in his term, "disjunct" (Appadurai 1990). In my view, this leads to a kind of revised transactionalism (Metcalf 2001a), but for present purposes I want to emphasize that Central Borneo is a region that has manifested this quality of disjuncture for centuries, as the communal histories recounted below amply demonstrate. Moreover, it is clear that previous generations of ethnographers found the same problem elsewhere. I am told by those who knew him that Meyer Fortes, for one, understood only too well that his characterisations of Talle culture were always partial and provisional. His reaction was to drive his colleagues insane by constantly hedging every statement he made with caveats and exceptions (Metcalf 2002a:96–7). He described the Talle – the name his informants gave for themselves – as a "congeries" of tribes. The root meaning of the term is "heap." Just so, we are dealing with heaps of tribes. Why this issue did not bring mid-twentieth-century ethnography to a grinding halt is not clear. Putting it charitably, there was a clear job to carry out, and quibbles would have to be left for later. The most pressing intellectual need of ethnographers in mid-century was to drive home the reality of cultural difference, of the vast array of possible ways there were for humans to live their lives (Sahlins 1998). One must concede that they succeeded brilliantly in making their point, and that some form of cultural relativism is now virtually inescapable for anyone who is reasonably well read. In the process, however, the issues that are now most pressing were swept under the rug. The dangers of reification were not adequately confronted, and that lapse left anthropology vulnerable to deconstructive criticism.

My response to this dilemma is radical but not nihilist. It is not to jettison the concept of ethnicity, but to de-essentialize it. In other words, the goal is to treat ethnicity as itself a cultural construct – and, indeed, one that is key to understanding longhouse communities. I offer a "cultural account" of ethnicity in Borneo in the same manner as David Schneider (1968) in *A Cultural Account of American Kinship*. The crucially relativist character of that account is made clear in the postscript to the second edition, where Schneider (1980:121) displays his irritation at a junior colleague who had tried to generalize (i.e., make widely applicable, or even universal) the "core symbols" that Schneider had found in American kinship, such as "blood" and "love." The whole point was that those core symbols were *not* universal; instead, they were part of system of meaning that was characteristically and peculiarly American.

In the same way, I turn my back on such hopeless questions as how many tribes there are in Borneo, or worse yet, what ethnicity might be, essentially and universally. Instead, I show how ethnicity appeared in the thoughts and actions of longhouse-dwelling people, and how it was constituted by, and constitutive of, their communities. How ethnicity appears elsewhere requires other studies by other authors.

Rehabilitating Ethnology

What this amounts to is the reinvention of the moribund discipline of ethnology to serve the needs of contemporary ethnography. There is a certain perversity in this proposition, I realize. The term "ethnology" has for long had a musty air about it, something left over from the nineteenth century, evoking only museum collections. In the twenty-first century, when so much of what seemed secure even a couple of decades ago is now questionable, surely ethnology is doubly dead.

Anthropology is, however, remarkably parsimonious with its concepts. Nothing ever seems to be finally thrown away, like the proverbial attic in Maine containing a box marked "string too short to save." When, for example, Claude Levi-Strauss began writing about totemism in the 1960s, the subject had become a minor curiosity relegated to courses on intellectual history. He dusted off the Australian material that had intrigued Durkheim at the turn of the twentieth century and found a new use for it – a very proper piece of intellectual bricolage. Totemism is central to *The Savage Mind* (Levi-Strauss 1962), a book that had enormous influence within anthropology and beyond. Such a spectacular precedent might set anyone looking for obsolete terms to rehabilitate, but it is one thing to find them and quite another to find a way to recycle them. Meanwhile, ethnology has exactly the character of leftover bits of string, wrappings from boxes whose contents are now forgotten. Is there really any way to save it?

Levi-Strauss was clearly drawn to the anthropology of an earlier age. As has often been remarked, his *The Elementary Structures of Kinship* (Levi-Strauss 1969) looks more like Lewis Henry Morgan's (1870) *Systems of Consanguinity and Affinity of the Human Family* than ethnographic studies such as Meyer Fortes' (1949) *The Web of Kinship among the Tallensi*. Clearly, what appealed to Levi-Strauss about late-nineteenth-century anthropology was its grand sweep. When the discipline was in its infancy, it captured the public imagination in a way that it has never done since. Its objective was nothing less than the discovery of the whole history of mankind: the evolution of technology, society, and religion; the rise of civilisations old and new; and the diffusion of people and culture across all the continents. It is the last item on the list that gave rise to the new science of ethnology, which immediately took on a taxonomic function. Despite all that happened in anthropology in the succeeding century, it is the original definition of ethnology that persists in the authoritative *Oxford English Dictionary*: "the science of human races and their relations to one another and their characteristics" (1984:425). "Races" were to be classified to reveal the different branches of the human family tree, from which could be deduced the routes involved in "the peopling of the world."

It is difficult now to recover the excitement generated by so ambitious a program, but those of us who are teachers have seen it often enough in the eyes of undergraduates new to anthropology. Perversely, it is then our job to extinguish their enthusiasm by reciting a familiar list of charges: racism, ethnocentrism, faulty logic, and so on. It is hard not to sound begrudging. The trick is to separate the issues from the methods. The intuitively reasonable premise that what is most simple in human cultures is also most ancient does not fit the known facts. Consequently the celebrated Comparative Method cannot be relied on. Similarly, trying to distinguish "races" by measuring bodily features of people all over the world produced, in the end, results that were totally garbled and open to as many interpretations as there were experts. Nor is it possible to argue that the advent of computers would now make the project feasible. It would remain a question of "garbage in, garbage out." Just why this great scientific project was so complete a failure is an interesting question, one that has many lessons to teach students of the history of science, but that is not the issue here. The point is that ethnology as conceived in the late nineteenth century was unmistakably dead by the mid-twentieth century.

After its early heyday, ethnology persisted only in a weakened form. When the term was used, and that rarely, it signified loosely the overarching project of which ethnographies were the particular manifestation. In effect, ethnology had become "the science of human *cultures* and their relations to one another and their characteristics."

The project of reconstructing "the peopling of the world" led an even more shadowy existence. There were still those interested in the diffusion of culture traits and the reconstruction of prehistoric contacts or migrations, but the time depth involved was shorter. There could obviously be no grand reconstruction of the branches of mankind because the traits in question were, by definition, impermanent – that is, subject to cultural change. There was still room, however, for interesting speculation and discoveries. For example, the spread of Southeast Asian cultigens to Africa clearly was an important factor enabling the expansion of Bantu people through the tropical rainforest belt and into the vast savannahs to the south (Wolf 1982:41–2). Moreover, specialists in different regions of the globe continued to trade information among themselves, despite the unfashionability of ethnology as a subdiscipline. In the bars of convention hotels, they could be heard asking questions in the form: "I've heard that there are some X people living over at Y. You ever been up that way?" Ethnology took on a hobbyist quality, demoted from journal articles to gossip. There is often a guilty air about these insider conversations, as if every valuable snippet of information was implicitly preceded by some disclaimer: "I don't really believe in all this, but." What could account for the contrast between professional invisibility and lively discourse? My answer is that ethnicity is the last of our standard technical terms still understood in essentialist terms. Moreover, that is a survival, if I may use the word, of the discredited assumptions of nineteenth-century anthropology.

The Process of De-Essentializing

The process of de-essentializing basic concepts has not been painless. Think, for instance, of the traumas inflicted on the study of kinship during the past few decades. There was a time, not so long ago, when it seemed obvious that kinship studies provided the bedrock of anthropology. Kinship theory appealed comfortingly to a universal logic; after all, everyone surely had a mother and a father. Moreover, it was clear that stateless societies were run predominantly according to kinship principles, and even the

6

institutions of kingship were only superimposed on those of localized clans and lineages. Finally, ethnographers were able to demonstrate an amazing variety of kinship systems that could be analysed in terms of a few basic principles, so showing how diversity arose out of a common human nature. Most gratifyingly, kinship studies generated a vast elaboration of jargon, a specialised knowledge that justified the very existence of the discipline. To become an anthropologist was primarily to master the use of that technical language. This cheerful professional self-confidence was undermined by dissident voices in the 1960s and collapsed entirely in the 1970s, when two of the foremost exponents of kinship studies, one in England and the other in the United States, announced that all of this theorizing was faulty and required radical revision (Needham 1974; Schneider 1977). Kinship studies were increasingly marginalised in anthropology curricula. Empty at its very centre, it seemed as if anthropology would fall apart. This was not, of course, what was intended by Needham and Schneider. What they had argued for was the abandonment of an essentialized understanding of kinship as something directly consequent on biology, and therefore universal.

Religion, conceived of as a universal human attribute, underwent a similar process, although with less trauma. Most ethnographers of comparative religion are by now resigned to the fact that there is no watertight definition of either religion or ritual. For many theologians, it is still shocking to discover that the Manus Islanders, for example, lack all notion of gods, creators, or an afterlife. As Reo Fortune (1935) describes it, the Manus look forward to nothing more than becoming sea slugs, thousands of which litter the floor of the lagoon over which their houses are built. For those of a missionary bent, it would be easy to say that the Manus simply have no religion. The ethnographer, however, notices something else. Not only do the Manus have a clear code of morality, but a strict one at that. Are not morals something we expect to find tangled up somehow with religion? Adding morality to the list of defining features is not going to help, however. What is really going on in such a process of definition is not isolating a category of human experience, but framing a theory of it. To say that religion consists of belief in gods is a shorthand way of arguing that almost all humans – with maybe a few appallingly primitive exceptions – inherently have a belief in gods or, better, a God. This is the kind of argument that appealed to Thomas Aquinas.

Only one approach to defining religion shows a way out of this dilemma, and paradoxically, it is provided by that arch-definer, Emile Durkheim. A religion, he says, is a "system of beliefs and practices relative to sacred things" (Durkheim 1965 [1912]:62). He declined, however, to define "the sacred," insisting that it was so varied that one could not know in advance what it might be from one place to another. It might be an idol or a *churinga*, but it could as easily be something immaterial, like a myth. Instead of a list of possible sacred things, Durkheim offers us a test for locating the sacred wherever we happen to be. Look out he says for "negative rituals," those signs of dread and awe that invariably surround the sacred. Durkheim's test is not always easy to apply, but it has this huge virtue: instead of telling us what religion is in advance, it tells us to go and search for what there might be out there that connotes religion. In this way, Durkheim shifts the emphasis from essentialism to nominalism. The question is not whether certain people have a religion or not, but what sorts of things are going on in various parts of the world that are religion-like, or remind us of religious things elsewhere. It is an invitation to explore. If we discover a place where religions are radically different from anything described previously, so much the better. We might call this an open door policy to religion.

De-Essentializing Ethnicity

How then might we manage an open door policy to ethnicity? The hesitation that we have comes from the fact that ethnicities have provided our units of study. If we lose our grip on that essential category, do we not undermine the validity of all ethnography, past, present, and future? In his influential study of Quebecois nationalism, Richard Handler (1988) grasps the nettle. Instead of writing as others did before him about what constitutes the uniqueness of the Quebecois people in terms of cultural contribution and historical experience, he shifts the view to how Quebecois themselves go about constructing this uniqueness, that is, how they tell it to themselves, remind themselves periodically about it, and seek to propagate it among their fellow Quebecois. It turns out that there is a lot of this activity in Quebec, providing rich material for Handler's account. Even car license plates bear the motto "Je Me Souviens." As an ethnographer, he is agnostic about the existence of Quebecois national culture – he is neither for it nor against it – instead, he defines his job as finding out how it is structured as a discourse. He shifts his view, as it were, through 90 degrees. Instead of looking at the grand façade of Quebecois nationalism, he looks at it from the side, to see what is propping it up.

Nationalism is not synonymous with ethnicity, so applying Handler's approach to central Borneo requires some readjustment. In the longhouse communities I studied in the mid-1970s, there was no such cultural self-awareness as one finds everywhere in Europe. All the intellectual apparatus that Handler describes as characteristic of Western notions of national identity, and the struggle to preserve it, were absent. There were no "nationalist" activists warning against the loss of identity and the risks of cultural pollution. This is not to argue that longhouse people were incapable of chauvinism – on the contrary – but it was not expressed in terms that we would recognize as nationalistic. It had a different quality about it, which it is my task to convey.

The crucial point is that deconstructing either nationalism or ethnicity – a mission for which contemporary anthropology is well equipped – does not imply that we will stop talking about nationalisms and ethnicities, as if they had suddenly ceased to exist. On the contrary, our job is to track them down in all their exotic manifestations, just as we have done with religions. As a general description of what this involves, Handler borrows from Bernhard Cohn the term "cultural objectification," and that is the focus of Section V. My argument is that cultural objectification in central Borneo is accomplished primarily through ritual. It does not follow, however, that ritual is the glue that holds longhouse communities together, as in the classic Durkheimian model of solidarity. For one thing, longhouse communities do *not* stay glued together; their histories are full of rivalry, collapse, and dispersion. Ritual consequently plays an ambiguous role, providing a mode of subversion as often as a tool of control. In making this argument, the model I develop is adapted from Levi-Strauss' "totemic operator."

The Reality of Communities in Borneo

Having de-essentialized ethnicity, it would be foolish to reify the even more slippery term "community." We are all accustomed to the politicians' invocation of the word to imply a cosy integration, a uniformity of opinion and culture that they claim either to represent or are to be in touch with. If a politician in a major American city begins talking about the "Hispanic community" or the "African American community," we know he or she is imminently about to engage in ideological conjuring tricks and fakery. Used in an ethnographic context – the "Nuer community?" – it would be hard to know what was implied.

Nevertheless, I use the term frequently because I can offer a specific definition of what I mean in reference to central Borneo, namely, the inhabitants of those impressive buildings with which I began. Longhouse communities not only had a concrete existence, they were also separated by miles of jungle from their nearest neighbours. This is not to suggest that there have not always been connections between longhouses involving transfers of people and goods – on the contrary, we see how important they were in Chapter 7, Moreover, there are a two caveats. First, residents are often away from the longhouse at their farms, perhaps for extended periods, so that the house has an abandoned air. Second, longhouses have to be rebuilt, often at new sites, and meanwhile, people are housed in shacks. Both conditions are temporary, however. It remains true that, until recently everyone in central Borneo belonged to one longhouse community or another, and their lives revolved primarily around those communities. Other places and communities were alien.

That technical and locally specific definition of community means that I can not use the term in any other sense, nor am I tempted to. Prior to the colonial era, longhouse communities were sovereign polities. There were no larger tribal or ethnic "communities" in anything like the same sense. Consequently, when I speak of communities, I mean longhouse communities and nothing else.

Ethnicity Is an Object of Research, Not a Preliminary to Research

If ethnology is to be rehabilitated and ethnicities are to be held up for inspection rather than taken for granted, it follows that we must get down to details. The problem in central Borneo is that there are literally hundreds of ethnic labels. Moreover, each has a contrastive quality, having relevance only in regard to other labels. There is nothing in this of Levi-Strauss' "structure" – no orderly arrangement of parts, let alone predictable "transformations" (1966:279). The reality is far messier and far more historically contingent. In the following pages, I am guilty of retailing, not just one ethnic label, but dozens. Everyone who talks about central Borneo does the same – it is that kind of place. This can easily take on an air of positive obfuscation. Worldwide, there are no more than a handful of Borneanists who would recognise most of these labels, and there are some that have never before appeared in print. True, a certain tolerance for ethnic labels is part of the *metier*. Who could imagine a properly trained graduate student who did not know the difference between the Nuer and the Dinka, for instance, and of how many people outside the discipline could the same be said? The tangles of ethnology in central Borneo, however, would strain the patience of a saint.

This complexity has had the effect of stalling theoretical discussions before they started. That is to say, the provision of an adequate ethnic taxonomy seemed a logical and necessary first step, and nothing could be done until we had a firm grip on who lived where. That this was true of colonial administrators is no surprise, since postcolonial theory has taught us that sorting people into groups is a technique of control. Oscar Salemink (1991:248) quotes the maxim of a French officer in Vietnam: "Name your tribes, and you are half way to controlling them." By this standard, administrators in Borneo performed poorly, seeming never to finish finding new labels and juggling them about endlessly. But it was also true of professional anthropologists. When they arrived on the scene, they cheerfully continued with the same project and found it as challenging as the amateurs had done. The quest became an obsession, obscuring everything else. The ethnography of Borneo unfortunately provides an apt example of what recent critics of the concept of culture have found most claustrophobic about anthropology.

Consequently, the challenges of writing ethnography are particularly sharp in the case of Borneo. They call for an equally drastic solution. Specifically, my tactic is to turn the proposition that has so impeded Borneo ethnography on its head: *ethnicity is not a preliminary of our research, but a goal.* Instead of assigning or arguing about labels, we have to begin with what they mean to those who use them. This is an empirical task; there is no avoiding the details.

Ethnicity and Community

What it is *not* an option is to simply discount ethnicity in central Borneo. It is pervasive, it inflects everything. When travel writers and administrators lumped together all the people of the interior as "Dayaks," they hid a great range of cultural diversity. If these authors do not specify the exact location where they saw or were told about something, their observations are mostly useless. Worse, they miss a major dynamic in peoples' lives.

Not to keep any rabbits up my sleeve, I state simply at the outset my major finding concerning ethnicity and community: longhouse communities are the sites of production of cultural differentiation. Without the institution of the longhouse, ethnicity in central Borneo would be something other than it is. Consequently, ethnicity and community are two sides of the same coin, so that neither can be understood without the other. In this way, the two research questions that I outlined at the beginning turn out to be the same question.

"Ethnographic Riches" versus "Need to Know"

As it happened, my initial fieldwork was based in a community with particularly complex ethnic affiliations. There were at Long Teru no less than eight different labels that residents would produce in different contexts when asked to identify themselves. Moreover, none of these were intended to deceive – they were just trying to be helpful. But every community can offer at least three names, and have done so routinely over the years, to try to get outsiders (missionaries, government officers) to understand. But instead of pausing to consider what kinds of information different labels were intended to convey vis-à-vis other labels, most outsiders focussed on finding out which was the "right" one.

Over the twenty-seven months of my first fieldwork in the mid-1970s, and in subsequent visits totalling nearly four years, I have visited about two-thirds of the longhouses spread out over the watershed of the Baram River, comprising more than sixty communities (listed in the Appendix). At each one, I wrote down ethnonyms (i.e., names people gave to describe their own ethnic affiliation) and tried to work out what they implied. Invariably, this meant long narratives about past communities. Moreover, narratives were not shared by everyone in the community, so that the process needed to be repeated or amended several times. In addition, I have pored over colonial archives and missionary records in London and Leiden, and in the Malaysian state of Sarawak, which includes the Baram watershed. The result is what is often referred to, with heavy irony, as ethnographic riches. In writing this book, my first task was to sort through a trunk full of assorted notes and photocopied material, some now beginning to fade. Then I needed to start writing as quickly as possible in order to bring the material together usefully before the details went out of my head again. I was also prompted by the thought that if I did not do this soon, I never would.

I can hardly expect the same effort of memory from my reader. Consequently, I have adopted a few strategies to keep my argument moving forward. The first is to focus on cases that demonstrate the point I am trying to make, and for which I have historical records with which to calibrate and augment indigenous oral history. One extended narrative, in particular, runs through Sections I and II. The ins and outs of that story are complicated enough, but it is I hope possible to follows the main actors – individuals and communities – throughout. Inevitably, I will be accused of picking atypical cases, to which I respond in advance that there is no such thing as a "typical" longhouse community, and to imply that there was would be the worst possible ethnic reification. For the same reason, there can be no question of "sampling." On the contrary, I have purposely chosen examples that neatly demonstrate processes that are nevertheless pervasive throughout the region. The region's history is indeed dramatic, and I have no intention of making it dull. As to how the processes that I describe apply elsewhere in Borneo, that is for others to decide, applying their own regional expertise. I believe that there is some general validity in them, and the best thing that can happen is for my account to stimulate further discussion.

My second strategy to aid the reader is to apply a strict criterion of "need to know." That is, the details that are provided are directly relevant to the argument. It would be absurd to proceed without naming communities and ethnicities, even without the disservice that would do to the ethnographic record, but I will not pull labels out of a hat that were last mentioned many pages prior. There are only a few that are mentioned throughout the book, and they should quickly become familiar.

Histories, Narratives, and Archives

One of the professional anthropologists who tried his hand at sorting out ethnicities in Borneo was Edmund Leach. After World War II, when a portion of the island came for the first time under direct British rule, the newly installed colonial government decided it needed the help of anthropologists in planning the reconstruction of the war-ravaged country. Leach was asked to tour Sarawak and design a program of research aimed at understanding indigenous social and economic systems. Given the developmental goals, it is not surprising that the projects he recommended focussed on the largest populations (Leach 1950). They resulted in several classic ethnographies: Derek Freeman (1970 [1953]) worked with the Iban, swidden agriculturalists found across much of the central part of the state; Stephen Morris (1991 [1953]) with the Melanau, a people of the central coastline, now mostly Moslems; William Geddes (1957) with the Bidayuh, swidden agriculturalists concentrated in the southwest; and Tien (1953) with the Chinese, who mostly immigrated during the nineteenth century and are concentrated in the towns.

Leach makes it clear, however, that he was more interested in the small, dispersed communities in the mountainous northeastern corner of Sarawak. Perhaps they reminded him of his research with the Kachin of Burma, and indeed, it is not hard to see them as part of that great sweep of "hill peoples" found across Southeast Asia. The connection is seldom made because the indigenous languages of Borneo belong to the Austronesian family, whereas those of the Kachin hills are Tibeto-Burman. Consequently, the two regions are partitioned between different culture areas, and this has obscured many interesting points of comparison. For my purposes, the most important is their location adjacent to the ancient trading routes converging on China, and it is pursued in Chapter 7.

Leach's *Political Systems of Highland Burma* is one of a handful of ethnographies that seem never to be outdated, whatever theoretical fashions come and go. Consequently, I have every reason to pay close attention to it as a comparative case. Moreover, Leach was confronted just as I am with "ethnographic riches" in the form of endless details of cultural variation. Each village (*kahtawng*) or village cluster (*mare*) had its own narrative of original settlers, their descendents, and later immigrants. By way of illustration, Leach describes in detail the community of "Hpalang" (a pseudonym), comprising some one hundred and thirty homesteads strung out irregularly along a mountain ridge. It requires nearly forty pages to do so because the community narrative was hotly contested. What was at stake is soon made clear: social standing within the accepted rules of the hierarchical (*gumsa*) forms of Kachin society.

Hpalang provides Leach's case study because, as he says, it was the community he knew best. No doubt he collected similar oral histories elsewhere, but he gives no details, having famously lost his field notes "as a result of enemy action" (Leach 1964:312) during the war with Japan. It has often been suggested that the clarity of Leach's account was a result of having no data beyond what he could remember without his notes. That lack, it is argued, allowed the underlying social processes to stand out clearly, uncluttered by distracting details. I have no such resort. For better or worse, I still have my field notes, so I must struggle that much harder to make my account clear.

The advantage of lost field notes is overstated, however. It discounts the mass of information available to him from archival research. As Leach describes it, "I made a very thorough study of government records and other publications relating to the area, mainly from sources preserved in the India Office library" (Leach 1964:312; Burma was administered during the colonial period as part of British India). Indeed, this data ranged far wider than Leach's personal experiences of Kachin village life could possibly have done, providing him not only with a regional perspective, but also a historical one as well. Leach was decidedly not in the position of studying a "people without history," in Eric Wolf's (1982) famous phrase, as other ethnographers of the epoch imagined themselves to be.

The Archaeology of Ethnicity

The result is a pervasive historicity, in which local narratives of communal origins are integrated with archival materials accumulated over many decades. Here, again, Leach provides me with a model because longhouse communities are narrated in the same way as was Hpalang, and I also had access to extensive colonial archives. Indeed, the colonial records of northern Sarawak begin even before the area was annexed, for reasons explained in Chapter 4. This gives me the advantage of data about social conditions upriver, particularly warfare and slavery, from before colonial "pacification." The crucial source is the *Sarawak Gazette*, a charmingly eccentric publication that changed its format several times over the years. My citations of the *Gazette* mirror changing fashions. For the most part, I provide the number of the issue, and the year of publication. For more details see page 96.

My goals, however, are not those of a historian, nor do I plan to engage the ongoing debate on the cultural construction of the past (Dening 1988; McDonald 1996; Roseberry 1991; Troulliot 1995). Instead, the objective is to see longhouse communities, not as static "institutions" in the manner of structural-functionalism, but as dynamic responses to changing geopolitical circumstances. These circumstances include the existence of an ancient trading network, a coastal state drawing on Islamic roots, and two different colonial regimes. Since, by my hypothesis, each longhouse community was a potential site of production of ethnic differentiation, it follows that I am also unravelling how ethnicities come into being and fade into irrelevance. We might call this an archaeology of ethnicity in central Borneo.

The Political Systems of Highland Borneo

Leach begins *Highland Burma* with what now seems like a breathtakingly daring move: he decides simply to ignore cultural variation. Faced with an inconveniently messy situation, similar to that in central Borneo, he sidesteps it and proceeds directly to the sociological issues that interest him. The second paragraph of his book states succinctly: "The population with which we are concerned is that which occupies the area marked KACHIN on Figure Int–01. This population speaks a number of different languages and dialects and there are wide differences of culture between one part of the area and another. Nevertheless, it is usual to refer to the whole of this population under the two heads Shan and Kachin. In this book I shall refer to the whole region as the *Kachin Hills Area*" (Leach 1964[1954]:1, capital letters in original).

Imitating Leach, the population with which I am concerned occupies the area marked ORANG ULU on Figure Int–01, comprising communities that vary widely in language and culture. I refer to the whole region as the hinterland of Brunei.

The population of the hinterland has fluctuated over the past 150 years. To give some idea of scale, however, in 1973 there were fifty-six longhouses in the Baram watershed, housing about 16,000 people. (For details, see Chapter 14 and the Appendix.) As for the city of Brunei itself, it was once the centre of a trading empire whose influence reached from the southern Philippines to the Malay Peninsula. Its prestige was at its height when Magellan visited in 1521, so the earliest Portuguese referred to the whole

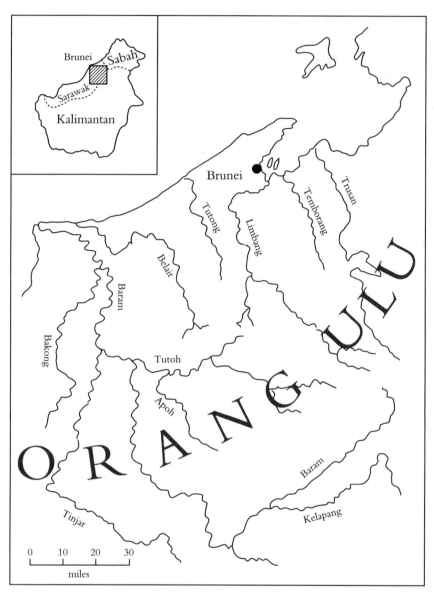

Figure Int–01. Brunei and its hinterland.

vast island – larger than either France or Texas – by the name of the city. This label persists in the corrupt form "Borneo" (Hall 1981:269), but is rejected by Indonesian geographers who have substituted the name Kalimantan. This causes no confusion here, however, because the immediate hinterland of Brunei is what English colonists called "Borneo proper."

Shan Is to Kachin as Malay Is to Orang Ulu

As for the "usual" distinction made between Shan and Kachin in the Kachin Hills Area, it is neatly matched by the similarly conventional contrast between Malays and Orang Ulu in the hinterland of Brunei. The category Malay resembles Shan in that it designates people hierarchically organised in small states that gained much of their power from control of international trade, and participated in a major world religion (Buddhism for the Shan, Islam for the Malays). Meanwhile, the Kachin "occupy the hills where they cultivate rice by the slash and burn techniques of shifting cultivation. The literature throughout the past century has almost always treated these Kachin as if they were primitive and warlike savages, so far removed from the Shans in appearance, language and general culture that they must be regarded as of quite different racial origins" (Leach 1964:1). The same is true if the labels Orang Ulu and Malay are substituted for Kachin and Shan.

In the following pages, Leach neatly deconstructs this hoary distinction, using the example of an informant whose family had been for several generations both Shan and Kachin. Again following Leach, I could easily repeat the demonstration for the Brunei hinterland. In fact, the majority of people classified as Malays are not descendents of immigrants from the Malay Peninsula, but simply of local converts to Islam. Even the Sultan of Brunei himself claims descent from indigenous heroes who founded the state prior to the arrival of Islam. Transgressing the distinction in the opposite direction, leaders of longhouse communities have for centuries accepted or assumed Malay titles such as Orang Kaya and Temonggong, and boasted of important Malay family connections. Nor would they hesitate to give themselves the air and graces of Malay aristocrats to impress their neighbours, all the while voicing deep resentment at Malay assertions of hegemony. In short, whatever borders existed between Malay and Orang Ulu worlds were extremely permeable and subject to constant renegotiation.

The artificial tidiness of the Shan/Kachin distinction also serves to homogenize the latter, and Leach's next move is to attack that tendency:

> The problem, however, is not simply one of sorting out Kachins from Shans; there is also the difficulty of sorting out Kachins from one another. The literature discriminates between several varieties of Kachin. Some of these sub-categories are primarily linguistic, as when Jinghpaw-speaking Kachins are distinguished from Atsi, Maru, Lisu, Nung, etc.; others are mainly territorial, as when the Assam Singpho are distinguished from the Burma Kachin, or the Hkahku of the Upper Mali Hka area (Triangle) from the Gauri, East of Bhamo. But the general tendency has been to minimise the significance of these distinctions and to argue that the essentials of Kachin culture are uniform throughout the Kachin Hills Area. Books with titles

such as *The Kachin Tribes of Burma; The Kachins, Their Religion and Mythology; The Kachins, Their Customs and Traditions; Beitrag zur Ethnologie der Chingpaw (Kachin) von Ober-Burma* refer by implication to all the Kachins wherever they may be found, that is to a population of some 300,000 persons thinly spread over an area of some 50,000 square miles. (1964:3)

In the ethnographic literature on Borneo, there is the same tendency to lump together all kinds of interior populations. Books such as *The Pagan Tribes of Borneo, The Natives of Sarawak and British North Borneo,* and *Over der Geneeskunde der Kenja-Dayak in Central Borneo* have uncertain coverage, potentially expanding to hundreds of thousands of people throughout the island. The catch-all label "Dayak" has the same indeterminacy.

One Society Integrating Many Cultures

Having pointed out the dangers of homogenizing the Kachin, Leach makes no effort to "sort out the Kachin from one another." Instead, he shifts topics: "It is not part of my immediate problem to consider how far such generalisations about the uniformity of Kachin culture are in fact justifiable; my interest lies rather in the problem of how far it can be maintained that a single type of social structure prevails throughout the Kachin area" (Leach 1964:5). Leach's notion of social structure was heavily influenced by the programmatic statements of A.R. Radcliffe-Brown, even though Leach goes to great lengths to distance himself from the prevailing orthodoxies of the day. He firmly rejects the equilibrium model of functionalism and insists on the necessity to incorporate some conception of historical change, whatever the difficulties involved. It is currently a platitude that structural-functionalism's ahistoricism is artificial and limiting. Having abandoned it, Leach was in a position to revive part of the original program of British structuralism. Leach vigorously attacks the concept of "a society" separated off somehow from others around it, and this allows him to re-emphasize the connective quality of social relations. In practical terms, marriages linked villages one to another right across the Kachin Hills. That is what makes Leach's analysis convincing and allows him to escape the finicky description of mere tribelets. Even more striking, it explains why people who live next door to Kachin effectively become Kachin. One intermarriage, and whole communities are drawn into relationship of *mayu* and *dama* (wife givers and wife takers). It is nothing less than a model of cultural imperialism at work, and this aspect is as exciting today as it was in the 1950s.

As an aside, we might note that Leach was hoisted on his own petard when he accused Claude Levi-Strauss of sloppy research for indiscriminately lumping together the Chin and the Kachin, even though they are divided by a swathe of Burmese lowlanders (Leach 1961:78). In the English edition of *The Elementary Structures of Kinship*, Levi-Strauss (1969:236) suavely turned the critique aside by noting the all-important structural similarities, and pointing out that Leach admitted as much in his foreword to the second edition of *Political Systems of Highland Burma*: "Viewed overall, Chins turn out to be even more Kachins than most of us would have expected" (1964:xv).

In Leach's attack on the notion of "a society," there is more than a hint of the critique that is now being made of the notion of "a culture." That Leach should have chosen to make the case in connection with the former rather the latter is a product of his training. In the internationally influential British anthropology of his time, culture, as distinct from society, had been pushed into a backseat. Leach himself does the same thing, with a casualness that now seems cavalier:

> My view as to the kind of relationship that exists between social structure and culture follows immediately from this. Culture provides the form, the "dress" of the social situation. As far as I am concerned, the cultural situation is a given factor, it is a product and an accident of history. I do not know *why* Kachin women go hatless with bobbed hair before they are married, but assume a turban afterwards, any more than I know *why* English women put a ring on a particular finger to denote the same change in social status; all I am interested in is that in this Kachin context the assumption of a turban by a woman does have this symbolic significance. It is a statement about the status of the woman. But the structure of the situation is largely independent of its cultural form. (1965:16)

Given this dismissive attitude to culture, it is easier to see how Leach could have begun his book by boldly pushing ethnicity aside. Meanwhile, Levi-Strauss had framed a concept of structure far broader that of his English contemporaries, in which this segregation of the cultural made no sense. By the time of the second edition of *Political Systems of Highland Burma*, Leach (1961) was beginning his own flirtation with French structuralism. Moreover, it would not be long before Victor Turner (1967) would have a great deal to say about the symbolism of such things as wedding rings and hair.

The Hinterland of Brunei Is Not a Culture Area

In the end, however, what makes Leach's approach no longer attractive is, ironically, that he is encumbered by the implicit assumption of a culture area. Despite his preference for the sociological over the cultural, Leach assumes a region within which some conception of what constitutes marriage applies uniformly, and that uniformity is what makes the Kachin Hills area interesting for him. Meanwhile, the notion of a discrete "culture area" carries the same baggage as the notion of "a" culture: the world is no more paved with the former than the latter.

To avoid that trap, I base this study on a region that could not conceivably be regarded as a culture area. Within the hinterland of Brunei, there are populations speaking languages that are also spoken by people across the mountain divide in Indonesian Borneo and to the south in the watershed of the Belaga. I am talking about the former, not the latter. The label that I give them, Orang Ulu, looks innocent enough. It is a phrase in the Malay *lingua franca*, meaning Upriver People. But such ethnonyms are, as I have already suggested, an object of research, not a preliminary. Upriver People certainly do not constitute any kind of "tribe." Instead, they share a certain historical experience that needs to be spelled out, but that shared history means that there is nothing random about the area I am marking off. It corresponds to an ancient trading network, which influenced the dynamics of communities and the process of colonial annexation, and much else besides. Within this region, I am concerned, as was Leach, with transactions that link people and communities together, and whatever conviction the argument carries depends on the real existence of those transactions. In contrast to Leach, however, I am concerned with commercial and cultural transactions, rather than the status and role consequences of marriage alliance.

Can Central Borneo Be Seen as One Society?

Consequently, I cannot follow Leach's example and set aside "culture" as he defined it. For certain purposes, it might be reasonable to claim that people across central Borneo share certain features of social structure in a similar manner to the Kachin. Specifically, there was a marked tendency for people of the highest status to marry their peers in other longhouse communities, even if those other communities were at a considerable distance. Moreover, these elite marriages undoubtedly contributed to relations of dynastic alliance. In that sense, it could be argued that the whole of central Borneo comprised one vast "society" – that is, a continuous social fabric. There are, however, three features that make this argument less convincing in Borneo than it was in Burma. First, the notion of alliance shared across the region was far less complex in the former, amounting to little more than a truce. In one upriver language, such alliances are called *pang buno*, "the end of war." There was none of that juggling for superiority so typical of the Kachin Hills, no superiority of wife givers over wife takers, no necessity for elite families to marry in a circle so as to avoid risking any kind of slight. Indeed, there was hardly even any ritual involved, other than a large drinking session. Second, all such considerations applied only to a tiny minority. No one else's marriage implied alliance, in the terms made famous by Levi-Strauss. Third, in many parts of the interior, and especially in the hinterland of Brunei, it was as common for elite families to have marriage alliances with coastal Malay people as with distant longhouse communities. Although there were remarkable exceptions, the mountains of central Borneo interrupted social contacts more effectively than the hills of the Kachin. Consequently, a river drainage, right down to the coast, constituted more of a social whole than the people of the interior in general.

A version of Leach's modus operandi is used in Jerome Rousseau's (1990) brilliant synthesis of ethnographic data from across the entirety of central Borneo. He surveys a diverse archive, much of it written in the nineteenth and early twentieth centuries, in Dutch, English, German, and other languages. His goal, however, is to say something about the peoples of the region in general. Consequently, he is obliged to identify a culture area, and the criterion he selects for inclusion is neither linguistic nor regional. Instead, like Leach, he selects a feature of social organisation, namely, the existence of marked hierarchy, involving distinct classes of aristocrats, commoners, and slaves. There are, however, several large longhouse communities within his culture area that do not have classes. To say which ones, I have to mention a few ethnic labels without explaining them – all in good time. The longhouses of the Berawan people do not have distinct social classes. I know this because I worked in them, and I can report that when residents are asked to separate the aristocrats from the commoners (it is illegal to identify former slaves), they cannot do it. If pressed, they coolly assert that everyone in the community is of noble birth. They even have a cycle of myths explaining how this came about. It is a remarkable inversion of what we are so accustomed to in the West – a people pretending to be class ridden when, in fact, they are not. Because some of my results were already published when Rousseau's book appeared, he takes a few pages to deal with this "problem" (1990:212–4).

Leaders and Aristocrats

Meanwhile, I am suspicious of the proposition that the rigid class systems that Rousseau found among the Kayan of the Belaga River Valley really were characteristic of the whole of central Borneo. I found a distinct countercurrent of egalitarianism wherever I went in the watershed of the Baram that reminded me of the working-class attitudes I knew as a child in

England. Commoners conceded the power of the upper class, but reserved the right to mock them behind their backs. It might be argued that what I saw and heard in the 1970s was a symptom of the breakdown of longhouse society. That argument can, however, be stood on its head. Perhaps firm boundaries between classes were a by-product of the colonial situation. The British administrators – mostly middle class, as elsewhere in the Empire – certainly preferred to think of themselves as dealing with the *crème de la crème* of upriver society, and see the commoners as loyal and respectful followers. A nice example is provided by an early administrator in the Baram region, Charles Hose, whose adventures are recounted in Chapter One. Hose was clearly a snob, and an insecure one at that. As his autobiography (Hose 1927) reveals, he toadied outrageously to secure an honorary degree at Cambridge. Meanwhile, in Borneo, he was perpetually describing this or that longhouse host as "a fine old chief," dignified in bearing, and descended from a long line of the same. In the illustrations to his books, some of his chiefs have a noble air, but others project no charisma at all and stare into the camera with a distinctly shifty look.

It is my hunch that class distinctions in longhouse communities were more permeable and unstable before the population movements and endemic warfare of the second half of the nineteenth century. (How these were caused by the collapse of an old trading economy and the penetration of new Western products is described in Section III.) I cannot dignify my hunch by calling it an hypothesis, however, because there is no conceivable body of data that can ever now be discovered that will confirm or deny it. What I can say with some assurance is that class was a much less conspicuous feature of the communities in the lower Baram and Limbang regions than it was further upriver – even if they did not manage to be quite as exclusively aristocratic as the Berawan – and these are the communities that provided the majority of the population of the hinterland of Brunei.

There is, however, no need to reach any firm conclusions about class and rank. The issue has already been explored in an interesting exchange between Rousseau (1979, 1980) and Derek Freeman (1981). What is mobilised here is simply the notion of leadership, and there is no dispute that longhouses everywhere in central Borneo were founded and maintained as communities by those who could exert strong leadership (Alexander 1992). Even where there are supposedly rigid class systems, there are always multiple candidates for the role of leader because there are no rules of descent that can limit the succession to one man only. A successful leader tries to find an able man to follow him, and so provide continuity to the community, but he is by no means limited to sons or brothers. He is just as likely to support a son-in-law, or rather to marry his daughter to a promising young man. Adoption is another possibility, even adult adoption, as practiced by Roman emperors. It is not to be denied that these notions of leadership imply inequality, but its nature has more in common with that pattern of competitive feasting that Thomas Kirsch (1973) found character-istic of upland Southeast Asia than with rigid class systems. In longhouse communities, leaders who won out in competition with others are found retroactively to have glittering genealogies. It is these people who concern me in Section II.

On the Irrelevance of Kinship

In tune with my emphasis on politics, trade, and religion, there is little in this book concerning the topic of "kinship," at least as conceived of in Leach's day. That does not mean, however, that I owe posterity another mono-graph. On the contrary, I consider kinship organisation to be largely irrel-evant to longhouse communities, and in this I agree with Jerome Rousseau (1990:98). This proposition ought not to be too surprising, given that data from Borneo played a major role in undermining that brand of kinship studies developed in Africa and grandly called "descent theory." It was Freeman's data on the Iban of Sarawak that put the final nail in its coffin by showing that there were small-scale, technologically simple societies – then called "primitive" – that lacked corporate groups based on descent or, indeed, any other kinship principle (Freeman 1970 [1955]). It was true that Iban longhouses were often built around a few closely related or allied families, and new members were soon linked to them by marriage. But no kinship principle lay behind these agglomerations, and no Iban claimed it did. Instead, they grew up around enterprising men, who were happy to recruit followers by any and every criterion available.

A logical move for Borneo ethnographers might have been to stop talking about kinship altogether and turn to ritual, politics, and economics, which are what longhouses are really about. Instead, they became fascinated with the concept of the kindred (Appell 1976). Several variants were found, but kindreds are by definition ego-centred groups that live, change, and die with the individual. They cannot have the kind of corporate continuity that descent groups have. Meanwhile, the key mode of sociality – the longhouse itself – had been forgotten, lost behind a veil of misplaced kinship "theory."

Tanks and Longhouses

As it happens, an alternative approach had already been suggested in a second ethnography by Leach (1962), this time set in Sri Lanka. However, it did not receive the same attention as his book, *Political Systems of Highland Burma*, perhaps because villagers in Sri Lanka did not count as "primitives." In *Pul Eliya*, Leach argues pragmatically that conversations that his contemporaries might have imagined were about some abstraction called "kinship" were, in fact, about shares in the limited supply of irrigation water. The water came from communal reservoirs, or tanks, that had been built long ago as part of the amazing irrigation schemes put in place by successive Sri Lankan kings. Whatever kinship connections there were had to fit themselves to the tank, not the reverse.

The longhouses of central Borneo are not fixtures of the landscape to the same extent as tanks in Sri Lanka. They can be extended or rebuilt as necessary to accommodate the inhabitants, and indeed, active communities are almost always in the process of reconstruction or repairing some part of their longhouse. But – and it is an important but – people are not distributed around a longhouse the way students are assigned rooms in a dormitory. On the contrary, living space is vested in discrete corporate groups that persist over generations and own property in common. The terms used in the languages of the region to describe such groups mean, simply, "room," and that is the gloss I use here. When Upriver People speak of "a room," they are more often talking about a group of people than a physical structure. This connotation is not conveyed by the English word, so to remind the reader of the special meaning of the word "room" here I often say "coresidents of a room." The layout of longhouses is described in Chapter 1. By comparison to rooms, houses themselves are corporate in a weaker sense. The total population of a longhouse owns nothing in common, not even the structure itself. They do share communal obligations, however, such as the duty to support and participate in longhouse festivals, as described in Section V.

What this means is that at any given moment the coresidents of a room are as firmly fixed as the pilings underneath them, which indeed they own. Everyone must be in one room or another. Farms are made by rooms, and their produce is owned by the coresidents and eaten at a common hearth. There is no obligation for a room that has stocks of rice to share with neighbouring rooms whose farms have failed, even if they house siblings or parents. In short, kinship no more provides the structure of longhouses than it does that of villages in Sri Lanka.

Room Affiliation: Birth and Adoption

The anthropological reflex of talking kinship dies hard, however. It will be immediately reactivated by the observation that the majority of children are affiliated to the rooms in which they are born. If this looks like a statement about descent, it is not; it is a statement about geography. It is hard to imagine a child being born in some place other than where his or her mother gave birth. But postnatal motherhood is more negotiable. There are a whole series of taboos and omens that seem designed to make parents give up their children for adoption. If there is anything unusual about the birth, such as a breach birth, new parents must be found. The same follows any bad omen – of which there seem to be an endless supply. A mother must not see a corpse or a carcass, and, more obscurely, must not throw sticks at fruit bats. Her husband must not engage in hammering nails or tying knots. Moreover, if an infant is sickly or fails to put on weight, the parents will "give it away" in order to "change its luck."

This strategy is not as wrenching as it sounds. Children are usually adopted by close relatives of the mother, often a sister or cousin. That means they only move a few rooms down the longhouse, and not infrequently to the room next door. Nevertheless, the result is striking, and a survey at one longhouse found almost one-fourth of children had been adopted (Metcalf 1974b). Meanwhile, mothers who "begged" a child from luckier relatives were often themselves childless. A woman with several children might even promise her next before it is born. The effect is to distribute children more evenly among rooms, reducing the chances that any "room" – that is, a corporate group existing over several generations – might die out. Paradoxically, there is pressure to share children between rooms, but not food: conativity in place of commensality.

Room Affiliation: Marriage and Remarriage

The other way to become a resident of a room is to marry into it. In theory, it would be possible for a marriage to occur between existing coresidents of a room, for example, if a widower married his deceased wife's sister, but I never heard of such a case. However, I did know of a woman – a famous beauty – who had first married an older man, then later his son, who was of her own age, and then later again his son's son. Neither the son nor the son's son were her sons; her children were by other husbands. The complexity of this woman's living arrangements was unusual, but divorce and remarriage are common enough that there is considerable internal mobility between rooms.

In some longhouse communities, men must as a rule move into the room of their brides, rather than the reverse. Where that is the case, an older woman often lives in the same room as one of her daughters, or even

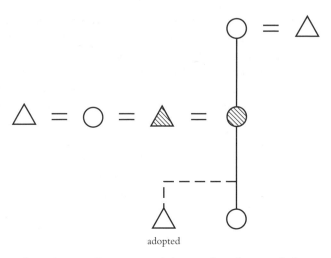

Figure Int–02. Room containing no first-degree relatives.

granddaughters, while other daughters live next door. This matrifocal tendency does not, however, produce anything resembling a matriline. On the contrary, the older woman's brothers and sons have all become members of other corporate groups in other "rooms." Indeed, they have likely become heads of household in those rooms.

In short, residence trumps kinship, and one striking example will serve to underline that. It concerns a man who married into a room occupied by his wife's parents and her two children by a former marriage, one of whom was adopted from another community (Figure Int–01). When his wife died, there was no question of the husband leaving – he was the head of household, part owner of all its resources, and responsible for its continued existence as a corporate group. If he had moved out he would have left behind only old folk and young children, and there would have been no one to do the heavy labour on the farm (see Figure Int–02). Under these circumstances, he arranged a marriage to a younger woman whose own room agreed to let her move in with him. Not long after, the man died in an accident. His new wife, like her deceased husband before her, had no intention of leaving the room in which she already had a stake, and so married a second time, her new husband joining her according to the usual rule. That marriage worked well, and the coresidents settled down to a normal family life: a "family" in which there are no two people who are first-degree kin (child, sibling, or parent). Moreover, a much desired goal was achieved, namely, three generations of women living together. The fact that these women shared *no* consanguineous relationships was neither here nor there.

Segmentation of Rooms

I have emphasised the continuity of rooms, but longhouses are rebuilt from time to time, on average about once a generation. If the population has grown, the new house will be longer than the old one, which is to say that it will have more rooms. So why were these rooms not simply built onto the old structure? The answer is that rooms segment by producing rooms next to each other, not stuck on at the ends. When segmentation occurs, it means not only that a new space is created, but also a new corporate group, a new "room," is founded. While the old longhouse existed, rooms – in both senses of the word – grew more crowded. An older man acting as head of household might have several younger men in his room, perhaps married to his daughters. This would have the advantage of increasing farm production, but would also increase the number of mouths to feed. Before long, the younger couples might choose to make separate farms, so gaining independence, and simultaneously decreasing the chances that everyone would be left hungry by a single disaster, such as flooding or pests. In that way, segmentation would be incipient, waiting only for the construction of a new house to become explicit. In terms of space, such rooms become filled with grandchildren, and consequently, noisy, sociable, and full of life – a thoroughly desirable state of affairs in the view of most Upriver People. The architectural modifications that followed such fullness are described in Chapter 1. Often, they involved moving kitchens to separate buildings and constructing little alcoves for married couples. In old longhouses, such rooms become labyrinths of corridors and alcoves – little worlds to themselves. The rooms of important leaders tend to grow rapidly because spouses are recruited for both sons and daughters, sometimes from other longhouse communities.

When rooms segment in a new house, they form a row of rooms, side by side. One of these rooms remains notionally "the room of origin," that is, a continuation of the accommodation space that was torn down during the rebuilding. This room is the one in which the parents continue to live, often that of their youngest daughter. This "room" has existed in previous longhouses as far back as memory reaches. Each of the others is an offshoot, now seeking to maintain its corporate existence in longhouses to come.

"Houses" and "Rooms"

My account of the internal arrangements of longhouses may bring to mind recent discussions of what has come to be called "the house" (Carsten and Hugh-Jones 1995; Howell and Sparkes 1999). Confusingly, "the house" in longhouse communities is not the house itself, but its constituent "rooms." Houses are agglomerations of "houses." Luckily, I can set such confusions aside because "house theory," as it has come to be called, presents itself as a kind of revivalist kinship theory. The idea was proposed by Claude Levi-Strauss (1983) as an afterthought, when he came to realize that societies organised around descent groups were in the minority among "primitive" peoples, despite what British anthropologists had told him when he was writing his magnum opus on kinship (1969). House societies were seen as an alternative, one structured around the kinds of group interests, in miniature, that characterised the royal "houses" of Europe. It is a hypothesis-saving device, like the kindred, and I have no need of it. The crucial issues in understanding longhouse communities concern politics, economics, and religion, and these have been staples of anthropology for a long time.

Order of Presentation

A final caveat: since my topic is ethnicity, it may seem strange that an inventory of ethnic labels in the Brunei hinterland is delayed until the fourth of six main sections of the book. This is consistent, however, with my conclusion that ethnicity is an object of research, rather than a preliminary to it. A mere list of proper names makes no sense without an understanding of the nature of longhouses (Section I), their communal politics (Section II), and the pattern of trade that linked them together (Section III). The only major topic that fits in after Section IV is religion, and that is because longhouses assimilating people of widely different ethnicities provide my crucial examples in Section V. Section VI describes the experiences of longhouse communities as they became subjugated to the nation-state, so connecting the upriver world of the late nineteenth century with the one that I knew firsthand, starting in the mid-1970s.

Having outlined my strategy, and set kinship firmly aside, I can begin with my description of longhouses.

Part I

Longhouses

Chapter 1

Longhouses

Structures housing multiple families are not, of course, unique to Borneo. There are traditional forms of architecture elsewhere that have been described as "longhouses" – written as one word or two, hyphenated or not. The first were Amerindian, as the *Oxford English Dictionary* (OED; 1991) notes in its definition: "a house of unusual length, spec. the communal dwelling of the Iroquois and other American Indians." The term is by no means a technical term of anthropology and was undoubtedly in common usage among English settlers long before it was enshrined in the ethnographic record. Nevertheless, it is the influence of Lewis Henry Morgan's pioneering account of the *League of the Ho-de-no-sau-nee or Iroquois* (1851) that is indicated in the OED entry. Elsewhere, Morgan gives this description of Iroquois longhouses:

> generally from fifty to a hundred and thirty feet in length, by about sixteen wide, with partitions at intervals of about ten or twelve feet, or two lengths of the body. Each apartment was, in fact, a separate house, having a fire in the centre, and accommodating two families, one upon each side of the fire. Thus a house one hundred and twenty feet long, would contain ten fires and twenty families. (1965 [original 1881]:315)

Morgan's illustrations of free-standing houses show light structures of poles covered with bark, standing directly on an earth floor. Evidently, the famous longhouses were simply larger versions built in the same way. By the time that Morgan made his study, most Iroquois villages consisted of scattered single-family houses, and longhouses were rare. Previously, when Iroquois had feared raids from hostile neighbors, villages were more compact and often surrounded by a stockade (Morgan 1965:314–15).

Houses of Unusual Length

Having gained currency, the term "longhouse" was readily applied elsewhere, or more likely reinvented. For instance, in forested parts of their colonial possessions in Southeast Asia, the French discovered peoples who built impressive joint homes. Georges Condominas describes one variant:

> The striking thing about the exterior appearance of Hmong Gar dwellings is their length – in Sar Luk two are almost forty meters long – and their massive roofs. Actually, all you see is roof. On either side of a ridgepole three to four meters high, a double thickness of thatch pitches to within sixty centimeters of the ground and thus conceals the greater part of the low wattled walls. The roof is rounded off at either end of the house. Doors are low, narrow openings cut in the front wall. A rattan arch supports the edge of the roof, permitting one to pass in and out. (1977:7)

The exceptionally long houses that he mentions accommodated a couple of dozen couple of dozen people divided between four households, each with its own hearth and rice store. Most were smaller, with only two or three households.

There were also examples from Melanesia. In the highlands of New Guinea, there were a great variety of domestic structures, often with separate accommodations for men and women. Roy Wagner describes alternative designs used by the Daribi, the largest of which was preferred in locations where there was a high risk of attack:

> The house erected in a new area is usually a *sigibe'* ("arrow-house"), a two-storey longhouse elevated from the ground and originally built with a bark floor and walls supported by a wooden framework and leafed with sago leaves. Like a block-house, a *sigibe'* is built for defensive advantage; women live on the first floor, while the second floor serves as the men's quarters and as an effective shooting platform in the local type of warfare, which consists in surrounding the house of an enemy. (Wagner 1967:18)

An outer ring of defence was provided by the gardens, which usually surrounded the house on land sloping away from it and are a tangle of fallen tree trunks and vines. The largest group that can occupy a house together is a clan (*be*, meaning "house"), comprising perhaps a few dozen men and a total population approaching a hundred, but it is evidently not a common occurrence (Wagner 1967:18–24, 34, 109, 151).

Other examples can be found in island Southeast Asia beyond Borneo. Roxana Waterson's beautifully illustrated volume on the indigenous architecture of the region contains a picture of a remarkable multifamily house of the Manggarai of western Flores. It has a massive thatch roof with a ridge approximately thirty feet above the ground, and reaching almost to the ground. Just visible from the rounded ends is a floor raised several feet above the ground (Waterson 1990:37). According to the ethnographer C. Nooteboom (1939:238), there had been houses of this type that could house hundreds of people. The majority of the Manggarai, however, lived in smaller houses with conical roofs. The insides of the Manggarai longhouses were gloomy and smoky. The Dutch authorities decided they were unhygienic and tore them down. Used to their neat bungalows, the colonists were apparently not impressed by the shade and coolness that a high roof can provide or the luxury of escaping from the intense tropical light.

First Sights of the Longhouse

Impressive as they are, the longhouses of the Iroquois, Hmong, Daribi, and Manggarai pale in comparison to those of central Borneo, in terms of both population and construction. Some impression of their scale can be gained from early eyewitness accounts. Spenser St. John was the British Consul-General to the Sultan of Brunei in 1851 when he made a visit to the Kayan people of the middle reaches of the Baram River (Figure Int-01). He navigated a couple of hundred miles upriver on board his steamer, the *Pluto*, along the winding lower course and into broken, hilly country, until he arrived at a place he calls "Longusin." His first sight of it made a great impression on him, he tells us, a whole complex of longhouses "built on lofty posts, on hills of various heights, yet appearing to be clustered together, while nearby were numerous little rice stores, neatly whitewashed. I never saw a prettier-looking place." Entering one of the buildings, he found it "very long, with a broad covered verandah, as a public room, and a sleeping-place for the bachelors, while off it were separate apartments for the married people, the young girls, and children. The roof was of shingle, the posts of heavy wood, the flooring of long and broad rough planks, the partitions of the same material, with small doors about two feet above the floor, leading into the inner rooms" St.John 1862:97–105). St. John estimated the population of Longusin at about 2,500, or five hundred families. That seems high, but one of his hosts boasted that a longhouse was considered small that did not contain a hundred families. St. John was already familiar with longhouses elsewhere in Borneo, such as those of the numerous Iban to the south. But the ones he saw along the Baram were larger and more sturdily built. Even within Borneo, the longhouses of Upriver People were impressive, and remained so throughout the nineteenth and twentieth centuries.

At the time of St. John's visit to Longusin, the watershed of the Baram was nominally a possession of the Sultan of Brunei. In fact, the Sultan exerted very little influence over the warlike Kayan. It was not until the 1890s that the region was brought under effective government control, and it was not the Sultan's government. Instead, the area was "pacified" by District Officers of a dynasty of English gentlemen, the once-famous "white Rajahs" of Sarawak, who carved out for themselves a private kingdom in northwestern Borneo. The man primarily responsible for the extension of Brooke rule throughout Baram was Charles Hose. His memoirs are more flamboyant and self-serving than St. John's, reflecting a change in the national mood in Britain. Raised on the derring-do literature of High Imperialism, Hose flagrantly romanticizes his role. His first visit to an upriver longhouse occurs in the context of a confrontation with a restive chief called Aban Jau, who occupied a major tributary of the Baram, the Tinjar. In the best tradition of English boys' magazines of the period, Hose arrives unannounced and almost alone in the very lair of the rebel leader:

> With a boat's crew of some ten or twenty men we hurried up the Tinjar River, and in five day's time reached the vicinity of Aban Jau's Long House, without anyone in the village being aware of our approach. Leaving the boat more or less hidden at the landing place a short distance from the house, and taking only two followers with me as guard, in the grey twilight of the dawn I ascended the ladder of the house.... As it was one of the first of these Communal Houses that I had seen I was much struck with it, although Heaven knows my attentions were needed elsewhere. It was about a quarter of a mile long and was supported on magnificent big wooden piles, with strong plank floors. Massive piles of ironwood supported the roof at a height of some thirty feet from the ground, and the floor was supported by the same piles at a level seven or eight feet below the cross beams of the roof. The projecting eaves of the roof came down to a level midway between the roof beams and that of the floor, and the interval of four or five feet between the eaves and the floor remained open along the whole length of the front of the house, which faced the river, save for a low parapet, which bounded the floor along its outer edge. The width of the floor was about fifty feet, the whole space between roof and floor being divided into two parts by a longitudinal wall of vertical planks which ran the whole length of the village.

This wall lay not in the middle line, but a little to the river side, that facing the river being somewhat narrower. The other and wider part was divided by transverse walls at intervals of some twenty-five feet so as to form a single row of spacious chambers of approximately equal size. Each such chamber was the private apartment of one family, in which father, mother, daughters, young sons, and female dependents slept and ate. (1927:50–1)

Hose estimates the population of this impressive building at seven hundred. Counting "outlying communities," Hose reckoned that Aban Jau could muster some 5,000 followers.

Construction of the Longhouse

Eighty years later, during my first fieldwork in the mid-1970s, Aban Jau's Communal House was only a memory, but it had not quite disappeared. At another place many miles down river, supporting another longhouse, I was shown pilings that had once been part of the house that Hose saw. They were about two feet in diameter, stood twelve or more feet above ground, and must each have weighed many tons. That they had survived a century without rotting through, despite being part-buried, is testament to the durability of the wood that Hose calls "ironwood," locally *bilian*, which survives tropical humidity better than iron ever could and is also impervious to termites. These old pilings could only have been moved by river. However, bilian is too dense to float, so they must have been transported on rafts. The labour involved was formidable: assembling rafts from tree trunks of lighter wood cut for the purpose or brought down by the river after heavy rains; manhandling the pilings out of their holes and lowering them carefully down the riverbank, using only rattan cables, levers, and wedges; and then unloading and setting them up in the new location. I was told with evident pride that these pilings had been moved several times, partaking in generations of longhouses, and providing a material link to communities going back even before Aban Jau's time.

Nevertheless, practical motives were emphasized: the pilings were moved because they were too valuable to leave behind. Replacing them with new ones of similar size would require finding suitable trees, and they are rare. This is not peculiar to bilian; tropical rainforests typically contain many species, with specimens of each scattered widely. Having located bilian trees of the right size, there is then the labour of felling them using only axes. This is a task of days, made all the more difficult by having to work on a flimsy temporary platform built above the widespread buttresses. These buttresses are an adaptation to the thin soils of the forest floor, which provide unfirm anchorage for the roots of the great trees. The buttresses help stabilize them

35

in strong winds. Once felled, trees must be cleared of top hamper, and then somehow rolled, dragged, and maneuvered through the jungle for a considerable distance, in all probability further than a previous longhouse site is from the riverbank. Finally – and except for the odd lucky find near the longhouse site – it is necessary to move the logs by raft anyway. Meanwhile, the old pilings are of proven durability, and already cut and shaped. Some are carved with a crude, deeply incised design, often a simple spiral, and this lends them an individual character.

There were other timbers preserved from former longhouses. The floor was made of thick boards like the "long and broad rough planks" that St. John saw at Longusin. They resonated to the footfalls of people striding down the veranda, but they were too massive to bend at all under the weight of a mere person. Some ran through two or three adjacent rooms and reached sixty feet in length. In breadth, they often measured about twenty inches, and three in thickness. They had been made by splitting segments from hardwood trees chosen for their straight trunks, and then squaring the wedge-shaped segments with adze and saw. The rippled pattern of cuts made by the adze could still be seen, despite the passage of innumerable bare feet, which polished the surface to a deep ebony (see Figure 01-01). These planks, all by themselves, contributed to the quality of longhouse life in the 1970s. They gave a feeling of solidness – one might almost say respectability – that is not achieved in houses elsewhere in Southeast Asia that use lighter materials, especially bamboo. Moreover, they connected rooms in more ways than one; it was, for instance, almost impossible to move around the house at night without stepping on a long plank and waking up someone sleeping on the other end of it.

The building that I saw in the 1970s certainly differed in details of design and construction from the one that captured Hose's attention. Nevertheless, he would have recognized it immediately, and there was much that remained just as he described it. Moreover, it was still the case that virtually all indigenous people living in the Baram watershed maintained residence in one longhouse or another. It was a universal mode of residence, in contrast to the Iroquois, Hmong, and Daribi longhouses, which were only built in exceptional circumstances. Despite the absence for decades of any serious threat of attack – or at least any attack for which they could provide defence – people continued to live in longhouses. Even as the twentieth century closed, although so much else had changed, longhouses persisted. Despite the wholesale destruction of the rainforest by unregulated commercial logging, they were, if anything, larger and more elaborate than ever.

The ancient pilings that I was shown in the mid-1970s may still be supporting a longhouse, and they are indeed more valuable than ever because there is no chance now of finding trees that could furnish replacements of

Figure 01-01. Entertaining guests in a Berawan longhouse in the 1910's. To the right is a fireplace kept burning for the benefit of the heads hung above it, which are evidently old. The wooden looks on the hosts' faces are no doubt due to the presence of the camera. (From Hose and McDougall 1912, Vol I, plate 69.)

similar proportions. They evoke the continuity of longhouse communities, but paradoxically, they also demonstrate the evanescence of particular longhouse communities. In their wanderings, these ancient timbers manifest a restless mobility that contradicts the apparent permanence of the massive structure itself.

The Spaces of the Longhouse

The floor plan of longhouses was simple enough: the veranda running down the river side, the row of apartments behind. Ethnographers have busied themselves distinguishing the floor plans preferred by different ethnic groups, but Upriver People entering a longhouse they had never visited before immediately knew their way around. The most obvious difference between them was, of course, their length, which Upriver People described in terms of the number of doors opening onto the veranda, one per "room." At the bottom end of the range, there was some possibility of confusion: was a three-door longhouse really a separate community, or simply a joint farmhouse of more sturdy construction than usual? What the inhabitants had to say on the matter often reflected subtle political dynamics. Under certain circumstances, such as bitter factionalism or high mortality in recent generations, even a few "doors" might claim independent status. Elsewhere, larger populations might claim that their "real" residences were to be found in a nearby community, even though the structure they occupied had every appearance of a longhouse. As we see in Chapter 5, such ambiguities are not random. On the contrary, they are crucial to the dynamics of longhouse communities. At the other end of the scale, longhouses were common with forty, fifty, or sixty doors, and some were even bigger. In the 1950s, Long Laput in the middle Baram had one hundred doors in a single longhouse half a mile in length (MacDonald 1958:270). Further upriver, level sites large enough to accommodate so long a building are rare, and so a community may comprise several longhouses, as at St. John's "Longusin."

Other differences in floor plan were minor. In some communities with marked social hierarchy, the apartments of the leading families in the middle of the building were larger, and the veranda in front of them wider, to accommodate public gatherings. But in all longhouses, the leading families tended to live near the middle, whether or not the structure made that explicit, and travellers without personal contacts in the community knew perfectly well where to seat themselves to await the attentions of their host. Hospitality was the duty and prerogative of politically active men because no one travelled alone and every party of travellers had a leader. Consequently, every arrival took on the quality of a state visit. As outboard motors became

Figure 01-02. Veranda of a Sebop longhouse in the 1910's. The pattern of adze cuts on the planks of the floor are clearly visible. The room immediately in front of the camera was evidently a wealthy one. Against its wall are stored two valuable large gongs, and a small cannon on wheels. To the left of them is a mortar for the pounding of rice, upside down. (From Hose and McDougall 1912, Vol I, plate 64.)

more common in the 1950s and 1960s, the political aspect became less marked, but the conventions of Upriver hospitality remained firmly in place. It was taken for granted that the government-appointed headman (*Tua Kampong*) of a community would offer food and accommodation to all travellers, important or otherwise. Nor was there anything grudging in their welcome; young people were often excited to have strangers in the community and took the opportunity to hold parties, with drinking and dancing until dawn. Travellers sometimes found it necessary to camp out for a night on some stony strand at the riverside, just to catch up on sleep.

Such hospitality hints at the social nature of the veranda. When Hose made his elaborately staged entrance to Aban Jau's house, he knew enough simply to take a seat on the mat outside Aban Jau's room. In so doing, he became a guest. What was unusual about his arrival was that it occurred at dawn. Regular visitors arrived in the afternoon, having spent the day on the river. Only those with evil intent skulked about in the jungle all night and emerged suddenly at dawn, in a sudden rush and with war whoops.

Hose deliberately mixed his signals so as to generate an air of tension where none was needed. As we see in Chapter 4, by the time of Hose's visit, Aban Jau's military adventures were over. Even so, it strikes me as unlikely that he succeeded in sneaking into the house unnoticed. Even before dawn, there are always sleepless old ladies in the kitchens, stirring up the fires to boil water. The point is that once peacefully inside, he became part of the social life of the community, however eccentric, and the response was to make breakfast rather than pound the alarm gongs.

Had Hose lingered on the veranda, he would have seen communal life ebb and flow throughout the day, as I did in the 1970s. In the relative cool of the morning, it would have been busy with people bustling to and fro, working on various chores. The most insistent was the daily pounding of rice, to free it of its husk ready for cooking. Pairs of women worked together, standing on opposites ends of a massive wooden mortar about six feet long. A few handfuls of unhusked rice were put in the bowl-shaped receptacle in the middle of the mortar, and then each woman in turn threw down her double-ended pestle, which stood about her own height and weighed as much as thirty pounds. Pestles had wide rounded ends, with a narrower shaft in between so that they could be held with a loose grip. This prevented the shock of impact being transmitted through the arms, so that women could keep up the work for hours at a time if necessary, for instance, before a longhouse festival. Even so, it was heavy work, and women found ways to lighten it by beating out rhythms or having races to see which team could go fastest. For all this percussion, the floor of the longhouse provided a sounding board, so that in myths heroes on a quest knew they were approaching a longhouse not because they saw it, but because they heard it. While arching their backs smoothly to lift the pestles with minimum effort, the women were all the time neatly pushing the scattered rice back into the mortar with their feet, so that they gave the impression of dancing. Every few minutes, it would be time to load a new batch of rice, and the women could take a moment to chat, smoke homegrown tobacco, and engage in repartee with whoever was passing by. Sharp-tongued older women were often the winners in these verbal skirmishes, and between bouts of pounding, laughter echoed down the veranda.

Men's work mostly took them off the veranda. The only chore they performed there that approached the repetitiveness of pounding rice was making and mending fishing nets, and it was usually left to older men, who alone had the patience. The veranda gave them room to spread out their nets, and the work an excuse to sit in a favorite spot, join the women's banter, exchange reminiscences with their peers, or tell stories to the children. Younger men always seemed to be rushing about, engaged in everything from household repairs to arranging work parties. In the morning, no one who was not ill lay abed, but as the midday heat built, activity slowed, and the house took on a somnolent air. In the late afternoon, the house revived, as people resumed their chores, began preparing the evening meal, or simply sat staring at the river sliding by below them. It was at this time of day that the term "veranda" – universally applied by colonial officers – seemed most appropriate. Frequently, convection clouds built in the mountains during the day and toward sundown released their moisture in violent downpours. Everyone raced to grab their washing. Those on the veranda huddled together in the sudden chill, rolled themselves a cigarette, and resumed their contemplation. During quiet times in the longhouse, this routine was invariable because, being close to the equator, dawn was always at 6.00 a.m., give or take a few minutes, and sundown at 6 p.m.

Evening activity on the veranda was more variable. During busy times in the agricultural cycle, when many people were away at their farms, there would be little stirring along it, and no light apart from the occasional wick lantern set outside a door. The line of lanterns, twinkling off into the distance, gave the house the feeling, not so much of being abandoned, as enchanted. At other times, however, and especially after the harvest, there were little gatherings in every second room, and a constant traffic of people up and down the veranda, pairs of girls arm in arm, young men strolling and laughing. The veranda became a boulevard, a place to see and be seen. This sociable season was interspersed with festivals – weddings, namings, annual festivals, and the like – and then the veranda became not only the avenue between gatherings, but the site of them as well, often involving a large part of the entire community. In the 1970s, most longhouses had a few kerosene-burning pressure lanterns, and their presence on the veranda indicated a celebration of some kind in progress. If one walked away from the house, the hubbub could be heard a mile away through the quiet jungle, not to mention the sounds of gongs and drums. The veranda was also the scene of banquets when there were many visitors in the house, and the hosts took pride in the row of food trays extending for hundreds of feet along it. The trays contained a variety of dishes, including fish and game, besides mountains of rice, and guests were lined up on both sides of them. Such occasions were the climactic moments of the community, and they took place in the most communal of spaces.

The dimensions that Hose gives for the "spacious chambers" that lay on the landward side of the "longitudinal wall" would have applied equally well to many longhouses in the 1970s. As to their contents, Hose would have found them sparsely furnished: no chairs or tables, only mats. Valuable brass ware, including gongs and trays, might be stacked against the wall, and there might be a few boxes for storing cloths. By the 1970s, there were a few items of furniture – but not much. Still at that time almost no one had chairs, but everyone seemed to have acquired a wardrobe with a mirror on the door, cheaply manufactured from plywood and purchased from a down river bazaar. A more fundamental change, however, was the universality of mosquito nets. I can find no record of the first introduction of so prosaic a trade item into the Baram watershed, but it must have been early in the twentieth century. There is folklore concerning them – to wash them in the river is said to cause a general disaster – and "to enter the mosquito net" has become the standard way to refer to sexual activity. However, it requires machine-made fabrics to provide a uniform mesh fine enough to keep mosquitos out while allowing air through, and I know of no indigenous substitute. Every longhouse apartment had multiple mosquito nets strung from the rafters, each creating a little personal space in a manner that presumably did not apply in Hose's time. The simplest arrangement was a cone-shaped net that was tucked in around a sleeping mat or thin cotton mattress at night. During the day, it could be hitched up by tieing it into a single knot, while the mat or mattress was neatly rolled up. Married residents made more permanent arrangements: a box-shaped net hung over a wooden frame. This gave more space and better ventilation, and allowed for thicker mattresses. The next step was to build low walls, so as create something like a bedroom. Flimsy as they were, these partitions chopped up the space inside apartments in various ways. Some couples preferred to sleep near the central wall, others near the back, with single people here and there in their own little tents, square or round.

As longhouses aged, apartments accumulated structural eccentricities. Hose talks as if all the rooms in Aban Jau's house were the same size, each containing a nuclear family. That might approximate the truth in a newly built house, but demographics soon confused matters. A couple fortunate enough to have many children could rapidly find their apartment crowded with in-marrying spouses and grandchildren. When a new house was built, each of these couples had the opportunity to build their own room beside the parents' "new" room, which nevertheless notionally persists as the "room of origin" of all its descendents. Consequently, longhouses grew from inside, and not just at the ends. Another implication of this mode of division of rooms was that a thriving community of, say, forty doors could easily expand to sixty at the next rebuilding, and the population of old longhouses might be greater than the number of "doors" indicated. Meanwhile, a crowded room had no way to expand but backward. Its interior spaces under the main roof of the house became segmented into sleeping spaces and sitting areas, and then extensions of various kinds were built on the back with their own low roofs. Viewed from the landward side, the house seemed to be pushing out roots toward the damp jungle. These tended to be longer near the center of the house because leading families were more likely to attract in-marrying spouses both for sons and daughters, but even here there might be a room housing, say, a widow with an unmarried son, and they had no need for extra space.

This description of what I might call "deep" rooms – since they are all the same width – might make them sound gloomy, a kind of longhouse slum, especially as there are, of course, no windows as such in the side walls or the roof. But the reverse is true. In the tropics, it is always a relief to enter the shade, and deep shade is positively luxurious. During the day, sufficient light permeated from the veranda, which was lit from its open side, from the back of the room, and inevitably from the odd hole in the roof. Far from being forbidding, I found them enticing – always an open area somewhere for lounging and entertaining casual visitors, with assorted valuables stacked here and there, and perhaps old family photographs taken at a studio in a down river bazaar. There were always thick mats made of split rattan to sit on, and sometimes cheap linoleum below them. Then there was some kind of a corridor, wide or narrow, weaving past all kinds of interesting nooks and crannies. Nor were these places closed to nonresidents – nowhere was – because one might very properly be headed out into the kitchen.

As rooms were pushed backward, so were their kitchens. In uncrowded rooms, the kitchen was set up directly at the back, tucked under the eaves of the main house. It consisted of a large hearth consisting of a box, perhaps eight feet by four, sitting directly on the floorboards and filled eight inches deep in clay for insulation. On top, a couple of small fires might be kept at the same time, with pots suspended above or balanced on trivets. Around the hearth were water jars, knives, and cutting boards, and remarkably neat stacks of firewood. It was a matter of pride among housewives that their sticks of wood were all sawn to the same length, split to the same size, and stacked – one might almost say shelved – with military precision. Kitchens were seldom untidy for long. They did, however, take up considerable space, so they were the first thing to be moved out of the longhouse, into a separate standing building. This also had the major advantage of reducing the chances of a kitchen fire burning down the whole longhouse – a disaster that persists in the memories of many communities. To avoid descending to the ground, kitchens were connected to the longhouse by walkways, like little piers, and this gave the same impression as a common form of Austronesian house built out over shallow lagoons, except what lay below was mud and coarse weeds rather than tidal flats. Having built such a pier, the opportunity existed to build covered spaces beside it, perhaps extending the main roof at a shallower angle, or alternatively raising a ridge pole at right angles to it. The result was a more complicated roof line than is usually associated with the rectangular form of the longhouse.

There is no doubt, however, that the main roof of the longhouse was its most impressive feature. Hose estimates the height of the roof in Aban Jau's house at thirty feet, with the cross-beams seven or eight feet above the floor. If the floor stood a similar distance off the ground, it meant that half the height of the building consisted of the roof. In addition, the roof extended out beyond the floor and came down to within five feet of it on the veranda side, so that wide eaves gave additional shade from the sun and protection against swirling rain. Indeed, viewed from the river side, longhouses appeared to be mostly massive, high-pitched roofs, standing atop rows of pilings. As Hose emphasizes, the framework of the roof – cross-beams, longitudinal beams, props, frames, and rafters – was as massive as those supporting the floor. This was necessary because roofs were heavy, being made of shingles cut from ironwood, that is, the dense and rotproof *bilian*. Such a roof could last a lifetime, and its components could even be reused in a new longhouse, but it did require maintenance because tiles were liable to split or move around in strong winds.

The space under the roof was empty, so that it provided a reservoir of relatively cool air above the house. Its eaves caught every breath of air moving in the light breezes of midday and circulated them through the longhouse. There was nothing to impede air flow because all the walls separating rooms from the veranda and from each other were kept low, never extending above the roof beams and often even lower than that. Both over the veranda and inside rooms, all kinds of odds and ends were stored in the rafters, such as old fishing equipment and half-carved paddles. Strong boxes containing the most serious valuables, particularly beads, were also stored in the rafters, safe from the prying fingers of children. Things stored in the attic were often dusty, but not sooty, because the space was large enough for smoke from cooking fires to disperse.

The longhouse itself, however, did not exhaust the social spaces of the community because those around it were used almost as much as those inside. Upriver People are shocked if it is suggested that they live in the jungle. Only the hunting and gathering Penan people do that, and they are generally looked down on for doing so. To them, it is obvious that the longhouse and its environs constitute a refuge of civilisation in contrast to the dank and threatening forest. If one walks away from the longhouse on any small track, one immediately gets the point. The sunlit area around the longhouse, although it may be too hot for comfort at noon, nevertheless begins to seem appealing.

The strip of land between the longhouse and the river was the most frequented. To describe it as the front lawn is perhaps stretching things, but it was kept clear of weeds and vines. On evenings when there was no rain, children gathered to play football, cheered on by adults sitting on the veranda, which neatly furnished the bleachers. The open space was also used in many rituals, or phases of rituals. Prayers were often made in front of the house at sites consisting of lines of sticks holding eggs, as well as other paraphernalia (Metcalf 1989:73–80). They were constructed anew on each occasion, but marked by planting bushes of croton whose red-tinged leaves, suggestive of sacrifice, made a visible record of previous rites. Prayer sites were always in the open, but along the edge of the river were planted various kinds of useful palms, notably those that furnished betel nuts. Used as a mild stimulant, chewing betel provided another common pastime, and older people could often be found together sharing a fresh batch. Mixed with lime, it makes the mouth water and colours the saliva bright red, so that evidence of previous sessions is everywhere to be seen. Old people were astonishingly adept at spitting through holes in the floor, but even their aim was sometimes lacking. Collecting nuts was the job of agile young boys because the palms grew high enough to make it difficult to dislodge them with sticks. Consequently, even in long-established houses, where a veritable grove of mature palms spread along the riverbank, it was still possible from the veranda to see under them to the river beyond.

Under the palms was a favorite spot for all manner of construction jobs. There was nearly always a canoe being built somewhere, a new hull being carved from a tree trunk or having side planks attached. Many were small, fifteen feet or so, but others were big enough for long distance travel, that is, at least thirty feet. Old boats were drawn up for repair, although some were obviously beyond it. Various sheds contained tools and outboard motors, if there were any, usually of smallest type. Similar bits and pieces accumulated underneath the longhouse itself, even though it was considered unclean because of refuse falling from above. Toddlers, for instance, do not wear diapers, so the standard practice was simply to wash their feces through cracks in the floor. Since children wandered anywhere, there was no telling when a bucket of water would come sluicing down. Nevertheless, such detritus was biodegradable – or at least it was until tinned food and plastic-wrapped candy became common. When longhouse people gave the polluted nature of old longhouse sites as a reason for moving, however, they were not thinking of the accumulation of rubbish but of malicious spirits, who also lurked under the house. Even so, the great bulk of the longhouse above provided the deepest shade available, so it was not uncommon for men to take a nap there at midday, in a carefully chosen spot, and after shooing away the chickens that roosted there for the same reason. Usually, there were convenient piles of lumber, newly sawn or salvaged, and more old boats. Sometimes there were ancient outboards, rusted beyond all hope of repair.

The open space in the front of the longhouse was intersected by raised paths, often just a string of logs, which allowed passersby to avoid the mud after heavy rains. They led to the riverbank, and then, more or less steeply, down to the river. The choice of longhouse sites depends on many factors, which are discussed more in Chapter 5, but it was obviously advantageous to pick a place not prone to flooding. Consequently, the riverbanks in front of houses tended to be high, and after rain they became a morass of soft mud. Needless to say, Upriver People can from infancy run up and down logs one foot in diameter balanced at an angle of forty-five degrees while carrying heavy loads, even if the logs are slippery with mud brought up on other peoples' feet. For me, to contemplate the climb and the ignominy of failure was sometimes daunting, and at houses I did not know well, I would attract a crowd on the riverbank watching to see if I would make it. At the bottom of the inclined logs were others floating in the river, often rafted together to provide docking for canoes. Usually, there were half a dozen of these rafts in front of the longhouse, so that everyone had convenient access to one. They were the scene of bustling activity in the early morning and again at sundown, when people came to bathe. Clothes were also washed there, and the morning gatherings on the rafts were a time for gossip and ribald teasing of those suspected of amorous adventures during the previous night.

At either end of the longhouse, small vegetable gardens, more or less well tended, stretched along the riverbank. If pigs were kept in pens, rather than being allowed to roam free as normal, they were kept here. As sites for new rooms, the ends of the longhouse were undesirable. Those already living at the ends might be perfectly respectable, although hardly belonging to the elite, but only low-status newcomers would build there after the community was established. By doing so, they signalled their lack of proper connections in the community, and such additions of single families were in practice rare. This is the reason that the residents of overcrowded rooms in the center of the longhouse had to wait for a new longhouse before gaining elbow room.

Finally, it must be emphasized that the description I give applies only to a completed longhouse, but many communities went for years at a time without them. If a house burned down, or if people moved to a new site, there was obviously an immense amount of work to be done assembling the necessary timber before construction could even begin, let alone be completed. Even assuming that there was no internal dissension about where to build or whether to stay together, a community might well be reduced to living in a row of shacks strung out along the riverbank and made of whatever materials came to hand, including bamboo for floors and palm leaves for roofs. These shacks would gradually be improved with plank floors and shingle roofs, as circumstances allowed, producing a kind of ragged pseudo-longhouse. Meanwhile, some people would be more active in getting their section of the new longhouse finished, others less so, so that the temporary structures persisted well after some people had already moved in. In fact, by the time the tardiest were established, the first room would need repair, so that the cycle of building never really ceased. The crucial point, however, is that everyone found living in insubstantial shacks unsatisfactory, not to say, humiliating. The only proper way to live was in a longhouse, and of that, no one had any doubt.

Moving about the Longhouse

In many accounts, the veranda of a longhouse is described as the main street of the village, but this is an oversimplification. Not since the Middle Ages has any street in a Western country been the scene of such a range of activities – productive, social, and religious. Moreover, the metaphor underestimates the complexity of traffic patterns inside the longhouse.

The walls between rooms were, for the most part, hardly barriers at all. Consequently, there was another constant movement of people that paralleled that along the veranda, at a slower pace, and with more intimacy. As has been pointed out, adjacent rooms generally contained siblings, or at least cousins. In a previous building, some of these people may have shared one room, and for them there was one that was their "room of origin," to which all had equal access. The casualness with which they moved around their new spaces was easily extended to in-marrying spouses and, of course, their children. Consequently, the walls between rooms always had plenty of gaps in strategic locations. In the seating area, there were perhaps walls of sturdy vertical planks six feet or so high, giving a somewhat formal air. But even here, it was possible to peep through cracks to see what was going on next door, if for example there was sudden laughter, and no inhibition whatsoever at immediately calling out to enquire. Further to the rear, one simply stepped through a gap, ducking or wiggling as needed to avoid half-finished framing. One could not speak of these spaces as doorways, because there was no door and never would be. It was more likely that the wall would be knocked down entirely, if, for example, it was necessary to create a large cooking area for a feast.

The permeable walls between rooms were related to an apparent indifference to anything we might call privacy. Christine Helliwell (1993) is the only ethnographer I know of who has captured this basic quality of longhouse life. What she describes is the absolute frankness of the "gaze," as we have now come to reify it, and its failure to oppress anyone, except perhaps the ethnographer. She recounts an incident when, suffering the usual fieldworker's angst, she put a piece of cardboard over a hole in the wall so as to create a tiny corner in which to hide. Her neighbour, in all kindness, took the cardboard down, explaining simply that she could not see her with the cardboard in the way. Helliwell describes spaces constructed to allow constant mutual visibility, and much of what she says resonates with Baram longhouses, even though the ones she knew were far away to the south, in the western province of Indonesian Borneo. The longhouses of the Kelabit in the far headwaters of the Baram River had no internal walls whatsoever (Harrisson 1959:24). There was division of space in social terms, that is, hearths and sleeping areas associated with particular small groups of people, but the crucial point is that from anywhere in the house one could see at a glance what was going on along its whole length. In most longhouses in the Baram watershed, this was not so, but even so anywhere (except the interiors of mosquito nets – those havens of marital intimacy) was open to inspection. The only real doors were those that gave access to and from the veranda, but they were seldom closed except when everyone inside had gone off to the farms. There were also occasions when doors were closed because of a ritual prohibition, marked by hanging a bunch of leaves on the door. At other times, to close a door was to invite a passerby to immediately open it again, and ask why it was closed in the first place – in exactly the same manner as Helliwell's piece of cardboard.

With our Western stereotypes of the Foulcaudrian "surveillance" of the police state and our suburban horror of meddling neighbours, it is hard to empathize with the negation of privacy as a positive value. It is nevertheless at the heart of longhouse sociality, and it is reflected in everything from religion to bodily functions. Some contexts bring both ends of the spectrum together. As I have described elsewhere (Metcalf 1982:33–45), no one who died in the longhouses died alone, but in a room crowded with neighbours. There was a vague notion that those assembled somehow aided the sick person, but the principle sentiment was simply that it was an event of concern to the entire community, and no private matter. I never heard anyone assert this as a rule because it was too obvious to need stating. Indeed, the reverse was hardly expressible. Birth was the same, although the mother-to-be was carefully hidden behind a wall of mats, and draped in a sarong. Even the midwives operated only by touch. Nevertheless, everyone in the room followed developments minute by minute, discussed how things were going, and grew alarmed when the mother groaned in pain. After a successful delivery, a wave of exhilaration ran down the entire longhouse.

As the case of childbirth indicates, openness to the public gaze coexisted with modesty about nudity and bodily functions. I have already described bathing at dawn and dusk as a social event. A man might avoid a raft already occupied by married women, but bathing was generally mixed, and some horseplay between girls and boys was tolerated. Even in same-sex situations, however, people were careful to keep their pubic areas covered at all times. In the 1970s, men bathed in swimsuits, women in sarongs. Similar rules applied as regards defecation. That is, people kept themselves decently covered, but showed no embarrassment. The sarong – worn alike by men and women around the house – was a convenient garment in this regard. First thing in the morning, people walked sleepily into the jungle, passing others without comment, to find a spot to squat, their sarongs tucked up at the back. Later in the day the rafts were often used, and some were fitted with a small box on the down river end, with walls a mere couple of feet high. If a canoe full of people happened to arrive from the farms while you were occupying the box, no one felt any compunction in handing you things to hold as they unloaded the boat.

Traffic to and from the rafts constitutes a third, lateral traffic pattern. The route directly from riverside to kitchens was travelled frequently by people carrying water. In Hose's day, water was carried in long tubes of the widest bamboo, tied together in bundles. In the 1970s, the usual container was an old kerosene tin, equipped with a tumpline that went across the forehead and allowed the water container to be balanced on the back, walking in a slightly stooped position. Full of water, the tins weighed about forty pounds, but nevertheless it was children who did most of the hauling of water, so acquiring their sure-footedness. There were seldom any stairs down to the ground at the back of the house because it was used only as a dumping ground for kitchen waste. Even chicken coops were built up at the level of the veranda, although fowls were mostly allowed to roam free. Leaving the house from a kitchen consequently meant walking through a room, across the veranda, and down the nearest notched log or steps. This route was travelled by everyone but the halt and infirm dozens of times every day. Meanwhile, there were the more or less frequent visits next door, from which one might go on again, as occasion suggested. Business several doors away prompted stepping out onto the veranda, and there were always excuses and even demands to do so. It must be conceded, however, that people from one end of the longhouse might go days or weeks at a time without visiting the other end, and when they did, showed reserve in intruding too far into the rooms of people they knew less well than their immediate neighbours. In short, although almost totally lacking anything that Westerners might call privacy, there were innumerable subtle nuances in the social spaces that longhouses provided.

One more traffic pattern remains to be discussed, less obvious because illicit, and that was through the attic. It was the route used by unmarried young men on their visits to girls with whom they had an understanding, and it was a hazardous one. At night, people barred their front doors leading onto the veranda, and, as noted previously, no one could tiptoe from room to room without waking up people sleeping on the same floorboards. Moreover, girls who were a suitable match often lived several doors away. So, the adventurous youth climbed up into the attic when the whole house was finally asleep and edged his way along the roof beams, cluttered as they were with all sorts of odds and ends. All this was done in darkness because the little wick lanterns that people kept burning in their rooms cast only a small circle of light and did nothing to illuminate the vast space of the attic. Arriving at his lover's room, he had to descend noiselessly, making sure to select the right mosquito net. Whether parents were genuinely unaware of these visits is unclear. Certainly, a measure of sexual experimentation was allowed to the young people, provided that the proprieties were strictly observed. First, it was unthinkable that any respectable girl would enter the mosquito net of a boy. Second, the credible denial of the parents had to be maintained, that is, everything had to be done discreetly. Third, the young man had to be gone well before first light or face an immediate shotgun marriage.

It was these nocturnal adventures that provided the mainstay of gossip and teasing at the rafts during the early morning bath. At times when the longhouse was full and there were many gatherings in the evenings in this room or that, it would be the young men who stayed up latest. Then there would be all kinds of plotting and giggling. A shy boy with a crush made a perfect victim. He would be assured that the girl had sent clear signals of her willingness to receive him, and then he was coaxed to drink while he was plucking up courage. The most hilarious result was that the victim would miss his step and crash down on the floor somewhere along the way, but even novices usually managed to succeed in their trysts. Longhouse opinion was seldom wrong when it detected an attraction between a man and a woman, despite the fact that there was never any public display of affection.

What moved about the longhouse most freely was conversation, which seemed never to cease. People joined a conversation, and left it again, or it fragmented into kitchens or down to the riverside. Even at night as people settled down to sleep, they talked from where they lay directly into the attic, which provided a kind of echo chamber. There would be long pauses so that it seemed everyone was finally asleep, but then a voice would come drifting in again from somewhere, worrying at some issue or other. When that open-ended conversation lapsed, there was nothing but the whispering of lovers inside their mosquito nets.

The Longhouse as Fortress

In contrast to the incessant movement around the longhouse, there was a quantitative and qualitative difference in traffic between communities. This is not to suggest that such traffic was insignificant. On the contrary, links between longhouses had major consequences, as we see in Section III. Moreover, communities could and did fall apart, and then their margins became hazy. Nevertheless, for much of the time, and in many places, there were clear boundaries between the populations, if not the territories, of different communities. That is, everyone belonged to one longhouse community or another. It is this feature that allows me to use the expression "community" in the first place. Moreover, there were ritual occasions when a community was formally closed off and no one was allowed to enter or leave. This condition was indicated by white flags posted on the riverbank at either end of the house. In the 1970s, the headman was empowered to fine on the spot any passerby who so much as touched one of the rafts in breach of this prohibition, and that included people from down river. During the nineteenth century, longhouses were ritually closed in this way when epidemics were reported in nearby communities, and anyone who approached was liable to be driven away or even killed. One shamanistic technique to exclude evil influences involved building mystical barriers around an entire longhouse made of spiky creepers that resembled nothing so much as barbed wire.

The segregation of communities in this way hints at the military function of longhouses. Hose describes in some detail the type of warfare practiced in the Baram and Limbang watersheds in the nineteenth century, and his account carries weight because he talked to warriors with plenty of experience from the decades before colonial "pacification," and even employed them on his own punitive expeditions (Hose and McDougall 1912:I:170–4). There are also firsthand accounts from coastal people, who had every reason to know about the warlike activities of their upriver neighbours.

Warfare mostly consisted of raids, and the whole point was to catch a community unprepared and take it in the first rush. The approach was consequently stealthy, involving canoes hidden at some distance and a secret camp with no cooking fires. Then scouts were sent to assess the defences, and when all was prepared, the predawn rush. Attempts would be made to set the house on fire and generally cause panic. As Hose and McDougall describe it:

> The calm stillness of the tropical dawn is broken by the deep war-chorus of the attacking party, by the shouts and screams of the people of the house suddenly roused from sleep, by the cries and squeals of the frightened animals

51

beneath the house, and the beating of the alarm signal on the *tawak* [gong]. (1912: I:172, parenthesis added)

The objective – apart from glory – was loot, especially the valuables acquired in trade with the coast. Another goal was taking slaves, as we see in Chapter 9. The amount of killing varied. Wounded defenders were often dispatched on the spot, and even women and children were killed in the first minutes, but the majority of residents frequently escaped into the jungle. There were few occasions when wholesale massacres occurred.

A third motive for attacks was the taking of heads, but the evidence is ambiguous about just how prevalent this was. During colonial times, heads were prominently displayed on the verandas of virtually all longhouses in the Baram and Limbang watersheds, so there is no doubt that the communities there practiced headhunting. Moreover, heads were required to terminate mourning after the funeral of an important person, and on these occasions, small war parties were sent out to collect them. In fact, the term for headhunting in many languages in the region translates as "war in small groups." But these prowlers were not about to attack longhouses. Instead, they preferred to sneak up on single victims, such as old ladies out collecting firewood. People on lonely farms were vulnerable, providing a strong motivation for adjacent farms. Finally, the inoffensive Penan foragers were often the targets of raids.

What is less clear is what part headhunting played in warfare not "in small groups." The Iban to the south of the Baram had by reputation an insatiable desire for heads, but this was not the case with Upriver People. Although heads were believed to bring fecundity to the community in terms of large crops and many children, their maintenance required food offerings and keeping a fire constantly alight below them. They could also be vengeful, and only old men who had already led full lives would dare touch them. Women and children hardly cared to go near them, shrinking against the wall if they needed to pass. Consequently, most communities kept only a few heads, and the impression is that warfare only marginally involved the taking of heads, as a by-product of deaths in combat, and seldom afterward in cold blood (Hoskins 1996; McKinley 1976; Metcalf 1996).

Having succeeded in overcoming a longhouse, the attackers had no thought of pursuing those who escaped into the jungle. On the contrary, they were anxious to grab what they could carry and retreat as fast as possible to their camp. The defenders, finding themselves not pursued, might well regroup in the forest and try to cut off the attackers as they straggled back along forest paths burdened with heavy gongs or valuables boxes. These were among the few occasions when pitched battles occurred in the open, although I did hear stories of raiding parties meeting half way between longhouses and fighting it out on a stony strand. Meanwhile, if the defenders managed to summon allies from nearby houses, they might outnumber their attackers and turn the tables on them completely. It was not unknown for war parties to be annihilated, so that hit-and-run tactics were the rule.

Moreover, a longhouse already alerted to the possibility of attack could be an extremely hard nut to crack with the weapons available. Each man carried a short sword and a spear. The swords were a variant of the ubiquitous *parang*, and here I must use the Malay word because there is no English equivalent. It was heavier than is suggested by the term "bush knife" and slimmer than a machete. The blades were about twenty inches long, and two wide at the outer end, narrowing toward the handle. They were slightly curved like a sabre and designed to deliver heavy slashing blows, whether at the limbs of trees or enemies. War *parang* were among the most beautiful artifacts of Upriver People, made of fine steel with an excellent temper, often intricately chased and incised. The surfaces were also slightly hollowed to favour the cutting motion, left or right handed. Handles were carved from deer's horn and decorated with tufts of dyed goats' hair.

The warrior's spear was also a more elegant variant of an everyday implement, which was used to finish off wild pigs rounded up by hunting dogs. In war as in hunting, spears were used for thrusting rather than throwing, and consequently, they were sturdily built, with a solid shaft and a heavy blade about two inches wide and ten long. By way of protection, warriors carried light wooden shields, also elaborately decorated. It was large enough to mask a large part of the body against projectiles. More important, it was used to fend off blows, or better yet to trap the blade of an opponent's *parang* if he were so unskillful as to attack with a simple downward chop. The *parang* was then bound to slice into the upper end of the shield, but could not split it lengthwise because it was bound together laterally with rattans. Consequently, the *parang* became stuck in the shield and could be jerked out of the attacker's hand, leaving him defenceless.

This technique for disarming an opponent gives some idea of the hand-to-hand fighting, always in the form of a melee, and lacking coordination once fighting began. In the 1970s, it was one of several manoeuvres demonstrated to me by older men, who became excited talking about military matters. It was surprising how many still owned the full panoply of war, even though the last opportunity to make use of it had been in their fathers' or grandfathers' time (see Figure 01-03). They even talked occasionally as if they expected the nation-state would wither away in due course, leaving them once again to their own devices. A generation later, such notions had entirely disappeared, marking the familiar triumph of modernity, that is, the future over the past. In addition to *parang*, spear, and shield, older men often

Figure 01-03. Tama Jok of Long Teru. Even in the 1970's, it was surprising how many older men still had available the equipment of a warrior: spear, sword, shield, war-cloak and bonnet. (Picture by the author.)

Figure 01-04. A Kayan longhouse protected by a stockade. Though relatively flimsy, the stockade would be extremely difficult to take at a rush, especially under fire from poisoned blow-guns darts shot from within. A well-prepared longhouse was a difficult nut to crack, using only the weapons available to Upriver People. (From Hose and McDougall 1912, Vol I, plate 100.)

had war cloaks made of bear or goat skin and caps made of woven rattan, some decorated with beads and feathers. These were in the 1970s still in demand for the male version of the dance called *ngajat*, which was always a feature of longhouse entertainment. Considered as body armour, however, cloaks and caps could not have provided much protection against anything but glancing blows, and the emphasis was clearly on agility and rapid sallies.

By all accounts, fighting with spear and *parang* was soon broken off when one side began to prevail, and this further emphasizes the importance of surprise in attacking a longhouse. If the residents did not flee at once, they might throw down the ladders leading up to the veranda, especially as these usually consisted of nothing more than a notched log. The attackers had now to climb up, and while they were trying to do that were targets for blow-pipe darts shot from above. These devices hardly count as weapons because they were normally used only for hunting small game. Nevertheless, the darts, although mere slivers of bamboo incapable themselves of causing serious injury, had their points armed with a most effective poison made from the sap of a jungle tree (Hose and McDougall 1912:I:215–9). Hunters reckoned that there was time enough to smoke a cigarette between shooting a large monkey with a dart, and the animal falling dead to the ground. Whether a human would die from such a dose depended evidently on where he was hit. Moreover, it might take a long time to disable him, and this explains why blow-pipes were not much used by the attackers. For the defenders, however, they could be effective in delaying the attackers, who were obliged to juggle their shields around while trying to stand up one of the heavy log ladders. Certainly, no one was indifferent to being hit, let alone multiple times.

Since the construction of longhouses was generally flimsier at the back than the front, attackers might try to go underneath the house and attack there. One technique was to make a roof of shields over their heads, like a Roman testudo. Another was to turn a canoe upside down and crowd in underneath it. It was hardly possible to chop through one of the huge pilings that supported the main structure, like the ones I saw in the 1970s that had come from Aban Jau's house. But the attackers only needed to cut or knock askew a few of the lesser supports by the kitchens to bring down a section of floor. Once they were inside, panic was likely to overtake the shocked residents. A cool-headed defender might respond by pouring down boiling water from the kitchens, but there were no other projectile weapons available. In the nineteenth century, ethnologists puzzled over why it was that people who had advanced to the stage of using iron tools had failed to discover the bow. It is, of course, a nonissue of the type generated by dogmatic theory. Bows were sometimes made – as toys. For hunting, they are ineffective because the dense vegetation seldom allows a clear shot. For pigs or deer, a combination of dogs and spears brings the best results. In regard to small game in the lower branches of trees, such as birds and monkeys, they are easily shot with darts. Moreover, the blow-pipe, being drilled from a long piece of hardwood, is most easily handled in a near vertical position. A bow is difficult to shoot at such steep angles, and arrows are impossible to recover in the dense underbrush. Pressed into service as a weapon, blow-pipes could be thrust through crevices in the floor and walls, but once the enemy was inside the house it was too late for that.

Clearly, the primary defensive feature of a longhouse was its height. Hose says that verandas stood "ten to thirty feet above the level of the ground" (Hose and McDougall 1912:I:178), but it is unlikely that those of Upriver People ever approached the top end of this range, except perhaps over uneven ground. Hose was probably thinking of the "great houses" of the Melanau people, as described by Stephen Morris (1991:42). The Melanau lived in the swampy coastal region to the southwest of the Baram watershed, near the mouth of the Rejang. Since large pirate fleets from the southern Philippines often swept along these coasts, the Melanau built especially tall houses, often fortified with cannons. Perversely, when the first English Rajah, James Brooke, set about suppressing piracy in the region, the Melanau were sometimes targeted for harbouring pirates. An engraving published in the *Illustrated London News* at the time (reprinted in Tate 1988:43) shows a British man of war attacking a Melanau house. The amazing height of the building is apparent, even allowing for artistic licence. Examples that reached Hose's thirty feet were still to be found in the 1970s.

However, even floors only ten feet above ground provided a formidable defence against attackers armed only with sword and spear. This feature is sufficiently obvious that we must remind ourselves that houses raised on stilts are found in many parts of Southeast Asia. The arrangement has many advantages. It escapes the mud below; it allows disposal of kitchen waste, soon cleaned up by free-roaming chickens and pigs; and it greatly improves ventilation. In Borneo at least, there is another major advantage. An elevation of only a few feet greatly reduced the number of insects, and anyone who has passed a night on the jungle floor knows what a blessing that is. Consequently, it is not surprising that during the twentieth-century longhouses continued to be at least eight to ten feet above the ground. Even so, longhouses retained a martial air in the 1970s. The bulk and height of the building conveyed a sense of security, and rumours of headhunting persisted (Metcalf 1996).

In the nineteenth century, when some leaders could muster forces of hundreds of men, many longhouse communities felt the need of a second line of defence. Stockades were for the most part not defended like the walls of a castle, but simply used to slow down the attackers and force them to expose themselves to a shower of blow-pipe darts. Meanwhile, the defenders had time to organise their resistance. As Hose and McDougall describe it:

> When a household gets wind of an intended attack, they generally put the house in a state of defence by erecting a fence of vertical stakes around it some three yards outside the posts on which it is supported and some six to eight feet in height. This fence is rendered unclimbable by a frieze consisting of a multitude of slips of bamboo; each of these is sharpened at both ends, bent upon itself, and thrust between the poles of the palisade so that its sharp ends are directed outwards. This dense jungle of loosely attached spikes constitutes an obstacle not easily overcome by the enemy; for the loosely fitting bamboo slips can neither be hacked away nor removed individually without considerable expenditure of time, during which the attackers are exposed to a shower of missiles from the house. A double ladder in the form of a stile is placed across the fence to permit the passage of the people of the house. (1912:I:179)

In addition, a community alerted to an impending attack could sew the paths around the house with punji sticks, that is, slithers of sharpened bamboo with fire-hardened points. These proved effective in the Vietnam War against soldiers wearing boots; their effect on bare feet can only be imagined. Small streams where raiders might camp were sometimes blocked, or even booby-trapped, with logs designed to fall on canoes pushing inland.

One might imagine that the easiest way to take a longhouse would be to set fire to it, but this was not as easy as it sounds. The main framework of well-established houses was made of dense timbers like the amazingly tough *bilian*, as were the massive floor planks. No doubt such wood will burn if heated to a high enough temperature, but an old *bilian* piling was not about to catch fire if a handful of blazing straw was held against it. The same applies to the shingle roof, assuming someone could throw a brand up there. Fire became a more practical weapon once the house's defences were breached because interior walls were usually made out of flimsier stuff, and the smoke and flames contributed to the general confusion. Old or rickety houses may perhaps have been burned down, but they were more vulnerable to other forms of attack as well.

There was no equivalent of siege warfare, but there were cases of long-houses being taken by treachery. In the 1850s, Spenser St. John – the same man who was impressed by his first view of the longhouse community at "Longusin" – collected the following account from a Brunei nobleman of how a "Murut" house in "Blait country" was taken by "Kayan" attackers. The ethnic labels that the nobleman uses are vague, no doubt because he had no interest in the diverse tribes of the infidels. We have more to say about who they were in Chapter 9, but for the moment suffice it to say that the community "had often been attacked, but, as a strong stockade had been built around it, they had defied the enemy." The account continues:

> One day a fugitive party of three men and several women and children were seen flying from the jungle towards the Murut village. Some armed men went out to meet them, and they said that they had run away from the Kayans, and were now escaping pursuit. They proved to be Muruts of a distant river, who had been captured and held in slavery by the Kayans. The Blaits received them with hospitality, and offered them room in their long village houses that contained 150 families. The fugitives, however, said they preferred keeping their party together, and asked leave to build a temporary hut against the inner side of the stockade. Permission was granted, and they lived there six months, working at a farm with their hosts.
>
> One of these men, after the gathering in of the harvest, stayed out till sunset, and explained it by saying that he had been hunting, and that the chase had led him further than he intended. It was a dark night that followed; and about four in the morning, a large party of Kayans crawled quietly up

to the stockade, and found an entrance prepared for them. The posts had been removed by the stranger Muruts, who had gradually cut through the wood that formed the inner wall of their temporary shed. When sufficient were within the defences, a loud shout was raised, and fire applied to the leaf houses. The villagers rushed out to be cut down or captured. In the confusion and the darkness, however, the larger portion escaped, but left about a hundred and fifty bodies and captives in the hands of the Kayans; and I am not sorry to add, among the former were the three treacherous men who had caused the awful scene. Some of the attacking party not obtaining heads, quietly possessed themselves of those of their three allies. (St. John 1862:I:91–2)

It is a story that says much about the violence of the times, but the point here is that the attackers resorted to trickery because they could not take the longhouse by frontal assault.

If that was the case, perhaps the defensive function of longhouses was their entire *raison d'être*, and we need seek no further for an explanation. The problem with this proposition is that it immediately takes on a chicken-and-egg quality: people lived in large, defended communities because *other people* lived in large, defended communities. But warfare existed in regions of Southeast Asia where people lived in small dispersed clusters of lightly built houses, as, for instance, in Renato Rosaldo's (1980) description of the endless raiding and killing between tiny Ilongot settlements. The same applies to much of the New Guinea highlands and elsewhere. Meanwhile, it would hardly be satisfying to explain the construction of castles in medieval Europe by saying that they were built by warring lords. That much is obvious, and the question remains why those lords and their castles existed. But if the military function of longhouses cannot explain their existence, *tout court*, considered as a feedback phenomenon it has real impact. In Chapters 4 and 9 we see how the arrival of large parties of immigrants from across the mountains destabilised the military situation in the Brunei hinterland and led to the formation of megacommunities able to defend themselves against the new threat. Consequently, we are led back to historical processes, rather than one-line explanations.

There is one more factor to be considered about the attack and defence of longhouses – the introduction of firearms in the nineteenth century. On the coast, the use of gunpowder had been known for centuries, at least since the arrival of the Portuguese, if not before. Malays were proficient in the use of cannons, as is evident in another drawing from the *Illustrated London News* (Tate 1988:37) showing an attack on a Malay fort, supposedly a pirate lair. The fort has two storeys and resembles a longhouse. The ground floor houses the heavy cannon mounted on wheeled carriages, as in European warships of the time. On the upper floor, there are only swivel guns, that is, light cannons, about four feet long, with a calibre of two to three inches. Too heavy to pick up and aim like a rifle, they were held in a simple U-shaped mount resembling an oarlock. They could be moved about the veranda as needed, and inserted in holes drilled here and there along it. They were easy to aim from the inboard end, and to load, by swivelling the gun around to reach the muzzle. Even the small shot thrown by such swivel guns, or gingels, could be devastating against the lightly built hulls of Malay vessels or the ship's boats of landing parties from British warships. Moreover, loaded with grape shot they could be effective at repelling a charge and could maintain a more rapid rate of fire than the larger cannons. They were the standard weapon of the light, fast-sailing pirate ships that cruised the coasts of the South China Sea in the eighteenth and nineteenth centuries.

In the mid-nineteenth century, guns still remained largely a Malay monopoly in the Brunei hinterland. St. John repeats a story told to him by a senior nobleman, Pangiran Mumein:

> He is always telling the story of his fight with the Kayans, which exemplifies how easily these men were defeated by the use of musketry. Some years since, Pangiran Mumein hearing that the district of Temburong was invaded by the people of Baram, collected his followers and guns, and proceeded thither. When they came in sight of the Kayans crowded around a village, the Malays became alarmed, and wished to retreat; but their leader sprang forward and fired a brass swivel at the enemy; it fortunately took effect on one, and the crowd dispersed. Recovering from their fright, the Borneans fired volley after volley into the jungle, and celebrated their victory by loud beatings of gongs and drums. The Kayans, still more frightened, fled in all directions.

The Pangiran worried, however, that such easy victories might be a thing of the past:

> Pangiran Mumein justly observed that as long as the Kayans were unacquainted with the use of firearms, it was easy to defend the country; but that now the Bornean traders were supplying them with brass swivels and double-barrel guns, he thought that the ruin of Brunei was at hand. But the fact is, that though the Kayans are now less frightened at the noise of heavy guns and muskets than they were, they seldom employ them in their expeditions in the jungle, as they can not keep them in working order. (St. John 1862:I:87)

What prevented longhouse people from keeping their guns in working order was not the guns themselves, but difficulty in obtaining and preserving gunpowder. Chemically, gunpowder is simply a mixture of saltpeter, carbon, and sulphur, but in powder form it is difficult to handle and ignite, and rapidly absorbs water and becomes useless. To be effective, it has to be formed into grains, a process called "corning," and then sieved to get grains of various uniform sizes, finer for hand-held guns, coarser for cannons. Uniformly grained gunpowder, carefully kept dry, was a convenient and effective propellent, but Upriver People had a lot to learn about it. Malays sold them inferior locally made mixes, which were near impossible to keep dry while travelling in wet jungle. Upriver People – and Malays, too – often left guns loaded for days or weeks at a time, so that when they came to be fired the charge was too damp to ignite. In this situation, guns were often abandoned because it was difficult and time consuming to pull the old charge out and reload. All in all, the Pangiran need not have worried; I can find no evidence of muskets or the double-barrelled hunting guns that he mentions ever being used by Upriver People in warfare. Heavier guns, swivels, and cannons were kept in longhouses where it was feasible to keep powder dry. In so far as they were used militarily, guns therefore favoured defenders and not attackers.

The military use of cannons is only part of the story, however. As we see in Chapter 6, their real value was as prestige goods, if not almost a form of currency. For that use, the fickleness of gunpowder was neither here nor there.

The Longhouse as Metropolis

Inevitably, my description of how people lived in the spaces and environs of longhouses in general makes them sound more uniform than they were. In fact, they varied a great deal in the impressions that they made on visitors. Some were grand, others seemed more intimate. Some exuded vivacity, so that one was surrounded by kids the moment one touched a raft, and once inside, by adults keen to exchange news. Others houses looked run down, or projected a depressed, abandoned air. Part of this had to do with the season of one's visit, but there were also noticeable differences in community *esprit*. Some houses had reputations for frequent adultery, others were riven by internal rivalries, and so on.

There was, however, one thing that almost all houses embodied: the sense of being a metropolis, the cultural center of what I can only call a nation. In the 1970s, it was common for people to contrast themselves as members of a particular longhouse community against all other Malaysians, of whatever ethnicity, put together, as if they were equivalent. Before colonial annexation, longhouse communities were sovereign entities, and all relations with other communities were foreign relations. Even in the

1970s, there was a kind of stateliness in the reception of travellers, as if they were delegations from other communities. This lay at the basis of Upriver hospitality, which often surprised Westerners, who probably thought that people with such a martial reputation would lack civility. That prejudice fails to grasp indigenous politics.

There is a caveat that must be added to the proposition that communities were politically independent. Historical links with other communities were often acknowledged. Also, the prestige of particular leaders often extended beyond their own communities, so that their precedence might be admitted by leaders in other houses. This was especially true among the more hierarchically inclined Kayan and Kenyah communities. This did not, however, give them any direct authority. When a community separated itself from another, it stated its ultimate sovereignty. Even in the colonial era, when chiefs and paramount chiefs were appointed, they often found it difficult to exert their influence outside their own communities.

Consequently, history among Upriver People was the history of communities. I made a point of collecting these narratives, and I was struck, not by how alien they seemed, but how familiar. They resembled nothing so much as the history of Britain that I had been taught as a child, and only ever half understood. I remember being amazed to learn that the Scots came from Ireland. This seemed utterly confusing. Did that mean the Irish came from Scotland, and who exactly were the Picts, and who built Stonehenge, and who was Boadicea? As it turns out, my childish questions were perfectly good ones, and even as an adult, I am hard put to find the answers. As I immersed myself in the narratives of longhouse communities, it became easy to see them as grand actors on a global stage. Imagine an English or French historian, or both together, sitting down to explain to an audience of Upriver People what the Hundred Years War was all about – they would, incidentally, be fascinated – and you have some idea of the kinds of discussions I got from longhouse historians. Imagine the ethnic subtleties – if Bordeaux was an English town, why did almost no one there speak English? What did they speak? What's this about the English kings coming from France? – and you are forewarned of what is to follow in stories concerning longhouse communities.

It takes time to absorb the consciousness of a longhouse community as metropolis. Colonial officers did not stay long enough in any one place to feel it, except perhaps vaguely, when in the company of a distinguished leader. The experience they lacked was of the other half of the life of Upriver People, the half spent away from the longhouse at the farms. I will not say much about the techniques of slash and burn agriculture using "dry" (i.e., nonirrigated) or "hill" rice since a large literature exists on the topic. Suffice it to say that farms were usually too far away from longhouses

Figure 01-05. What longhouse life was really all about. Sebop men singing at a longhouse festival sometime in the 1950's. (Picture taken by Hedda Morrison, from her book of photographs entitled *Sarawak*, 1965: 275.) By permission of Alastair Morrison.

to allow commuting back and forth each day, so every room in the long-house also had a farmhouse, more or less flimsy. In former times, when attacks on outlying farms were an ever-present threat, farmhouses were often built side by side so that they resembled small longhouses. In those days, I was told, security took precedence over production, and farms were smaller. Consequently, people were forced to rely more on jungle produce, particularly wild sago.

Life at the farms was hard. Work began soon after sunrise and ended not long before sunset. People took time off in the early afternoon, but there was nowhere to escape the heat. The small farmhouses were hot, and the jungle full of insects. In the evening, the only lighting was from wick lanterns, and after a hasty meal, everyone was soon asleep. Near harvest time, when dry weather was earnestly looked for, bathing was often difficult. Tiny streams dried up, leaving only muddy water holes, and then people went to sleep not only tired but dirty – a privation sorely felt by Upriver People. During the harvest, everyone was frantic to get the crop in before some disaster wiped out the year's food supply. Growing hill rice is a risky business. If it is too wet early on, it is difficult to burn off the felled trees and underbrush. If there is no rain after planting, the seed will not germinate. Most important, there must be dry weather in the weeks before the harvest. Sudden squalls, with violent winds and lashing rain, could leave the whole crop rotting in the mud. Meanwhile, the climate of Borneo is fickle. This is the less glamorous side of longhouse life; the anxieties of hill rice agriculture.

Consequently, everyone eagerly looked forward to getting back to the longhouse. There was, to begin with, the considerable luxuries of the longhouse, appreciable only by comparison with the farms: space, shade, and a cool river in which to bathe. There was the promise of small treats: homegrown tobacco and betel, and perhaps shop-bought biscuits, sugar, and coffee. Upriver cuisine was always simple: rice or sago, salt, various leafy plants, and fish or game as available. But at least in the longhouse it could be properly prepared and eaten at leisure. Finally, there was rice wine, which was seldom available at the farms. It was made by cooking rice, rolling it into balls about four inches in diameter, and allowing it to ferment in large glazed jars. After a few days, a milky liquid ran off, which is usually described in the literature as rice "wine." Later, water was added to make a second batch of wine, which was clearer but less tasty.

In addition to these luxuries, there was the excitement of seeing new faces. Children were keen to meet age-mates who had gone with their parents to other farming areas, but adults shared their expectation because they, too, had friends they had known since childhood. There was the promise of social life in the evenings, climaxing in the weeks after the harvest. This period constituted an informal ritual season. Many communities had annual festivals at this time, and marriages were scheduled to take advantage of plentiful rice supplies. There were also parties held simply because the young people wanted them, and they were occasions for displays of the performing arts, dancing and music, enjoyed by young and old alike. The most appreciated dances were performed solo, and skilled dancers were much admired. They usually appeared last, after everyone else had taken a turn. The accompaniment for dancing was provided by a three-stringed instrument carved from a single piece of wood, sometimes augmented by gongs and flutes.

The longhouse was also the place for communal gatherings of a legal variety. Disputes between coresidents, about everything from assaults to the ownership of fruit trees, were settled in town meetings. Half the community might attend, crammed into the largest room available. Nominally, community leaders presided over these events, particularly the headman, but everyone could have their say about what was right and fair. The only effective resolution was consensus, summed up by the headman. Stiff fines could be imposed, especially on continual wrongdoers who had exasperated their neighbours. The most extreme measure was expulsion. These occasions provided an opportunity for leaders to display their knowledge of community history and custom, and their own political skills.

To Lack Longhouses Is to Live in the Forest

In short, the arts, entertainment, civil society, history, and law − all the things we associate with major cities − were invested in the longhouse, and each longhouse was its own metropolis. If I asked Upriver People why they lived in longhouses, the answer was a blank stare. Did I think they were animals, that they would live in the forest? When I told them that there were people not very far away, in Indonesia and the Philippines and New Guinea, who had no longhouses and lived all the time at their farms, they were not at all surprised. They had always known that not everyone shared their level of civilisation. It was not long before I absorbed their view of things. Those other people simply lacked something; how boring it would have been to have had to do fieldwork there.

Chapter 2

Longhouse Communities

To begin with a negative, longhouse communities are not the building blocks of ethnicity. Why this is so is neatly demonstrated by the community whose longhouse Hose described, the lair of the infamous Aban Jau.

Aban Jau's Community

In almost the first mention of Aban Jau in the colonial records, he is already threatening to raid a town on the coast. In the report, he is described as "the Kyan chief of Tinja" (*Sarawak Gazette* 1876:120). Given that the Kayan had the most warlike reputation of anyone in the Baram watershed, the ethnic attribution is reasonable. Nevertheless, it is wrong; neither Aban Jau nor his followers would have described themselves as Kayan. Within a few years, colonial administrators had learned that not all troublesome chiefs were Kayan, so they reclassified him as chief of the Sebop. This is better, but still inaccurate. To begin with, there are problems of orthography. The ethnic label also appears in the records as Sibup, Sibop, and Sebob, and all of these sound odd to a native speaker. Clement Langat Sabang (1991:21), himself Sebop, prefers the spelling "Chebup," but for the present moment we leave such niceties aside.

Aban Jau was not "chief of the Sebop" because there were certainly people who called themselves Sebop (or Chebup, or whatever) but did not

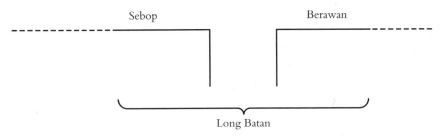

Figure 02–01. Long Batan people were neither a kind of Sebop nor a kind of Berawan.

acknowledge him as their leader. They may have barely heard of him. This we know from colonial later records and from the extensive oral histories of the communities involved. Moreover, a substantial part of his following was not Sebop at all. Their autonym comes down to us in the colonial records as "Berawan," although the name they use among themselves is Melawan, and Sebop people say Belau'un. Aban Jau was, however, no more chief of the Berawan than he was of the Sebop, so of what exactly was he chief? The answer is that he was the leader of the community that Hose visited. It was called Long Batan because at that place a tiny side stream called the Batan flows into the main Tinjar River, which itself flows into the Baram. In short, Aban Jau was chief of the Long Batan people, and if that sounds like another ethnonym, then it is.

This one instance hints at the fecundity of longhouse communities in generating ethnonyms. Every communal alliance, every new arrangement of community membership, has the potential to produce new ethnicities. Meanwhile, the histories of longhouses are of constant movement, as a result of both internal dynamics and external circumstances. Consequently, every close inspection of the fabric of particular longhouse communities reveals yet more ethnonyms. Moreover, nothing guarantees that new categories will be compatible with old ones. Long Batan people were neither a kind of Sebop nor a kind of Berawan. Potentially, Aban Jau's community constituted a whole new "tribe," created under the very noses of colonial administrators. So much for ethnicity in Borneo as an essential, hereditary, or inherent trait.

Place and Ethnicity

It might be objected that I am mixing up place names like Long Batan with ethnic names like Sebop, but so are the people using those names. That is the nature of ethnicity in central Borneo.

If Aban Jau's Sebop followers wanted to distinguish themselves from other Sebop, they called themselves Long Taballau. Used in that way, the name implied that there was a *previous* longhouse at a place of that name. For me to find out where it was requires locating the Taballau River, but I cannot find it on any map. This is not surprising if it is as small as, say, the Batan stream, which I could have paddled past without noticing if it had not been pointed out to me. No one I talked to in the 1970s remembered exactly where the Taballau was, except to say that it was far away, in an entirely different watershed. Invoked as an ethnonym, the term "Long Taballau" meant that a good number of the ancestors of the Long Batan Sebop came from there – although not all – and other Long Taballau people were to be found in communities other than Long Batan.

The crucial point is that the community building that went on at Long Taballau was significant enough to cast a long shadow down the generations. On one of his visits to the Tinjar, Hose took time off from his administrative functions to measure a few heads at Long Batan, no doubt hoping to win credit for moving forward the great nineteenth-century project of ethnology. What is interesting about his results a century later is not the cephalic indexes he reports, but the ethnic categories under which he sorts his data (Hose and McDougall 1912:II:Tables A–C). Trustingly, he takes his subjects' self-identification at face value: five described themselves as "Sebop," but three as "Tabalo." Consequently, in his taxonomy, Tabalo had achieved equal standing with Sebop as an ethnicity. Note also that the prefix "long" has been dropped, disguising the origins of the ethnonym in a place name. This observation might set us looking for a Sebop stream in that other river system across the mountains, and indeed, there is one, large enough even to be shown on a map.

The process of place names becoming ethnonyms demonstrates the character of longhouse communities as the sites of production of ethnic differentiation. Just how much differentiation occurs at any particular site is variable, but having once occurred it is remarkably persistent. In the 1970s, there were still people in the Tinjar Valley who called themselves Long Taballau and Long Batan. Neither term means quite what it did in Hose's time, which is only to say that a lot happens in a century. The crucial point is that differentiation occurred at both Long Taballau and Long Batan that outlasted the longhouses that once stood in those places. I can in fact make a strong statement in this regard: all the descendents of the people who lived together at Long Batan a century ago, wherever they now live, retain shared peculiarities that mark them off from other people, including other Berawan and other Sebop. In Chapter 10, I give specific examples, but for the moment what we need to notice is that a process of sharing *within* a community simultaneously drives wedges *between* communities.

If the analogy of wedges rings a bell, it is probably because of Darwin's famous description of the "hundred thousand wedges" of evolution constantly creating new species by splitting old ones apart. Darwin has no patent on the simile, however, and ironic as it may be, there are similarities between speciation and ethnic proliferation in central Borneo. What is different is, of course, the ethnicities remain culturally cross-fertile, however distantly related, as if cuckoos might mate with crocodiles. What is intriguing in the present case is the way that longhouse communities manage to produce an equivalent of speciation; perhaps we should call the process "ethnification."

Narrating Community

Luckily, it was until recently not difficult to gather information about ethnification. In the 1970s, I never failed to elicit elaborate oral histories wherever I went. Often I was referred to someone regarded as especially knowledgeable, and the result was less an interview than a social occasion. Longhouse residents crowded into the narrator's apartment, and children were sat down in the front row. Such narratives clearly constituted a genre. They did not occur just for my benefit but formed a regular part of life in the longhouse. Indeed, knowledge of their communal history constituted a large part of people's sense of who they were.

Not surprisingly, there were segments in these narratives about heroes who climbed to the skies or fought dreadful foes, but their basic format was a list of place names, the former locations of the community. Many moves were relatively short – a few miles – but in most narratives there were instance of major migrations between different watersheds. Often place names were idiosyncratic and did not match places on any available map. If I asked about them, I might or might not get information that enabled me to mark them on a map, but in any event I would start a discussion that would interrupt the story and introduce all kinds of distractions. Moreover, there were often older people in the audience who were differently situated in the narrative. Any break in the flow allowed them to make additions and amendments. Usually, these did not take the form of corrections, but of subplots. I would find someone tugging at my arm, whispering that the narrator had forgotten to mention that while his people were at X, my new informant's people were at Y with some friends from Z, and remarkable things had occurred there. Evenings spent in this way tended to be long ones, and my notes so tangled up with proper names jotted here and there as to require several follow-up sessions. In short, collecting communal narratives was a major aspect of fieldwork, and it drove home for me their significance in shaping longhouse identity.

Reference to Location

Throughout central Borneo, locations are specified in terms of rivers. Longhouses are invariably built beside rivers, so ensuring running water for drinking and cooking, and the opportunity to bathe frequently. Travel is mostly by river. Swidden farms are seldom far from the valley floor, and hilltops remained virgin forest. Until recently, all long-distance travel was by canoe. Except when hunting or searching for jungle produce, journeys across land were usually portages between streams in the headwaters of neighbouring watersheds. As befits a riverine people then, most place names were constructed by reference to the confluence of rivers, using the familiar formula Long X, where X is the name of the lesser stream. We might speak of the river's "mouth," except that the term usually implies the place where it flows into the sea. These river mouths are inland.

There is a marked fractal quality to riverine geography. A map of the rivers across a slice of central Borneo, as in Figure Int-01, presents a confusing mass of lines out of which it is hard to make any sense. If we close in on a smaller area, with a larger-scale map such as Figure 02-02. the phenomenon recurs. Every time the scale is increased, ever more tiny streams appear, and each one produces a potential place name. In discussing likely fishing spots or hunting trails, longhouse people often name streams too small even for a small canoe, watercourses that outside the rainy season are no more than ditches. Consequently, the number of places that cannot be found on any map is always large. Were it not for the longhouse there, Long Batan would certainly not be shown on government survey maps, and indeed, the stream of that name is not. That is why it would be only by the merest chance that the site of the original Long Taballau longhouse could be located with any precision because it was abandoned before mapping began.

This pattern of riverine settlement has produced a way of referring to longhouse locations that is found in all local languages and was transferred into colonial English. If I speak of a house being "in" the Tinjar, I summon to the literal mind an absurd image of an underwater building, but in practice the usage causes no ambiguity. The preposition might be taken as short for "in the watershed of," except that the greater part of most watersheds remained uninhabited and under virgin forest. The local usage is evocative and appropriate, and I follow it here. If people speak of a place being "inside" a river, it usually means that the river in question is small.

As an example, the elderly Aban Jau moved his longhouse away from the banks of the Tinjar and "inside" the Termado.

Compared to their knowledge of rivers, Upriver People are only vaguely aware of mountains, and name only whole ranges and a few high points. There is, however, one upland region that is frequently mentioned in oral histories – the high, eroded volcanic plateau of the Usun Apau. Judging by the number of migration sagas that begin in the Usun Apau, it would seem that it must have been very crowded a few centuries ago. At the same time, however, few make any mention of neighbours there, and it is likely that populations moved in and out of different parts of the plateau at different times. Why they settled there in the first place remains a mystery. Direct archaeological evidence is lacking, and prehistoric sites would be hard to find because of the jungle cover and rapid rates of erosion (Bellwood 1985:13). One possibility is that the cultivation of rice found a particularly favourable niche there – when it finally arrived. As Karl Pelzer pointed out many years ago, the "pioneer settlement" of tropical Asia by swidden agriculturalists took centuries to unfold, and the interior of so large a landmass as Borneo – far bigger than any of the other islands of the archipelago – may have been one of the last places to be penetrated (Pelzer 1945, Revel 1988). If the first farmers thrived, increases in population would soon necessitate migration out of the narrow valleys that cut into the plateau, toward the gentler slopes down river. What this would not explain, however, is why the Usun Apau was apparently abandoned entirely by successive populations, and the best explanation for that seem to lie in external factors, of which more later.

Longhouse Communities and Speech Communities

To recapitulate, these place names and narratives of migration are worth collecting because they provide instances of ethnification. Traditionally, however, ethnographers have taken a more direct route, relying on linguists to sort out for them their ethnic classifications. The hazards of this tactic were pointed out many years ago by Dell Hymes (1968), and the Brunei hinterland provides clear examples of what he meant. The problem is not just that there are many languages spoken in the region, although that is true. There are places with even greater linguistic complexity, such as the New Guinea highlands. The languages that concern me are at least in the same family, the western branch of Austronesian (Bellwood 1979:121). Convenient as that is for research, it also makes for complications. So many words are closely cognate from one language to another that it is hard to distinguish divergence from mere borrowing, and this has classically been the stumbling block of historical linguistics (Teeter 1963). Communities have not been isolated from one another like islands in Polynesia; on the contrary, they have constantly been on the move, constantly encountering new neighbours. Habits of linguistic borrowing are common, as for instance in ritual languages that use a form of parallelism involving paired words (Metcalf 1989:38–41). Pairs are often formed with one word from the home community and one loan word. Being cognate, the pair often shows rhyme or alliteration. To use loan words demonstrates the cosmopolitan sophistication of the speaker.

Wary of generalizing about the distribution of languages, ethnographers in Borneo have tried to hold the issue at arm's length by substituting the term "isolect." An isolect is whatever is spoken at one particular location, regardless of how it fits in with others at other places. But even this move, radical as it seems, does not get us out of trouble. What, for instance, was the isolect of Long Batan? It will do no good to argue that Long Batan was two locations, by accident simultaneously occupied by both Sebop and Berawan. The whole point is that Long Batan acted as one community, its residents intermarrying and participating together in everything from hunting to ritual. As Hymes shows in his 1969 article, languages are not shared, modified, and kept alive by "tribes," but by speech communities. Between ethnicity and language lies an intermediate variable, which complicates any match between the former and the latter. Longhouse communities are perfect examples of speech communities.

Robert Blust, who conducted extensive linguistic research in the Brunei hinterlands in the 1970s, summarizes the results as follows:

> The linguistic situation in the basin of the Baram river of northern Sarawak is one of the most complex on the entire island of Borneo. Although all the indigenous languages of this region with the possible exception of Kayan-Murik belong to a single large and internally diverse subgroup . . . linguistic differences within the area appear only occasionally to reflect simple differentiation *in situ*. More commonly, as a result of centuries of migration along the major waterways speakers of closely related languages have become separated and interspersed among speakers of other, sometimes markedly different languages, in an intricate interdigitation of speech communities that plays havoc with the mapmaker's representation of language boundaries. (Blust 1984:101)

Under these circumstances, it is as hard to speak of "a language" as it is of "a culture." To deconstruct one is equally to deconstruct the other, but that no more means that I will stop talking about language variation than about I will about cultural variation. The data from comparative linguistics is invaluable, and I continue to cite it. It is only necessary to abandon the notion that somehow linguistics provides any final or definitive answers about ethnicity; always we must consider that intermediate variable, the unfolding fates of longhouse communities.

What Did They Speak at Long Batan?

Before returning to issues of migration, it is worth pausing a moment to wonder just how communication was managed at Long Batan. By the standards of the region, Berawan and Sebop are only distantly related, and certainly not mutually intelligible. Moreover, the Long Taballau migrated into Tinjar from a considerable distance, and there had not been a long period for accommodation. Was there some lingua franca? By the mid-twentieth century, a simplified version of Malay was almost universally spoken by Upriver People, and could be used to bridge over any lack of comprehension between them, in addition to its use as a language of trade with Malays and Chinese. A century prior, however, Malay was much less widely known. Certainly, there must have been a few people at Long Batan who had some Malay, or no one could have spoken to Hose, who certainly knew neither Sebop nor Berawan. Nevertheless, old people that I knew in the 1970s insisted that Malay had been rare among ordinary villagers when they had been children. Their claim gained support from a whole genre of antique anecdotes about embarrassing misunderstandings, usually of a sexual nature, between Upriver People from different communities. Finally, it is consistent with colonial reports of difficulties finding linguistic go-betweens in remote places. Nor was there any alternative lingua franca. In the Belaga Valley, Kayan was used in this way, but it arrived too late in the Baram watershed to compete with Malay.

We are left, therefore, with the Berawan and Sebop dealing directly with each others' languages. Did both parties become bilingual? Was one language imposed over the other? Or was there a more subtle accommodation, such that everyone spoke his or her own language and simply expected to be understood? This implies something less than bilingualism, but considerable skills in comprehension. What I observed at longhouse festivals was people constantly trying out their language skills and acquiring new ones. It was truly wonderful for an Anglophone to hear a lively discussion, full of interjections and good-natured interruptions, going on in a babel of excited voices, with a rumble of simultaneous translation for the less adroit. At Long Batan, it may well have been similar: a wide range of individual language skills coupled with a casual, taken-for-granted multilingualism.

As the community of Long Batan adapted itself to its own internal diversity, there was inevitably much linguistic borrowing, and that was still evident decades later in the speech of its descendents. In other words, the alliance of Berawan and Sebop created new language varieties in the same way that it created new ethnic varieties.

Community, Language, and Ethnicity: Mapping the Sebop Diaspora

Meanwhile, it is perfectly feasible to shift narratives of migration into reverse gear, as it were, and put people back where they came from. Luckily, the materials exist to do exactly that for the Sebop, and not just that component of the Sebop that were at Long Batan (Arnold 1955; Gockel 1974; Sabang 1991; Seling 1974). The result is to place all the people who now call themselves Sebop into a few adjacent valleys on the southern side of the Usun Apau, those of the rivers Seping, Menapun, Menawan, and Luar (see Figure 02-01).

That is not all that can be said about Sebop speakers, however. There are also several closely related variants spoken by people who do not call themselves Sebop (Blust 1972; Urquhart 1959). That is, we can reconstruct a linguistic cohesion for which no ethnonym exists. Just what community dynamics caused these languages to diverge and their speakers to disperse can only be a matter of speculation because they belong to an epoch beyond the reach of oral history. What the narratives can do is put the Sebop-speaking non-Sebop back in the same region south of the Usun Apau, and so reconstruct one component of that culture area that Rousseau (1990) describes as central Borneo. It would be an error to imagine, however, that there was ever some epoch of harmony and tranquillity predating the perturbations of the eighteenth and nineteenth centuries. Instead, there were surely other migrations, dispersions, and collisions that are simply beyond reconstruction.

From this Sebop homeland, people successively migrated north, along what was evidently a well-beaten path that led from the headwaters of the Menawan over the western tableland of the Usun Apau and down into the Para. The section on foot was necessary because the migrants were moving between major watersheds, the Rejang on one side and the Baram on the other. The migrants were presumably aware of this, even though they only moved from one barely navigable stream to another. The terrain is too rough for it to be practicable to haul canoes across the mountain ridges, so migrants had to abandon them on one side and cut new ones on the other. The abandoned canoes would have been a windfall for any travellers going in the other direction, pursuing jungle produce and trade. Not all Sebop migrated, however, so that remnant populations persisted in the Usun Apau area, allied with various Kenyah groups. Meanwhile,

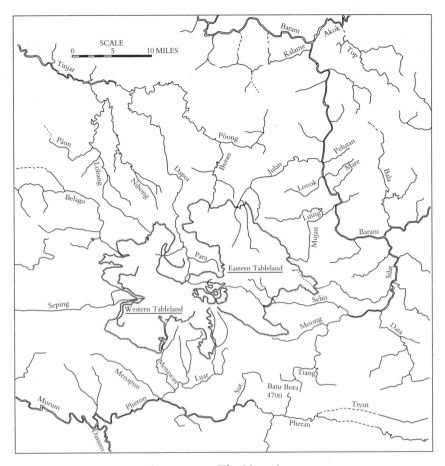

Figure 02-02. The Usun Apau.

those who joined communities in the Belaga watershed were locally called Sepeng (*Sarawak Gazette* 188:June 1882).

Among the close relations of the Sebop were the Lirong and the Long Wat people, who evidently arrived in the upper Tinjar in the first half of the nineteenth century. In Hose's lifetime, the Lirong were numerous and powerful, so much so that their arrival at one of his carefully arranged peace meetings nearly turned the event into a battle (Hose and McDougall 1912:II:295–6). However, at the beginning of the twentieth century, a cholera epidemic took a heavy toll on the population, and by the time of my fieldwork, the Lirong were reduced to one longhouse, with minorities in two or three other communities. The Long Wat people take their name from a former longhouse site in the Luar. A contingent settled in the valley of the Tinjar and became the Long Suku. The majority, however, moved on from Tinjar into the Apoh, a major tributary of the Tutoh, and we have reports of them there by the end of the nineteenth century. The *Sarawak Gazette* of May 1899 (no. 400) describes them as being at war with their neighbours in the Tutoh, so that trade in the region was at a standstill. After hostilities ceased, they promptly succumbed to internal rivalries and split into several longhouse communities.

In addition to Lirong, Long Wat, and Long Suku, there are other language variants closely related to Sebop, namely, those spoken by foraging Penan (Blust 1972). Until recently, the Penan practiced no agriculture and had no longhouses, and they suffered heavy discrimination. Longhouse dwellers often treated them as slaves. The persistence of foraging adaptations lends credence to the notion that rice agriculture came late to the Usun Apau. In fact, in the 1970s, I was told flatly by Sabang Chapu, headman of Long Loyang and the most respected Sebop leader of his generation, that his ancestors had lived exactly as the Penan did, and indeed that they simply were Penan. In contrast with many of his neighbours, he took pride in pointing out his connection with people whose knowledge of the forest is unparalleled. Nevertheless, Penan were generally excluded from Sebop society, demonstrating once again the lack of fit between language and ethnicity.

That the Penan lack longhouses and the kinds of communities that go with them has a further consequence: they were not subject to the mode of ethnic differentiation I describe here (Needham 1954a, 1955, 1958). In addition, they are mobile in ways that longhouse people are not. They often provided longhouse people with information about other rivers and acted as guides. As a result, they played a role as a kind of invisible connective tissue between longhouse communities.

Imposed Ethnicities

The example of the Sebop migrations shows how complex the entanglements of language, ethnicity, and community might be, but new complications were unwittingly added by the first colonial administrators. Not understanding what they were seeing, they imposed ethnic categories of their own invention. Since Upriver People were obliged to use these clumsy approximations to make themselves understood to their new masters the categories took on a life of their own and began to influence indigenous conceptions.

The key distinction imposed by the colonialists was the contrast Kayan/Kenyah. The first colonial administrators in the Baram watershed were aware of the aggressive and numerous Kayan, so much so that Aban Jau's military adventures were enough to get him initially classified as a Kayan.

Soon, however, it became clear that not everyone in Baram was Kayan, and the next ethnic label that came to hand was Kenyah. As it happens, Kenyah communities display more diversity among themselves in language and culture than the relatively homogeneous Kayan. Consequently, it was easy to stretch the term "Kenyah" to just about anybody in Baram who was clearly not Kayan. This included the Sebop, so that willy-nilly they became a subtribe of the Kenyah.

This spurious piece of taxonomy set in motion a series of bizarre repercussions. Early administrators had cultivated contacts with key Kenyah chiefs during the process of "pacification." What those chiefs gained from their cooperation was increased prestige, and their communities gained a reputation for aristocratic hauteur and refinement in the arts, such as music and dance. Those people newly classified as Kenyah began to model themselves on these elite communities, and their leaders assumed as much of the aristocratic manners of Kenyah chiefs as their followers would let them get away with. No sooner had they started down this path of acculturation, however, than administrators began to notice fissures in the Kenyah edifice that they themselves had built. They began to distinguish between the "true" Kenyah and those who now appeared as interlopers "passing" as Kenyah. The Sebop were caught in a trap: having aided the uncomprehending outsider by agreeing to be a type of Kenyah, they were then denigrated as poor cousins of the real thing.

At least one administrator-ethnographer had the sense to notice that if the Sebop were a kind of Kenyah, then by all logic foraging Penan should be, too, because their languages were very similar (Urquhart 1959). But this extension was intolerable, however, to the "true" Kenyah who looked down on the foragers. If, however, the Sebop are to be excluded, then we have people who cannot be fitted under the Kayan–Kenyah umbrella. The temptation then was to take all the "misfits" and put them under some new miscellaneous category. Hose – that indefatigable adventurer and dabbler in nineteenth-century anthropology – formed the theory that the nondescript non-Kayan non-Kenyah residents of the Baram watershed were remnants of a more ancient migration into the region, a primitive substrate. Similar theories were of course popular in colonial Africa at the same epoch, and the notion of a hidden proto-civilisation has its romantic appeal. The term he invented to cover these peoples was "Klemantan," and the term still circulates in the anthropological literature. For instance, it appears in Raymond Kennedy's *Bibliography of Indonesian Peoples and Cultures*, published by the Human Relations Area Files in 1945. There are, however, no communities that describe themselves as "Klemantan," and the category achieves exactly what one would expect: it makes things appear alike that actually have nothing in common. Just who Hose's Klemantan people really were is revealed in Chapter 8, but for now the point is that imposed categories only obscured the ethnological realities that they were supposed to reveal.

The temptation to invent nonindigenous super categories was not restricted to amateurs. During his 1947 visit to Sarawak, Edmund Leach was drawn into making yet another ethnic taxonomy of the peoples of Sarawak, refining those made by colonial officers before him. He rejects the Klemantan classification, which Hose had stretched to its breaking point. Having ridiculed Hose, however, Leach promptly substitutes a miscellaneous category of his own. Leach's term "Kajang" was not invented from thin air; it evidently had some currency to describe non-Kayan, non-Kenyah people in the Belaga watershed, but Leach extended it to cover populations like the Sebop and Berawan in the Baram watershed, where the term is unknown. The resulting construct, his Kayan-Kenyah-Kajang Complex (Leach 1950:54–5), is now enshrined in Borneo ethnography, but it is no more justified than Hose's Klemantan. It represents no indigenous ethnicity, and linguistically Sebop and Berawan are as distant from the languages in Belaga as they are from Kenyah. He, too, fell into the trap of imposing ethnicity, rather than studying ethnification.

Oddly enough, Anna Tsing (1993:52–3) argues in favour of such invented names. She worked at the opposite end of the island from Brunei, in a hilly region not far from the south coast. The people she worked among call themselves "Bukit," from the Malay word for hill or mountain. Tsing finds this term offensive, connoting "hillbilly," but it is not clear whether the term had those connotations for local people. It does not seem so different too Orang Ulu, or "Upriver People," an ethnonym that was used in the 1970s without self-consciousness and even with pride. To avoid the term "Bukit," Tsing makes up a name: she calls the people she worked with Meratus, after the mountain range they inhabit. She remarks that there are many different ethnic groups in the mountains, but she tells us nothing about what those groups might be. This strikes me as leaving a gaping hole in any ethnographic account of the region.

Swidden Agriculture Does Not Explain Migration

Community narratives are full of details about previous sites, but vague on the reasons for moving from one to another. Sometimes there is a dramatic incident: a miscreant calls down the wrath of the spirits, and the residents flee for their lives. Most moves, however, occur without comment, as if movement itself were a given. The genre is such that no one goes out exploring for good land, or sits around debating the pros and cons of migrating.

Nor is there any confusion or dispersion; everyone just gets up one day and moves, en masse. As we see in Chapter 3, there were occasions when migrations occurred in exactly this way, usually as a result of warfare, but in the majority of cases the motives for moving, let alone the process of migrating large distances, were more complicated and difficult to reconstruct.

It is usually assumed by outside observers that regular moves are simply a function of swidden agriculture, but this does not fit the facts. There are longhouse communities that stay put long after they should have moved, and others that never seem to settle down. An obvious example of the former is the massive longhouse community of Long Nawang, in the valley of the Apo Kayan River on the Indonesian side of the central mountain chain. When A.W. Nieuwenhuis visited it in 1900, he counted no less than seventeen longhouses there, each with twenty to forty family apartments (1904:II:410–11). A panoramic view of Long Nawang assembled from a series of photographs taken from a nearby hill shows an imposing spectacle: a dozen or more substantial longhouses grouped together in rolling terrain – a veritable city (Waterson 1990:60–1). Seventy years later, Herb Whittier found twelve longhouses on the same site, and because the jungle had been cut for miles around, it was necessary to travel a long way to find new land (Whittier 1973:90). Travel back and forth to farms had become a major chore, but still the huge longhouse community persisted. It may be objected that Long Nawang was an exceptional place, the cultural centre of the world of the numerous and influential Lepo Tau Kenyah and home to their most blue-blooded aristocrats, but that is just the point: where longhouses are built has more to do with politics and history than farming efficiency. Long Nawang may be an extreme case, but all longhouse communities are exceptional in their own ways.

Meanwhile, it is simplistic to imagine that a longhouse community systematically works out the land around itself until it is all used up, and then moves one quantum leap to the next available site, and so on. Contrary to that notion, you cannot tell the age of a longhouse by measuring the dispersal of the farms. Farmers do not work their way out from the longhouse, a slice at a time, like a caterpillar eating a leaf. Moreover, longhouse migrations do not proceed by equal steps. Instead, there are periods of relative immobility, and then sudden leaps into whole new river systems. Certainly, ecological factors are taken into account when a move is contemplated – not only soil quality, but also availability of game and jungle produce. However, none of these factors alone explain the migration paths that I recorded. Almost invariably, the motivation for long-distance migrations came from external factors, either warfare or trade.

Chapter 3

The Coming of the Brooke Raj

If there was one event that triggered the Sebop exodus from their homeland on the southern slopes of the Usun Apau, it was an unprecedented bout of mayhem known in the colonial literature as the Great Kayan Expedition. In 1863, the man who was to become the second Rajah of Sarawak unleashed on the unsuspecting communities of the upper Rejang a horde of eager and undisciplined Iban numbering, by his own estimates, some 15,000. His prestige was such that he could organise a war party of a size never before seen in the interior, but lacking any organised force of his own, and accompanied by just three other Englishmen, he could not keep it under control. The Iban laid waste an entire region, killing, looting, and burning. The refugees who fled further upriver set off a chain reaction that for decades destabilized communities deep in the interior, including those as far away as the Usun Apau.

James Brooke Goes Adventuring

This humanitarian disaster was totally at variance with the policies of the Raj, yet, it was a logical consequence of the administrative style it established. The first Rajah, James Brooke, founder of his own private kingdom in the highest romantic tradition, was born in Benares in 1803. His father was an East India Company official, who eventually rose to the rank of judge of the High Court. James spent his formative years immersed in an imperial ideology that celebrated the stupendous victories of Robert Clive in the previous century, but retained a certain generosity of spirit toward the subject populations and their cultures. It was this ethos that set Brooke's eyes toward the Malay Archipelago when he was invalided out of the Bengal army at only twenty-one years of age. Influenced by the writing of Stamford Raffles, he saw himself destined to rescue indigenous peoples of the islands from both rapacious Dutch colonialism and corrupt local rulers. In 1838, he published a "prospectus," presumably designed to attract backers, but which nevertheless renounces financial gain. Citing Raffles, he argues that territorial possessions are necessary to establish proper administration and facilitate trade, but that:

> any government instituted for the purpose must be directed to the advancement of native interests and the development of native resources, rather than by a flood of European colonisation to aim at possession only, without reference to the indefeasible rights of the Aborigines. (Runciman 1960:52)

This odd amalgam of military adventurism and humanitarian aspirations characterised the Brooke Raj throughout its history, surviving long after it had been swept aside in India itself by the bitterness of the Great Mutiny and the unbending Social Darwinism of the late nineteenth century.

After a couple of false starts, James Brooke sailed for Southeast Asia in an armed schooner financed from his father's estate. In his explorations, he happened to arrive in Sarawak at a moment when the local Malay potentates were faring badly against an uprising provoked by their own ruthless extortions, and they appealed to Brooke for help. This was the opportunity he was seeking. In a few brisk strokes, followed by conciliation, he managed to bring an end to the rebellion. Within a few months, he had so outmanoeuvred the chief Malays that their suzerain, the Sultan of Brunei, formally appointed Brooke over them, giving him the title of Rajah of Sarawak. With minimal resources, military or financial, Brooke then set about extending his control. He was so successful that, in time, the Raj all but gobbled up the Sultanate.

Brooke's first task was to bring to heel the pirates that infested the coast to the north of the Sarawak River, whose depredations had totally disrupted a once flourishing coastal trade. At crucial moments in his campaigns against them, Brooke was able to draw on the help of the Royal Navy, which maintained an antipiracy patrol in the South China Sea, operating out of nearby Singapore. As Robert Pringle shows in his magnificent *Rajahs and Rebels* (1970), the impression of power made by the presence of warships larger than anything else on the coast added as much to Brooke's prestige as their guns added to his firepower in attacking the pirate lairs. His enemies at this point were Malay notables, sophisticated in both diplomacy and warfare, who in effect operated much as Brooke had done. Able to mobilize only small forces from their core following of coastal Malays, they relied on recruiting the people of the interior to do the majority of their fighting for them. Having taken the lion's share of the loot, they left their fickle allies to collect the heads of their victims (Pringle 1970:73–8).

Since it was a couple of enterprising Royal Navy captains who put Brooke ahead of his Malay rivals, he had every reason to extend the category of "pirate" as far as he could. There were limits to the help he could receive, however, because the antipiracy patrols were needed elsewhere, controlling the much more formidable Illanan pirates of the southern Philippines. Consequently, as Brooke struggled to extend his control upriver, he had no alternative but to employ his old enemies against his new enemies. From the outset, we find him playing off the Iban of one rivershed against those of another. The ultimate sanction behind the *Pax Brookenensis* was a punitive raid, in which the Rajah in effect licensed one Iban population to make war against another, headhunting included. Whether Brooke cynically offered heads as a reward for service, or simply decided that he could not stop the practice, is a moot point.

Punitive Raids as an Instrument of Government

It was under the second Rajah, Charles Brooke, that the punitive raid reached its height of refinement. Charles' early service in the Raj had been spent on outstations, and he seems to have had a genuine admiration for the Iban, as well as fluency in their language and culture. By 1855, he already held the title *Tuan Muda* ("Young Lord"), in effect the Rajah's deputy, yet operated like an Iban leader, if on a somewhat grander scale:

> In June the Tuan Muda used Serikei as his base for an attack on Saribas Dyaks who had settled on the Jalau river, a tributary of the Kanowit. With a few hundred men, armed mostly with spears, as he possessed only 100 out-of-date muskets and a few rifles, he advanced into country that the Dyaks had thought impenetrable, and by burning the Jalau longhouses alarmed the Dyaks into abandoning raids for a year or two. The task of keeping the Sea Dyaks under control was now almost entirely on his shoulders. It was a hard task. He had to listen to and assess every rumour of hostile activity and usually to take action without any time to call on help from Kuching [the capital]. He had to work out his own system of jungle warfare, conscious that his few Malay troops were of little use except on water and that his Dyaks would usually act rashly or stupidly unless they were led by himself or by one or two

respected Malay chiefs. He was allowed only 30 pounds sterling a month for the upkeep of the district, which now comprised half the Raj of Sarawak. (Runciman 1960:131–2 [brackets added]; in this context, the terms "Dyak" and "Sea Dyak" refer to Iban)

Not surprisingly, things did not always go well, and during this period, there were several moments when dangerous uprisings threatened the existence of the Raj.

It is in this context that we find the Tuan Muda organising the Great Kayan Raid. In 1863, only five years before becoming Rajah himself, he was well aware of the fragility of his position. Consequently, when two Englishmen were murdered at Kanowit, far up the Rejang River, he felt his prestige required a major show of force. It was really the Iban that he was trying to impress, and paradoxically, he did it by recruiting them, including some recent enemies, to attack an innocent third party. The pretext was that the murderers had fled yet further upriver into Kayan country. Even at the time, Charles Brooke, hardened warrior though he was, had second thoughts. Directly after the Raid, he confessed: "There have been more dreadful sights in this campaign than I had bargained for. Many women and even children have been killed by our people . . ." (quoted in the account of the expedition by Baring-Gould and Bampfylde 1909:279–94). As Pringle argues:

> The results of the Great Kayan expedition went far beyond the gratification of the Tuan Muda's personal and official desire for revenge. By associating the Sarawak government with an Iban force of great size in such a way, he gave unwitting encouragement to Iban raiding against the ethnically distinct, far less numerous peoples of the upper Rejang. This was probably apparent within a few years to Charles Brooke himself. The Katibas Ibans, whose complaints about Kayan behaviour had spurred him to undertake the expedition, and who participated eagerly in it, did not remain his allies for long. Willing enough to take heads at government command, they were unwilling to stop when requested to do so. Charles soon regarded them as enemies, and felt compelled to send a series of punitive expeditions into the Katibas after 1868. (Pringle 1970:152)

The Conundrum of Iban Expansion

It is clear that Charles Brooke was as much used by his allies as he was making use of them, and the underlying issue in this perennial struggle was Iban expansionism. The Iban originate from the Kapuas River to the south and east of Sarawak, in what is now Indonesian Borneo, but in a few centuries they spread far to the north (Sandin 1967). By 1850, they had moved into the tributaries of the lower Rejang – a vast watershed – and were already pushing at the boundaries of Kayan and Kenyah territory, causing endless friction. What underlay this remarkable demographic and territorial expansion is one of the great conundrums of Borneo ethnography. There is no reason to believe Iban fertility rates were higher than those of other ethnic groups. Part of the answer has to do with what can only be called "cultural colonialism." That is, as smaller ethnic groups were intimidated or defeated, they effectively became Iban. Whether these subjugated people were sufficiently numerous to explain the Iban expansion is not clear. Meanwhile, it presented a major problem for the Rajahs, who vacillated in their policies regarding it. On the one hand, it involved the violence and instability that they were trying to control; on the other hand, it extended their rule. Wherever the Raj gained territory at the expense of the Sultan, the Iban followed. In the Great Kayan Raid, they provided the shock troops for Brooke's annexation of the Brunei hinterland. We can only imagine how the shock was experienced from the other side.

The Second Great Kayan Raid

Nor did the "dreadful sights" that set Charles Brooke musing about the Great Kayan Expedition stop him from organising another one in 1896, after he became Rajah. This second mass raid penetrated even further upriver and caused similar chaos, but it merits hardly a mention in official reports and is reported in none of the standard histories of the Raj. The reason for this lack of attention is that *no* European accompanied the expedition. Instead, the Iban raiders were left entirely to themselves, and there were no squeamish witnesses to report the results. There is nothing more than a self-satisfied editorial in the *Sarawak Gazette* reporting the expedition's "success" (366:July 1896). Some months later, a review of the preceding year's events remarks on the general peace and stability, with the minor exception of the raid on the "Kayan" of Belaga (*Sarawak Gazette* 372:January 1897). In the meantime, thousands of refugees fled out of Belaga watershed and into the Baram (*Sarawak Gazette* 368:September 1896, 371:December 1896).

On this occasion, however, we do have an account of the raid from the point of view of the victims. According to Sebop memories, the provocation was the murder of a Chinese trader in a bazaar in Belaga by a Lepo Jingan (Kenyah) man who was outraged, first, by being given short weight by a trader, and then being beaten up by the trader's henchmen when he complained. Evidently lacking the local knowledge to sort out the Lepo Jingan from other people in the region, the Rajah's council decided that the proper response to the murder was to give a handful of Iban leaders *carte blanche* to attack any and all communities in the Seping. Presciently, the Sebop leader expected no niceties of discrimination from the raiders:

> Ukun Ding exhorted us to flee. "Let us fight back," said some of his subjects, but Ukun Ding did not approve of it. So we fled. "Let us have pity on the children and the women. It is not our fault, but that of the Lepo Jingan." That is what Ukun Ding is said to have said. So we fled through the night and through the whole of the next day. We used torches and links on our flight. We went upriver, climbed the Menapan and crossed the Batait. When we reached there we made a shelter. Ukun Ding, who was our leader in those days, was in front because he carried the charms [house stones]. . . . As we reached Batait, the enemy had reached and burned the house at the Menavan. "Oooi! The enemy has already arrived" they shouted "look, the house is burning." The people broke up from there [i.e., panicked]. Ukun Ding said: "Don't leave the weak people behind. Don't leave the old people," said he as he came running to the back. And when he reached the back: "Go and carry your children and carry the weak ones on your back." (Seling 1974:331 [brackets added])

The last official mention of the raid came in a brief note in June 1897, reporting that hundreds of people had starved to death because of the loss of their food stocks and crops in the raid (*Sarawak Gazette* 377).

Part II

Longhouses and Leaders

Chapter 4

Aban Jau's Career

When Charles Hose made his theatrical entrance onto the veranda of Aban Jau's Communal House at Long Batan, the great man was already past his prime. He belonged to a previous era, before colonial "pacification," which makes him a useful example of the dynamics of leadership in longhouse communities. Moreover, we know a lot about his activities because agents of the Raj collected intelligence on what was going on in the Baram watershed for decades before the region was annexed. They did this in order to build a case for the annexation, to be made to a British government that had undergone a change of heart. Since the early days of James Brooke's anti-piracy campaign, crucially supported by ships of the Royal Navy, Whitehall had begun to doubt the wisdom of letting Charles Brooke swallow up the remaining territory of the Sultan of Brunei (Pringle 1970:81–2; Runciman 1960:174–201). Consequently, evidence was needed of chaos and violence within what was nominally the Sultan's realm, and Aban Jau had obligingly provided a fair amount all by himself.

In addition, Aban Jau casts a long shadow down the oral histories of the descendents of his followers at Long Batan. In the 1970s, those Sebop people, who also called themselves Long Taballau talked of him as a kind of George Washington. The descendents of his Berawan followers were more mixed in their assessment. Some denounced him as a tyrant, but everyone agreed that the community of Long Batan was his creation, and that without him it would not have existed.

Origins in the Usun Apau

Long Taballau tradition is clear that Aban Jau was born in the Usun Apau. About everything else in his early years, it is silent. We do not know if he led the migration into the Tinjar, or exactly when or why it occurred. Counting backward from the end of his career, we can estimate that he was born sometime around 1810. By mid-century, he was an established leader at Long Batan. The details of what occurred between those years had by the 1970s dropped over the horizon of oral history. We know that Long Taballau was in the Menawan River on the southern slopes of the Usun Apau, and the survival of the ethnonym surely means that there was a large and successful community there, but we do not know the names of its leaders. Evidently, after the move was made into the Baram watershed, they became irrelevant, and their names were abandoned along with their tombs.

We can only guess at the motives for the move into the Tinjar. It is possible that demographic pressures played some part. On the face of it, the Sebop "homeland" described in Chapter 2 was vast in comparison with its population, but the soils of the Usun Apau are not fertile, and what parcels of suitable land existed were not equally accessible. Consequently, a perception of relative overcrowding may have caused the Long Taballau to look north toward the comparatively empty Tinjar. Alternatively, the move may have been precipitated by rivalries between competing leaders, either within the parent community or between adjacent ones. Another important consideration would have been access to trade to the coast, for which the Tinjar has real advantages over the remote Usun Apau. The mayhem caused by Charles Brooke's Great Kayan Raid was not a factor, however, since the move occurred well before 1863.

Encounters with the Berawan

One thing is sure, however: the Long Taballau did not move at random into terra incognita. Trading links down river already existed, making use of the path that led from the headwaters of the Menawan into the Dapoi (Figure 02-01). As a result of those contacts, however intermittent, it is possible that marriage alliances already existed with the Berawan of Tinjar. Indeed, by some accounts offered in the 1970s, Aban Jau's mother was Berawan.

Berawan migration stories, like those of the Sebop, recount an origin in the Usun Apau. They insist, however, that the Berawan were alone there, and that the steep valleys cut into the southern side of the Usun Apau were abandoned before any of the ancestral Sebop arrived. One major component of the Berawan moved via the Nibong into the upper Tinjar, which proved to be a rich and attractive environment. Their stories tell of many longhouse sites occupied over several generations along a fifty-mile length of river that runs relatively straight along the northern edge of the Dulit range. On the left bank, the mountains drop dramatically into the fast-flowing river, whereas on the right there are several places where the hills draw back, leaving flatlands that were ideal for cultivation. Several sites were occupied repeatedly. The most fondly remembered was Long Dunin, where longhouses were built by folk heroes who climbed to the moon and learned the proper forms of rituals from spirits. So attractive is the site that it has seldom been left empty for long. In the 1970s, it was occupied by a group of Kenyah who arrived only in the early twentieth century.

In the early nineteenth century, the Berawan communities in Tinjar had a large stretch of country all to themselves, apart from a scattering of Penan. It does not follow, however, that they were out of touch with their neighbours, even ones who lived outside the watershed of the Baram. Genealogies collected in the 1970s show kinship links all the way to the Kejaman community in the Belaga River. The trip involved a tortuous route requiring sixty miles of river travel in three different watersheds and some arduous walking. The first leg took travellers by canoe to Long Tisam in Tinjar, then on foot to the headwaters of the Jelalong, a tributary of the Kemena. Having descended the Jelalong, they went upriver along another tributary, the Tubau. A path then led over difficult mountainous country into the valley of the Belaga River, where canoes were again necessary for the final leg (see Figure 04-01). Yet, the trip must have been made several times in arranging a marriage, and later by a large party of wedding guests. We need not assume that contacts between such distant communities were constantly maintained. They may have lapsed for years at a time, but even intermittent contacts were sufficient to allow cultural transfers. Examples are provided in the large repertoire of songs used at death rituals, some of which were nothing more than little games to pass the time during the long nights of the vigil. In the 1970s, elderly Berawan people could still remember songs they learned from Punan Bah visitors from the Kemena River and from Kejaman people from the Belaga.

In comparison, the route that led from the Sebop "homeland" into Tinjar was shorter and less troublesome. Out of the headwaters of the Menawan, a path led to a stream that flowed directly into the Tinjar. Hose walked the path and pronounced it "easy" (*Sarawak Gazette* 280:May 1889). Fifteen miles of walking followed by thirty miles down small streams brought the traveller to Long Lobang, the upriver end of the Berawan territory. I emphasize the ease of this transit because for outsiders – foreigners and people from the coast – it seems that the watershed of the Plieran (into which the Menawan flows; Figure 02-01) is infinitely removed from the Tinjar. Our spatial sense is conditioned by our modes of travel into the interior,

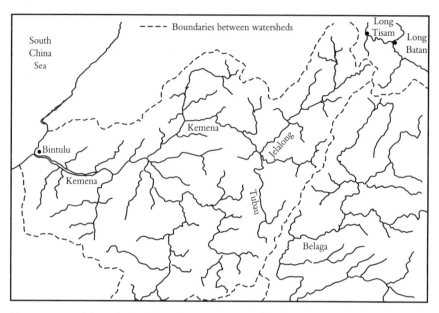

Figure 04-01. Watershed of the river Kemena, with adjacent parts of the Baram and Rajang watersheds, showing the route from Long Tisam in the Tinjar to the Belaga, via the Jelalong and Tubau. It also shows the vulnerability of Berawan longhouses near Long Tisam to raids from the Bintulu area, as described under "Threats of continuing violence" in Chapter 5.

beginning with launches in the wide lower reaches of rivers and transferring to ever smaller canoes once the rapids begin. Travelling in this way, even in the 1970s it would have taken weeks to get from Tinjar to Menawan. Upriver People turn this view inside out. Their historical experience orients them toward the mountains, which are everywhere in plain view. They see the rivers running out from the Usun Apau like spokes in a wheel, and until the advent of logging roads and migration to the coastal cities, it remained their reflex to travel via the hub, rather than all the way out to the rim (Metcalf 2008).

Consequently, we may be confident that in the early part of the nineteenth century at least some Sebop communities in the Usun Apau had knowledge of the Berawan, and vice versa. There may well have been a web of marriage alliances. What we do not know is how the Long Taballau migration into Tinjar was negotiated with the Berawan. Did the migrants first build a house for themselves somewhere far upriver, as far away as possible from their new neighbours as possible? If so, there is no mention of it. Or, at the other extreme, is it possible that the whole alliance was worked out before Aban Jau and his people set out, and that everyone involved had already agreed to join the megacommunity at Long Batan? Probably the truth lies somewhere between these two, but the details cannot be recovered.

One problem in dealing with this issue is that migration stories by their nature collapse the historical sequence of events. What they do is string together the names of consolidated longhouse communities, one following directly on another, as if everyone invariably moved en masse and by common consent. What they do not do is report periods of factionalism and dispersion, and it is only by comparing different versions that such phases can be deduced. As it happens, however, the Berawan stories agree that just before the Long Taballau made their move into the Tinjar, the Berawan there had been divided among no less than four longhouses scattered along the upper Tinjar, at Long Sijoi, Long Ugeng, Long Lamat, and Long Penuwan. Consequently, they were in a weak position to defend themselves against a large party of marauders. Yet, both sides agree that there was never any fighting between the Berawan and the Long Taballau, and the intentions of the latter clearly had to do with settlement not rapine. On the contrary, the vulnerability of the dispersed Berawan communities may well have given them an incentive to welcome their new allies, allowing them to draw together against a common threat.

Meeting the Kayan Threat

By the time of the Great Kayan Raid in 1863, the community at Long Batan was firmly established and Aban Jau at the height of his career. When the community was in its nascent stage, the threat of attack by Iban was remote. They were still far away to the south and only a distant rumour. Instead, it was the Kayan who were the immediate threat. Their expansion is another dramatic story in the ethnology of Borneo, rivalling that of the Iban. About the Iban there is a considerable body of information, including an exhaustive treatment of Iban oral history by Benedict Sandin (1967), himself an Iban. The equally intriguing Kayan expansion has received far less attention. I rely on the synthesis of Jerome Rousseau (1990), who draws on a variety of ethnographic reports as well as his own fieldwork among the Kayan of the Belaga River. For the peoples of the Baram, the Kayan and the Iban together must have seemed like the upper and nether millstones, steadily grinding them down.

The Kayan expansion began from across the mountains in territory that was later to be annexed by the Dutch, and then became part of Indonesia. They entered the Baram watershed from two directions, from the east directly over the mountains and from the southeast via the Rejang watershed. By the early nineteenth century, they were firmly established in the middle

Baram, with a number of large longhouse communities. It was one of these that was seen by Spenser St. John at "Longusin," and whose size and orderliness so impressed him (1862:II;104–5). The arrival of the Kayan transformed the political situation in the Baram. They were able to assemble war parties on a scale not seen before, and where previously most raids had been hit-and-run affairs with a few heads taken, now whole communities were liable to be annihilated, the inhabitants killed or enslaved. Some areas were virtually depopulated, leaving vacuums that would later be filled by Iban immigrants.

In this situation, the confederation that Aban Jau brought about made eminent good sense. The location of Long Batan was not on the usual path of Kayan war parties, which went down the Baram. No one, however, had failed to notice that there was a relatively easy path from Long Pata in the Baram to the headwaters of the Paong, which flowed into the Tinjar. Had a sizeable Kayan war party entered the upper Tinjar, they could have swept down river picking off small communities without encountering any serious opposition. It was this threat that the concentration at Long Batan was designed to counter.

Aban Jau's Diplomacy

Aban Jau went further, however. In addition to passive defence, he engaged in a positive diplomacy designed to make allies of the Kayan of the middle Baram. His success was marked by the marriage of his daughter Tijan to Nipa of Batu Gading, one of the most important Kayan leaders of the middle Baram. This woman proved something more than a pawn in a dynastic game, however. Strong willed and adventurous, she was said to be so beautiful that no man could resist her. Supposedly, the Tinjar – that beautiful river – is named after her, a conceit given credence by the fact that the Berawan have another, older name for the river: Meleteng. She had a series of divorces, and her repeated liaisons seriously complicated Aban Jau's diplomacy. Nevertheless, his alliance with the Kayan held, and with his flank secured, he had room to begin throwing his weight around. It was his military adventures that caused the first agents of Rajah Brooke to misclassify him as "the Kyan chief of Tinja" (*Sarawak Gazette* 120:1876).

Aban Jau's diplomacy was put to the test in 1870, in a series of alarms and excursions that were closely followed by the agents of Rajah Brooke. In Aban Jau's first appearance in the historical records, we hear confused reports of the massing of Kayan of the middle Baram to attack him. From the outset, however, Aban Jau's son in law Nipa would have nothing to do with the escapade, thus seriously undermining its chances of success. Finally, it emerges that this raid has been instigated by a Brunei adventurer named Nakoda Raman, who claimed the right from the Sultan to various taxes from the people of the Tinjar. Since the Sultan had never collected any such taxes, he was not giving much away. Nakoda Raman's bold plan was to use the unruly Kayan to help him collect them, no doubt with promises of a share of the loot and all the heads they could take. Also summoned to assist is Liar, who is reported to be "a chief of the Upper Tinga and very strong in fighting men" (*Sarawak Gazette* 44:February 1871). Liar was leader of the Lirong, who had arrived from the Usun Apau after the establishment of Long Batan and settled far upriver. Liar's power was soon to be undermined, however, by a smallpox epidemic that decimated his community. Even while his following was large, however, he declined to assist Raman and his allies, no doubt calculating that he had more to fear from bringing a Kayan war party into Tinjar that he could possibly gain from turning on his cousins, the Long Taballau Sebop.

Consequently, Nakoda Raman's scheme to enrich himself came to nothing. Nipa and Liar refused to cooperate, and only forty Kayan turned up to help him. So, after much blustering on all sides, with threats of wholesale death and destruction, the effort fizzled out without bloodshed. Nevertheless, the incident provided the Sarawak government with a convenient opportunity to fulminate against Brunei misrule:

> We had our doubts whether this talked-of expedition would ever really be organised, but when this was determined on, we imagined that the task of carrying it out, especially when a district as important as that of Baram was in question, would have been entrusted to a leader in whom his government had confidence enough to suppose that he was likely to do what they required effectively. If Nakoda Raman had not the necessary qualifications, we have a striking example of the folly and ignorance of his government; if he had, a no less striking example of their impotence. In any case, the spectacle of this gentleman mustering his 40 Kayans to take the field, with one or more luke-warm friends or possible enemies in his neighbourhood, is hideous in the extreme. After such a collapse, we shall perhaps not hear of another attempt to extort by force what the Bruneians have hitherto been content to extort by threats and cunning from their so-called subjects, although we fear the failure will not have the effect either of lessening an old evil, or of leading to the establishment of a settled and trustworthy government on the Baram river. The unlucky people there deserve a better fate than to be made the victims of the schemes and intrigues of petty chiefs, without a chance of waking the government that professes to rule them from the stagnation and indifference to wrong that characterizes the present Bruneian system. We feel sure that any effort to relieve these people by bringing them under a proper rule will command the good wishes and support of all who have the best interests of the Natives at heart. (*Sarawak Gazette* 44:February 1871)

This rhetoric was of course directed at London, since the poor beleaguered Sultan was surely past caring.

Aban Jau Makes Himself a Rajah

The extensive coverage that this incident received in several issues of the *Sarawak Gazette* says more about the activities of the Brooke regime than the misadventures of Nakoda Ramen. First, it was a factor in the founding of the *Sarawak Gazette*, which first appeared in 1870, the year in which the crisis began – if indeed there was a crisis. It was not exactly an official publication since it claimed an independent editorial policy, but it was funded by the Raj and usually edited by a senior civil servant. Its first issues resemble broadsheets, reflecting its propaganda function, but over the decades it took on a more sober air. Throughout the existence of the Raj, the *Sarawak Gazette* routinely published reports from the outstations, often excerpted from the official annual reports of District Officers, and is consequently an invaluable resource. It continued publication during the period of direct British colonial rule, and into the postindependence era, and it is frequently cited throughout the book. Attentive historians may notice that my citations are not uniform. In the early years, the *Sarawak Gazette* had no page numbers, so I generally give the number of the issue, as well as the month and year of publication. An almost complete run of the paper is held in the Public Records office in London, of which there is a copy on microfiche in the Southeast Asia collection at Cornell University. The series in the Sarawak Museum in Kuching is less complete.

The reportage of this incident also shows the efficiency of Brooke's spy network in the Baram area. Hearing rumours of a Kayan raid against Aban Jau, the Resident at Bintulu sent a Malay assistant to investigate, even though the events there were no official concern of the Sarawak government. The young man, Yusup, found Aban Jau in the longhouse at Long Batan alone with the women and children, his fighting men having gone down river to meet the expected Kayan war party. From this, we may conclude that Aban Jau's skills were not those of the general. On the face of it, to leave the longhouse itself ungarrisoned seems a risky tactic, but Yusup did not linger to find out what Aban Jau was planning to do if personally attacked. He does report Aban Jau's long-term strategy to retreat, if necessary, into the Usun Apau (*Sarawak Gazette* 44:February 1871). Later, a Chinese trader arrived in Bintulu with reports of the ignominious failure of the raid, which meant that Aban Jau's military acumen was not put to the test.

Nevertheless, Aban Jau seems to have taken his survival from Nakoda Raman's attempt at subjugation as a triumph over the Sultan himself.

Calculating that he had demonstrated his independence from Brunei every bit as much as Charles Brooke had done, he began to style himself Rajah and demanded the right to levy taxes in the manner of a Malay potentate (Metcalf 1992). These claims were inscribed on his door, as Hose noticed after he made his surprise entrance at Long Batan. His room, he tells us, "was distinguished by possessing a special door, a massive piece of ironwood about twelve feet square and three or four inches thick, with beautifully carved frame-work" (Hose 1927:51). The door still exists in the Sarawak Museum in Kuching, and it is impressive. It must have been carved from one of the spreading buttresses of a truly enormous tree.

The inscription on Aban Jau's door was written in Jawi, an Arabic script used for Malay (Herbert and Milner 1989:103). Hose's translation reads, "This is the door of Tama Long, The Rajah who exercises authority over the country of Tinjar." Tama Long is the same person as Aban Jau, the two names being examples of teknonymy, that is, naming someone by specifying a relationship. The practice has intrigued ethnographers of Borneo, and there is an extensive literature on it. For present purposes, we need only note that Jau was father (Tama) of Long and also a widower (Aban). Since a person may have several teknonyms over a lifetime (mother, grandparent, person whose parent, or child, or sibling is dead, and so on), the possibilities for confusion are multiple. Moreover, person or "body" names are constantly recycled. Consequently, it is easy to mistake two distinct persons for the same – for example, there may be several Fathers of Jau – or to fail to notice that two different names refer to the same person. None of this makes collecting oral histories any easier. The names of the long dead at least usually settle down, and in the 1970s, I never heard anyone refer to Aban Jau as Tama Long. There were old people who knew that he had been Tama Long, and that was important to me in untangling what I read in the *Sarawak Gazette*, which used the name he was known by when the entry was written.

Phillip Thomas, Curator of Malay documents at the Library of Congress, was kind enough to provide me with his own translation: "This place is the door of Tama Long, the Rajah who holds power in Tinjar district, controlling all trade." Hose's version, although not wrong, fails to catch the grasping quality of that final phrase. It is perhaps only a detail, but Hose affected an upper-class Englishman's disdain for "trade" or commerce, and would not have wanted to portray his hero as a kind of boxwallah. It was not, however, a detail as far as people in Tinjar were concerned, and by 1877 they were complaining to the Resident at Bintulu about Aban Jau's exactions, particularly his attempt to take two-thirds of the valuable camphor they collected (*Sarawak Gazette* 134:August 1877). Some communities planned to escape Aban Jau's bullying by moving further upriver. His Berawan followers were meanwhile threatening to move out of Tinjar entirely, into the Jelalong (*Sarawak Gazette* 151:March 1879). That would have taken them out of the Baram watershed into that of the Kemena and, consequently, brought them under Sarawak rule.

Despite these complaints, it is not clear how far Aban Jau could get away with playing the despot. When Berawan people spoke about him in the 1970s, they invariably described him as having a "swollen nose" (*kumbung cum*), implying pride, arrogance, and pomposity. It is a charge that Upriver People with pretensions to aristocracy avoid. On the contrary, modesty and self-restraint are the signs of good breeding, and boasting proves the lack of it. The resentment with which they recount Aban Jau's attempts at exacting tribute seemed to stem not so much from actual abuses as from custom scandalized at the very suggestion of it. Reading between the lines of the *Sarawak Gazette* reports, one gets the impression of a Tammany Hall politician rather than a mafia boss. There is violence aplenty; between 1872 and 1880, a whole string of incidents was reported in the *Sarawak Gazette* in which Aban Jau is implicated in the murder of traders, Malays and Chinese, and Iban and Kayan collecting forest products in Tinjar, not to mention the murder of Penan for their heads. It is not clear, however, that Aban Jau is the instigator of these crimes, and there is no hint of him swaggering around the countryside with a gang of armed henchmen at his back.

Aban Jau Raids the Coast

There are, however, examples of sabre rattling. In 1876, intelligence reached Sarawak that Aban Jau had assembled 2,000 men to attack Sibuti, a small coastal town to the west of Long Batan, within Brunei territory. This caused anxiety because one of the Rajah's most trusted aides, Hugh Brooke Low, was travelling back from Brunei by an inland route that would take him up the Tinjar, and there was a danger that he would blunder into the hostilities. The Resident at Muka tried to avert trouble by sending a messenger to tell Aban Jau that the Rajah would be angry if the attack went through. These are good examples of what we might call the Rajah's "forward policy" in Baram. When Low finally reappeared, it turned out that he had indeed encountered Aban Jau's war party. Entering the Tinjar, he met a Malay trader:

> A few reaches from the mouth, I fell in with Pangeran Achmat, of Lingga, who was on his way to the "kubu" [trading post] to buy tobacco. He told me that Tama Long [Aban Jau] was encamped some distance up the river, awaiting the return of a party he had sent to Sibutih. He had heard of my

intention to visit, and did not seem altogether pleased. I understood at once that he was disposed to regard me with suspicion, particularly so, as my companions were Dyaks, Tanjong and Bakatans, kinsmen every one of them, of people he had murdered a couple of years ago. We passed up the river quietly without adventure of any kind. At the entrance of Sungei Bok, a stream leading in the direction of Sibutih, we found a deserted hut, and on landing discovered traces of recent occupation, and were able to form a pretty accurate conjecture, that the war party had returned, and so it proved as we neared the camp at Long Tuyut, where we heard whooping and yelling. We were hailed as we approached, and after giving notice of our arrival, crossed to the opposite bank and bivouacked on the "karangan" [sand bar]. At daybreak I visited Tama Purai, whose acquaintance I had formed at Bintulu, and was by him introduced to his elder brother Tama Long. They were both of them courteous and plain spoken. The younger brother, as I surmised, had only just returned from the war-path. The elder had not accompanied the expedition, the bala [war party] seemed to have met with doubtful success, for they brought neither heads nor plunder and lost besides one of their most esteemed warriors, Tama Itang Lalo, Tama Purai's son. Avit was wounded in the arm. At Bintulu I was afterwards enabled to ascertain with accuracy the amount of damage done at Sibutih. Three men were killed; Sunan a Sibauch, Mat Bakir a Sarawak Malay, and Rebas, slave of the late Pangiran Suliman Damit. Awang Singa was wounded in the foot. I learnt upon enquiry that this expedition was undertaken to punish the Orang Kaya Ladong and his friend Lebaai for their refusal to deliver up certain slaves that had run away to Niah and Sibutih. After this interview the camp broke up, and we went upriver in the wake of the bala. Two days more, and we reached the village, where we stayed ten days. Tama Long pressed me to live in his house, and take my meals there; and as he now showed a disposition to be friendly, I humoured him, and was gratified beyond measure when he informed me on the eve of my departure that my visit had been a source of unmixed pleasure to himself and his family; that this was the first time he had had the honour of entertaining a white man, as before me no European had ever visited Tinjar. Tama Long has a magnificent physique; he is of a tall and commanding figure, and although his hairs are grey, his limbs are still strong and powerful. He looks a chief every inch of him, and is without exception the most intelligent native I have ever chanced to meet. His conversation is full of interest, and he proved himself as willing to give as to receive information. In character he is proud, passionate, and jealous of his power. These qualities have rendered him unpopular throughout Barram, where he is more feared than loved. (*Sarawak Gazette* 122:August 1876 [brackets added]; note also that Orang Kaya and Pangiran are Malay titles)

Once again, we find Aban Jau hanging back from the fighting, and despite his imposing appearance, it is his conversation that really impresses Low.

The image of Aban Jau as a man of words rather than deeds – a politician rather than a general – fits with the way events unfolded at Sibuti. The leading figure there was the Pangeran Suliman, who, in those unquiet times, had already taken the trouble to fortify his residence (*Sarawak Gazette* 120:June 1876). If illustrations of similar structures from the same period are any guide, this would have included a stockade defended by several small cannons. Consequently, those residents of Sibuti who had not fled had ample time before the attack to move their valuables inside the stockade and prepare their weapons. Having sacked the rest of Sibuti, Aban Jau's warriors made no attempt to rush the stockade. Did Tama Purai try to rally his people for such an all-out attack? Was there some council of war in which he was outvoted? Did his son, Tama Itang Lalo, die while trying to win glory by some bold stroke? Of these details, we unfortunately hear nothing, but it is evident that the power of command of Aban Jau and his lieutenants were strictly limited. They could whip up enthusiasm for an adventure, but they could not maintain it in the face of reverses.

During the journey in which Low visited Aban Jau, he settled another old feud concerning a slave. Travelling south along the coast of Brunei, only a short distance from the city itself, he found the inhabitants of the small Belait River (Figure 01-01) in fear of their lives:

> My arrival found the Belaits busy palisading their houses as they expected an attack from Tinjar. On inquiry into the origin of their feud with Tama Long, I ascertained that only one man of them all was to blame in the matter, the Orang Kaya Sbandar to wit, who refused to surrender a runaway slave and a stolen jar belonging to that chief. Years ago the Sebops and Berawans invaded and slaughtered a number of persons in revenge for some of their friends who had been put to death by the people of this river. In this attack, the Orang Kaya was the principal sufferer, as his brother Raup was slain, and his nephews Siloo and Rampak taken prisoner. Rampak was subsequently ransomed for three piculs, but Siloo grew up in bondage, and married a Murut of Buan named Sadi, a fellow-captive. Soon after his marriage, Siloo managed to escape, and took with him his wife, his wife's daughter by a previous husband, and a gusi jar belonging to his master. Siloo and his wife were now both dead, but Sibai remained a full-grown woman. As the Orang Kayas of Belait were anxious to put an end to the feud with Tinjar, and were eager to pacify Tama Long, I recommended the immediate restoration of both slave and jar, accompanied with a promise of ransom for Siloo and his wife, provided always that Tama Long was moderate in his demands. The Orang Kayas at once adopted my advice and desired me to confer with the refractory Sbandar, to whom I had no sooner unfolded the resolution of his brother-chiefs than he at once offered to return both jar and slave, and further

begged me to convey them to Tinjar as I was going that way, and to do all in my power to keep Tama Long at home. I promised to do my best, and the Orang Kayas seemed please, for they felt relieved as if from a great danger. As this village was under the thumb of the Pangiran Pamancha, whose son had turned a deaf ear to their pleas for assistance, I sent a line to Brunei (to prevent any misunderstanding) to say that I had been commissioned by the Belaits to appease Tama Long with the offering before mentioned. (*Sarawak Gazette* 121:July 1876 [parentheses in original])

This story has several interesting details. First, we have Low, the Rajah's emissary, settling disputes between people entirely within the Sultan's realm and notifying the Sultan afterward. Second, the adventures of Siloo and family hint at the circumstances of slaves within Aban Jau's household, which was such that they could not only escape down river – a long journey – but also do so carrying a heavy burden. A "gusi" is the largest type of Chinese jar traded upriver, some standing several feet tall and having great value. One reason why Siloo might have stolen the jar was to make himself welcome back in Belait. The Orang Kaya Sbandar, having been forced to give up the jar, does not scruple to hand his niece back into slavery.

Most important, however, we see that Aban Jau's earlier raids on the coast had been more destructive and more profitable. A "picul" is a Chinese unit of weight, equivalent to about 133 pounds, and Low assumes that his readers understand that it is paid in brassware, probably a mixture of gongs of various sizes, and small swivel cannons. The four hundred pounds (three piculs) of such elite goods paid as ransom for Rampak was a small fortune, and the deal that Low promoted would have provided yet more. Presumably, the attack on Belait occurred sometime in the 1860s, about the time when Aban Jau was at the height of his power. Even then, however, Aban Jau's warriors might not have succeeded so well had the inhabitants trusted less in the security of Brunei and fortified their houses, as did the Pangiran Suliman at Sibuti.

Aban Jau's relations with the Brooke Raj were, to say the least, ambivalent. In 1875, he was reported as telling the Kayan of Upper Rejang not to pay their taxes, but to take an independent stance like himself (*Sarawak Gazette* 106:August 1975). These are the Kayan who were supposed to have been "pacified" by the Great Kayan Raid, although in fact the majority had retired upriver and left the smaller ethnic groups to take the brunt of the Iban attack. Just four years later, Aban Jau is volunteering his services to the Rajah to mount an expedition against those same Kayan in punishment for crimes that they had committed in the Baram, although not to any of Aban Jau's people. That is, he expects to be hired as a mercenary to attack the Rajah's own subjects. His offer was politely declined (*Sarawak Gazette* 168:September 1880).

Outmanoeuvred by the Rajah's Men

The cession of Baram in 1882 made a confrontation inevitable. By then, the anarchy that Rajah Brooke had been documenting for two decades finally convinced the British government to withdraw their objections and the Sultan to despair of further profit from his largest remaining province. The first Resident, a former naval officer named Claude de Crespigny, initially gives credit to Aban Jau, if somewhat begrudgingly, for maintaining order: "It is due to Aban Jau, however, to state that the Tinja was not affected by the anarchy" (*Sarawak Gazette* 207:April 1883). It is not long, however, before a showdown occurs, and it appears to concern a case of headhunting – a very proper disciplinary issue. From the outset, however, there are odd aspects to this case. First, Aban Jau tries to stay on the right side of the Resident by announcing in advance his intention to take heads. De Crespigny reports:

> Aban Jau sent down a letter by Tama Tinggang to inform me that the wife of his son Long has lately died, and that according to custom Tama Long will go on ulit either up Tinjar or to the head of the Baram. I must not say another day that I was not told. Wants some white paint, and writes whoever passes Tama Long's house in order to trade must pay a tetawak [small gong]. (*Sarawak Gazette* 221:June 1884 [brackets added])

Note that *ulit* is, significantly, the Iban word for headhunting; Aban Jau uses it because that is the word used by the Rajah's administrators. At first glance, the last sentence seems unrelated to what went before, but that is not so. The paint that Aban Jau wants is probably to make the large supporting posts of the mausoleum that he is constructing for his daughter-in-law stand out dramatically against the green backdrop of the jungle. A white lead-based paint manufactured in England was commonly available in coastal areas for use on the hulls of ships as protection against barnacles and marine borers. Also, the small gong payable to Tama Long is not another of Aban Jau's taxes. It is rather a fine for the ritual infraction of disturbing a longhouse in full mourning.

The crucial element in the message, however, is that it is taken for granted that the Resident understands that the mortuary rites of an important person constitute the most pressing possible need for heads. De Crespigny himself describes the necessity to "appease the manes" of the dead woman

Figure 04-02. Charles Hose giving final instructions to a party of Kayan engaged on a punitive raid. It seems impossible that Hose travelled around in the jungle wearing white ducks and a pith helmet, but apparently he did. (From Hose and McDougall 1912, Vol II, plate 209.)

(*Sarawak Gazette* 222:July 1884), and although that hardly describes the full eschatological significance of headhunting (Metcalf 1996), it will do for the present. To Aban Jau's frank statement of intent, de Crespigny's reply is interestingly prevaricating:

> Wrote to Tama Long in Tinjar ordering him on no account to go on ulit, and saying that I should be glad to see him to send him against some enemies of government, but without mentioning names. (*Sarawak Gazette* 221:June 1884)

De Crespigny was evidently willing to nominate a suitable target for homicide. In the event, Aban Jau made other arrangements, which he might reasonably have believed would demonstrate his willingness to comply with the Resident's prohibitions. As Charles Hose describes it in his memoirs, Aban Jau:

> sent ten men to the Sultan of Brunei, and bought a slave from one of the ministers, the Bandahara, for the equivalent of one hundred and fifty to two hundred dollars . . . which was supplied in the form of camphor, rubber,

and other jungle produce. As the slave purchased was an old man of little marketable value, the minister added a beautiful piece of cloth of gold-thread made in Brunei, and a large jar or vase of Chinese make to be used for burial purposes. The return journey was duly begun, but the poor old slave was an encumbrance as he could not keep up with the others on the march. The party therefore decided that, as it was his head that was wanted, the rest of him was not only superfluous but a nuisance. They accordingly cut off his head, and left the body by the jungle path. Word of the mission had, however, reached us, and I was allowed to assist in intercepting and capturing them as they entered the Baram District with their gory trophy. (Hose 1927: 48–9)

What Hose fails to mention is that the party that went to Belait had called at the new government outstation at Marudi on their way down river and had actually carried letters from de Crespigny to Pangiran Mauai (*Sarawak Gazette* 222:July 1884). A path leads from Marudi into the headwaters of the Belait River, making it an easy route to the coast, and so to Brunei. The path was also easy to watch, facilitating the interception and capture in which Hose was "allowed" to assist.

It is evident that Aban Jau was deliberately entrapped. De Crespigny certainly knew why Aban Jau's followers were going to Belait, but he did not point out to them that dispatching a slave would be considered a breach of the prohibition on headhunting, even though it could not possibly result in any kind of revenge attacks. Consequently, Aban Jau's men, having served as his postman, had no qualms about delivering themselves into the Resident's grasp. For their troubles, they were all put on trial, convicted, and shipped off to jail in Kuching. The jar and fabric were forfeit, but more significantly Aban Jau was fined one hundred piculs, or over six tons of brassware. The interesting thing about this stupendous fine was that it could not conceivably be paid in serving trays and small gongs; the weight could only be made up with the cannons that defended Long Batan. De Crespigny was pulling Aban Jau's teeth. Aban Jau fulminated, threatening to attack the new fort at Marudi, but there was nothing he could do.

What lay behind this elaborate entrapment was not headhunting at all, but an economic issue in which Aban Jau represented the views of many leaders in Baram. Not surprisingly, Upriver People associated the Iban with the most violent aspects of Brooke rule and deeply resented their presence. Noting the problems Iban had caused in the Limbang River to the north, Robert Pringle explains:

Along the much larger Baram river and its tributaries there was similar friction between the inhabitants and itinerant Iban produce seekers, with the Government again initially on the side of the Ibans. In 1884 the first Baram Resident, C.C. de Crespigny, told a reluctant Kenyah chief that he could either allow the Ibans to work produce in his area, in which case the Government would allow him to levy a toll of one-tenth of whatever they collected, or that the Rajah might well order them to work there anyway without further reference to him. De Crespigny was irked when the Tinjar Sebob chief Aban Jau refused to allow a party of forty-five Ibans from Banting to work produce in his area. The Resident noted with approval that at this time over 200 more Second Division Ibans were reported en route to the Baram for the same purpose.

No one knew better than the Sarawak Government that bands of young Ibans supposedly looking for gutta percha were capable of creating endless trouble, especially when there were human heads to be gained thereby. Gradually, officers appointed to the newly acquired rivers began to see things more from the local point of view. In 1888 A.H. Everett listened with sympathy when the Kenyah chief Aban Nipa (Tama Oyong) complained that Ibans were denuding his country of jungle produce. Everett recommended that the Ibans should in future work only in completely uninhabited streams. (Pringle 1970:268–9)

Pringle quotes Everett as follows:

The Kayans and Kenyahs are now quite conversant with the methods of working and are, as they truly say, dependent on jungle produce to pay their tax to government and as the Dayaks will still have the choice of numerous uninhabited streams . . . in which to work and, as moreover, they have for over four years had their pick of the gutta producing districts, they can have no ground for complaint. (*Sarawak Gazette* 269:June 1888)

In resisting de Crespigny's Ibanocentric policies, Aban Jau was in the right of it, as even future Residents conceded. What distinguished Aban Jau's reaction from that of other disgruntled leaders was that he took direct action. He closed off the Tinjar with a rattan cable and threatened death to any unwanted intruders that crossed it. This was a direct challenge to de Crespigny's tenuous authority, to which he did not dare respond directly for fear of uniting all the Kayan and Kenyah chiefs of Baram behind Aban Jau. His Machiavellian solution was to frame Aban Jau on some other charge entirely, the hoary issue of headhunting. The manoeuvre worked because the Kayan chiefs of the middle Baram – Aban Jau's in-laws and oldest allies – did not back him up. Instead, he was isolated, and his influence diminished.

The Last Years

From then on, the attitudes of Residents to Aban Jau were dismissive. According to De Crespigny's successor,

> He has had a bad character all his life among his own people, as well as among strangers; always wishing to elevate himself above his proper mark; to fine or otherwise bully; never really dangerous, but full of capriciousness; sometimes very humble, and at other times just the contrary. The first Resident (the late Mr. C.C. de Crespigny) tried everything he could to bring him into a reasonable path and to act through him as chief, and his successors have done the same. Aban Jau is now, however, between seventy and eighty years of age and so is scarcely expected to change his character. (*Sarawak Gazette* 238:November 1885)

It is interesting to compare this assessment with that made by Hugh Brooke Low a decade earlier. There is in Low a willingness to see the genius of the man, while de Crespigny and his successors see only an obstacle in establishing the control of the Raj. As a final humiliation, he is reduced to a mere supporting role in Charles Hose's adventures. The defanged and domesticated Aban Jau is described as "this fine old Chief." Hose devotes a whole chapter of his memoirs to Aban Jau, entitling it "A Rob Roy of Sarawak" (1927:48–59).

The Longhouse as Tomb

The irony of Hose's breathless account of Aban Jau's Communal House is that it was already well past its prime when he arrived. Just before his visit, the *Sarawak Gazette* reports that Aban Jau had begun to make the move "inside" the Termadoh (278:March 1889). That is to say, he was abandoning the site on the banks of the main river and retreating to one hidden in an adjacent side stream. When completed some months later, the new house had a much smaller population than the Long Batan community at its height. The move marks the end of Berawan participation in Aban Jau's community, and even his Sebop followers were drifting away. The contrast with just five years previously is marked. After de Crespigny arrested Aban Jau's people on the track near Marudi, he listed the names and identities of those apprehended. Four were Sebop, and four were Berawan. There was one Kayan, listed as a slave. The final man was a Maloh, from far to the south. The Maloh developed a speciality in working silver for jewellery and travelled widely throughout the interior practicing their trade. A small part-Berawan, part-Maloh community still existed in the middle Tinjar in the 1970s. Such was the cosmopolitanism of Aban Jau's metropolis at its height.

The Long Batan community consisted of several longhouses. This is not unusual; in the first description of longhouses quoted in Chapter 1, Spenser St. John (1862:97) describes a cluster of longhouses "built on lofty posts, on hills of various heights, yet appearing to be clustered together." At that site in the middle Baram, the terrain was evidently too broken to allow a single house long enough to accommodate the whole community, so it was built in several sections. Consequently, the concept of the "longhouse community" must be taken to mean not only the community of a longhouse, but also a community of longhouses. At the site of Aban Jau's community at Long Batan, there is a considerable plain, quite large enough for a single longhouse, but the riverbank is curved. By all accounts there was a row of three longhouses in an arc facing the water, connected by small bridges and surrounded by a stockade. The major Berawan house was at the downriver end, but intermarriage soon broke down any real segregation.

In the 1980s, there was once again a longhouse at Long Batan, although it is overshadowed by a much larger community of Long Pokun Sebop right next door. The site is an attractive one, and it is not surprising that it was reoccupied by the wave of Sebop immigrants who arrived after the Great Kayan Expedition of 1863. Most of the Long Taballau Sebop by then lived elsewhere, but a few had moved back to Long Batan and were able to point out to me the monuments associated with their famous ancestor, including several grand mausoleums and the pilings of his last longhouse "inside" the Termadoh. There is, however, no tomb for Aban Jau himself. At first sight this seems odd, especially since the *Sarawak Gazette* (314:March 1892) reports the construction of an "immense mausoleum" for him. In fact, there were too few people left for any major construction effort, and when Aban Jau lay dying, he instructed his last faithful followers to lay him out in state in the middle of his longhouse apartment, and then to simply abandon the place. Appropriately, the longhouse itself became Aban Jau's tomb.

Chapter 5

Aban Jau's Successors

There were aspects of Aban Jau's life and times that were unique, but the arc of his career was not at all exceptional. Time and again, we find the names of important leaders associated with the fluctuating fortunes of longhouse communities, so that we might think of the longhouses themselves as having a life cycle to match the man's. For all his bravado, Aban Jau failed to impose his ideas of what his role should be, and his end shows that failure – steadily abandoned and finally alone in his empty house. His case is instructive because it represents an extreme example of a general tendency. Moreover, his times cannot be contrasted with a previous epoch of peace and stability. As far back as oral histories reach, there is evidence of struggle between communities and rival leaders within communities. Consequently, Aban Jau's career represents not novelty, but an intensification of processes that had happened before and would happen again. To prove the point, it is only necessary to follow the fate of the people who abandoned him to his fate in his empty longhouse.

Aban Jau's Rivals

Even at the height of his career, Aban Jau had rivals. In the Seping (Figure 02-01), the Lepo Anan leader, Tama Lian Avit, assembled a large community of even more diverse elements than those at Long Batan. When Hugh Brook Low visited in 1884, he found six longhouses, three of "Lepu Anans," one of

"Lepu Sawa," one of "Klabits," and one of "Savop" (*Sarawak Gazette* 220: May 1884). The prefix "Lepu" (also written Lepo, Leppo, and Lepo') indicates Kenyah ethnicity, meaning simply "house." The presence of Kelabit people in the Seping is a surprise, but there is a connecting route to the Kelabit highlands via the Silat River, passing to the east of the Usun Apau. In the nineteenth century, the Silat Valley was repeatedly occupied by communities escaping enemies on one side or another, and was often a no man's land between warring parties. Finally, the "Savop" component comprised yet another element of the Sebop, a remnant that had survived the Great Kayan Expedition of 1863. This one longhouse within Tama Lian's community was all that remained of a much larger population that had been ravaged by smallpox, as de Crespigny discovered during a visit in 1882. Other refugees had fled to Belaga, where they were referred to as "Sepengs" rather than Sebop (*Sarawak Gazette* 188:June 1882).

Predictably, the relationship between Aban Jau and Tama Lian Avit was stormy. It began amicably enough, with a visit in 1878 by Tama Lian to the funeral of Aban Jau's wife (*Sarawak Gazette* 147:November 1878). The next year, the relationship had blossomed to the point that a marriage was proposed between Tama Lian and Aban Jau's daughter, an alliance useful to Aban Jau in case his position in Tinjar became untenable, and he was obliged to retire south, back toward the Usun Apau (*Sarawak Gazette* 155:July 1879). Aban Jau's attempts to use his daughter for dynastic purposes were repeatedly frustrated by the woman herself, however, as recounted in Chapter 4. Aban Jau should already have understood how wilful his beautiful daughter could be because she had just divorced her first husband, a powerful Kayan chief of the middle Baram. Perhaps Aban Jau believed that having lost an ally to the north, he had better recruit one to the south. But relations with Tama Lian soured, and he rapidly became more of a liability than an asset. The problem was that Tama Lian, or his brother Lijau, stirred up trouble constantly by making raids into the Baram watershed, particularly into the Silat country. Even on the way home from the funeral of Aban Jau's wife, Tama Lian had ambushed a party of Uma Pliau Kayan and taken four heads, supposedly in revenge for a raid they had previously made on his house in Seping (*Sarawak Gazette* 147:November 1878). Aban Jau did not need to be making enemies among the Kayan, and within a few years we find him offering his services to Rajah Brooke to make a punitive raid against Tama Lian (*Sarawak Gazette* 168:September 1880). What was strange about this proposal was that Lian was nominally a subject of Sarawak, presumably under the protection of the Raj, whereas Aban Jau was not. Perhaps Aban Jau saw the irony in this, since Tama Lian had previously claimed to be under the protection of the Rajah, and so immune to counterattacks (*Sarawak Gazette* 160:December 1879).

Intra-Berawan Rivalries

What Aban Jau and Tama Lian Avit most obviously had in common was that they had built defensive alliances, and then tried to use them to project their own power over whole river systems. Neither succeeded, and their followers drifted away as their grandiose ambitions became evident.

The first independent leader of the Berawan to emerge from Aban Jau's shadow was Tama Lire. No sooner had the Baram watershed been ceded to Sarawak than he appeared at Marudi to complain about Aban Jau (*Sarawak Gazette* 203:December 1882). Soon after, the *Sarawak Gazette* reports his scheme for six "tuahs," or elders, to "desert Aban Jau and move into Luak" (207:April 1883). The name Luak refers to a large, shallow lake that drains into the lower Tinjar. On the banks of the lake, there was a community that had been there for time immemorial. At that time, it was the only one in the swampy lower Tinjar. Consequently, Tama Lire was proposing to lead the residents of a handful of rooms at Long Batan half the length of the river and attach them to another community, in order to escape Aban Jau's domination.

As Aban Jau's grip loosened, Tama Lire grew more ambitious. Within five years, the Berawan had entirely abandoned Long Batan, and Tama Lire was established in his own longhouse not far down river. There was a problem, however. Tama Lire had not succeeded in assembling at his new house all the Berawan who were leaving Long Batan – so tidy an outcome is not in the character of longhouse dynamics. Instead, the decline of Aban Jau brought on a period of bickering, dispersion, and competition among possible successors. Old factions resurfaced – if indeed they had ever been fully submerged – and new ones emerged, each with its own agenda. Tama Lire's struggle had only just begun.

The factions with which Tama Lire had to contended dated from a time before the arrival of the Long Taballau Sebop in Tinjar, when there had been four separate Berawan communities in the upper stretches of Tinjar, at Long Sijoi, Long Ugeng, Long Lamat, and Long Penuwan. Apparently, each had achieved enough persistence and continuity of leadership that their names provided ethnonyms still cogent in the 1970s. Yet, everyone's narratives confirmed that there had been an epoch before this dispersion when all Berawan of Tinjar had shared a single longhouse community. Such unity had in fact occurred several times, and those communities were the high points of oral history, fabulous in their riches and glory. Given such happy memories, it is puzzling that some brief period of disharmony had not simply been forgotten. One might have expected that the structural opposition Berawan/Sebop at Long Batan would have suppressed internal differences and that a generation of intermarriage would have blurred the edges of old categories.

The survival of ancient factions teaches several lessons. First, one ethnicity does not erase another; people are perfectly capable of announcing multiple allegiances or attachments at the same time. Putting that in political terms, the leading families of the Berawan continued to jockey for position throughout the Long Batan period, and this is further evidence that Aban Jau was not such a despot as to eliminate all other voices but his own. In fact, the same factionalism took place among the Sebop element. The *Sarawak Gazette* records a quarrel between Aban Jau and his former general, Tama Purai, bitter enough that the latter threatened to move back into the Usun Apau, taking a large part of his brother's following with him (147:November 1878). Unfortunately, we are not told what the quarrel was about, but it was not fully resolved for some years. Had it actually produced a split, the two parts of the Long Batan Sebop would undoubtedly have produced new ethnonyms. Second, intermarriage may complicate category distinctions, but it was not a process unique to Long Batan. Marriage had occurred within and between all previous communities, without erasing pre-existing ethnonyms. When the Long Sijoi Berawan lived at Long Sijoi, and the Long Ugeng at Long Ugeng, and so on, those communities were not endogamous. As with all ethnonyms, the point is never tidy boundaries. Instead, it has to do politics, meaning the rivalries between aspiring leaders, and the community dynamics that produces. Third, there is nothing inevitable about the process of ethnification. For instance, the Long Sijoi might have been assimilated into the Long Ugeng, or the reverse, to the point that both ethnonyms would have lost cogency. It just so happens that they did not, and in general, what is remarkable is the tenacity of such hoary divisions. If the analogy is not too far fetched, we might say that the place of ethnonyms in longhouse politics is more like that of parties within a state than national differences between states. If there is a Republican president in the United States, this does not eliminate the differences between interests within the Democratic Party, progressives, labour unionists, centrists, and so on. Moreover, it would be ludicrous to suggest that intermarriage between Democrats and Republicans endangered the existence of either party.

After the Long Batan community broke up, Tama Lire had the edge over his competitors because he led the Long Sijoi, who were the most numerous. A rival soon appeared however, in the person of Aban Avit, leader of the Long Ugeng. The loyalties of Long Lamat people were divided, and many Long Penuwan went their own way, joining up with Sebop and Lirong elements and moving upriver from Long Batan, as opposed to down river like the rest of the Berawan. A joint Berawan/Sebop/Lirong community still existed in the 1970s at Apogun in the headwaters of the Tinjar.

In addition, Tama Lire had the ear of the government. In 1884, after Aban Jau had been framed for the murder of the slave and so brought to heel, Tama Lire was put in charge of all Berawan and Penan in Tinjar. In his report, de Crespigny remarks that he delayed announcing this appointment in order not to irritate Aban Jau, but now saw no need to delay (*Sarawak Gazette* 221:June 1884). Within a short time, he was given the formal title of Penghulu (Government Appointed Chief), and for the next three decades, we hear of him dutifully collecting head taxes.

However, Tama Lire squandered his early lead over Aban Avit by indecisiveness. In 1899, on his way home from the Torres Straits expedition, Alfred Court Haddon spent some time in Sarawak and accompanied Charles Hose on a trip up the Tinjar. Haddon reports:

> Although Taman Liri is a *penghulu* . . . he complained that the long Tobai people had left him and had gone to live with Aban Avit at Long Tisam, a little higher up the river, the latter chief having enticed them away. Hose questioned some of the friends of the long Tobai people, who stated that the reason for the latter not wishing to live with Taman Liri was that he constantly shifted his house, and that he did not fulfill his annual promise of building a really good house. They were sick of living in this unsatisfactory manner, and therefore went to live with Aban Avit, who also was a Berawan, and who had a very good longhouse at Long Tisam. Hose told Taman Liri it was unreasonable to expect people to shift their house every year, as the greater part of their time was taken up in house-building, and their plantations suffered in consequence.
>
> We next visited Aban Avit, who certainly had a much better house than Taman Liri. Owing to the influx of people, the house was being extended. When we walked over the framework of the extension, we were cautioned to be careful not to fall through. This warning was not given solely to save us from injury, although a fall of some fifteen feet would not be particularly pleasant, but because if anyone fell off a house in process of building a new house would have to be built elsewhere, as would also be the case if a dog was killed in the house. (1901:335)

It cannot literally be true that Tama Lire had uprooted his community every year. What was probably going on was that he was trying to work out the location that best suited the distribution of his followers' farms, and one can imagine him grinding his teeth in exasperation when Hose told him smugly that he was doing it all wrong. Meanwhile, Aban Avit's house was evidently a solid structure of the traditional kind, as we can surmise from the report that its floors were fifteen feet above the ground, and his strategy of emphasising the house over the site had evidently paid off. As for the "Long Tobai," they constituted a splinter group that had moved to Long

Figure 05-01. The longhouse of Aban Avit at Long Tisam whose establishment drew Berawan settlers away from the following of Tama Lire after the collapse of Aban Jau's community at Long Batan. (From Furness 1902: frontispiece.)

Tobai temporarily, after leaving Long Batan and before joining Tama Lire. It was, of course, for the adherence of such groups that he and Aban Avit were struggling. We do not know whether the Long Tobai people were of Long Sijoi origin, or Long Ugeng, or Long Lamat, or a mixture of these, but in any event the name did not survive. By the 1970s, it had been forgotten, which is to say that it had only passing significance. In my jargon, it never achieved cogency.

Selecting the Sites of Farms

In addition to political rivalries, there was a second major centrifugal tendency that had to do with the dispersion of farms. Given the low population densities of central Borneo, it might seem that there was land and to spare. That was true in the sense that swidden farms could, in a pinch, have been made just about anywhere over huge tracts of empty land. But that is to ignore the techniques and preferences of Upriver farmers. What they were looking for was niches that satisfied various criteria, including suitable soil and topography. In a few swampy places, conditions approximated those of "wet" rice agriculture using irrigation, allowing cultivation year after

113

year. These valuable sites were seldom abandoned. However, flat land right on the riverbank was risky because any serious flooding could destroy the entire crop in one blow. Some slope was desirable for drainage, but if it was too steep a sudden downpour could wash away the new seed or germinating rice. Since there were also hazards from blight, and from pests like pigs, it was better to hedge one's bets by having several small fields rather than one big one. Monkeys were particularly loathed. A troop of macaques could, heartbreakingly, destroy an entire field of nearly full grown rice in one night. A site that allowed a number of fields, and a mixture of strategies was often preferred. Like farmers everywhere, longhouse people had a huge store of information on particular microenvironments and valued it highly. In addition, there were criteria having to do with access. Upriver farmers seldom moved far away from streams large enough to provide access by canoe, and that is why large tracts of virgin rainforest persisted until their destruction by commercial lumbering in the final decades of the twentieth century. Also, there was the thorny issue of distance from the site of the longhouse that had given Tama Lire so many headaches.

Finally, there was an important set of social criteria in selecting farm sites. Having invested time and effort learning the virtues and vices of a particular location, a farming unit – that is, the coresidents of a room in the longhouse – would not want to move to a totally different place the following year. Consequently, the site needed to have enough acceptable land to allow new clearings to be made for several years. Moreover, families did not want to be alone at these sites. No one wanted to present so easy a target for head hunters, and in addition, people preferred to work in groups. Indeed, there are phases in the agricultural cycle when work parties comprising several rooms proceeded systematically from field to field. Finally, farmers preferred old secondary jungle because it is easier to clear than primary jungle, while having lain fallow long enough for the soil to recover its fertility. Claims to such land consist of asserting that former residents of one's own room originally cut the jungle there. Consequently, and contrary to the nomadic stereotype of swidden agriculture, there was a strong conservative element in the choice of farm sites.

Selecting the Sites of Longhouses

This habitus shaped, of course, historical and geographical perceptions. For those Berawan preparing to leave Long Batan, the Tinjar did not flow between endless expanses of empty rainforest, as we might see it, but was instead an avenue connecting pockets of choice land. The terrain of each was known to everyone in the community, but associated with particular people, both alive and dead. Long Tabai was such a place, although no longhouse was ever built there. In fact, longhouse sites were often at none of these places because their selection had different criteria. Longhouses were almost invariably built within a hundred yards of a river, and careful attention was paid to the shape of the riverbank. If it was too high, access to the water involved slithering down a muddy bank, but if it was too low, the house would be flooded at every high water. If the river was too straight at that point, the current might be so swift as to endanger the children, who spent their time leaping into and out of the water. A few eddies were useful to provide slack water, provided they were not such as to undermine the bank or draw in too much of the driftwood that floated downstream after high water. Finally – Tama Lire's dilemma – they needed to be centrally sited for everyone's farms.

Exploiting Ambiguities of Residence

In the meantime, no hasty decision needed to be made about new longhouse sites because the process of abandoning Long Batan occurred by degrees. Even when the house was in its prime, its residents routinely left to go to their farms, a few families here, a few there, upriver and down, and sometimes they stayed for extended periods. Indeed, at times of sowing and harvesting, longhouses were often nearly empty, except for those who were too old or too young to work. All that was required for Aban Jau's fortunes to turn was for people to begin to spend more time at their farmhouses and less at the longhouse. Aban Jau might fulminate against the antisocial tendencies of those who too often left their longhouse rooms locked, and he might threaten fines if the rooms fell into disrepair. What he could not do – even if he had had a band of toughs at his back – was stop people from going to their farms. All he could accomplish by being heavy handed was to encourage people to stay away. Once their farmhouses became more elaborate than their longhouse apartments, the fate of Long Batan was sealed. Meanwhile, if several families built their farmhouses in a row according to the longhouse plan, there could be considerable ambiguity about whether they were still resident at Long Batan. Although these mini-longhouses had little chance of growing into major communities, they could certainly persist over long periods and steadily draw support away from failing communities. No doubt, Aban Jau made attempts to rally his followers, but he had then to reckon with the reputation for coercion that he had made for himself. When he finally chose to move his house "inside" the Termadoh, it was only because the house at Long Batan was half empty anyway, its echoing verandas a constant reminder of his failures and excesses.

While Aban Jau's position was being undermined by the ambiguities of dual residence, Tama Lire was busy trying to take advantage of them. When he was appointed Penghulu, he had managed to convince de Crespigny that his house, wherever it happened to be at that moment, was or would become the proper longhouse, and that all the other houses along the Tinjar were just elaborate farmhouses. It is that pretence that was unmasked during Hose's visit with Haddon. However, Aban Avit did not hold all the cards either because there was no way he could usurp Tama Lire's claim to the support of the large Long Sijoi faction. The result was a long standoff. For seventeen years, the Berawan of Tinjar lived in at least two different longhouses, not to mention those who effectively lived at their farms.

There was no inherent reason why the stalemate between Aban Avit and Tama Lire need ever have been resolved. For instance, if either one of them had decided to relocate to the upper Tinjar – or another river system entirely – it might have become permanent. That is what had happened a generation before, when the Long Wat separated from the Long Suku, as described Chapter 2. Nothing this dramatic occurred, however, and the different Berawan populations, dispersed along a relatively short section of the middle Tinjar, maintained close ties of marriage and ritual cooperation. In the predominant narrative, the final reunification in 1906 is attributed to the statesmanship of Tama Lire. He is portrayed as a level-headed man, lacking Aban Jau's irritable temper, persuasively urging the virtues of community and solidarity. Berawan history is not entirely narrated by the victors, however, and I soon found informants who were quick to point out that by then Aban Avit was in poor health. Moreover, the site of the newly combined house was at Long Tisam, where Hose and Haddon had seen the impressive new structure being built in 1899. In that sense, Tama Lire had joined Aban Avit, rather than the reverse, and that was perhaps the basis of their reconciliation.

Nevertheless, the house at Long Tisam is firmly associated with Tama Lire, and the decade of its prime is remembered as a golden age, a time of peace and plenty in which new trading opportunities brought wealth in traditional valuables and ritual life flourished as never before. Another feature marked the completion of a longhouse cycle. For the house at Long Tisam, ancient pilings were recovered from the abandoned site at Long Batan. Each belongeded in theory to a particular room, if it still existed, but they required so much effort to move that only a renewed community had the manpower and resources to reclaim them. As for the planks, they were no doubt removed earlier and shipped to other, more temporary sites. One has the eerie image of former longhouse-mates, Sebop and Berawan, bumping into each other at the abandoned and overgrown site of Long

Batan as they pick over what was worth moving and what was too rotted to use again.

Continuing Threats of Violence

There is a curious footnote to this, however. The issue of the *Sarawak Gazette* that reports that Tama Lire had collected his people together and built a fine new house of fifty "doors" (i.e., rooms) appeared in March 1906 (number 483), and the new unity was apparently achieved in the nick of time. The previous issue contained the startling report of a large Iban war party, estimated at 1,000 men, preparing to attack the middle Tinjar. These Iban are reported as coming from Mukah and Bintulu, both areas on the coast that had supposedly been fully under Sarawak government control for decades. Evidently, the war party had moved inland by ascending the Kemena River and then the Jelalong, and so to a path leading to the Tinjar not far upriver from Long Tisam (Figure 04-01). Although the force was, astonishingly, assembled and moved upriver without any interference, a rumour luckily reached the ears of the Resident at Bintulu. He dispatched a contingent of Sarawak Rangers (i.e., uniformed soldiers armed with rifles – probably themselves Iban) just in time to intercept the war party near Long Tisam (*Sarawak Gazette* 482:March 1906). The Iban were ordered to return home, but sixty of them refused to do so, brazenly claiming legitimate business. These were arrested and fined $5 each, and $25 for the four "ringleaders." Given their obvious mass homicidal intent, and the enormous fines visited on Aban Jau in a much less settled time, the sanctions seem absurdly light.

This incident must have been a considerable shock to the people at Long Tisam, who were the obvious target, even though the whole watershed was reported to be "armed to the teeth for war." It certainly confirmed the wisdom of Berawan reunification. Indeed, it may have promoted it because people from Long Tisam used the route along the Kemena to the coast and were well aware of the growing numbers of Iban in the Bintulu region. No one had forgotten the Great Kayan Raid of 1863 or the even more destructive one of 1896.

A Successful Handover of Leadership

Unlike Aban Jau, Tama Lire went to some pains to ensure an orderly succession. Although he had outlived Aban Avit, he was himself ailing. So he selected an able young man, his nephew Tama Tiri, and set about training him to assume the role of Penghulu. Tama Tiri was soon delegated to collect taxes and deliver them to the Resident in Marudi, where he had a chance to make a good impression (*Sarawak Gazette* 550:February 1910). Tama Lire was in a position to influence the Resident's decision since only a short time before that he had been held up as a model to the still dispersed Sebop remnants from Long Batan (*Sarawak Gazette* 530:April 1909).

Tama Lire's strategy succeeded with the Resident, and Tama Tiri was indeed appointed Penghulu in his place. Not surprisingly, things did not go quite so smoothly at Long Tisam itself, however. After Tama Lire's death in 1913, factional disputes re-emerged, and Tama Tiri found himself challenged on all sides. Disgruntled parties spent more and more time at their farmhouses, and once again creating ambiguities about exactly who was a resident of the longhouse and who was not. Luckily for Tama Tiri, no leader emerged of the stature of Aban Avit, so he was given the time he needed to establish himself. The end of this phase is marked by the removal of the community from Long Tisam to a new site at Long Miri sometime about 1925.

This case is instructive because it shows what continuity may be expected in longhouse communities. Tama Lire's plans for the succession were in the end successful. In most Berawan tellings of it, the golden age of Long Tisam flows seamlessly into that of Long Miri, and the names of Tama Lire and Tama Tiri are invoked with equal regularity, so that to begin with I mistook them for the same man. The similarity of their names also fooled the Kuching-based editors of the *Sarawak Gazette*, who went on reporting the activities of "Tama Liri" after they had announced his death. Oral histories also reveal less generous voices commenting on Tama Tiri, voices that were soon to be raised again. The essential point, however, is that Tama Tiri's standing was not secure until he had built a new longhouse at Long Miri. To accomplish that, he had to contain the centrifugal tendencies that had dispersed the Berawan of Tinjar after the collapse of Long Batan and threatened to do so again. The new longhouse at Long Miri, ever after associated with his name, was in part the evidence, in part the instrument, of his success.

Tama Tiri died not long before the arrival of the Japanese in 1942, and the disruption of his death is consequently mixed up with the greater confusion of the war. Like other people in the Baram, Berawan tell of hiding in their farmhouses to avoid the Japanese, but the Japanese rarely bothered to go far upriver. In the 1970s, old people vividly remembered an occasion when Japanese soldiers with an officer arrived, demanding that they hand over their entire rice crops. They complied, and were forced back on sago and other jungle produce to survive. The end of the war did not bring the restoration of the Brooke Raj that they had known before it. Instead, the war-ravaged country was ceded to Britain, and there were new district officers with different ideas about the future of Upriver People. As the British colonial order established itself, Tama Tiri's successor, Tama Are, was appointed headman but he was not given the title of Penghulu. Instead, that office moved downriver, to Long Teru.

Tama Are established himself at a site only slightly down river from Long Miri, at Long Jegan, as if to emphasize continuity. Building there had begun before the war, and when the Japanese arrived, there were five doors completed and several more under construction. After the war, construction resumed, and Tama Are was successful in holding the community together. When I arrived at Long Jegan in the mid-1970s, Tama Are's longhouse was still in place, together with supporting posts that had been moved from Long Batan to Long Tisam and then Long Miri. At first glance, it appeared to be a single imposing building, several hundred yards in length. A closer inspection revealed small breaks of perhaps four feet, crossed by bridges complete with railings. In that way, they were still there – the separate houses of the Long Sijoi (down river), Long Ugeng and Long Penuwan (in the middle), and Long Lamat (upriver) – just as they had been at Long Batan.

Old Rivalries Re-Emerge

In the 1970s, the old factionalism flamed once again into secession. Uking, a grandson of Aban Avit, announced that he would take the Long Ugeng people away from Long Jegan to a new site at Long Teran, some miles down river.

Uking was convinced that the extensive and productive land around Long Teran would be lost to a flood of Iban immigrants if it were not occupied. To help him hold the land, he invited Kayan settlers from the middle Baram to join him, preferring them to the Iban. He claimed the right to do because the site had been opened up by Long Ugeng people. Uking was charismatic, but unstable, sometimes agreeable and sometimes domineering, but always jealous of his power, just as Aban Jau had been. His proposals caused uproar at Long Jegan, and the leadership of the Long Sijoi ridiculed both his claims to Aban Avit's mantle and his apocalyptic views; they were convinced that the postindependence government would defend their rights. Within two decades, however, the influx of Iban exceeded even what Uking had predicted, and the government did nothing. Meanwhile, Uking's community thrived, despite its ethnic mix of Upriver Peoples.

The Life Cycle of Longhouses: A Model

It must be emphasized that what I am proposing here is a model, a simplified account abstracted from many different historical narratives. In general, places that figure prominently in migration stories are associated with the names of particular leaders. Just how messy the details can be is illustrated by Tama Lire, who nearly lost out to Aban Avit in the long-running competition for leadership of the Berawan of Tinjar, and won in the end only by outliving his rival and taking over his longhouse. Nevertheless, in the 1970s, it was Tama Lire's name that was associated with the Golden Age of Long Tisam, when the Berawan had enjoyed stability and wealth, and successfully repelled their most violent enemies, the Iban – with a little assistance from the Resident.

The career of Tama Lire was less dramatic than that of Aban Jau, and he had no Charles Hose to make him into "a fine old chief," but he is for that very reason a better example of the routine fusing of leaders and communities, so that one may speak of the life cycle of longhouses.

It is the nature of such models that they deal with time in terms of process. That is, the life cycle is portrayed as constantly unfolding in all communities, at its own speed and on its own timetable. This process provides a kind of sine wave that underlies genuine historical change, but it must not be mistaken for that change. The forces that were to buffet longhouse society in the nineteenth and twentieth centuries were external, and it is to them that I turn in Section III.

Part III

Longhouse and Trade

Chapter 6

The Sultan's Fence

Of all the leaders of longhouse communities in the valley of the Tinjar, Aban Jau stands out not only because of his hubris, but also because his career straddled the period when Upriver People lost their turbulent independence and came under colonial control.

In his rehabilitation of the humbled Aban Jau as "A Rob Roy of Sarawak," Charles Hose quotes several of his "picturesque sayings." Among them is this remark, half plaint, half boast:

> Your Rajah may govern the down-river people; they are inside the Sultan's fence and he had the right to hand them over. But over us he had no authority; we are the tigers of the jungle and have never been tamed. (Hose and McDougall 1912:II:283)

Picturesque as his wording may be, Aban Jau's argument was perfectly reasonable. As far as he was concerned, the political manoeuvring between Rajah Brooke, the Foreign Office in London, and the Sultan in Brunei, leading up to the "cession" of "Baram," was absolutely meaningless. The annexation of the whole watershed had no more legal basis than any other colonial land grab.

The protest fell, of course, on deaf ears, but it reveals something of the world in which Aban Jau grew up, a world divided between those who did and did not live "inside the Sultan's fence." Since that was the world in which the institutions of longhouse life were shaped, it is now necessary to turn attention to the nature and location of the fence. It was not, it turns out, a very formidable barrier, but then it never had been; it had more to do with connection than separation.

Gilding the Lily: Murder at a Funeral

By way of transition, I begin with a vignette, a series of incidents that occurred along the Tutoh River in the 1870s. The Tutoh is the second largest tributary of the Baram after the Tinjar, but whereas the latter leads south away from Brunei, the Tutoh hooks to the west, directly behind the territory of what the British called "Brunei proper" (Figure 01-01). Consequently, where the Tinjar was a relative backwater insulated from the convulsions of the nineteenth century, the Tutoh provided the major highway from the upper Baram to Brunei, and bore the full brunt of warfare. Wanting to know more about this highway, the Rajah sent one of his most trusted aides, Hugh Brooke Low, to explore it in 1876. Low bore the Brooke name because his father had been a close friend and admirer of the Rajah (Pringle 1970:120n). Not surprisingly, given the sensitivity of the area and the blatant intention to spy, the Sultan denied permission for the itinerary. Undeterred, Low took another route, travelling south along the coast, and then up the Belait River and over into the lower Tutoh on foot. Later, he went by canoe up the Tinjar River and so back to Sarawak territory, but not before encountering Aban Jau on his way home from a foiled raid on Sibuti, as described in Chapter 4.

Low reported the intelligence he collected in Tutoh, including a drama that climaxed in a murder at a funeral. The funeral was in a Berawan longhouse some distance upriver. In accordance with custom, both then and a century later, the corpse was displayed on a special throne (*teloren*), dressed in all his finery, and surrounded by all manner of valuables (Metcalf 1982:36–44). While a corpse is seated on the *teloren*, it is proper for people to pay their respects as they arrive. Women engage in a formalised dirge, throwing their long hair forward over their faces. Men are more restrained, muttering under their breath, or simply standing mute, eyes downcast. At this particular funeral, however, something outrageous occurred. There were Brunei traders at the longhouse, Moslems, of course, and one of them was tactless enough to ridicule this pagan usage, pointing to the corpse and laughing. "Stung to fury," Low says, a nephew of the dead man pulled the sword from the sheath at his dead uncle's waist and cut down the offender on the spot (*Sarawak Gazette* 12:August 1876).

This violence came at the end of a long series of provocations. The traders, who called themselves Burong Pingai, began their dealings in any particular community by making gifts of valuables, such as brassware, to the leading men. These gifts were to be repaid with jungle produce, but the products they wanted cannot be accumulated rapidly, so the Burong Pingai sat down to wait. In the meantime, they battened off their hosts and, as the weeks went by, made a thorough nuisance of themselves. First, they behaved in a high-handed fashion, often tapping their stomachs to remind their hosts that they had yet to eat any of the profits of their trade. Second, they seduced the wives of men away in the jungle, luring them on board their boats with trinkets and fine fabrics. Finally, they employed every available form of bad business practice, lying and cheating so as to defraud their long-suffering hosts out of whatever gains they had made.

It must be remembered that Low had reasons to paint as black a picture as he could. One of the goals of his trip was to document cases of Brunei misrule, so that the Rajah could win the approval of the British government for his annexation of more Brunei territory. It was not the fault of the traders that rounding up sufficient volumes of jungle produce is a slow process, and they certainly provided a service in making luxury goods available upriver. The types and amounts of such goods owned by leading families shows that the trade had gone on for centuries, presumably to the interest of both parties, and it may be that traders always had to put pressure on unsophisticated longhouse people in order to spur them into economic activity.

Evidently, there were those in the Berawan community who wanted to see things patched up. The victim of the murder had been a mere boy, and a slave at that. Ironically, he had himself probably come originally from a longhouse community. So the Berawan chief, Orang Kaya Panglima Ipui, offered to replace the slave with one of his own and, in addition, pay brassware to the tune of "373 catties of guns." This he regarded as *ganti nyawa*, "a replacement of the soul," that is, a final settlement. But the Burong Pingai traders wanted more and appealed to the Sultan to impose a much larger fine. Growing impatient, their leader, Nakhoda Rahman, decided to avenge himself. He and a few followers rowed up to an isolated Berawan farmhouse and murdered a boy standing unawares by the riverside. Then they fled down river, with Berawan boats in hot pursuit. The pursuers managed only to shoot one of the attackers in the arm with a poison dart from a blowgun, but they found two of Nakhoda Rahman's associates lingering upriver and killed both of them. One was a Burong Pingai, the other a man from Sumatra.

Berawan fury at the treachery of Nakhoda Rahman, who had accepted *ganti nyawa* and then killed the boy, soon spread to communities in the

Baram, who had their own grievances. The result was a total breakdown in trade:

> The Burong Pingais were expelled from Baram 18 months ago and have not dared to come back ever since. In Tatau [Tutoh] it is certain death for an individual of that race to show his face. They are unpopular everywhere, and wherever they have set their feet, they have managed to embroil themselves with the natives. (*Sarawak Gazette* 12:August 1876)

For Low, this murder and mayhem was grist to the mill, further proving what the Rajah had been telling the British government for years about the chaotic conditions in Baram. For my purposes, however, the incidents have other lessons.

Outside the Sultan's Fence

The first lesson concerns the longhouse communities existing in the Tutoh in 1876. Low's account is specific about them: there were just two, one near the confluence with the Baram and another some hours' travel upriver. Although Low was not to know it, there were other communities in the far headwaters, but they were isolated by a narrow gorge containing nearly impassable rapids and played no part in the politics of Baram. Meanwhile, the two communities in the navigable lower part of the river were very much caught up in Baram politics, as Low's account demonstrates. Both were remarkable establishments, containing an even greater mix of people than Aban Jau's community at Long Batan. The more upriver of the two communities comprised two longhouses of "Long Patas," and one of "Trieng." The other community had four houses, accommodating the "Longkiputs, Tanjongs, and Batu Belahs." Needless to say, each ethnic label needs unpacking to make sense of it, but we postpone that for Section IV. Suffice it for the moment to say that the Long Pata and Batu Belah were elements of the Berawan, whom we already met at Long Batan. The Long Kiput were first cousins, but the Tanjong were recent arrivals in the area, having come all the way from the Rejang watershed to the south. As for the Tring, we come to them in a moment.

In addition to having multiple longhouses, both communities were enclosed within a stockade, built in the manner described in Chapter 1. The reason for this high state of military preparedness is not far to seek: it was a response to Kayan raids that in the previous decades had brought to the lowlands warfare and destruction on an unprecedented scale. Just what set off this chaos takes some unravelling because it was both a cause and a symptom of the decline of Brunei. One obvious feature, however, was the migration of Kayan into the Baram watershed. Of course, there was nothing exceptional about the migration per se; on the contrary, such population movements had been a feature of central Borneo as long as it is possible to make out. But the arrival of the Kayan in Baram was so sudden, and in such strength, that it sent shock waves throughout the region.

Kayan oral history places their homeland in the upper reaches of Apo Kayan River, far to the east of Brunei, across the mountains. From there, different streams of settlers moved east toward the coast, south into the watershed of the Mahakam, and west into Sarawak. The reason given for the emigration is overcrowding (Hang Nyipa 1956), and ecological degradation was advanced. In the late 1890s, the Dutch explorer Anton Nieuwenhuis found that even far up the tributaries there was no primary forest, and only clumps of secondary growth amid rank grasses (Nieuwenhuis 1901:1061). This situation is relatively rare in central Borneo because overall population densities are so low, and it demonstrates how numerous the Kayan were when the out-migrations began, sometime in the eighteenth century. They crossed the mountain chain onto the Sarawak side in two parties. One moved into the far headwaters of the Rejang, south of the Baram watershed, and by 1800, their hegemony over the indigenous peoples of the region was apparently well established. From there, some moved on again into Baram about 1830. Meanwhile, other Kayan arrived directly from the Apo Kayan (Rousseau 1990:331–2). Within a short time, a series of large Kayan communities were established, effectively occupying the entire middle reaches of the Baram.

In the face of the Kayan incursion, other communities retreated into tributaries such as the Pata and the Akar, where they were defended behind difficult rapids. This is not to imply that the Kayan invariably provoked hostile relations on all sides, nor that their neighbours were timid and unwarlike. There were from the start alliances sealed with leading families of non-Kayan communities. In Chapter 4, for example, we noted Aban Jau's policy of maintaining close links with the Kayan, despite the fact that he was already tucked away and moderately secure in the upper Tinjar. What these alliances show is the flexibility of indigenous political institutions. Moreover, once they had arrived in Baram, a new factor entered Kayan calculations, if indeed it had been one of their motives for moving there in the first place: greater access to the trade goods available on the coast. That interest turned their attentions down river, so that there was little point attacking other upriver communities that were only as rich or as poor as themselves.

When I speak of "access" to trade goods, I am purposely ambiguous about how access was achieved. There is no reason to believe that Kayan communities did not engage in trading expeditions, such as had occurred in Baram for centuries. They certainly lost no time taking control of the caves near Batu Gading, which furnished birds' nests much prized in China for making soup. This activity indicates a willingness to trade jungle produce for manufactured luxury goods. However, there was also a strong temptation simply to help themselves, and expeditions bent on plunder rapidly escalated by an internal logic of their own. As St. John was told by his hosts on his first visit to a Kayan longhouse, they preferred to take slaves rather than heads, and in their attacks, they killed only those that resisted (St. John 1862:I:104). In this way, large Kayan communities grew even larger, meaning more fighting men and bigger raids. The social status of slave was one for which Kayan communities had evidently always provided. Hose claims that:

> An unmarried slave of either sex lives with, and is treated almost as a member of, the family of his or her master, eating and in some cases sleeping in the family room. Slaves are allowed to marry, their children becoming the property of their masters. Some slave families are allowed to acquire a room in the house, and they then begin to acquire a less dependent position; and though they still retain the status of slaves, and are spoken of as 'slaves-outside-the-room,' the master generally finds it impossible to command their services beyond a very limited extent, and in some cases will voluntarily resign his rights over the family. (Hose and McDougall 1912:I:70)

Jerome Rousseau (1990:173–9) paints a less happy picture of the slave's lot, but for the moment the point is that slaves were integrated into the community and performed the same kind of work as commoners. When the Kayan arrived in Baram, their raids down river supplied new labour on a scale than had ever occurred in the Apo Kayan. Each input freed up men to participate in yet more raiding, and so on.

Those people in the lowlands who failed to organise themselves adequately for defence paid a heavy price. In mid-century, Kayan war parties large enough to crush small or poorly defended communities swept through the Tutoh watershed, and the Tring people (St. John's "Trieng") were virtually annihilated, either by death or enslavement. Only a remnant survived, by joining the defensive confederacies of the Berawan and Long Kiput. Whole stretches of the Tutoh River were left empty. It should be emphasized that the Tring were not overrun because of meekness. On the contrary, they had a reputation as fierce warriors, bordering on the berserk. Where they failed was in adapting to warfare on a new scale.

The Tutoh was, however, only the beginning; even worse devastation occurred in the Limbang River (Figure Int-01). Kayan war parties reached the Limbang by means of a short portage between watersheds. It involved travelling up Melinau stream on the Tutoh side, and then down the Madalam into the Limbang. When St. John got to the summit of this ridge in 1858, he found traces of an old Kayan camp, and noted that the tiny riverlet nearby had been "improved into a sort of canal" to allow easier passage of war canoes (St. John 1862:II:6). The portage itself had been made into a "road":

> This road is cleared about two fathoms broad, and then trunks of small trees are laid across and secured about a yard apart. I followed it once for upwards of two miles. The Kayans, on reaching this spot, haul their boats (tamuis) along the road, and considering that some of their tamuis are sixty feet long, it is a work of infinite labour, but three or four crews lay on to one boat and gradually moved the whole fleet over. (St. John 1862:II:54–5)

The road was so much travelled in the nineteenth century that Berawan could still point it out to me in the 1970s. They refused to camp in the area, however, because it was haunted by the ghosts of a party of Tring trying to escape into Limbang, mostly women and children, who had been caught there and massacred. Their bones can still be found in a small cave into which the bodies were thrown.

St. John was prepared for what he found on his expedition up the Limbang. Before leaving Brunei, he discussed the situation there with Pangiran Mumein, whom he describes as the Sultan's "prime minister," and who later became Sultan himself. Consulting with his followers, the Pangiran listed no less than forty villages that had been destroyed by the Kayan within the previous ten years – an amazing toll, considering the scale of the societies we are considering. Since coastal people tended to be undiscriminating about the ethnicities of Upriver People – remember that Aban Jau was described in the earliest colonial reports as a Kayan chief – it is possible that others were aiding and abetting in the mayhem. The raids made in force, however, the ones that had annihilated whole villages, clearly were Kayan because only they possessed the resources of manpower involved.

It is surprising that the Pangiran allowed St. John's expedition to proceed, when he would later prohibit Hugh Brooke Low from entering even the lower Limbang. But St. John was the British Consul General to Brunei, whereas Low was an agent of the Rajah, and the Sultan was relying on British help to restrain his ambitious neighbour. Ironically, Low accompanied St. John on the 1858 expedition anyway, and so was able to carry back information on the devastation in middle Limbang, whose surviving inhabitants had fled upriver. St. John refers to these refugees as the "Adang Muruts." The Adang River is a tributary of the Limbang, but sufficiently difficult of navigation as to impede raiders. Moreover, the refugees joined forces with the people already settled there, who were close cousins, as we see in Chapter 8. This strategy worked well on at least one occasion, when a Kayan war party two or three hundred strong ventured on from the Adang into the headwaters of the Trusan where "contrary to the usual Murut custom, a large force quietly collected, and before the Kayans had killed above two women and a child, they were attacked in the rear and fled" (St. John 1862:II:55). Remarkably, and quite by accident, St. John had already seen the effects of this attack from the other end, from the Kayan side. When he visited "Longusin," the pretty Kayan village in the middle Baram described in Chapter 1, he found some houses there in mourning. A Kenyah chief had just brought the news that a lone survivor of the Kayan raid into the Trusan had stumbled into his village, naked and half starved. The defeat was a considerable blow to the Kayan chiefs whom St. John describes as "so conceited that they consider themselves superior to all except ourselves" (1862:I:118). Evidently, the chiefs were willing to concede an equally exalted status to their English visitor on account of the deep impression made by St. John's steam launch, not to mention the display of fireworks that he put on for them.

For the most part, however, the Adang people failed to combine against the Kayan, and instead fell to feuding among themselves. This tendency St. John found frustrating; at one point during their 1858 expedition, he and Low wanted to take shelter in some huts they saw on a nearby ridge. They were both weak from loss of blood because of leech bites suffered in walking through dense jungle, and chilled to the bone from torrential rain, but their guides refused to take them there on the grounds that their folk were feuding with those in the huts. St. John and Low found their own way there and fired their weapons in the air to warn everyone away (St. John 1862:II:98). Arriving finally at a less than impressive village, St. John remarks: "from the clearings that are seen on every side, there must be a very fair population assembled around these hills; but their continual petty quarrels have no doubt a bad effect on their prosperity and their power to resist their great enemy" (1862:II:104).

Under these circumstances, large Kayan war parties for the most part found easy pickings:

> The recent history of the Adang people is a good illustration of the injury done by the Kayans to the surrounding tribes. They formerly lived in the Adang river, but extended their farms to the entrance of the Madalam; but they have gradually been driven back, until they have abandoned the Limbang waters, and now drink those of the interior of the Trusan, the whole country from the Madalam being now jungle. I do not imagine they are nearly so

numerous as they were, as in the last great Kayan foray they suffered awfully. They were, I believe, all collected in their villages at some great feast, when the Kayans, about 3,000 strong, set upon them; the first village was surprised, the fighting men slain, the rest taken captive; the few fugitives were followed up so fast as almost to enter together the second village with their pursuers, where the same scene again took place. The burning of these villages, and the beating of gongs and talawaks gave notice to the rest, and all who could fled precipitately over the Adang range, followed by their relentless foes, who killed and captured a very great number. (St. John 1862:II:103)

The choice for longhouse communities in the path of Kayan raiding is clear: either they organised themselves into megacommunities like those that Low found in the lower Tutoh, or they faced extinction.

Inside the Sultan's Fence

There was one other option: to retreat "inside the Sultan's fence." Just what that constituted, however, and how much protection it offered varied from place to place. For most, it meant beginning the process that throughout Sarawak is called *masok Melayu*, literally, to "enter Malaydom." This implies not only conversion to Islam, but also taking on Malay social and cultural practices. Probably the great majority of people in Sarawak who call themselves Malay are descended from indigenous people who underwent this process. In the hinterland of Brunei, whole communities have made the transition within historical memory. There were several communities in the lower Baram and its smaller tributaries that escaped the Kayan onslaught by fleeing westward toward the coast.

The protection afforded by Malay coastal settlements was of two kinds. First, the estuaries that provided their harbours were those of tiny rivers draining only coastal lowlands and swamps, such as the Belait (Figure 01-01). Consequently, raiders descending the Baram in large war canoes could not approach them without venturing out to sea, and the Kayan were not prepared to do this. Not only were their canoes prone to swamp in any ocean swell, but they also would have made easy pickings for Malay sailing boats armed with even light cannons. Such locations were not entirely proof against attack, however. At the height of their depredations, some Kayan war parties left their canoes and walked overland to surprise communities in small coastal watersheds. Two examples were given in the discussion of the longhouse as fortress in Chapter 1. They involved the treacherous betrayal of a fortified longhouse in Belait and an attack from the Limbang overland into the Temburong country.

A second defensive advantage gained by those who "entered Malaydom" was to profit from Malay organisational and military skills. Given the defeats that Brunei had suffered, and was about to suffer, it is easy to dismiss those skills until one remembers how competently Aban Jau's attack on Sibuti was thwarted (see Chapter 4). The wily Pangiran Suleiman was alert to trouble brewing, and wasted no time bringing his entire community and its valuables inside his stockade. He even managed to inflict a few casualties by taking pot shots at Aban Jau's men, who were left with nothing to do but burn down a few huts and retire ignominiously. Unfortunately, we know nothing about Suleiman's career before this event, but his stoutly defended house suggests that he had learned something from the warfare then occurring along the coast. He may even have had first-hand experience, and anyone familiar with the appalling methods of Illanun pirates would have found little more than a minor inconvenience in Aban Jau's raid.

The mention of piracy raises the issue of Brunei's decline as a maritime power. To address that issue requires us to broaden our perspective beyond the hinterland of Borneo in the nineteenth century. Describing the disruption wrought on many of the port cities of island Southeast Asia, D.G.E. Hall, doyen of Southeast Asian historians, has no hesitation in attributing a massive upsurge in piracy to European incursions:

> In the Malay world it was an evil so old, so widespread and with so many facets that even when the European powers in the nineteenth century decided that it must be stamped out it baffled all their efforts for many years. For it was an honorable profession which was connived at, promoted, or even directly engaged in by the highest potentates in that strange Malay world of Raja Brooke's memoirs and Joseph Conrad's early novels. And nowhere else in the world is geography so favourable to piracy.
>
> There can be no doubt, however, that the particular phase that was acute in the eighteenth century and "a great and blighting curse" in the nineteenth arose mainly out of the disorganisation of native commerce in the archipelago by the impact of the Portuguese and the Dutch during the sixteenth and seventeenth centuries. And by comparison with the Portuguese filibustering methods of enriching themselves, the systematic and carefully calculated methods by which the Dutch built up their trading monopoly caused so much ruin to the native peoples and disintegration to their governments as to have constituted the biggest single factor in the situation. Thus it was that, with the weakening of the control of the V.O.C. [Dutch East Indies Company] itself over its island empire in the eighteenth century, the way was open for piracy to increase to what must have been unexampled proportions. And it is ridiculous to attempt to explain it away by the argument that it was only in the eighteenth century that European writers began to make a clear distinction between a pirate and an honest trader. (Hall 1981: 568–9 [parenthesis added])

Brunei suffered on both accounts, first from Dutch domination of international trade, and second from the wholesale piracy it provoked. In the Lesser Sundas, the Bugis and Moluccans embarked on careers as freebooters, but the most dreaded pirates of all established themselves much closer to Brunei, in the small islands just off the northeast coast of Borneo. In the first half of the nineteenth century, the people variously called *Illanun, Iranun, Lanun,* the "Pirates of the Lagoon," and the Balanini or Balangingi sent out fleets every year numbering several hundred boats of fifty to one hundred tons with crews of forty to sixty. Their effect on unprotected coastlines can easily be imagined. Sulu became their commercial headquarters and grew wealthy in the process (Warren 1981). Ironically, Sulu had once been a tributary of Brunei, and its Sultans originated from the Brunei royal house (Brown 1970:144). Nevertheless, it steadily extended its influence into northern Borneo and wrested control of trade routes away from Brunei.

This overview of Brunei's worsening geopolitical situation helps put Kayan depredations in the hinterland in perspective. If they were not the cause of Brunei's decline, however, at mid-century, they came close to administering the coup de grace. As St. John describes it, a Kayan war party 3,000 strong "in March and April 1857, kept the capital in a state of great alarm" (St. John 1862:II:34). They sent taunting messages to the Sultan, threatening to lay waste his entire country. Unable to eject them, the Sultan was reduced to bribing them to go away. Nor was this the first time; the same thing had happened in 1855 (St. John 1862:II:57). The Sultan must have known very well what result he could expect from paying Danegeld, since in better times his predecessors had extracted it often enough from others.

These repeated crises make clear the flimsiness of the "Sultan's fence," even in his own backyard. For the people of lower Limbang, harassed and exploited on all sides, it was a time of incessant ordeals. Their Brunei lords, starved of income from external trade, became ever more demanding. Indeed, if the stories recounted in St. John's memoirs or in the editorial pages of the *Sarawak Gazette* are to be believed, it is clear that the pangiran were busy killing the goose that laid the golden egg. So extreme were their extortions that their villages became so impoverished as to cease to function. Some were without food, forcing their inhabitants to live in and off the jungle. In addition, some pangiran engaged in acts of violence that called their sanity into question. St. John tells, for instance, of the son of an important noble who took a Murut girl as a concubine. Tiring of her, he planned to sell her into slavery, but instead her father paid a large fee to get her back. When she later married a fellow countryman, however, the noble fell into "a most unaccountable fit of jealousy," had the husband abducted and tied up, and then cut the man to pieces with his own hands (St. John 1862:II:86–7).

For the Rajah's agents, such abuses could only be seen as a symptom of Brunei's collapse. Not long before, a few decades at most, the communities of the lower Limbang had been wealthy, secure, and populous. They stood to gain both from supplying the capital with agricultural produce, and from acting as middlemen in the trade in jungle produce between the interior and the coast. As was true in city states elsewhere in island Southeast Asia, non-Moslem communities had always been an essential part of the ideal model of the Brunei state, constituting a periphery, or series of peripheries, to the Islamic centre, personified by the Sultan and his nobles. In this sense, Islam functioned in much the same way as Hinduism had before it, providing charismatic resources that were by definition limited. Consequently, Islam was not an actively proselytizing force in Brunei. Meanwhile, those on the periphery may have had a lesser role, but they enjoyed facilities unavailable to their less civilized cousins upriver, and so maintained an interest in the continuity of the state.

It was this social contract that collapsed in the mid-nineteenth century. Certainly, there had been abuses and violence before. The Tring, as noted previously, had a fierce reputation and had been known to make headhunting raids on communities in the lower Limbang. There had even been minor wars between the communities themselves, in which the pangiran had made no effort to intervene unless their own interests were threatened. These clashes, however, rarely disrupted communal life for long; rather they serve to show the degree of autonomy enjoyed even by those "inside the Sultan's fence." Having conceded that they owed various taxes and customary services to their lords, they were left to handle their affairs in a manner not so much different from those outside.

The Open Backdoor

Just how low Brunei's fortunes had sunk was made clear by the denouement of the Kayan threat to the capital in 1857. As St. John reports it, the Sultan collected every fighting man he could find and sent them up to oppose Kayan. As the forces approached each other, however, neither side showed any willingness to join battle. For two months, there was a stalemate during which the commander of the Brunei forces, the devious Pangiran Mokota, engaged in a secret diplomacy with the Kayan chiefs. Eventually, he gave out that the Kayan had agreed to return home and promptly marched his small army back to the capital. In fact, what he had done was to deliver into their hands the whole Murut community of Balat Ikan, against whom he had a personal grudge. Sure enough, the Kayan laid waste to the village, killed its inhabitants wholesale, and left burdened with booty and captives.

"This," says St. John bitterly, "was the Bornean plan of getting rid of an enemy" (St. John 1862:II:56).

The Murut should not have been surprised. Makota had used a similar stratagem on the previous occasion when a Kayan war party had threatened the capital, in 1855. On that occasion, however, he had also collected a huge bribe from the Murut communities, supposedly to be used to buy off the Kayan. (St. John says, "100 pikuls of guns," meaning brassware amounting to many thousands of pounds.) This bribe he coolly pocketed himself, while deflecting Kayan aggression onto some harmless Tabun people, relatives of the Tring, living further upriver (St. John 1862:II:56–7). What may have fooled the Murut yet again in 1857 was that they lived down river from a fort established at Blimbing near Nanga Medamit specifically for the purpose of closing the river against raiders. Its guns menaced the river and should have been sufficient to prevent the Kayan passing. The garrison, however, were Visaya – another of the ethnicities found in Limbang – and they allowed the Kayan through. Moreover, they failed to beat their alarm gongs, so ensuring that the people of Balat Ikan would be taken unawares. St. John says that the lead Kayan boat hailed the garrison commander and told him that they would leave the Visaya people alone if they made no trouble, but it seems more likely that he had already been bribed by the devious Makota (St. John 1862:II:56–7).

For all his intrigues, however, Makota's was clearly a strategy of desperation. He may have bought the Sultan a little more time, but in the end he did him no service because he sowed the seeds of rebellion among the Murut. Indeed, there had already been uprisings. In 1850, a party of Bruneians trying once again to dun people for imaginary debts were murdered, and one of the party was a nephew of the Sultan (St. John 1862:II:44–5). In 1858, Makota himself was murdered by the Visaya that he had double crossed (St. John 1862:II:170). As events gathered momentum, Brunei administration in the hinterland ceased to function. By 1884, the Trusan watershed had become unsafe for Bruneians, and even the local Malays favoured annexation by Sarawak (Baring-Gould and Bampfylde 1909:345). The same year, there was an armed uprising in Limbang, and rebels marched toward the capital. Only the arrival of a British gunboat saved the city from being overrun (Runciman 1960:186–7). At this difficult moment, the Sultan died and was succeeded by an heir whose legitimacy was challenged by many Brunei nobles.

By 1880, the entire hinterland of Brunei was ready to fall into the hands of Rajah Brooke, leaving only a remnant of the ancient state, totally surrounded by its erstwhile vassal. The Baram watershed was the largest slice and the first to go. As we saw previously, Tutoh and Baram had been closed to Brunei traders ever since the incident of the murder at the funeral. Consequently, there was no profit to be had there, either for the Sultan himself or for any of his nobles. Worse, the Berawan and their allies assembled at Long Kelejeo remained openly hostile after the affray with the Burong Pingai, even though the Sultan had refused to come to the traders' assistance. In 1876, Low said of the people at Long Kelejeo: "I suppose it will be the Sultan's policy to cajole them into a good humour, as they guard the approaches to the capital, and woe to the imperial city should she ever draw upon herself the wrath of the warlike tribes of Barram" (*Sarawak Gazette* 122:August 1876). With his backdoor wide open to renewed Kayan raids, the Sultan had little choice but to cede Baram, in the hope that Rajah Brooke could at least control the Kayan threat. The cession of Baram occurred in 1882, rapidly followed by Trusan in 1884. The Limbang watershed was more difficult for the Sultan to give up: it was close to the capital, and losing it would cut the Sultan's remaining lands in half, with pieces on either side of Brunei Bay. It was also his only remaining source of jungle produce. Nevertheless, in 1890, he faced up to the inevitable and relinquished what he could not hold.

In this way is history made: the tactless laughter of a Moslem slave at a Berawan funeral precipitated a permanent redrawing of the map of Southeast Asia.

The Persistence of Trade

To say that everyday life somehow continued amid all this anarchy and violence is stating the obvious. Nevertheless, it is surprising to find to what lengths people in the hinterland of Brunei would go to maintain patterns of trade that had existed for centuries. Even after the middle Limbang had become a dangerous no man's land, Murut still travelled through it in pursuit of trade. St. John reports that people from the Adang still travelled down to Brunei, and took months doing it. This he attributes to a necessity to hunt for their food as they went along. Moreover "time is of no value to them, as they generally start after the harvest, and many parties are said to have taken six months" (St. John 1862:II:26). What St. John overlooks is how long it took to accumulate a store of jungle produce worth the bother of trading down river. The abandoned valley may have provided rich pickings, but the process was still slow. Meanwhile, constant vigilance was needed; St. John records an occasion when a large party of Murut, a hundred strong, was surprised by three times that number of Kayan and badly mauled (St. John 1862:II:36). Yet, despite the effort and risks, trading expeditions continued.

Another example is provided unwittingly by Low, in his account of the Tutoh. He arrived from inland, having walked over from the valley of the

Belait with a local dignitary and his followers as guides. "At the entrance of a small stream called the *Kelajiu* is a shed dignified by the name of 'kubu,' and here I was invited to put up by Sabdulah, one of the Sultan's revenue collectors. The Penuroh Haji Mat Nasir lived in his prahu [boat] which was beached and moored to a raft" (*Sarawak Gazette* 121:July 1876 [brackets added]). *Kubu* means literally a fort, and it was the standard word used throughout the Brooke Raj to denote an administrative outstation. As either one, Low found the "shed" unconvincing. It speaks volumes, however, that what the Sultan's agents built at Long Kelejeo obviously had no military or administrative function. Instead, it was a warehouse. The Sultan's supposed revenue collector was a man so lowly that, in a society awash with titles, he is simply Sabdulah. Given that the people of the Tutoh were not accustomed to paying taxes, his real function was clearly as a watchman. In contrast, Sabdulah's neighbour boasted a mellifluous title, even though he lived equally modestly on his beached boat. But the Penuroh Haji Mat Nasir was a trader, however humble, and trade was what had always mattered to Brunei.

Chapter 7

Premodern Upriver Trade

About trade in the hinterland of Brunei, two things stand out: first, Brunei's exports consisted largely of jungle produce, and second, the tokens of high status in Upriver longhouse communities were manufactured goods imported from Brunei. These facts alone are sufficient to show how closely the histories of coastal and interior societies were enmeshed.

What is not clear is *how* these two things were connected, which is to say that data about the organisation of trade in Brunei's hinterland are scarce. By the time Westerners began observing Brunei, its ancient trading system was heavily disrupted and far sunk in decline. Meanwhile, written records from Brunei are primarily concerned with courtly matters and preserve few of the mundane details of trade. Finally, the oral histories of long-house communities provide only sketchy information about trade before the colonial epoch. Nor is there much likelihood that archaeology will shed new light on the situation. In the swampy terrain, ancient living sites are difficult to locate and vulnerable to riverbank erosion.

The situation is far from unique, however. In his analysis of rainforest collectors and traders in the Malay Peninsula before the nineteenth century, F. L. Dunn remarks that "little or nothing seems to have been recorded concerning the trading relationships of the hinterlands and secondary [i.e., less important] ports in this period" (1975:115 [brackets added]). His reaction, however, is not to discount the importance of this trade, but to piece together data from several disciplines – anthropology, history, and ecology – to provide as clear a picture of it as possible. I do the same.

Considering the formation of Philippine lowland societies, Karl Hutterer states flatly that trade was crucial to a whole range of social features:

> population movement and the establishment of coastal population centres acting as focal points for multifaceted commercial relationships; the establishment of networks of communication and trade penetrating islands and reaching across the archipelago; the development of social stratification and the emergence of political leadership independent of kinship organisation. (1974:297–8)

As we have already seen, the same considerations apply in Borneo, yet little has been done to study their effect. This is a case where social anthropologists must take their cue from archaeologists. The distribution of artefacts is clearly meat and drink for the archaeologist, whereas an abstract concept of culture has allowed Borneo ethnography to remain stuck in a paradigm of culture areas.

Port Cities of Southeast Asia

Meanwhile, there is a vigorous literature on the trading centres of Southeast Asia. Anthony Reid remarks that in Southeast Asia, "that meeting place of oceans and waterways," port cities were a "dominant element" in contrast to most other regions of Asia where inland cities held supremacy (1989:55). This was particularly true, he continues, for the sixteenth and seventeenth centuries, the period when Brunei was at the height of its influence. Reid laments that "Royal inscriptions and chronicles are primarily concerned to show the all-pervading role of the court as the centre of the city, and there have been no sources remotely comparable to the Geniza documents of Cairo to reflect the economic activities of the middle and lower classes." The Geniza is, however, unique; an extraordinary jumble of bills, receipts, and tallies preserved by Jewish traders who could not destroy any paper bearing the name of God. Even had a similar cache existed in Southeast Asia, the rainy climate, in contrast to perpetually dry Egypt, would not have allowed it to survive.

The resources of historians in Southeast Asia are not so different from those in say, medieval Europe, and Reid attributes the failure to use to the full the sources that do exist to "the academic pre-occupation with establishing the 'uniqueness' of the independent, economically dynamic European port city. In emphasizing the dichotomy between East and West, scholars from Webber to Braudel have encouraged a stereotype of the 'traditional'

Asian city as 'enormous, parasitic, soft and luxurious'" (Reid 1989:55; the final phrase is a reference to Braudel 1968:4). Moreover, the familiar analytic apparatus of core and periphery established by Immanuel Wallerstein (1974) is of less value where, as Thomas Gibson argues:

> each zone was characterized by a distinctive, 'semi-autonomous' political economy, loosely integrated within a larger region. Core agrarian states, semi-peripheral maritime states and peripheral tribal groups each maintained distinctive economic, political and ideological institutions, all the while interacting with one another on all those levels. (1990:1)

Nevertheless, Wallerstein's emphasis on "world economies," particularly the Asian world economy, is entirely relevant (Abu-Lughod 1989:291–314; Chauduri 1990:383–7).

What is beyond doubt is the central importance of international trade in shaping the polities of the archipelago for 1,000 years before European contact (Cushman 1993. Kathirithamby-Wells and Villiers 1990). The first generation of Western historians to pay close attention to Southeast Asia shared this premise, although they disagreed about the details. G. Coedes (1948) emphasized the expansion of Hindu civilisation, giving rise to an influential image of "Greater India." J.C. van Leur (1955) objected to the passive role assigned to Indonesian peoples, especially in view of their long maritime traditions, and O.W. Wolters (1967) focussed on indigenous trading states, particularly Sri Vijaya. In the several editions of his magisterial *A History of Southeast Asia*, the first published in 1955 and the last in 1981, D.G.E. Hall returns repeatedly to the organisation of transoceanic and inter-island trade.

Just how well established these trade routes were is shown by the sailing instructions written for ship masters in both Arabic and Chinese. J.V. Mills compares the Chinese and Arabic documents available before 1500 for the waters around the Malay Peninsula, and shows that it is possible to recognize the same features in both – capes, shoals, and harbours – and correlate them with modern charts. Among his conclusions is that "Arab trading ships, progressing eastward, penetrated to Malayan waters about AD 700: Chinese trading ships, progressing westward, found their way to Malayan waters about 795" (Mills 1974:56). Note that these were direct trading voyages; indirect contacts via local intermediaries had occurred much earlier. According to Mills' reconstruction, Arab sailors were initially the most active, reaching China soon after 724, but by 1178 Chinese merchants had broken the Arab monopoly and were sailing directly to India. Chinese hegemony in the Indian Ocean reached its zenith in 1421 with the massive expeditions of the celebrated Admiral Cheng Ho, but even after the decline

Figure 07-01. Arrival of a British naval delegation at the palace of the Sultan of Brunei in 1846. The houses of commoners can be made out across the waterway. (The picture originally appeared in *The Illustrated London News*, reprinted in Tate 1988: 66.)

of the imperial navy large junks regularly plied from Canton to ports in Southeast Asia.

A Portrait of Brunei

Borneo lies only slightly off these trading routes, which hugged the mainland coast (Figure 07–02). Nevertheless, by the fifth century, there were contacts with emporia on the east coast of the Malay Peninsula. Direct trade between Brunei and southern China was established in 977 by a trader who was evidently himself an Arab. His name is given in the archives as P'u Lu-hsieh, a sinicized form perhaps of Abu Luhayy (Mills 1974:9). This cosmopolitan interchange resulted in an envoy being sent from the ruler of Brunei to the Emperor, led by one P'u A-li (Abu Ali). Similar exchanges, invariably interpreted in the imperial records as tributary missions, were repeated intermittently until 1425 (Brown 1970:133; Groeneveldt 1880). Brunei's influence was greatest, however, during the sixteenth century, after the conversion of its ruling elite to Islam. At its maximum extent, the Sultans' suzerainty extended along the whole northern and western coastline of the Borneo, so that for the first European visitors it was natural to name the

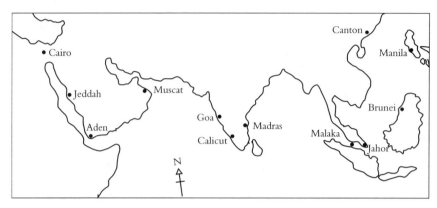

Figure 07-02. Location of Brunei in the pre-modern Asian world economy.

island after the city. Brunei power extended into the southern Philippines, but not without competition from the rival sultanate of Sulu, and before long from the Spanish (Horton 1995; Hughes-Hallett 1940, Nicholls 1975).

The first tentative English contacts with Brunei were not made until the late eighteenth century. Thomas Forrest leaves this description of the city in 1779:

> The town of Brunei is situate (sic), as has been said, about ten miles up the river from Pulo Chirming. The houses are built on each side of the river upon posts, and you ascend to them by stairs and ladders as to the back doors of warehouses in Wapping. The houses on the left side, going up, extend backwards to the land, each in a narrow slip. The land is not steep, but shelving; every house has therefore a kind of stage, erected for connection with the land. There is little intercourse from house to house by land, or what may be called behind; as there is no path, and the ground is swampy: the chief communication proves to be in front, by boats.
>
> On the right going up, the houses extend about half a mile backwards, with channels like lanes, between the rows; so that it would seem the river, before the houses were built, made a wide bason (sic) of shallow water, in which has arisen three quarters of the town, resembling Venice; with many water lanes, if I may say so, perpendicular and parallel to the main river, which here is almost as wide as the Thames at London bridge, with six fathoms water in the channel; and here lie moored, head and stern, the China junks; four or five of which come annually from Amoy, of five or six hundred tons burden. The water is salt, and the tide runs about four miles an hour in the springs. Some of the houses on the right side are two stories high, which I never saw in any other Malay country, with stages or wharfs before them, for the convenience of trade . . .
>
> In those divisions of the town made by water lanes, is neither firm land nor island: the houses standing on posts, as has been said, in shallow water; and

the public market is kept sometimes in one part, sometimes in another part of the river. Imagine a fleet of London wherries, loaded with fish, fowl, greens, &c., floating up with the tide, from London bridge towards Westminster, then down again, with many buyers floating up and down with them; this will give some idea of a Borneo market. (Forrest 1779:380)

The Exports of Brunei: Herbert's List

Forrest was preceded by Captain John Herbert who sought to make a treaty on behalf of the East India Company in 1773. His plans were frustrated by Sulu pirates, who attacked and totally destroyed the small establishment that he set up to the north of Brunei, at Balambangan (Hall 1981:536). The same pirates were making heavy inroads into the trade of Brunei itself, but Herbert nevertheless found the city still at that date fabulously wealthy. In addition to camphor, he lists its exports as "gold, diamonds, bezoar, lignum, aloes, musk, civit, benjamin, amber, dragons blood, wax, rice and rattans" (quoted in Logan 1848a:525). The gold and diamonds came from Brunei's domains on the far western end of the island; early sources mention Sambas and Sukadana. Whatever rice was exported almost certainly came from near the capital, whose Kedayan subjects were among the most productive farmers in the region. It was impractical to ship rice in bulk, and it was consequently sold mostly for provisioning the trading vessels themselves.

All the other items on Herbert's list are jungle produce. Each is worth attention, since we must follow it back to its source. Some products are, to the modern mind, exotic to the point of being bizarre. We should not, however, assume that they seemed so to the visiting Englishmen. As traders, they were well aware of the demands of the Chinese market. Moreover, European medicine of the age depended on cures not unlike those used in China. The traders had every reason to respect Chinese medical knowledge, which was certainly superior to their own. A study of T'ang exotics by Edward Schafer (1963) gives details of the uses of these products.

Bezoar enjoyed a great reputation as an antidote to poisons of all kinds, and it is sufficiently valuable that some provinces sent it to the Emperor as tribute. Bezoar is, properly speaking, a concretation occasionally found in the fourth stomach of various ruminants, notably the bezoar goat. For medical purposes, however, the category was expanded to include other kinds of stones found in the entrails of animals (Schafer 1963:191–2). As new varieties were imported into the empire, each was assigned special properties in a virtuoso display of the science of the concrete (Levi-Strauss 1966:1–33). Borneo's contributions comprised gallstones taken from various species of long-tailed monkeys, especially macaques. According to Hose and

143

McDougall (1912:I:155), "they are formed of concentric layers of a hard, brittle, olive-green substance, very bitter to the taste." Stones were also taken from the intestines of porcupines.

So much for the consumption of bezoar stones, but what about their "production"? Not surprisingly, there are no written sources on the subject, but it is not difficult to make a few simple inferences based on what we know of the modes of livelihood of shifting agriculturalists in the interior of the island. First, a caveat: simply because monkeys roam freely in the forests all over Borneo, we should not assume that they are more numerous the deeper one travels into the rainforest. On the contrary, the canopy is so high in mature rainforest as to be relatively inaccessible, and food supplies are better on the edges, along the banks of rivers and near clearings. Since secondary forest was until recent times found even near the coast, monkeys might be found almost anywhere.

Wherever shifting cultivation was practiced, however, there were sure to be monkeys, and the monkeys were sure to be a pest. It is astonishing how much damage a troop of monkeys can inflict on a rice crop. In a few hours, a large part of the product of a whole season of hard work can be lost, and it is not surprising that monkeys are often spoken about as a kind of universal enemy of mankind. They do not even eat the crop, they simply trample it down. Consequently, when harvest time is near, farming families routinely patrol their fields to head them off, even at night. Moreover, monkeys provide an easily obtained source of meat. Perched in the lower branches of trees, they are relatively easy to shoot with that most characteristic Bornean weapon, the blow-pipe. Indeed, it may be the prevalence of monkeys as game that had caused the wide distribution of the weapon. At the end of the nineteenth century, it seemed a great mystery that people that knew the use of iron nevertheless lacked the bow. But in dense vegetation, a bow is virtually useless for hunting large game such as pigs and deer. What is needed is dogs to round up the prey and spears to finish it off. Meanwhile, firing a bow directly upward is clumsy, whereas a long, relatively heavy blow-pipe is most easily handled in that position. The knowledge of effective dart poisons completes the technology. They induce heart failure in the prey without tainting the meat, and I was often told with satisfaction that there would be time to smoke only half a cigarette before a grown monkey would hop once to another branch, and then fall dead at their feet.

How then does the collection of bezoar stones relate to this pattern of hunting and vermin control? It was surely impractical for forest-dwelling people to go out hunting monkeys in order to harvest bezoar stones. Stones are rare in healthy monkeys. To shoot and butcher hundreds of monkeys in order to find one or two was not a rewarding use of labour. A better strategy was to go about one's business, scaring off monkey troops and shooting the odd one for the pot, until a stone happened to appear.

The next consideration is how such accidentally found bezoar stones became commodities. Stones with mystical provenance were valued by longhouse people, as for instance if their discovery was predicted in a dream or if they had anthropoid shape. Usually such stones are geological, but metabolic stones found their way into bundles of charms attached to swords or used by shamans. Consequently, such stones may have had intrinsic value to longhouse people, but it is another thing entirely to realizing their exchange value on the coast. Moreover, if it was impractical to shoot monkeys in order to find stones, it was even more so to travel long distances to trade just one or two. Bezoar stones are one example of what we might call *fortuitous commodities*, and they call for a particular kind of trading system. Let us see what further examples there are on the list.

Lignum refers to precious wood of various kinds. The most obvious in a Southeast Asian context is lignum aloes, and aloes is indeed the third item on Herbert's list. What else might Herbert have been referring to? Very dense wood from various parts of the world were referred to as lignum vitae, and the most likely candidate for the title in Borneo was *bilian*, which the *Oxford English Dictionary* (OED) describes as "the ironwood of Borneo" (1991:135). *Bilian* is immune to rot and termites, and is consequently in great demand for the pilings of building, especially those that stand in water, as in Brunei. It is laborious to work, however, and must be moved about on rafts because it does not float. There was certainly a market for *bilian* in Brunei, but it was not feasible to move *bilian* from far away, which restricted the trade to the immediate vicinity of Brunei Bay. Consequently, it is unlikely that longhouse communities far upriver were in a position to profit from exporting *bilian*.

Aloes, however, is a different story. It was always in high demand and actively sought out by traders. According to Schafer, it was the favourite aromatic substance in T'ang China. Its many names, Malay *gahru*, Portuguese *aguila*, Hebrew *ahaloth*, all derived from Sanskrit *agaru*, testify to how widely it was traded. It was important in Chinese medicine. Decocted in wine, it was used to alleviate internal pain, and as a fumigant, it was believed to cure ulcers and wounds. Meanwhile, made into incense, its use in "every sort of ritual and private purpose was enormous" (Schafer 1963:164). Small objects such as writing brushes were sometime made out of aloeswood, but the boy-Emperor Ching Tsung was scolded by his guardians for indulging in the excessive luxury of having a little kiosk built out of the precious stuff.

Aloes is "a product of various trees of genus *Aquilaria*, native to Southeast Asia. The aloeswood of the incense trade is heavy, dark, diseased wood, distinct from the lighter, softer wood around it. It is saturated with resin and richly scented. Sometimes these pathologically fragrant patches occur in the shapes of men and animals, which increases their market value greatly" (Schafer 1963:163). This description is enough to makes it clear that aloes was also a fortuitous commodity. For centuries, it flowed at a steady rate out of the jungles of Borneo, but it must have been collected from over a vast area of forest. What this implies is a trading system that could collect small caches of aloeswood from far and wide. No great amount could be expected to accumulate in any one place or time, and so trading contacts did not need to be frequent. The trading network needed to be extensive, but it might also be slow moving and intermittent.

Musk and *civet* are of animal rather than vegetable origin, but considered as rainforest products, they have the same characteristics as aloes. Musk is an odoriferous substance secreted from a gland in various species of deer belonging to the genus *Moschus*. Civet is "a yellow or brownish unctuous substance, having a strong musky smell, obtained from sacs or glands in the anal pouch of several animals of the Civet genus" (OED 1991: 262). Deer of all kinds were of course hunted by longhouse people as game, but they are not common in the rain forest. Civet cats are even rarer, and in many communities hunting them was hedged about with supernatural dangers. Possession of civet skins was consequently a source of pride, and each such kill would also provide a tiny store of valuable civet perfume.

Benjamin, also called benzoin, is an aromatic resin obtained from the tree *Styrax benzoin* (Wheatley 1961:55–9). It was known to the Arabs as *luban Jawa*, "frankincense of Java," and was widely used as an apotropaic. In Chinese medicine, it was substituted for the more valuable "Arsacid aromatic" obtained from Syria and Iran (Schafer 1963:169–70). In longhouse communities, various resins had practical uses, such as sealing holes in boats, but the ones valuable as commodities were scarce.

Amber is a fossilized resin, usually translucent and yellow-brown in colour. It played a part in Chinese jewellery similar to coral, being used in pendants and prayer beads. Such pieces had mystical connotations, and were supposed, by association with their own preservation, to promote longevity (Schafer 1963:247–8). Within Borneo, it does not seem to have been much used for jewellery, so odd pieces found on the jungle floor would be valued only for trade. There is no record of people mining amber, so that its availability as a commodity would have been entirely fortuitous.

The final three items on Herbert's list cannot be described as fortuitous commodities because they could be located readily enough, if labour was available. For the sake of completeness, however, *dragon's blood* was a name given in China to various bright red substances that were supposed to be desiccated blood. In Borneo, the source of dragon's blood was the fruit of relatively common palms of the genus *Daemonorops*. It was used as an astringent and prescribed for haemorrhages (Schafer 1963:211). In Southeast Asia, it was used as a dye and would have been the most effective red dye available to interior people.

Wax had uses that would have been as familiar to European traders as to Chinese. In addition to candles, beeswax was used to seal receptacles, and so no doubt travelled along with some of the other trade items on Herbert's list. In China, wax had medicinal usages – Schafer (1963:193) tells us that mixed with an egg and taken in white wine it would stop haemorrhaging in pregnant women – but presumably it was obtainable from sources much closer to home than Borneo. Upriver, it would have been available as a by-product of collecting honey and used in wick lanterns.

Rattan, the final item on the list, is downright prosaic. It is furnished by the long woody stems of climbers of the genus *Calamus* or *Rhapis*, which are widely found in tropical rainforest. Schafer (1963:259) remarks that finely made rattan work from Annam was admired at the imperial court, but this was because of its workmanship not its materials. The modern associations of rattan are of course with furniture and wicker work, but the tough, pliable material had innumerable practical applications in premodern Southeast Asia. It was used in house construction, and in boats for rigging and for lashing planks. At the time of Herbert's visit, it would have been available in Brunei in much the same way as rice, and it implies no involvement of longhouse communities. Only in the twentieth century did it become practical to export it in bulk.

The Exports of Brunei: Other Precious Commodities

Herbert's list of the commodities available at Brunei is intriguing for two reasons. First, he was himself a trader alert to the possibilities of profit, and consequently his list is no idle inventory. Second, it was made well before the colonial era, and is therefore our best guide to the city's former exports. The best European account of Brunei at the zenith of its power is given by Pigafetta (1525?), the historian of Magellan's voyage. However, Magellan was an explorer rather than a trader, and the only commodity to which Pigafetta draws attention is camphor. By the time of Herbert's visit in 1773, the European role in the carrying trade of Southeast Asia was established, but not dominant. Brunei was already suffering from the competition of other indigenous maritime powers, but its ancient trading network in the interior of the island was evidently still functioning. Consequently, Herbert's list gives us the best picture of the commodities that emerged from that network. It is confirmed by Pin-tsun Chang's (1991:164–86) analysis of imperial revenue records from ports in southern China around the year 1600, which often indicate the origins of taxable commodities. There are, however, other items that might have occurred on Herbert's list. First, we must backtrack to deal with the item singled out by Pigafetta.

Camphor is a volatile crystalline substance with a characteristic odor that was "extravagantly admired in T'ang" (Schafer 1963:167). It was an ingredient in incense, and worn in amulets and in clothing it had erotic associations. It was recommended for eye troubles, including cataracts, and mixed with musk made a prophylactic against a range of ailments. It was evidently imported from Borneo and Sumatra in significant quantities for centuries (Wheatley 1961:101–5; Wong 1960:88).

According to Hose, "camphor is formed in the crevices of the stems of old trees of the species *Dryobalanops aromatica*, when the heart is decayed leaving a central hollow. The tree is cut down, the stem split up, and the crystalline scales of pure camphor are shaken out on to mats. It is then made up in little bundles wrapped in palm leaves. The large flake camphor fetches as much as (English pounds) 6 in the Chinese bazaar" (Hose and McDougall 1912:I:152). I find no reference to the consumption of camphor by longhouse residents, so that whenever camphor was collected it was from the outset intended for sale. It does not follow, however, that people went looking for camphor trees to cut down. Hose's account makes it clear that it is only the rare old tree that produces the crystals in its decayed core. The most likely scenario was that a hunter would come on a suitable-looking tree and note its whereabouts. Later, a work party would arrive to collect whatever small store of crystals happened to be inside.

Consequently, camphor was another fortuitous commodity. Hose's account speaks of camphor gathering, as if it were an industry, but this was only practicable after the establishment of "Chinese bazaars" in the colonial era, and as an adjunct to collecting gutta. In the modern era, camphor found new markets; for a while it was required in the production of celluloid for photographic film.

Rhinoceros horn is not mentioned by Herbert, but we know that it was imported into Canton from the Indies "in such quantities that the near extinction of the Indochinese rhinoceroses in modern times can in large part be attributed to the China trade of T'ang" (Schafer 1963:241). The species found in Borneo was the smallest in Southeast Asia, *Rhinoceros sumatrans*, whose horn was in particular demand (Schafer 1963:226). Powdered, it was prescribed as an antidote to all kinds of poisons, but it was more often treated as "a precious substance, suitable for the jeweller's art, and could be transformed into little boxes, bracelets, paper weights, knife hilts, and chopsticks, all objects which were also made from ivory" (Schafer 1963:241). Jewellery made of it was fashionable in the imperial court, but supplies from

Borneo must have been rare. Nevertheless, Hugh Brooke Low found a small quantity on sale in the bazaar at Belaga, far up the Rejang River (*Sarawak Gazette* 220:1884).

Hornbill casques are mentioned neither by Herbert nor Schafer, yet at least a few reached China where they were carved into elaborate ornaments or utensils, in the manner of rhinoceros horn (Chin and Datan 1991:11). Casques are hollow chambers on the tops of the beaks of various kinds of *Bucerotidae*. The largest come from the rhinoceros hornbill, *Buceros rhinoceros*. For longhouse people, the tail feathers of hornbills – white with a broad black band – were the favoured decoration for war bonnets and cloaks. The casques were carved into delicate ear pendants and had warlike associations (Langub 1991:73).

The Exports of Brunei: Bulk Commodities

One item is conspicuous by its absence from Herbert's list.

Birds' nests are a famous Borneo export item, and at first sight they appear to be luxury items of the same order as camphor and rhinoceros horns: highly exotic in China, and available to be appreciated only by those of the richest and most sophisticated tastes. The nests in question are those of the swiflets that nest in the vast caves found in scattered limestone outcroppings in half a dozen places in the Brunei hinterland. They come in various qualities, the most prized being almost translucent (Leh 1993). They are made by *Collocalia fuciphaga*, whose sticky saliva not only makes up a large part of the nests, but also glues them high up on the walls of the cave (Hose and McDougall 1912:I:156). Only by means of perilous scaffoldings made up of bamboo poles lodged here and there in the walls is it possible to climb up and detach the nests. At their destination in China, the nests were made into a soup legendary for its delicate flavour and invigorating qualities (Blusse 1991).

There is, however, a marked difference between rhinoceros horn and birds' nests as commodities. While horn might turn up a piece here and a piece there, birds' nests were available, literally, by the boat load. It is this difference that causes what Mark Cleary sees as a paradox: the volume of exports of an apparently "ancient" trading commodity actually increased during the colonial era. This is a surprise because what any simple model of economic modernisation would predict is the replacement of indigenous "jungle products" by "the new 'colonial' commodities" such as "plantation rubber, oil, minerals and sawn timber." Yet, between 1881 and 1940, the value of birds' nests exported from Sarawak and North Borneo (now Sabah) more than tripled (Cleary 1997:30, 41). This is something of an illusion, however. The export of birds' nests was more the creation of the colonial order than a survival from a previous era.

Jerome Rousseau quotes St. John (1862:I:111) to suggest that the long-house communities in the Brunei hinterland were unaware of the value of birds' nest until the arrival of the Kayan. The irony here is that the Kayan immigrants came from an area much more remote from trade than the Baram watershed. Berawan claimed that they knew full well of the caves near Long Laput in the middle Baram ever since they inhabited the same location on their own migrations down river. The difference according to them is that when the Kayan arrived, they asserted sole ownership of the caves, whereas previously they had been exploited by occasional work parties from various communities. If this were true, it indicates not a special liberality on the part of the Berawan, but a difference in trade opportunities. The source of birds' nests most accessible to Brunei in precolonial times were the massive caves at Niah, which are easily reached directly from the coast. It is entirely possible that they were capable of supplying the entire demand for birds' nests at Brunei town even at the peak of its trading prosperity in the sixteenth century. In the first reports from the area in the *Sarawak Gazette*, it is noted that the caves are firmly in the possession of local Malay potentates, who used local Penan to gather the nests, and then shipped them up the coast to Brunei (106:1875).

What went up in the twentieth century was not supply but demand. Unlike the handful of sailing junks that in previous centuries arrived each year at Brunei, steamships operating out of the new port of Miri could export virtually unlimited quantities of nests, bound for China. It was at that time that Kayan proprietors tightened their grip on the caves in the middle Baram and began selling in bulk to Chinese traders operating from the upriver bazaar established at Long Lama around 1905 (Chew 1990:76). One of these Kayan proprietors was a granddaughter of Aban Jau, and her wealth earned her the sobriquet among colonial officers of the "Dollar Princess" (MacDonald 1958:272–82). Intriguingly, the wholesale logging of the forest in the 1980s brought to light caves that had not been previously noticed or exploited because they were too far from any major river. The revelation set off a veritable gold rush among people traditionally excluded from the birds' nest trade, especially Iban immigrants, leading to another surge in exports. When the trade was in Brunei hands, such increases in production would have served only to depress prices to the point where the nests would not have been worth collecting.

Pepper was at one time an important Brunei export, but its production had little to do with longhouse communities. It was instead Chinese settlers that Forrest found growing pepper on plantations close to Brunei in the 1770s. By the 1840s, however, they had gone, victims of Brunei's declining control over its sea lanes (Low 1848:55–6). Only in recent decades have Upriver People experimented with pepper as a cash crop, and with mixed success, given unstable world prices.

The Lack of Infrastructure

What comes out clearly from this review of the jungle products exported from Brunei during its heyday is that the most valuable were commodities of the fortuitous kind. Consequently, it comes as no surprise to find that there was no specialised class of collectors. Instead, anyone working or travelling in the jungle might discover them by chance. The volume of such commodities was low everywhere, but their value high. Presumably, they accumulated in small caches in all upriver communities. How then did they make their way to the coast?

The first thing to note is the lack of any trade infrastructure such as was found even in remote parts of mainland Southeast Asia. To speak of an "infrastructure" may give an illusory notion of regular transportation, and how far that is from the case is neatly illustrated in Charles Fitzgerald's (1973) account of his travels in southern Yunnan in the 1930s. It is a mountainous region, and the roads between dispersed pockets of population were the merest tracks. Where they had been "improved" with stones thrown into muddy patches, they often became almost impassable to pack animals, stumbling on the insecure footing. Meanwhile, landowners planted prickly bushes on either side to restrict travellers to the path. Bridges were hazardous, and bandits common. Travel was frustratingly slow:

> No Yunnanese would think of starting on a journey unless he allowed for a possible week's delay, through bad weather or – formerly a paramount consideration – delay due to unsafe roads and banditry. When the roads were still infested with robbers it was not uncommon for all travellers to wait in the last town below some dangerous pass until the authorities agreed to provide an escort, or until there were sufficient wealthy travellers assembled to pay for one. My arrival in one such town, some ten years ago, was hailed with delight, since I already had the escort which the local authorities were unwilling to provide for nearly fifty or sixty other travellers and four caravans of forty mules. (Fitzgerald 1973:209)

For all the inconvenience of this travel, there were a whole range of institutions catering to the traveller. In addition to the roads themselves, there were inns or caravanserais providing food and accommodation, however spartan. There was a class of muleteers and porters who made a hard living by constantly travelling back and forth over particular stages, many of them

Min Chia people. Chinese Moslems were also prominent in the carrying trade, underlining their role in the introduction of Islam into China (Winters 1979:7). Even on byways far from major arteries, transportation was a speciality of Moslems (Gladney 1991:32).

Whatever the hardships of travel in mountainous regions of mainland Southeast Asia, there is no doubt of the immense social impact of long-distance trade. Once again, Edmund Leach's famous study of Highland Burma provides illustrations, mainly in his chapter, "The Evidence from Kachin History" (1964:227–63). This chapter is often overlooked, and not surprisingly so, since Leach begins it by announcing that he himself is bored by the mere facts. There are, however, some interesting facts in this chapter that bear importantly on his main argument. It becomes clear that the differences between Shan people in the valleys and Kachin in the hills has to do with more than a contrast between wet and dry rice cultivation. In addition to better soil, the valleys provided the thoroughfares for mule caravans travelling between Burma and China. Shan princes flourished according as the traffic through their valleys afforded sufficient tolls.

Leach mentions tea going northwest to China, and rice and salt moving in the opposite direction (1964:235). To the latter, we can no doubt add manufactured products like ceramics and fine fabrics. Upwardly mobile (*gumsa*) Kachin chiefs emulated the princes as far as they could and, by providing armed guards, operated elementary protection rackets. Also, from an early date, they added regional products to the trade that are reminiscent of those exported from Brunei to China:

> A number of early Chinese works published at various dates between A.D. 350 and A.D. 1000 make reference to the "wild and troublesome *b'uok* tribes" living apparently in the mountains to the west of Yung Ch'ang, whose land produced "rhinoceros, elephant, tortoiseshell, jade, amber, cowries, gold, silver, salt wells, cinnamon and cotton trees, hill paddy and panicled millet." This seems to be a population inhabiting the Kachin Hills and though language and culture may have changed, the tribal name has stuck. Modern Maru called Jinghpaw speakers *p'ok*; the Shans of Hkamti Long used to refer to their Kachin serfs as *kha-p'ok* (serf *p'ok*); Jinghpaw itself might be written *chying-p'ok*... (Leach 1964: 238–9)

Leach leaves no doubt that for both Shan and Kachin, the existence of trade routes had a direct impact on communal organisation and social hierarchy.

The Alternative: Trading Expeditions

In the hinterland of Brunei, no such trading infrastructure existed: no roads, no inns, and no muleteers shuttling backward and forward. Most significantly, there was nothing resembling the caravans that criss-crossed mainland Southeast Asia. Instead, the circulation of commodities relied heavily on *trading expeditions*. By this, I mean that autonomous communities organised parties of their own people to travel long distances, sometimes almost to the far terminus of the network, in order to trade directly with similar communities. Such contacts were infrequent and irregular, in remote communities occurring only perhaps once or twice in a generation.

The evidence of such expeditions is everywhere in the ethnographic literature, even if there are no day-by-day accounts from the participants. Some of the earliest issues of the *Sarawak Gazette* contain mentions of trading expeditions from remarkably far afield.

When a tiny bazaar (i.e., a few shops) was established at Belaga in the far headwaters of the Rejang River before the annexation of the Baram watershed, it drew customers from across the mountain range in what is now Indonesian Kalimantan. In 1879, a trading expedition arrived there from the middle Mahakam, having journeyed by canoe to the very headwaters of the Mahakam, abandoned their canoes, walked over into the Balui, and there built new canoes before descending to Belaga bazaar – a stupendous voyage (*Sarawak Gazette* 150:February 1979). It is amazing that people in Mahakam even *knew* about the new bazaar in Belaga; clearly, someone had been travelling back and forth through the vast expanses of unoccupied jungle. In 1885, the same journey was made by more than three hundred "Peng Kayans" and "Ukiets," who, not satisfied with the urban amenities of Belaga, went on to Kapit in the middle Rejang (*Sarawak Gazette* 231:April 1985). In 1900, the trade goods in Belaga bazaar were completely exhausted by parties of Uma Kulit arriving all the way from the Apo Kayan in Kalimantan (*Sarawak Gazette* 410:April 1900).

Such long-range trading expeditions continued to be made right into the 1980s. In his narrative of travels with Penan companions in the central highlands, Eric Hansen describes encountering a Kenyah party returning to Kalimantan from Sarawak:

> A nearby rustling and crunching of twigs caught my attention. Something large was moving towards us on the trail. Bo 'Hok and Weng instinctively slipped cartridges into their shotguns, eased the breaches shut, and waited quietly. Staggering into view a man suddenly appeared on the narrow game trail. He was bent double beneath the weight of what looked like a large hardwood box. His arrival came as a surprise because we hadn't seen any other human being in six weeks. The man was dressed in blue satin jogging shorts, black high-top tennis shoes without socks, and a red T-shirt. It wasn't until he got closer that I recognised what he was carrying. It was an old-fashioned treadle sewing machine mounted on a cast-iron frame within a hardwood cabinet. I knew there wasn't a village for more than eighty miles

in the direction from which he was walking. I stared at him in disbelief. He walked up to us and with a half-smile, raised his eyebrows slightly in greeting, then lowered himself to his haunches, gently placing the heavy machine upright on the ground. Cast into the metal base I read the word "Singer." (Hansen 1988:145)

A moment later, a man came clanking down the path festooned with metal cooking pots. Behind him, another with a twenty-five-horsepower outboard motor and two rainbow-coloured golf umbrellas. And so it continued – chain saws, jerry cans of gasoline, tape recorders, plastic buckets, and tins of biscuits. Stopping to talk and smoke, "the men sat on the jungle floor surrounded by their remarkable loads with expressions of total nonchalance. They might have been simply returning from the corner store with a bottle of milk and the newspaper."

In historical perspective, such remarkably long and arduous expeditions were no doubt exceptional, reflecting the political and economic circumstances of particular epochs. Nevertheless, they show the lengths to which interior people would go in order to trade. In the late nineteenth century, Sarawak was a refuge of stability in a volatile region, and presented better opportunities for equitable trade than the almost equally distant coast of Kalimantan. Nevertheless, as in Europe before the railway age, transport by river was always faster and easier than elaborate portages such as Hansen witnessed.

Travel by river also required considerable manpower, however. The canoes employed were not the simple dugouts used by families to go back and forth to their farms. Instead, the sides were built up with one or two planks. They required crews of a few dozen or more. When colonial officers began to move about the interior, they had ample opportunity to experience river transportation. Charles Hose leaves this description:

> During a day's journey the crew of a boat will from time to time lighten their labour with song, one man singing, the others joining in the chorus; and if several boats are travelling in company the crews will from time to time spurt and strive to pass one another in good-humoured rivalry. At such times each crew may break out into a deep-pitched and musical roar, the triumphal chorus of a victorious war party.
>
> In the upper reaches of the rivers there are numerous rapids, and here and there actual falls. The boat is usually propelled up a rapid by poling. Each member of the crew has beside him a stout pole some eight or nine feet long; and when the boat approaches a rapid, the crew at a shout from the captain, usually the steersman, spring to their feet dropping their paddles and seizing their poles. Thrusting these against the stony bottom in perfect unison, the crew swings the boat up through the rushing water with a very pleasant

motion. If the current proves too strong and the boat makes no progress, or if the water is too shallow, three or for men, or, if necessary, the whole crew, spring into the water and, seizing the boat by the gunwale, drag it upstream until quieter water is reached.

It is necessary for a man or boy to bail out the water that constantly enters over the gunwale while the boat makes the passage of a rapid. All through these exciting operations the captain directs and admonishes his men unremittingly, hurling at them expressions of a strength that would astonish a crew on the Cam or Isis: "matei tadjin selin" (may you die the most awful death) is one of the favourite phrases. These provoke no resentment, but merely stimulate the crew to greater exertions.

Sometimes when much water is coming down after heavy rains, the current is so swift in deep places that neither paddling, poling, nor wading is possible. Then three or four men are landed on the bank, or on the boughs of trees, and haul on the boat with long rattans, scrambling over the rocks and through the jungle as best they can.

The passage downstream in the upper reaches is even more exciting and pleasurable. The crew paddles sufficiently to keep good steerage way on the boat, as it glides swiftly between the rocks and shallows; as it shoots over the rapids, the steersman stands up to choose his path, the water splashes and gurgles and leaps over the gunwale, and the men break out into song. The smaller waterfalls do not check its onward rush; as it approaches a fall, several men near the bow stand up to see if there is sufficient water; then as they resume their seats all paddle with might and main until the boat takes the leap. Occasionally a boat is upset during such an attempt, and rarely one or two of the crew are lost from being hurled against rocks and drowned while stunned.

In making a long journey, nights are passed if possible in friendly villages. When no such villages can be reached, the night is passed either in the boats moored to the bank or on the river bank. In the former case, the leaf mats, of which each man carries at least one in his basket, are used to roof the boat; in the latter case a rude hut is quickly built, a framework of saplings lashed together, roofed with the mats, and floored at a level of some feet above the ground with bamboos or slender saplings. On camping in the evening and before starting in the morning, rice is cooked and eaten; and about mid-day the journey is interrupted for about an hour while the party lands on the bank, or, if possible, on a bed of pebbles, to rest and to cook and eat the mid-day meal. (Hose and McDougall 1912:I:132–4)

As Hose's description makes plain, expeditions involving several boats required elaborate organisation. Sometimes war canoes carried as many as a hundred paddlers, but a crew of about sixty was more common. As Hose describes it, six men were needed to steer such boats, two on the first bench and four on the last two. In each pair, one man draw his paddle toward himself, struggling to draw the bow or stern over, while his neighbour levered his paddle against the side, and it took all six working in unison to turn the canoe. Even in the 1970s, it was possible to get an impression of the power of these massive canoes because they were still raced at the biannual Marudi "Regatta," originally organised as an outlet for competitive urges by Charles Hose during the process of "pacification." At the beginning of a race with a dozen boats a mist of spray rose into the air from hundreds of paddles striking the water at the same moment, so that the canoes disappeared behind a screen of their own making.

In the lower reaches of the major rivers, below the rapids, river transport was considerably easier. Indeed, the main Baram provides a broad avenue reaching far into the interior. From the mouth, one can travel a couple of hundred miles upriver, at least as far as Long Kasih, without encountering any navigational difficulties. Even measured as the crow flies, this is more than a hundred and fifty miles, across the coastal plain and into the foothills. Of the main tributaries, the Tinjar is the most accessible because it flows through a broad valley. There are no serious rapids until the headwaters are reached. The Tutoh is extremely difficult in its upper reaches, and the people living there were known as some of the best boatmen in Borneo, but one could go as far as Long Terawan without difficulty. It is only the rivers that flow into the Baram above Long Kasih, notably the Pata and Akah, that are hazardous along their whole length. Consequently, a surprisingly large part of the Baram watershed is readily accessible by river.

Under these circumstances, roads such as those maintained – or not maintained – throughout Yunnan were irrelevant to trade in the hinterland of Brunei. As for inns and caravanserais, travel was not regular enough to support such institutions. Instead, it was longhouse communities themselves that provided hospitality. In the twentieth century, there was an elaborate etiquette of upriver travel, specifying where one should stay and what to expect in the way of entertainment. It would be a mistake, however, to assume that the same applied in the precolonial era. No doubt there were already established forms, especially among the elites and during longhouse festivals, for the reception of visitors from neighbouring communities, or even from far afield. But all of this assumes peaceful relationships between hosts and visitors, and that was far from universally the case. Descending the main rivers, where there were many large longhouses in succession, often meant running a gauntlet of ancient enemies. According to the missionary Hudson Southwell (personal communication), as late as the 1930s, parties of Kelabit travelling down the Baram from their homes near the headwaters would not pass Kayan longhouses during the daytime. Instead, they would camp upriver of them, and then drift quietly by during the dead of night, sticking to the middle of the river and hoping to go unobserved.

On the return trip, they paddled quietly by at a similar hour, hugging the opposite bank. This stealth was the result of a series of raids and murders in the 1890s, culminating in a Rajah-authorized punitive expedition against the Kelabit (*Sarawak Gazette* 472:May 1905). If suspicions ran this high in the 1930s, they must certainly have inhibited casual hospitality in the previous century, when there was outright warfare between communities in Baram.

Consequently, long-distance trading expeditions needed to be made in force. As such, they were hardly be distinguishable from war expeditions. One can imagine the delicate balance of suspicion on all sides. Indeed, at times of political unrest, the same tensions and ambiguities emerged as on the coast, where legitimate trade and outright piracy often went hand in hand. No doubt there were times when innocent mercantile ventures turned opportunistically into raids, if travellers found downriver communities weakly defended. Perhaps that was the origin of the great Kayan expeditions of the latter half of the nineteenth century against the people of Tutoh and Limbang, and eventually of Brunei itself. Moreover, there are stories of hosts murdering their travelling guests for the sake of whatever commodities they were carrying. One version of Aban Jau's demise told at Long Batan in the 1970s was that he had murdered visitors staying with him, and so incurred a curse.

Brunei's Trading Communities

It would be wrong, however, to assume that all trading expeditions headed down river. It is evident that Brunei's traders were active in pursuing commerce upriver. Moreover, in contrast to overseas trade, which was tightly controlled by the Sultan, there was room for individual enterprise in upriver commerce. Traders came from particular neighbourhoods within Brunei, and it is for this reason that my definition of trading expeditions speaks of contacts between autonomous communities.

A nice example is provided by the Brunei traders we met in Chapter 6. They identified themselves as Burong Pingai – a name that functioned in much the same way as the ethnic labels of their Upriver customers. If we trace the Burong Pingai back to Brunei, we find that there was a ward of the city with the same name. Moreover, its inhabitants had a strong sense of community, such that they gave themselves air and graces, and looked down on their neighbours just a stone's throw away across the water lanes. In his description of the city, St. John (1862:II:252–65) lists thirty such wards, each associated with particular specialisations, some mundane, such as fishing or husking rice, and some technical, such as working iron or casting brass.

Many wards were centred around the residences of important nobles or court officials. The impression that St. John conveys is of an Italian city of the Renaissance, such as Florence or Sienna; a place not so much united by a common culture as precariously balanced between intense rivalries. In some ways, if on a larger scale, Brunei resembled longhouse communities like Long Kelejeo, with its mixture of ethnicities. That similarity again draws our attention to the subtle connections between societies upriver and down, and the truly indigenous nature of both.

> Burong Pingai was one of half a dozen wards that St. John reports as active in upriver and international commerce, and was home to some of the wealthiest traders. Moreover, the enterprise of Burong Pingai was made clear in a myth that gave them a key role in the founding of the Sultanate. Their ancestors, they claimed, were descended from "Muruts," i.e. indigenous people of the lower Limbang river region (Maxwell 1996). They became Moslems, however, as a result of a spectacular coup: the abduction of the daughter of the Sultan of Jahor.
>
> This is the tradition or history: they were, as usual, cruising down the Gulf of Siam, looking out for prey, when they observed a prahu [galley], gaily dressed out with banners, pulling along the coast. They gave chase, and soon came up with her, and found the daughter of the Sultan of Jahore, surrounded by a bevy of pretty attendants; they seized them and carried them off to Brunei, and presented the lady to their chief, who married her. When the father heard of it he sent a great deputation of nobles to entreat the Murut to turn Mohamedan, and marry his daughter according to the custom of that religion. He made no difficulty, but on the contrary, invited the nobles to remain and take wives in that country. Many did, and it soon became a great rendezvous for the Malays; in fact the other twenty kampongs [villages] are descended from odds and ends of strangers, together with their wives, taken from among the aborigines. The rajahs [nobles] all say they are of Jahore descent. (St. John 1862:II:87–8 [brackets added])

Colourful as it is, this account fails to explain the origin of the curious name Burong Pingai, which translates literally as "white bird." The phrase occurs, however, in story collected by Don Brown, who conducted fieldwork in Brunei in 1967–8. According to this version, the Sultan of Jahor sent a mystical "white bird" to locate his missing daughter. "The princess told the bird to tell her parents that she was in Brunei wed to a descendent of the gods and thus of one family with her father. The princess' happiness, plus the fame and glory of Brunei, persuaded the Sultan of Jahor to come to Brunei and install Awang Alak Betatur as Sultan" (Brown 1970:135). Awang Alak Betatur is the name given in Brunei court annals for the man who became the first Sultan, Muhammad (Maxwell 1996). Even so, we are still

left guessing about the community called "White Birds," and one must look
elsewhere in Brown's ethnography to find the metaphorical link between
birds and people: "the people of Burong Pingai are descendents of people
of Jahor who came to Brunei when its first Sultan married a princess of
Jahor" (Brown 1970:55).

If the three legends together manage to provide a coherent rationale for
the name, they fail to resolve other ambiguities:

> Firstly, as a people of Jahor are the Burong Pingais of high status (Jahor is a
> prestigious place in the Malay world) or of low status (foreigners as compared
> to the "true" Bruneis)? Secondly, were those people of Jahor who established
> Burong Pingai slaves or servants (sent as part of the wedding arrangements,
> for example) or were they of high status in Jahor? In the absence of historical
> data such questions can only elicit controversy. Thus when I quizzed the
> headman of Burong Pingai on his ward's origin he acknowledged that the
> people of Burong Pingai cared for the pet bird of the Jahor Princess (the ward
> is ostensibly named after that bird). But he went on to say that this indicated
> nothing about the origin of his ward – anyone who insisted that he knew
> the truth about the origins of people who lived so long ago was simply a
> liar. Moreover, he said that all men were created by God, and that was the
> important point about their origin. (Brown 1970:55)

The headman's down-to-earth scepticism is justified by a properly Islamic,
if uncharacteristically egalitarian, sentiment. Note, however, that the speech
attributed to princess of Jahor, delivered to the "White Bird," contains a
throwaway line whose implications are downright blasphemous: that both
Sultans are descended from gods. The claim serves as a reminder that a state
drawing on Indic notions of sovereignty long predated the Brunei Sultanate
(Singh 1984:14–16). Its power was maritime, profiting from the rich trade
between southern China and the Straits of Malacca (Bellwood and Matussin
1980). This epoch is evoked in the story of the capture of the Jahor princess,
which portrays the ancestors of the Burong Pingai "cruising" as far as the
Malay Peninsula.

Set out side by side, it is evident that the legends are contradictory, portraying the Burong Pingai as both heroic indigenes and high-class foreigners.
Their neighbours meanwhile could dismiss them with similar inclusiveness
as either thuggish provincials or imported menials. Such elaborate snobber-
ies hint at the social complexity of Brunei. By the time of Brown's fieldwork,
the institutions of government had undergone bureaucratic "rationaliza-
tion" under British influence, so that it was not possible to reconstruct the
functioning of the state in precolonial times. Even so, his written and oral
sources are sufficient to demonstrate the endless imbroglios of ethnicity and
rank (Brown 1970:11–33, 86–118).

Given what we have already learned about the hinterland, it will come as no surprise that "in Brunei tradition, the state was ethnically plural from the earliest times" (Brown 1984:31). Needless to say, we know next to nothing about the population from which came the original founders of Brunei, or whatever protostate it was that first emerged somewhere around Brunei Bay, other than that it was indigenous. It is a safe guess, however, that it was in no sense homogeneous. In court annals, the founders are described as Murut – the same term given to St. John (Sweeney 1968). As we see in Chapter 8, however, this is a particularly slippery ethnic label. To this population was added various foreign elements, in addition to the Malays, nobles or servants or both, who accompanied the princess from Jahor. The second Sultan is said either to have been Chinese, or to have married a Chinese. All these elements together make up the Bangsa Brunei, the ethnic Bruneis, but that is only the beginning. The state of Brunei also contains Moslems who are not Bangsa Brunei, such as the Kedayan, skilled rice farmers inhabiting the subcoastal belt (Maxwell 1997). Also, Moslem are the people called "Belaits" and "Tutongs" living near the rivers of the same name. These people comprise part of the majority of Brunei citizens that Brown describes as "Non-Brunei Subject Peoples," but also included in this category are peoples who were not Moslem, such as the Visaya and Dusun (Bernstein 1997). Meanwhile, there are still those who call themselves Murut, supposedly the people who founded Brunei but never converted to Islam.

Cross-cutting this ethnic complexity were issues of rank. Within each and every community, there were those of high status, and inevitably, the traditional polity had to take account of this standing. The humblest farmers had their "headmen" and "land chiefs," whose elite status made them equal to at least the lower orders of Brunei aristocrats. Meanwhile, the Sultan reserved the right to appoint a bewildering array of officials: viziers, *cheteria*, *pehin*, and *menteri*. Who now was to say whether a wealthy Dusun secure in his income from rice outranked a Brunei aristocrat of the middling sort, whose family's trading ventures had not been doing well of late?

Moreover, this refers to a Brunei shrunk to its present borders. But even at the beginning of the nineteenth century, two centuries after its prime, Brunei still controlled a thousand miles of coastline, along which dozens of major rivers flowed into the north China Sea. Each watershed contained its own locally resident "Malay" communities, complexly descended from local people and immigrants, and multiple indigenous ethnic groups of varying degrees of sophistication. The largest river of was the Rejang, and near its mouth the numerous and worldly Melanau people, although still adhering to their own religions and elaborate systems of rank (Morris 1980, 1991), played a part in coastal trade not much inferior to the Bruneians themselves. Their subject status was marked only by the fact that their trading system was included within Brunei's; that is, it depended ultimately on Brunei as the emporium of overseas imports and exports.

As the Melanau case illustrates, to speak of Brunei "controlling" the coast means dominating trade along the coast. Certainly, there was a territorial aspect: there were nobles invested with fiefs who levied taxes on the farming communities under their direct control. But, as is often remarked, the indigenous states of Southeast Asia conceived of themselves not in terms of territories administered and boundaries defended, but rather as ritual centres with dependent populations (Anderson 1972; Tambiah 1976). For a maritime power like Brunei, what mattered was control of river estuaries. In some rivers, the Malay presence comprised little more than a trading post; in others, there were substantial populations of fishermen and farmers. Nowhere, however, did Brunei control reach far upriver because that was unnecessary for the domination of trade.

In the mid-nineteenth century, Singapore was the major trading partner of Brunei, but in the precolonial period the major trading partners were more diverse (Brown 1970:67; Wong 1961). The links to southern Chinese ports, particularly Canton, were crucial, but there were others, to the Malay Peninsula, the Riau Archipelago, the southern Philippines, and beyond. Within Brunei, nobles maintained trading connections overseas, either by fitting out their own ships or by purchasing cargoes arriving in Brunei. It was the latter commerce that was most easily controlled by a strong Sultan, acting through his viziers. Nobles not only maintained personal followings in their own wards of the city, but also had officials acting for them in their appanages, either outside the city or further away along the coastlines to the north and south. These local officials in turn maintained their own followings, and supervised taxes and trade in villages belonging to their lords. Coastal trade moved either directly to Brunei, or from region to region along the coast. Through this network, jungle produce was funnelled from far and wide into warehouses owned by the most powerful men in the realm.

Longhouse communities were connected to this trading network by intermediaries. Nowhere is there any hint of Upriver trading canoes, with their numerous crews, paddling down the water lanes of Brunei city, stopping at the steps of houses and palaces to engage in barter. The Sultan, lacking regular armed forces, would surely not have taken kindly to bands of heavily armed pagans wandering around his capital. It follows that the exchange of commodities occurred at communities in the hinterland, either just inside or just outside "the Sultan's fence."

The Burong Pingai at Long Kelejeo

It is unlikely that the wealthy men of Burong Pingai who financed trading ventures went along themselves. Instead, they found reliable followers to undertake the enterprise for them. Such men were often called *nakhoda*, meaning simply captain or skipper. It is noticeable, indeed, that throughout Brunei history the title Nakhoda constantly jostles the verbose formulae of inherited rank, as if to suggest the practical realities of trade that underlay courtly affectations. In earlier times, nobles evidently played a more muscular role. Brunei's fifth and most famous ruler, Sultan Bulkiah, had himself been a sea captain, under the name Nakhoda Ragam (Brown 1970:63). Moreover, the title was easily applied to leaders of trading expeditions upriver because the boats employed were not so different to those used in the coastal trade. Not needing to navigate through rapids, they had more beam that the canoes of Upriver People and were built like seagoing craft of planks over frames. Consequently, they were better adapted for carrying freight. As Upriver People invariably remarked in the 1970s, where they could not sail Malays preferred to "paddle backward," that is, row their boats.

Berawan accounts make it clear that the Burong Pingai were well established at the multiethnic longhouse community of Long Kelejeo, where they had built houses along the riverbank, inside the stockade. Their presence attracted trade from further upriver, sufficient for it to be worth establishing the "*kubu*," or store house, that Low sneered at. But the traders were not content to sit and wait for customers. As is made clear by all the to-ing and fro-ing in Low's account, summarised in Chapter 6, they ranged from a base at Long Kelejeo further up the Tutoh, and also down the Tutoh into the Baram. There must have been an elaborate Malay folklore of adventurers who journeyed into wild country seeking to make their fortunes from their sophistication and cunning. We met an example in Chapter 4, that of Nakhoda Raman who turned up in the middle Baram in the 1870s coolly announcing that the Sultan had granted to him the right to tax Aban Jau's people in Tinjar, and expecting his Kayan hosts to go and collect it for him. Nakhoda Raman was a trader, when he was not meddling in regional politics.

It is important, however, to note that the presence of Burong Pingai did not mean that Long Kelejeo had come inside "the Sultan's fence." On the contrary, when the Burong Pingai made trouble, they were forcibly expelled. Consequently, Long Kelejeo provides an example of what we might call a "forward base" outside Brunei territory. The circumstances that had brought so large a longhouse community into existence were unique to the epoch, with all its instability and warfare. Nevertheless, there is no reason to believe that such forward bases had not occurred previously, before the Kayan migrations into Baram. This would explain the otherwise puzzling feature that there is no ancient site near the river mouth of the Baram associated with Malays. However, the last fifty or so miles of river wound through a region of unproductive swamps, and there was a more direct route via the Belait River and into the Tutoh. Consequently, forward bases like Long Kelejeo were nothing new.

Longhouse trading expeditions heading down river ended either at one of these forward bases, or at something similar inside the Sultan's fence. For a party from Baram or Limbang, the most likely terminus was one of many large non-Moslem communities in the last thirty or so miles of the lower Limbang. Each owed allegiance to a Brunei aristocrat (*pangiran*) who took a large share of the profits. In the late nineteenth century, the *Sarawak Gazette* made much of the appalling abuses – extortion, murder, and rape – visited on these communities by corrupt Brunei *pangiran*. The anger it provoked caused uprisings, culminating in the cession of the Limbang watershed to Sarawak in 1890 (Runciman 1960:192–4). By then, however, the region had been ravaged by Kayan raids, and the whole Brunei economy was in a state of collapse. In previous centuries, such abuses would have been counterproductive. It would have been in everyone's interests that the non-Moslem villages in the lower Limbang remained thriving communities, with a solid agricultural base and enriched by trade.

In sum, if we imagine the spatial organisation of Brunei in terms of annular rings, then the Sultan and his ministers stood at the centre of the city, surrounded by the various wards. Beyond them came the non-Bruneian Moslem subjects, then the non-Moslem subjects. At the periphery, Brunei influence did not end abruptly, but simply faded away. Above the rapids, there were people for whom the existence of Brunei was little more than a rumour. A reasonable hypothesis might be that the size of trading expeditions, in terms of manpower and quantity of trade goods, was proportional to the distance from the centre, and their frequency inversely proportional. But even in lowland areas, the nature of jungle produce and the constant threat of attack meant that trade moved by means of community-based expeditions. Another way of thinking of this is that trade in the Brunei hinterland moved in a series of pulses, rather than a constant flow.

Elite Commodities Going Upriver: Brassware and Ceramics

There is one remaining element of trade into the interior to be considered, and it neatly confirms the picture we already have of it. The goods given in exchange for jungle produce were such as to support the social system that assembled them. The list is brief compared to the esoteric jungle products exported from Brunei. It comprised just three main elements: brassware, ceramics, and beads, all of which were associated with elite status in longhouse communities.

Brassware came in many different forms. There were household utensils of various kinds: trays large and small or raised on stands, wick lamps, boxes for betel nut and lime, jars and kettles, all of them available in plain designs or elaborately decorated. These objects were in everyday use, especially when there were guests. At other times, brassware was stacked in a corner of the apartment, out of the way but not out of view. There were gongs ranging in diameter from six inches to three feet. The music of gongs accompanied many longhouse festivals, and for that purpose, they were laid horizontally on a frame strung with rattans, from largest to smallest. The player sat behind the frame and struck the raised dome at the centre of each gong with wooden sticks, producing a sound like the familiar *gamelan* orchestras of Java. Large gongs were suspended vertically, and the largest kind hung was used to summon people in case of a death, a fire, or an attack. To own large gongs was a sure sign of high status. At grand events, leading men used them as thrones.

The largest brass objects were cannons (Shariffudin 1969). Aside from their use in warfare, their sheer weight in metal made them valuable. An editorial in the *Sarawak Gazette* of April 1975 (100) noted that the Melanau distrusted money and preferred to own cannons, which were often seen tied vertically to the main posts of a house. A man's wealth was estimated in terms of piculs of guns, and bride prices were set in them. The same applied in longhouses in the Brunei hinterland, and stories of grand marriage alliances of the past never fail to emphasize the canoes of the bridegroom's party on the point of sinking because of their fabulous cargoes of brassware. In short, brassware provided the most readily available and readily negotiable medium for the expression of elite status. In contrast, the other wealth objects – beads and ceramics – moved around much less fluidly, for the most part passing only by inheritance to a handful of heirs.

All this brassware, crucial to upriver society, was produced in Brunei. This fact promotes the city to what Immanuel Wallerstein (1976:I:231–2) calls the semiperiphery of the Asian world economy. Since brass working continued into modern times, we have good descriptions of its methods (Lim and Shariffudin 1976). Victor King offers this account of the "lost wax" technique used in Brunei:

> Around a moulded or fashioned core of refractory clay or wood, the desired object was made in molten wax; fine details were sometimes cut or etched

into the wax. Raised surfaces could be modeled in. The sheets of wax corresponded to the thickness of the metal eventually to be produced. Then an outer encircling mould of clay and padi husk would be produced, leaving a hole for the wax to drain out. For solid items a solid wax replica was made with an outer layer of clay. Heat was applied to the mould from a furnace to melt the wax inside. Liquid metal was then poured into the space to replace the wax. The mould was allowed to cool gradually, and the outer clay surface was chipped off, revealing the brass casting underneath. Of course, the metal would then have to be filed, smoothed, cleaned and polished. (King 1991:156–7)

Using these techniques, master craftsmen in Brunei produced beautiful brassware, with elegant forms and delicate decoration. Their methods did not, however, lend themselves to mass production because every cast had to be broken in order to extract the casting. This applied as much to plain wares as to the most elaborate, so that there must have been many workshops in Brunei during its heyday. As Brown (1970:66) remarks, the production of brassware must have been prodigious given the amount found throughout the interior, but Hugh Brooke Low remarked in the 1840s that it had fallen off to such a degree that Brunei traders were obliged to import brassware from Java (Low 1848:159–60). By then, the casting of large cannons had already ceased, but they had previously been made in a wide range of types, some elaborately decorated with dragons' mouths or carrying lugs in the shape of fish (Shariffudin 1969). The foundries needed to caste such large objects could hardly have been located in the wooden houses of the city, so there must have been industrial sites on dry land.

One final point: Brown (1970:66) points out that Brunei's supply of brass came largely from melting down Chinese coins of low denomination. Nothing could make plainer the transition between a cash economy and one where a man's worth was measured in cannons. St. John (1862:278) noted that he often heard prices quoted in terms of weight of gunmetal even in Brunei itself.

Ceramics provide the prime example in Asia of manufactured goods that, in Wallerstein's terminology, were produced in an economically advanced core and exported to a backward periphery. For centuries, Chinese export wares found there way all over Southeast Asia, and for the student, they have the great advantage that they can be readily identified by means of their shape, decoration, and glazes. There is an immense literature devoted to them. For Borneo, Lucas Chin's (1988) guide to the collection in the Sarawak Museum is a valuable source, and its illustrations give some idea of why Chinese jars were so prized by indigenous people. Longhouse people in the Brunei hinterland were not, however, such avid collectors as the

165

Melanau or the Iban. In the 1970s, displays of conspicuous wealth in long-house apartments featured brassware more often than jars. Nevertheless, there were always jars of the largest kind, three feet or so tall, ready for the brewing of rice wine. Although plain, with monochrome glazes in deep browns or blues, they were often old and valuable. Each jar is evidence of a major transaction in years gone by, involving the accumulation of considerable amounts of jungle produce and an expedition down river to trade it for the jar. The demand for these massive jars persisted into the twentieth century, and in the 1970s, there was a Chinese pottery outside the town of Miri on the coast that still produced creditable replicas of them. It was in graveyards that I saw the most highly decorated polychrome jars, visible inside the rotted shells of tombs raised on wooden pilings or lying shattered on the ground. Smaller ones had been used for the storage of bones after secondary treatment of corpses, and there were occasionally large ones that had been used for primary storage (Metcalf 1977).

The Importance of Glass Beads

The most important markers of elite status in the Brunei hinterland were beads. Longhouse people displayed an endless fascination with them. There was until recently a large folklore on beads, with an elaborate nomenclature, reflecting the great variety of sizes, shapes, and colours in which they were found (Anonymous 1984; Colfer and Juk 2001; Janowski 1998; Munan 1988, 1991, 1995). In contrast to brassware, beads were generally kept out of sight. Necklaces of carefully arranged beads were worn during longhouse festivals and on other important events, but many aristocrats owned far more beads than they could wear at any one time. On any given occasion, they chose a necklace as a businessman chooses a tie. In the heavy wooden boxes used to contain beads, usually stored away in the rafters, there were also loose beads waiting to be strung. Strings of beads were constantly being dismantled and arranged in new orders by whoever in a family apartment was knowledgeable about them, often an elderly woman (Lah and Munan 2001). Stringing beads was a high art: they had to be arranged in careful graduations of size from smallest in front to largest at the back. A successful creation served to show off polychrome beads, without using combinations that were considered garish. The most valuable beads were unprepossessing, dull blues with their surfaces scuffed, but everyone recognised the great antiquity that such wear implied. Finally, strings had to tapered so that the bigger beads, which had larger holes in them, did not jiggle about on the string any more than the little ones. Bead strings were made of yarn rolled together between finger and thumb, and they were fragile and prone to rot. Consequently, necklaces were seldom worn outside the longhouse for fear the string would break and the beads be lost.

There was an air of secrecy about beads that perfectly fitted notions of rank in many of the longhouse communities in the Brunei hinterland. An important person did not boast; to do so was immediately to discredit whatever claims were being made. Beads could be worn discreetly when the occasion called for it, and for those in the know, they said plainly enough who a person was, but beads collections were never in my experience put on display in their entirety. So much was this the case that it frustrated my efforts to study bead classification systematically. Only on a few occasions was I allowed to look inside the valuables boxes of important people, and each time I was stunned by what I saw there, a veritable Aladdin's cave. There was jewellery in gold or silver, often of curious design or with inset precious stones, armlets made of rows of what appeared to be ivory bracelets, and decorations presented by the Rajah. The predominant item, however, was beads – not only beaded necklaces, but also boxes of loose beads numbering in the hundreds or even thousands. It would have been fascinating to discover whether the beads considered the most rare and valuable in one community were the same as those in others, and whether that evaluation genuinely reflected antiquity and rarity. To discover this would, however, have required a research effort greater than I could manage alone, and I fear that the chance is now lost.

The mystery of beads extends to their origins. For the archaeologist, beads have the advantage that they are almost indestructible. As Peter Bellwood points out, in the Early Metal phase dating back to 1,000 BC, they are found associated with bronze artefacts in sites across Southeast Asia. Examples from excavations in central Java show cylindrical and barrel-shaped beads entirely similar to those still to be found in central Borneo (Bellwood 1985:246, 299). However, beads are hard to date. Upriver connoisseurs readily distinguish old beads by the wear around the hole, an effect that cannot be faked, but over how many centuries it occurred they do not know. It is also difficult to pinpoint the places where beads were manufactured. Stylistic classification soon meets the obstacle that the same basic designs were produced in many places over many centuries, and only the most sophisticated chemical analysis could hope to distinguish the raw materials from different production sites.

Much research remains to be done concerning the origins and distribution of beads in Southeast Asia, but a valuable beginning has been made by Peter Francis (1986, 1989a, 1989b). In several papers from the Center for Bead Research in Lake Placid, New York, he collates material from archaeological excavations and museum collections around the Indian Ocean and

South China Sea. He identifies a type of monochrome drawn glass beads of "rather dull and limited colors," which are found everywhere across the region, from the African coast to eastern Indonesia (Francis 1989a:4). The technology for manufacturing them originated in southern India, but was easily portable because the necessary materials for glass working are found near many a beach in Southeast Asia. Alastair Lamb (1965:95) suggests that "nomadic" groups of Indian artisans established themselves all over Southeast Asia, wherever there was a demand for beads. Francis identifies several production sites in Southeast Asia. Those nearest to northwestern Borneo were Oc-eo, an ancient trading city on the southern tip of what is now Vietnam, Sating Pra on the Malay isthmus, and Muara Jambi in Sumatra (Francis 1989a:6–7).

Consequently, the oldest glass beads in longhouse collections may not have been imported from very far away. As Heidi Munan (1991:178) remarks of the glass beads found in Sarawak, most are certainly of Indian manufacture, "but not necessarily made in India." Some may have been manufactured by immigrant craftsmen no further away than Sarawak's own beaches (Everett 1908; Harrisson and O'Connor 1968). The basic ingredients are quartz sand and soda, which can be made by burning seaweed. (Potash from wood ash is another alternative.) Clay, marl, limestone, or lead added to molten mix improved the durability of the glass. Temperatures of some four hundred degrees Fahrenheit needed to be achieved, but this is within the range of a simple clay furnace attached to a pair of bellows made from wood and leather (van der Sleen 1964:19–21).

Even if some beads were produced locally, however, their existence implies a Sarawak integrally involved in a South Asian world economy from an early date. It is significant that one of the oldest Sanskrit inscriptions in Southeast Asia was found in Borneo, associated with a sanctuary dedicated to Siva (Coedes 1968:18, 52). Moreover, there are beads in Borneo that are almost certainly of medieval Venetian origin, although their frequency may have been exaggerated (Harrisson 1950:210). Since no one imagines Venetians setting up factories in Southeast Asia, the existence of these beads is dramatic proof of the westward extension of the ancient world economy of which Borneo was a part. The simplest beads, however, were much older: relatively large, round, and tinted a deep blue with copper oxide. Such beads have been made in South Asia for five millennia.

Subsequently, the variety of beads proliferated almost ad infinitum. They were made be winding glass around a core while still malleable from the furnace, or drawing it out into long cylinder, which was then snapped into pieces. With minor modifications in technique, beads could be made that were globular, cylindrical, or shaped like a barrel, a truncated cone, a convex bicone, or a chamfered cylinder. Glass of two or more colours, using different mineral additives, can be layered, wound in intertwined patterns, formed into cylinders that are then drawn out, or appliquéd onto the core before it cools to produce spotted beads, stripped beads, zoned beads, spiral lines, undulating lines, mosaics, chequers, stars, chevrons, or a combination of these. The beauty and diversity of beads is remarkable. As I can attest, sorting them into their varieties can rapidly become an obsession. For the novice, W.G. van der Sleen's *A Handbook on Beads* (1968) is an excellent introduction. Peter Francis' (2002) magnum opus *Asia's Maritime Bead Trade, 300 B.C. to the Present*, provides the advanced seminar, but what is most striking to me is that the same process of classification, naming, and evaluating was occurring in many upriver longhouses as late as the 1970s.

In all this trading activity, China is not conspicuous. Given the importance of China as a consumer of jungle products and supplier of ceramics, this is surprising. (Braghin 1998) may provide a clue to this situation because she shows from archaeological data that beads were only intermittently popular with Chinese elites. They are found in tombs from the Liangzhou period (3,000–2,000 BC), but disappear during the Shang (1,500–1,000 BC). In the Warring States period (475–221 BC), they reappear in small quantities, some made locally and others imported from the Eastern Mediterranean. Francis notes that some writers have denied that China ever exported beads. Against this, he quotes a guide to trade in the southern seas written by Chau Ju-kua, who was the chief customs official of Hangchow early in the thirteenth century. The guide lists commodities that were in demand as far away as Zanzibar, and in just three cases – Borneo, and two places in the Philippines – Chau specifically mentions beads (Francis 1986:2–3). Moreover, the kinds of multicoloured beads made in China are found in Upriver collections, but we know that by the seventeenth century the Dutch were substituting copies of the most popular types of Chinese beads. In the 1920s and 1930s, a German manufacturer produced yet more copies. I found them entirely convincing, but they did not deceive the discerning eyes of expert older women, and consequently, were worn only by the nouveaux riches.

In the preliterate societies of the Brunei hinterland, the durability, antiquity, and mystery of beads made them the perfect icon of aristocratic lineage. They constituted the very essence of nobility. There were ritual circumstances when beads were given away, but usually only a few at a time. Generally speaking, they were passed on only through inheritance. Any one collection might at the owner's death be shared among several descendents, but these same people were eligible to receive inheritances from other relatives. The ease with which bead collections could be assembled and dispersed again made them ideal markers of political transactions constantly in flux.

Cloth and Iron

Less durable goods than the trio of beads, brassware, and ceramics may have ben traded upriver, but the range of possibilities is limited. An item that immediately comes to mind is cloth because we know that there was an almost insatiable demand for it in the early colonial times. St. John reports that in the 1870s, Malay traders sold on credit in the Kayan houses of the middle Baram some 50,000 pieces of "grey shirtings and chintzes" (St. John 1862:I:112). In the 1880s, a Brooke official mentions cotton cloth as one of the luxuries that local people in Belaga "had not even dreamt of before" (*Sarawak Gazette* 176:June 1881). The point is, however, that these were cheap machine-made cottons imported from Britain – the very icon of the Industrial Revolution (Hobsbawm 1968:56). Meanwhile, in St. John's description of the various wards of Brunei town mentions only one centre of weaving. In the elite Kampong Sungai Kedayan, home to several important nobles and a centre of gold working, there were women engaged in the production of "expensive and handsome gold brocade" (St. John 1862:II:256). St. John refers to the celebrated *kain songket*, a deep red fabric woven with designs in gold thread. However, *kain songket* can hardly be thought of in the same terms as industrial cotton because, even more than beads, it was worn on only the grandest occasions. Indeed, it was often stored in the valuable boxes along with beads, unseen for years at a time.

A mundane item that may have been traded upriver is iron. St. John mentions blacksmiths in several of the wards of Brunei, some of whom produced magnificent examples of the Malay short sword or *kris*. We also know that iron was smelted on the coast from ancient times. At Santubong in the Sarawak River delta, excavations reveal what Daniel Chew (1990:52) describes as an "industrial-cum-trading zone" of considerable scale. Not only are there thousands of potsherds, beads, and coins, but also piles of iron slag, as well as evidence of furnaces (Harrisson and O'Connor 1968). Santubong reached its peak of activity in the twelfth century, when there may have been a permanent Chinese colony, in addition to a cosmopolitan collection of ships waiting for the change in the monsoon winds that would carry them back through the Straits of Malacca and across the Bay of Bengal.

Upriver People had, however, acquired the techniques of ironworking for themselves. Writing in 1912, Charles Hose insisted that "thirty years ago nearly all iron worked by the tribes of the interior was from ore found in the river beds, and possibly from masses of meteoric iron; and even at the present day the native ore is still smelted in the far interior, and the swords made from it by the Kenyahs are still valued above all others" (Hose and McDougall 1912:I:193–4). He goes on to describe in detail smelters employing bellows operated by two men, forcing air through a furnace containing charcoal mixed with ore. Similar furnaces were used for forging, using stone hammers and anvils. Starting with a bar of iron, elegant long blades were produced by repeated heating and shaping, and some were decorated with fretwork and chasing worked in while the metal was still hot. Blades were carefully tempered by putting them on a red-hot ingot of iron, so that the degree of reheating could be exactly controlled (Hose and McDougall 1912:II:193–7). The technical skills that Hose describes are impressive, and there is no reason to doubt his account. A half century earlier, the trader and adventurer Robert Burns has expressed the opinion that Kayan steel was better than that made in England because the ores of Borneo were better (Burns 1849, quoted in King 1995:167). As late as the 1970s, I saw forges built in the manner Hose describes, and used to reforge bush knives and utensils and even, miraculously, broken parts of outboard motors. Even so, it remains likely that the scarce supplies of iron upriver were supplemented by the products of the smelters that existed in Brunei. The constant clearing of farms for slash-and-burn agriculture is hard on tools. Even without breakages, constant resharpening soon wears them down, so there must always have been a great demand for iron from all available sources.

As for more perishable commodities, it is hard to imagine Upriver People exchanging their hard-won stocks of precious jungle produce, brought to market only with great effort, on mere comestibles. According to Kenneth Hall (1985:255–6), in the seventeenth-century, Brunei and Sulu sailors controlled the trade with the Spice Islands in what is now Eastern Indonesia. But there is no evidence of Upriver People gaining a taste for spices in their food. On the contrary, in the 1970s, I found them militantly opposed to *haute cuisine*, which they associated with coastal decadence. Their simple food was held up as evidence that they were plain folk and proud of it. Meanwhile, the leaders who organised down river expeditions surely had their eyes firmly set on the main chance: brassware and beads.

No doubt some room must be left for the whimsy of consumers. When St. John visited "Longusin," he saw in his host's apartment "no want of goods here, as they were heaped in all directions" (St. John 1862:I:120). He noted an old English table lamp, in addition to the usual brassware. His host had also acquired half a dozen English-made glass tumblers, having formed a taste for French brandy. This shows how far Western manufactures, in addition to those from India, China, and Brunei, were penetrating upriver by mid-century, well before colonial annexation. At that epoch, a Kayan chief wealthy from plunder might well indulge a little frivolity, but even in other communities and at other times, curious and unusual items had always found their way into family strongboxes, alongside the essential beads.

Every Longhouse Its Own Brunei

Before leaving the topic of manufactured imports, it is necessary to note that they did not constitute the only signs of rank available in longhouse communities. Indeed, in his summary of the symbols of social differentiation among the Kenyah of the Apo Kayan, Herb Whittier does not even mention them. He focuses instead on architectural features and artistic motifs restricted to aristocrats. For instance, the depiction of a full human figure, usually in a seated position, was restricted to an elite. These designs occurred in paintings on the walls outside the longhouse apartments of aristocrats and in beadwork decorating the backs of wooden baby carriers (Whittier 1973:161–226). In the twentieth century, the tiny beads threaded together to make such designs were bought at trade stores, but I was told that previously they were made from pigmented clay rolled around a wire and hardened in a simple kiln.

Once we begin to consider the legitimization of status within longhouse communities, however, we are drawn far beyond beadwork designs. In Section V, I argue that ritual was the crucial arena for the negotiation of leadership. For the present moment, what I am concerned with is the geographical and historical context within which those negotiations occurred, particularly trade with the coast and the expeditions that it required. Whatever indigenous concepts of inequality may have existed centuries ago before the rise of Brunei, as part of some ancient Austronesian heritage, there can be little doubt that they were modified and refined by ideas flowing upriver along with the beads and brassware. As Peter Bellwood and Matussin bin Omar argue (1980), concerning the development of the Brunei state:

> The input of new wealth would be channeled into the society as a whole through its highest ranking members, and these persons would enhance their personal wealth and political power at an increasing rate. Islam, with its codified rules of government and social status, simply speeded up a pre-existing process. In historical Brunei foreign trade was still controlled by the Pengiran Shahbandar, one of the five highest-ranking members of the state below the Sultan. Therefore, in the sense described, it is possible to see a definite role for those items of foreign trade that could be regarded as storable and inheritable wealth in the origins of the Sultanate of Brunei and its immediate pre-Moslem predecessor.

The process that shaped Brunei as macrocosm was reproduced in miniature in every longhouse in its hinterland.

Chiefly Patronage of Trade

Meanwhile, the strategy of Malay traders depended heavily on chiefly patronage. The endless crooked dealing of Brunei traders that Low and St. John delight in reporting cannot have been characteristic in the centuries when the trading system in the hinterland was still functioning, however intermittently. The fate of the Burong Pingai in the 1870s – expelled from both Tutoh and Baram on pain of instant attack – is proof enough of that. In establishing a "forward base," a party of traders had first to gain the trust and protection of some leader powerful enough to ensure their safety. One can imagine how delicate were the opening moves, and here is where the bravado of the *nakhoda* or captain came to the fore. Whatever small force he possessed, including perhaps a little gunpowder and a few guns, he was surely incapable of defending his party from any sustained attack. Consequently, he had to rely on the impression made by his own self-assurance, and the fabled riches and power of Brunei, manifested in a few tasteful gifts. Like other Western observers, St. John and Low were wrong to see only arrogance in the self presentation of Brunei nobles. At times, it had been a means of survival, an essential adaptation.

Even a single trading venture unfolded over a considerable period of time. St. John (1862:I:108) says that it took Malay traders upward of sixteen days to pull upriver as far as his "Longusin," and as much as thirty days if the river was running strongly after heavy rains. But that was only the beginning:

> The report given by Malays of the former system of trade pursued by the Kayans is curious. They say that when a native merchant arrived at the landing-place of a village, the chief settled the terms with him, and all the goods were carried up to the houses, and placed in a prepared spot, secure from pilferers. For a week no business was done, but the stranger and his followers were feasted at the public expense. After that, the goods were brought out and spread in the public room, and the prices fixed. The chief selected what he wanted, and the next in rank in rotation, till all the villagers were satisfied. Three months' credit was always given, but at the appointed day the produce in exchange was ready for the trader. I imagine the Malays would be glad to return to the old system. (St. John 1862:I:124)

We may take "Kayan" generically to mean all the people in Baram, just as Brunei Malays referred to all kinds of people as "Muruts." It was just such a system of trading that was being abused by the Burong Pingai in Berawan houses in Tutoh in the 1870s. Most of their crimes had come about because they had nothing to do but hang around the longhouse until jungle produce could be accumulated, so they passed their time molesting women, and they might have got away with that had they not also tried to cheat people by imposing spurious fines or taxes. In comparison, what is striking in the account given to St. John is the trust required on both sides: the Malays put themselves and their stock entirely in their protector's hands, and he and his followers, knowing nothing of international markets, had to assume that they were getting fair value on what they exchanged. It is a measure of how important trade was to both parties that so delicate a system ever worked, let alone working for centuries, as it manifestly did.

The account also makes plain the order of precedence in selecting goods, but it is doubtful whether the "prices" could really be settled in advance. The price had to have been set in terms of jungle produce, and no one knew what products were going to be available. Instead, the chief and his followers, when their turns came, reserved the right of first refusal for the choicest goods. What was left for the commoners was presumably plain brassware, a few beads, utilitarian ironware, and perhaps some fabrics. By the time of St. John's visit, a major item of trade was machine-made cloth, which was bought in large quantities by customers of all classes. Even then, however, the lion's share of trade goods went to the elites in each community.

What was happening during the three months before transactions were completed is not specified in the account. My argument is that it was not a series of frantic searches in the jungle for aloes-bearing trees, or the butchering of whole troops of monkeys in search of bezoar stones. Instead, every remote farmhouse had to be contacted to see what tiny stocks of jungle produce each had, and then neighbouring longhouse communities and *their* farmhouses – a gradual assembly of whatever had accumulated over years of hunting and making farms. The glamorous luxuries on display outside the chief's apartment were the bait, drawing to them as if by magic – the Sultan's magic – all those half-forgotten caches. We might note that this is exactly what the chief would have had to do had he planned his own trading trip, although his bait could be nothing more than promises. From this perspective, there was less difference than one might expect between Malay trading expeditions going upriver and longhouse expeditions going down.

Finally, the climactic moment, portrayed in St. John's account as a simple handing over, was surely when all the hard bargaining went on. The visiting traders could at last inspect their hosts' stocks of jungle produce and decide what they would exchange for what. This technique required no elaborate accounting because each party simply made up matching piles. One imagines a man of some importance eyeing a particularly fine gong with a raised dragon design, while shuffling bamboo containers filled with camphor, and trying to gauge how desirable a large hornbill casque really was to a trader studiously feigning indifference. If this is an accurate portrayal, there was no extension of credit at the beginning of the process, but only a statement by the traders of what sorts of things they were looking for, and in what quantities.

Viewed in this light, the trading system takes on a remarkably contemporary quality. The empire of Brunei, like other maritime states before it, reaching back to Sri Vijaya, did not depend on boundaries. It was not a colonial empire, like that of the British and the Dutch, but something closer to what Michael Hardt and Antonio Negri (2000) refer to as "Empire" in the abstract. Instead of overawing upriver chiefs militarily, Brunei co-opted them to help draw their own followers into commercial activity. The mark of this was the title most frequently accorded to prominent upriver leaders: Orang Kaya, "Rich Man." Although they disdained to pay taxes, the Orang Kaya in upriver communities were agents of Brunei's trading empire in just the way that Orang Kaya Temmonggong Lawai, busy harassing the Tring in Tutoh, was its "General," complete with his own army, provided to the Sultan free of charge. Only the strangulation of Brunei's maritime trade put an end to this subtle balancing act. As St. John's account makes clear, even the warlike Kayan could have been drawn in to the system, given time. The contempt of the Brookes was self-interested; Brunei's trading empire was in its heyday an effective and humane polity.

Trade in Isolated Communities

The description of upriver trade given to St. John clearly referred to a major community, with a large population and a prominent leader. Even so, there were clearly only a handful of Brunei traders, accompanied by perhaps a dozen servants or slaves to do the rowing. So as not to be simply robbed by any passersby, Malay traders needed the protection of a chief whose name brought respect. Even then, the trip required considerable daring, and bluff was by far their most valuable weapon. Each trader had to let drop his elite connections both upriver and down. No doubt, a certain style of dress and self-presentation was called for, but there were plenty of opportunities to practice those skills in the incessant competition for status at home. Indeed, since the same bluff was required in dealing with traders from overseas, one might reasonably argue that trade was the origin of that competition.

Prior to the Kayan incursion, however, most communities in the network were smaller than the large Kayan ones in the middle Baram in the nineteenth century. Such megacommunities as Aban Jau's Long Batan, or Long Kelejeo in the lower Tutoh, did not yet exist. Instead, each was split into several longhouse communities. In those more peaceful times, Malay traders could have operated with less fanfare. There was still danger of robbery and violence, to be sure, but it was also possible to cultivate a network of customers whose interest lay in continued trade.

An example of this older pattern of trade is provided by the Lelak of the Tinjar. They had been settled since time immemorial in the same location. In contrast to just about everyone else in the Baram watershed, they have no stories of migration. By their account, the Lelak always lived on the shores of the only sizeable lake in northern Sarawak, which lies in a shallow depression separated from the Tinjar by swamps. The lake is a couple of miles wide and mostly shallow, filling slowly through the swamps when the Tinjar is in flood, and retaining water when the Tinjar is low. It is a rich eco-niche; the lake provides ample supplies of fish, while the hilly side of the lake has several pockets of fertile soil, renewed annually by flooding.

In this little Eden, the Lelak managed to remain aloof from the petty wars between lowlanders. In the mid-nineteenth century, the Kayan of the middle Baram were only twenty miles away over the hills, but had their sights trained down river and did not notice the peaceful community on their back doorstep. When the advance guard of the Sebop entered the Tinjar, they made at least one raid on the Lelak, but were foiled by the swamps. Given plenty of warning, the defenders arranged an ambush in which the attackers were routed. One might assume that their obscure location would also have removed the Lelak from trading networks, but the reverse is true: they were strategically located between indigenous populations. Before the Kayan had arrived in the middle Baram, the Lelak were in a position to conduct trade with people to the north, south, east, and west. A short river journey to the north brought them to the mouth of the Tutoh, from where it was possible to reach Brunei via the Belait stream, the same route that Low travelled in the 1870s when he visited Long Kelejeo. To the south along the river were the Berawan communities of the upper Tinjar, while to the east lay the famous birds' nests caves of Batu Gading. Finally, to the west lay a veritable highroad to the coast, for those who had eyes to see it. When the river was in flood, it was possible to paddle a canoe directly through the swamps from the Tinjar into the Bakong, and via various streams to arrive at Sibuti – the same Malay trading post that Aban Jau's men were unsuccessfully attacking when Low found him skulking in his canoe a few bends upriver from the mouth of the Tinjar.

Consequently, the Lelak were in a location to maintain contacts upriver and down. Alternatively, they were the first stop for Malay expeditions headed upriver. As a result, the Lelak people were rich not only in rice and fish, but also in beads and brassware. That wealth was still to be seen in the 1970s, on those rare occasions when people opened their strongboxes, and I was given a few minutes to marvel at what they contained.

Jungle Produce in the Colonial Era

There is a final item of jungle produce that needs to be mentioned, even though it played no part in the trading system of Brunei.

Gutta-percha is a jungle product whose exploitation began only in the colonial era. Demand for it peaked early in the twentieth century, when it was required for such purposes as insulation in electrical wiring, dentistry, and making golf balls. It was gathered from any of a dozen different trees that were felled, ring barked every few inches, and bled of their milky sap. Congealed and pressed into slabs, it was sold to Chinese traders for modest prices. An inferior variety called *jelutong* was obtained by tapping a large tree that grows abundantly in swampy jungle, and commanded even lower prices (Hose and McDougall 1912:I:151).

Despite its relatively low profitability, gutta played a crucial economic and even political role in the early colonial phase. It prompted jungle gathering on a scale never seen before. Since gutta was common enough to guarantee a return on the effort, it became feasible to go on expeditions just to obtain jungle produce. Whatever *other* produce was obtained along the way became pure profit. When that shift occurred, the old pattern of accumulating fortuitous commodities was replaced by the direct exploitation of jungle for commercial gain. It is this kind of activity that is described by Hose and McDougall (1912:I:159–67) in their discussion of "the gathering of jungle produce," but they are wrong to imply that this is an ancient pattern. On the contrary, it became possible only after colonial "pacification" made it possible to travel about harvesting commodities in this way. Moreover, as noted in Chapter 5, it was particularly young Iban men who took advantage of the new opportunity. While Brooke policy favoured the Iban, they were allowed into the territory of Upriver People, over the objections of Upriver leaders, even though they stirred up trouble wherever they went. It was because of his resistance to colonial policy on this score that Aban Jau was framed for a crime he went to great lengths not to commit, and then fined so harshly as to impoverish him.

Part IV

Longhouse Populations

Chapter 8

The Linguistic Data

In order to understand the nature of Brunei's trading system in the hinterland, the previous chapter did not discuss particular longhouse communities. The goal, however, is to understand the impact of trade on those communities, so the next step is to assemble what we know about them. What makes this difficult is the disparity in data available for those that survived the Kayan raids of the late nineteenth century compared to those that did not. For the former, I have oral histories collected in the 1970s, often rich in detail concerning longhouse sites and political relations. For the communities that failed to survive, we must fall back on historical snippets, augmented by linguistic data.

As noted in Chapter 2, there are pitfalls in using linguistic data to make inferences about ethnicity or community. Such data have the advantage of systematic methods that produce reliable results. But – and it is a big but – in central Borneo words are borrowed so freely that any simple notion of distinct linguistic isolates with near boundaries is as questionable as a similar view of cultural ones. Language diversity is the result of innovation within speech communities, but our problem is precisely that we do not know what those communities were. Meanwhile, oral histories really are about communities, so there is a danger of mixing apples and pears. Putting it another way, if I now equate ethnic and linguistic taxonomies, I defeat the purpose of my argument.

The question then is how to make use of the linguistic data without falling into this trap. My answer is that linguistic taxonomy provides a step in an argument resembling the mathematical technique of successive approximation. This method allows calculations to proceed even when the exact value of any variable is unknown, or even unknowable. It depends on there being reasonable limits that can be placed on some variables. Estimates can then be used to calculate values for other variables, which in turn can be used to recalibrate the original estimates, and so on. The technique abandons precision, but there are occasions even in mathematics when exactitude is beside the point. The metaphorical equivalent in the present case is to tack back and forth between linguistic taxonomy and oral history, seeing how each successively refines our understanding of the other.

Utility of the Linguistic Data

Since all the indigenous languages of Borneo belong to the Western branch of the Austronesian family, they display high percentages of cognate words, indicating relatively close historical relationships and frequent borrowing (Dyen 1965). At the same time, the least densely populated areas in the centre of the island manifest bewildering linguistic diversity. It is this combination of overall similarity and endless difference that makes it as difficult to segregate languages as discrete ethnicities. In these circumstances, grand taxonomies must be dealt with carefully. What is needed are fine-grained studies that get closer to the level of individual speech communities.

It is my great good fortune that just such a study was conducted in the early 1970s by Robert Blust (1972, 1974). Blust found a ready supply of intelligent and knowledgeable informants in the high schools in Miri and Marudi. The students who boarded there came from communities throughout the Baram region, so providing him with detailed information, longhouse by longhouse. Blust summarises his major finding as follows:

> It is now possible to say with a high degree of certainty that all of the coastal languages between Bintulu in the south and Tutong in the north, and all of the non-Kayan languages of the Baram are descended from a language in which the first of like vowels flanking the reflex of PAN *S was regularly lost if it followed the reflex of PAN *b, *d, *D, *j, or *Z. I used the term "North Sarawak" for this proposed subgroup. (1972:13)

His summary is admirably concise, but it needs some explanation for those not familiar with the technical language he uses. Basically, Blust found a phonetic innovation in one subgroup of Austronesian languages that marks its members out as contrasted with others deriving from their common ancestor, Proto-Austronesian (PAN). The stars before letters indicate that they are reconstructed forms, rather than ones collected from speakers of living languages. Crucially, this finding does not depend on counting numbers of cognates, as do the more general surveys of Bornean languages (Cense and Uhlenbeck 1958; Hudson 1978). Consequently, it is not vulnerable to the most common pitfall of lexicostatistics, the confusion of cognates with borrowings (Teeter 1963). Instead, it rests on the more secure basis of phonological change.

For my purposes, the most important implication of this finding is to confirm the close connection between the peoples of the Brunei hinterland, including the ancient founders of Brunei itself. Blust's vowel deletion hypothesis is not framed in historical terms, but for my benefit he conjectured (personal communication) that the ancestral speakers of proto-North Sarawak arrived on the northwest coast of Borneo some time about 1,000 BC, as one element of the wide expansion of Austronesian-speaking peoples (Bellwood 1985:116–26). From there, they evidently spread upriver and into the mountain ranges of central Borneo. This is not, of course, to suggest a creeping 3,000-year migration to the east. We simply have no way of knowing how many oscillations and counter flows there have been over such an enormous stretch of prehistory.

It is also significant that Blust specifically excludes Kayan from the North Sarawak subgroup. Alfred Hudson (1978:32–3) criticizes Blust for taking too localized a view. Far to the southwest, he argues, across the mountains in Kalimantan, the Kayan-related languages display greater variety than they do in the Baram region, with isolects that show resemblances to Kenyah languages. For my purposes, this is just the point, however: the origins of the Kayan languages lie elsewhere, well away from the hinterland of Brunei. In parts of Kalimantan, Kayan and Kenyah languages have evidently coexisted and borrowed from each other for centuries. In Sarawak, by contrast, Kayan shows a relative uniformity across many different communities – a linguistic equivalent of what is called "founder effect" in population genetics. In Sarawak, the Kayan are recent arrivals.

Blust divides the North Sarawak subgroup into four smaller subgroups that he labels (1) Kelabit – Lun Bawang – Saban, (2) Kenyah, (3) Lower Baram, and (4) Bintulu. In addition, he further subdivides Kenyah into three categories. These labels are not significant in themselves. They are a mixture of place names and ethnonyms, intended only as descriptive tags. Languages of subgroup (4) need not concern us further because they are spoken only outside the Brunei hinterland, along the coast to the southwest (Morris 1953). As for the other three subgroups, their speakers figure prominently in the hinterland, and each requires separate discussion.

Before proceeding, however, a quick sketch of the general situation may make the details more accessible. It refers to the period just before the disruptions of the mid-nineteenth century. At that time, speakers of Blust's category (1) languages were found in the watersheds of the Tutoh, Limbang, and Trusan, and off to the north and east beyond the Brunei hinterland. The majority of speakers of category (2) languages lived across the central mountain ranges in what is now Indonesian Borneo, but substantial numbers had already migrated into the Baram watershed by mid-century. Others arrived later. Category (3) languages were spoken by populations indigenous to the Baram. Some had colonised the western slopes of the Usun Apau plateau at some ancient date, but had later moved back into the Baram watershed. For ease of presentation, I reverse Blust's order, beginning with category (3).

First Component: The Lower Baram Subgroup

Blust's research shows plainly that there is a subgroup of closely related languages that are indigenous to the Baram area and found nowhere else. Clearly, the speakers of these languages were a key element in the trading system of the Brunei hinterland. Despite their linguistic cohesion, their oral histories were diverse. In the 1970s, they comprised a dozen major communities. Half of these had no traditions of having lived anywhere other than the lowlands. The others had stories of migration from the Usun Apau (Figure 02–02). For the moment, I divide them into "highlanders" and "lowlanders." It must be emphasized, however, that in making that distinction I am pursuing historical *not* linguistic data, so putting into action my strategy of tacking back and forth between the two.

The "Lowlanders"

The lowlands are a region of swamps between the long loops of meandering rivers. There is little land not prone to flooding, and consequently, agriculture is a risky business. There is good fishing, however, and a ready supply of sago palms, whose pith furnishes a starch that was the staple of many indigenous coastal populations. The oral histories of communities in this region make it clear that they lived in independent longhouse communities that often squabbled among themselves. There was, for instance, friction between the relatively numerous and aggressive Narom people, who lived at various sites along the main Baram upriver from the junction with the Bakong River, and smaller populations "inside" the Bakong itself.

The latter organised an alliance and routed the Narom at a place still called Bukit Sa'ong ("Bloody Mountain"). The descendents of this alliance in the 1970s and 1980s used at least three ethnonyms. The Bakong lived near the tiny upriver bazaar of Sibuti. The Dali' lived in three small villages outside the small town of Bekenu, and the Miri lived in several villages in and around the bustling city of Miri on the coast (Zainah 1982). The Lelak people had close ties with the Bakong, but their location further inland allowed them to stay out of the feuds with the Narom. Their traditions tell of continuous residence near the only substantial lake in northern Sarawak, Loagan Bunut, which provided rich fishing.

What these narratives indicate is the scattered nature of subcoastal communities and their relative lack of contact with other populations. There was some intermarriage with small groups of Penan foragers, especially around Niah. On the coast itself, there were small, widely separated Malay villages. The nearest longhouse-dwelling peoples were further inland.

The "Highlanders"

The other components of the Lower Baram cohesion tell stories of living in the mountainous interior. In the 1970s, there were four large Berawan communities, one Long Kiput, and a scattering of small longhouses (Blust 1992,1998). Berawan migration stories begin on the western edge of the Usun Apau, not far from the homeland of the Sebop, as described in Chapter 2. Robert Blust (personal communication) suggested to me that these stories might have been fabricated in imitation of Kenyah narratives. In my experience, however, Berawan are not at all dismayed to be called un-Kenyah. On the contrary, they insist that there were no Kenyah in the Usun Apau when their ancestors lived there, and this claim is consistent Herbert Whittier's (1978:92–3) account of Kenyah migrations. Moreover, there is physical evidence of their presence adjacent to the Usun Apau, in the form of graveyards, with their distinctive monuments. These were pointed out to me in the headwaters of the Dapoi stream by Penan living locally. Longhouse sites could also be distinguished because of the fruit trees and areca palms long ago planted in front of them.

As the Berawan moved away from the Usun Apau, they split into two parties. One went north via the Dapoi into the valley of the Tinjar. The other went east via the Silat, before turning north along the Baram itself (Figure 01-01). This left the two on opposite sides of the Usun Apau, and that separation is still reflected in linguistic divergence. It would be a mistake, however, to overdramatize their departure from the Usun Apau. The ancestral Berawan lived in a world of small streams running out of a limestone massif. No great significance was attached to movements within this environment, whether north or east.

There is another population of "highlanders" who speak languages closely related to Berawan ones, the Long Kiput. They also claim the Usun Apau as their homeland, but their migration stories begin with them already settled in the Baram (Belawing Tingang 1974).

After abandoning the Usun Apau, these populations slowly moved down river, but not in one step. Instead, migration stories tell of favourite sites occupied, abandoned, and reoccupied a generation later. The mid-nineteenth century found one party of the Berawan in the upper Tinjar, and the other, together with the Long Kiput, in the middle reaches of the Baram. The former comprised four communities situated between Long Bok and Long Dunin, whereas the latter were at least three communities between Long Tutoh and Long Laput.

Second Component: The Lun Bawang Subgroup

At the same epoch, there were in the Brunei hinterland many speakers of the "Kelabit–Lun Bawang-Saban" subgroup of North Sarawak languages. I describe them by location.

The Tutoh Region

Beginning with the Tutoh, the aboriginal population is described in the colonial records as Tring, but by the time Charles Brooke finally annexed the region they were already a ghostly presence (Harrison 1956). What I can add comes mainly from Berawan narratives, which describe a numerous and warlike people, who gave no respect to the Sultan's representatives and often preyed on neighbouring Lower Baram peoples. They lived in relatively small longhouse communities as far up the Tutoh as the first rapids, and also in a major tributary, the Apoh. As evidence, I was shown ancient Tring graveyards in both Tutoh and Apoh, recognizable by the fragments of large jars used for primary storage of corpses. These were of Chinese manufacture, mostly with a dark brown glaze, and they had been cut at the shoulder to allow insertion of the corpse. The same practice occurred in Berawan communities, but the Tring cemeteries were well away from any known Berawan sites, and had been discovered only by accident during hunting expeditions. Some were in deep jungle, confirming a report that the Tring often preferred to live some distance inland from major watercourses.

Berawan narratives give no details, however, of the locations of particular Tring communities, evidently because their encounters were predominantly hostile. While they were still getting established, the newly arrived Berawan were kept on the defensive by Tring raids, and there were skirmishes between war parties from both sides near the mouth of the Tutoh, a location that controlled the trade routes from Brunei into Baram. The initiative in this struggle gradually passed to the Berawan, who organised an effective alliance. Under increasing attack, the Tring abandoned the lower Tutoh. When a party of Berawan moved as far upriver as the Melanau stream, the Tring were left with no safe refuge. The Sultan was so pleased to see his ancient enemies defeated that he invested the Berawan leader with the prestigious title of Temonggong, which we might translate as "General" (Brown 1970:109). In Berawan history, the Orang Kaya Temonggong Lawai cuts as large a figure as his contemporary, Aban Jau. What the Berawan began, the Kayan completed, but the Sultan handed out no titles to Kayan leaders. As we have seen, he had every reason to prefer his old enemies to his new ones.

The Limbang Region

Throughout the colonial literature, the indigenous peoples of the Limbang watershed are described as "Murut." This followed Brunei usage, but it mistook a descriptive term for an ethnic label. It means nothing more than "hill people" – the people that live in the hills rather than on the plains. As a way of classifying populations, it is not much different to Orang Ulu or "Upriver People," a phrase that in the twentieth century came to be applied to everyone in the hinterland of Brunei who was not Moslem ("Malay"), Chinese, or Iban. How this ragbag category became an ethnic group is described in Chapter 14, but for the moment the point is that the category Murut covered even more ethnic diversity than does Upriver People (Pollard 1933). After all, it hardly mattered to the nobility of Brunei what precisely their subject – and not so subject – peoples called themselves. The problem was that European observers took Murut to refer to a "tribe," and then were confounded to find fundamental differences of custom within it. There is in fact no ethnological mystery: the northern limit of Blust's North Sarawak subgroup lies not far up the coast from Brunei, and the languages found beyond that boundary have very different connections. As David Prentice (1970) has shown, they belong to the Idahan family of the North Indonesian branch of Austronesian, as found in the Philippines, in contrast to West Indonesian branch of Austronesian, found in much of the rest of Borneo. That a Brunei ethnic label should casually hop across so profound a linguistic divide is yet another example, were it needed, of the disconnect between linguistic taxonomy and ethnicity. It makes perfect sense, however, in terms of the structure of the Brunei state.

To avoid this confusion, Blust uses the term "Lun Bawang." The phrase turns out to mean nothing more than "people (*lun*) from here" (Crain 1970:30), but it is now used as an autonym by people throughout Sarawak's Fifth Division (Deegan 1973:23). The other peoples referred to as "Murut" live in the neighbouring Malaysian state of Sabah. Since that is outside the region that I am calling the hinterland of Brunei, I can now dispense with the troublesome term "Murut" entirely. From this point on it appears only in quotations from Brunei observers of the nineteenth-century scene. Even without it, however, we must still reckon with linguistic variation within the population that now calls itself Lun Bawang. Unfortunately, Blust's main emphasis was on Baram isolects, and he had only a few informants from Limbang. Meanwhile, the opinions of local people cannot be relied on. I was often told by informants that two mutually unintelligible languages were "the same," when what they really meant was that they had spoken both since they were children. Add to that the degree of borrowing between people living in neighbouring longhouses, or even the same longhouse, and only the most careful linguistic fieldwork can be expected to produce reliable results.

Sticking then to generalities, before the Kayan raids, Lun Bawang people occupied the whole Limbang River, including side streams such as the Medamit and Madihit, right up into the headwaters of the Adang. This is not to imply, however, that they enjoyed the same lifestyle. Reading between the lines of colonial reports like those of St. John and Low, it appears that some Lun Bawang communities were firmly integrated into the Brunei polity. The nearest, after all, were only a few miles from the capital, across a shallow lagoon at the western edge of Brunei Bay. They belonged to the appanages of Brunei noblemen, but also had leaders of their own who lived in a certain style and could even assert precedence over lesser Brunei aristocrats. Commoners lived in longhouses, but richer Lun Bawang evidently lived in Malay-style houses. It is significant that place names are often specified as Pengkalan X, where *pengkalan* means a pier or jetty, and X is the name of a leading man. Much the same was true of the Lun Bawang in the small Temburong River on the southern end of Brunei Bay.

In contrast, the Lun Bawang that St. John visited in the Adang spoke of Brunei in almost mythic terms: "it would appear incredible – the awe and fear inspired by the Sultan and his nobles in former times; and the idea was universal that the Bornean government was the greatest and most powerful in the world" (1862:II:106–7). St. John was interested in dispelling the myth, but found that difficult, paradoxically because the people in the Adang had so little first-hand experience with Brunei or Bruneians. St. John found their houses cramped, but he estimates fifty families in one (i.e., fifty "rooms"). He reports finding many beads, but not much brassware (St. John 1862:II:104–5). Between these extremes of sophistication and naïveté, subjection and autonomy, there must have been considerable variation in the middle reaches of the river. In addition, we know that people there offered outsiders a variety of ethnonyms. Since they were quite prepared to go along with the classification imposed by Brunei, they would have readily assented to being "Murut" just as longhouse people in the Baram are now content to be called Orang Ulu. They would not have produced the currently acceptable label Lun Bawang because it had yet to be used with the force of an ethnonym (Langub 1991). There are to this day people in Limbang who insist that they are Adang, not Lun Bawang. What they are saying, plainly enough, is that they are *not* "from here." Naming according to other home tributaries was frequent, even after Kayan raids had forced the abandonment of them. Finally, there were the familiar identifications with particular house sites, past and present. Unfortunately, it was even in the 1970s too late to obtain a comprehensive list of these.

In addition, there were communities in the lower Limbang that did not speak languages of the Lun Bawang subgroup, of which the most important were the Visaya, or Bisaya (Sandin 1977). Visaya is an Idahan language, and most of its speakers live in Sabah, where most are now Moslem. The Visaya of Limbang, however, stoutly resisted conversion, so maintaining their structural position within the Brunei polity. In the twentieth century, they rejected Christianity in the same way, and may ironically have been some of the last people in the Brunei hinterland to maintain their ancestral religions, despite the fact that they lived even closer to the capital than most Lun Bawang. Their villages were riverine, and where longhouses existed they were small, between four and ten doors. Villages were named for their jetties, or *pengkalan*, and it was undoubtedly from the Visaya that the Lun Bawang acquired the same practice. Indeed, the two peoples evidently lived side by side along the densely populated lowest reaches of the Limbang. One of their ethnonyms neatly matches the Lun Bawang usage: Jilama Bawang means simply people (*jilama*) from here (Bewsher 1959; Peranio 1972). Together their settlements made up what can be thought of as the suburbs of Brunei, and that makes even more shocking their deliverance by the devious Makota into the hands of the murderous Kayan in 1856, as described in Chapter 6.

Trusan, Lawas, and Beyond

Populations speaking Blust's "Lun Bawang" languages are not restricted to the Limbang watershed, however. As St. John discovered, the hills that divide the headwaters of the Adang from those of the Trusan were a haven rather than a barrier, and he saw plainly the cultural discontinuities as he travelled across them. The same is true in descending the Trusan and crossing over again into the Lawas watershed. In short, the people who now call themselves Lun Bawang comprise a large number of communities spread out over a considerable area. Before the Kayan raids of the mid-nineteenth century, there may have been even more, but the ethnographic record is insufficient to say much about their internal differences. Moreover, in the mid-twentieth century, almost all of them were converted to a fundamentalist variety of Christianity brought by Australian missionaries of the Borneo Evangelical Mission. This has suppressed many cultural differences and political cleavages. What we know from the colonial archives is that the populations of these watersheds were infamous for their incessant feuding and petty warfare, and this feature made them vulnerable to Kayan depredations.

Heading further into the interior, we find other speakers of Blust's "Kelabit – Lun Bawang – Saban" languages. Beyond the headwaters of both the Limbang and the Trusan lies a plateau intersected by small streams and with many fertile niches. By chance, an early European encounter occurred with people living in a tiny stream in the far headwaters of the Tutoh called the Labid. Asked who they were, they identified themselves simply as Pa ("people of") Labid. This was corrupted into "Kelabit," and that label was then extended to all nearby communities (Harrisson 1959:182). The effect was to make it look as if there was a neat ethnic boundary running around the plateau, with one tribe inside and another outside. Needless to say, that was an illusion. There is neither uniformity within, nor any sharp cultural disjuncture with neighbouring Lun Bawang communities. Considered as an element in the trading system of Brunei, the people of the Kelabit plateau were remote. Undoubtedly, they obtained such valuables as beads and ceramics, but there is no evidence of trading expeditions to anywhere inside "the Sultan's fence." Brunei traders knew nothing about them. Fundamentally, the people of the plateau were not riverine, and even in the 1970s, many of them resisted the label Orang Ulu or "Upriver People." From the point of view of the analysis offered here, they are marginal.

The last element in Blust's formula can be dealt with rapidly: the Saban constitute a tiny population on the far side of what is now the Sarawak-Kalimantan border (Clayre 1972). They are not relevant here. Moreover, if it had not been for the Kayan depredations, Blust would probably have labelled his linguistic subgroup "Tring – Lun Bawang – Kelabit," and that would better represent the important populations in the early nineteenth century.

Third Component: The Kenyah Subgroup

The Lower Baram and Lun Bawang languages are largely restricted to the Brunei hinterland – not so the Kenyah ones. On the contrary, the majority of Kenyah speakers live across the central mountain range in what is now Indonesian Kalimantan. There are also Kenyah communities to the south in the Balui region. Since my concern is only with the Kenyah of the Brunei hinterland, we thankfully need not deal with the daunting complexity of the signification of "Kenyah" as an ethnic label throughout central Borneo. Instead, I focus on the half dozen communities already established in Baram before 1830, that is, the beginning of the Kayan incursion. These early Kenyah immigrants were isolated from the major centres of Kenyah population in the Apo Kayan region of Kalimantan for long enough to take on a separate identity. Rousseau (1990:16) reports that Kenyah arriving in the twentieth century described themselves as Lepo Buau, or "real Kenyah," reproducing the implied inferiority to which the Sebop were subjected. This repeated contestation of authenticity is a measure of Kenyah diversity. Meanwhile, the early Kenyah immigrants into the Baram have an expression that groups them together with their long-standing Berawan and Long Kiput neighbours. They call themselves Lepo Pu'un, which we might gloss as "owners of the land" (*pu'un*, Berawan *puwong*, meaning "to own"). In addition, the Berawan describe these Kenyah as Lepo Umbo (*lepo* meaning literally house, *umbo* meaning root). We might gloss the phrase as "Kenyah with roots here."

Blust's linguistic findings fit neatly with indigenous accounts. His taxonomy distinguishes three subgroups within the Kenyah languages, of which the third corresponds to the Lepo Umbo. Their separation from the Lepo Buau may indeed predate migration into Baram. Herb Whittier (1978:93) reports that most Kenyah trace their origin to an area lying between the headwaters of the Iwan, Bahau, and Pajungan rivers. Some of these people later moved into the Usun Apau, but only after the Lepo Umbo had already moved on into Baram. This is consistent with Berawan claims that they were in touch with Lepo Umbo communities on the eastern side of the Usun Apau when they themselves lived on the western side. As migrants moved into the main valley of the Baram, they formed defensive alliances, which were later put to the test in the long war with the Tring. In particular, the people of Long Ikang were close neighbours and allies of the Long Kiput and

Berawan. In a manner now familiar, the Long Ikang Kenyah refer to themselves as either Long Sebatu or Long Ulai, recalling former communities where their ancestors had thrived. Meanwhile, the people now associated with Long San, who call themselves Long Tikan, stayed further upriver beyond the rapids. During the first years of the Brooke Raj in Baram, their chief, the famous Tama Bulan Wang, gave Charles Hose invaluable help in making peace, and so established his pre-eminence in the region. The prestige of his community and family persisted until the 1950s, when his grandnephew, Oyong Lawai Jau, became the first Temonggong appointed by the British in Baram District. In addition, Long Sela'an is a community in the upper Baram closely allied to Long San, while the people of Long Dunin migrated into the Tinjar sometime in the 1920s.

Blust's second Kenyah subgroup corresponds to the Lepo Buau, or "real Kenyah," as represented in the Baram watershed. If we extend our view across the mountains, we would see related communities stretching away to the east and south, across a large slice of central Borneo. What linguistic diversity there is among them is not known in detail, and much research remains to be done, if the destruction of the timber boom has not made it too late.

Finally, Blust's last Kenyah subgroup is already familiar because it is discussed in Chapter 2. It comprises the Sebop, Lirong, Long Wat, and their cousins who lived on the southern slopes of the Usun Apau, before Aban Jau arrived in Tinjar and before the Great Kayan Expedition of 1863. So, we come full circle – from the generalities of linguistic classification to the specifics of communities and their diverse histories.

Chapter 9

Disease, Slavery, Assimilation, Annihilation

The survey in Chapter 8 provides an overview of the populations that were involved in the trading network in the hinterland while it was still functioning, but many puzzles remain. It is difficult to be certain of even the most basic demographic issues, such as the approximate size of the populations involved.

Epidemics and Community Size

To hear people tell it in the 1970s, there was a previous epoch when longhouse populations were far larger. Repeatedly, I was told that in the old days when the women went to fetch water, the river would be reduced to a mere trickle. The implication was not that all communities were larger in the past, but that the one I was visiting had held a dominant place in the region. Their current reduced circumstances were explained as the result of disasters that caused heavy loss of life, so that what I saw was only a remnant of their former glory. Some disasters were caused by provoking kraken-like monsters that live at the bottom of the river. Others had to do with breach of a taboo, so that a longhouse and its inhabitants were turned to stone. In the muddy lowlands, there are only a few places where river erosion has exposed rocky outcroppings, and each is associated with a petrified longhouse.

It is easy to dismiss such boasting, but there may be some truth behind the myths. We know that epidemics of cholera and smallpox devastated some communities in the nineteenth century. In Chapter 2, we see that the Lirong branch of the Sebop was reduced by smallpox from major players in Baram politics, as it was when Hose held his peacemaking at Marudi in 1890 (Hose and McDougall 1912:II:293), to a community so small that it was advised by a district officer in 1909 to merge with others in Tinjar (*Sarawak Gazette* 530:April 1909). When visited by the Oxford Expedition of 1955, they stubbornly maintained their independence, while acknowledging their decline after the epidemic (Arnold 1959:173). Because smallpox was for centuries only a minor inconvenience in Europe and is now eradicated worldwide, it is easy to forget the appalling toll that it took on populations lacking previous exposure. Sheldon Watts (1997:84–121) not only documents its major role in the destruction of the indigenous peoples of the New World, but he also describes an outbreak in Scotland in 1720 that killed off most of the inhabitants of a remote fishing village. Its vulnerability was a result of nothing more than avoiding contact with the disease for a few generations. This case makes it easy to imagine how communities in the remote interior of Borneo could vary considerably in their response to smallpox epidemics. If some were decimated while others were not, the result would be rapid changes in the ethnic composition of a region. Presumably, this had been the case for centuries, so that epidemics constituted a wild card constantly disrupting the political game. Moreover, this could work in two ways: communities that avoided outside contacts might escape contagion altogether, but by the same token they failed to develop immunities that would defend them from catastrophic mortality at a later date. The Lirong may be a case in point because they had evidently managed to have hostile relations with just about everyone in Baram.

It is possible, however, that the *volkerwanderung* of the nineteenth century exacerbated the impact of epidemics. When Kayan raiders sacked down river villages, they may well have brought back new diseases along with their slaves. After his trip up the Baram in 1876 as far as the first rapids, Low reported:

> I next proceeded up the Baram as far as long Lusan, where Oyong Ngau now lives. He abandoned Batu Gadin on account of the smallpox, which carried off 200 persons in his own house; 1,888 are estimated to have fallen victims to this epidemic, and 8,000 Keniahs. Although I did not ascend the river above this point, I met several of the upriver chiefs, both Kyans and Keniahs, and among the latter, Paran Libut's brother Tama Peng Wang, who assured me that his tribe had been decimated, and that the upper Baram, which before was populous, was now a mere waste. Houses which a year ago could boast of

100 fighting men can now scarcely muster 10. Fortunately for the Kyans there was a Selimbu Malay, one Haji Unus, at Batu Gadin at the time, who understood inoculation, and did inoculate some 3,600 persons of both sexes, and though many died, many also were saved. (*Sarawak Gazette* 122:August 1876)

This account has several interesting features. Mainly, there is the oddly precise number given for Kayan casualties; one wonders who was doing the counting. In contrast, the estimate of Kenyah deaths must be a wild exaggeration. At the time, there could only have been a handful of communities in the upper Baram, and 8,000 Kenyah deaths would surely have annihilated the Lepo Umbo. What need not be doubted is the relative weakening of the Kenyah in Baram versus the Kayan. Finally, we note that there was a Malay resident in Oyong Ngau's community public spirited enough to spend a lot of time and effort to inoculate thousands of people, and trusted enough that he was allowed to do so. This hints at the degree to which Malays could be integrated into upriver communities: Haji Unus was not a government employee, he was a trader. His established position at Batu Gadin constituted what in Chapter Eight was called an "advanced base" of the Brunei trade network.

The difficulty of assessing the impact of epidemics prior to the beginning of historical records would seem to undermine all accounts of the ethnic composition of the Brunei hinterland, were it not for the stubbornly communal nature of oral history. We need to take account of the possibility that relatively small communities may once have been larger, as the myths claimed, but it is less likely that multiple communal narratives were collapsed into one. For instance, a cycle of Berawan stories recount the adventures of the folk hero Anak Tau, the Orphan Boy, who created major geographical features and originated the practice of bird augury. As a child, however, he was mistreated by the commoners, so that he later cursed them, and they died off. Only the aristocrats survived, I was told, meaning that every apartment in the existing longhouse represented a separate longhouse in former times. This myth neatly justified the proposition that all Berawan were aristocrats, but I did not collect a different migration story in each longhouse apartment. There were variants indicating all manner of fission and fusion, but not thirty or forty or more. The oral histories of the Berawan of Tinjar summarised in Chapter 4 show plainly enough that there were times when they were collected in one longhouse community and others when they were spread between four, or dispersed in farmhouses, but there is no suggestion that the Tinjar was ever lined with dozens of Berawan longhouses. Moreover, most reported longhouse sites can be associated with a graveyard, and this serves as a further check on inflated numbers of communities.

Oral histories provide a check on exaggeration, but early estimates of population remain suspect. Just after his account of the effects of the smallpox epidemic in the Baram, Low remarks that the population of the region had previously been overestimated. He was referring to the figures given by St. John, who had visited the same Kayan communities in the middle Baram. St. John describes his discussions about Kayan aggression with a leader named Tama Wan:

> He declared, however, that his great village, and twenty-one others, were averse to the practice of headhunting, but that over twenty eight other villages he had no influence. The above forty-nine villages he went over by name, and mentioned likewise the principal chief in each. They assert that a village was considered small that had only a handful of families, while a large one contained four hundred. If we may judge from the account he gave of the town opposite which we had anchored, he must have underrated considerably. He said this contained two hundred families; but after going over the numbers in each village-house, we came to the conclusion that there were at least five hundred families at Longusin. But as long as headhunting is considered an honourable pursuit, and the acquisition of Murut slaves enables the chiefs to live without labour, it will be impossible to put a stop to their forays. (St. John 1862:I:104–5)

Unfortunately, St. John did not record the list of communities reeled off by Tama Wan.

The total is not unreasonable, if we assume that the twenty one over which he claimed "influence" were those in the middle and upper Baram, and the remaining twenty-eight were those in Tinjar and Tutoh. Nor is it unreasonable that he knew such detail – that was after all his business as leader and statesman. Moreover, Tama Wan acknowledges that longhouse communities vary greatly in size. Consequently, Low's scepticism concerns population totals, and Tama Wan's arithmetic skills certainly did not extend that far. Hose remarks that his great Kenyah ally, Tama Bulan Wang, was unique among upriver chiefs in being able to use an abacus, and so keep an accurate tally of his transactions. Others could do no better than piling up the goods to be traded side by side (Hose and McDougall 1912:II: 211).

Instead of estimating populations, Low gives his own list of the "peoples" found in the various rivers. Gratifyingly, it largely matches the survey offered in Chapter 8, so that the main point comes through clearly enough: oral history in the Brunei hinterland is the history of longhouse communities. Their fortunes may rise and fall, but they remain the central actors in the historical drama, the main loci of trade, and the focus of our attention.

Relations with Brunei

There is another story that is as common in the lowlands as that of the women draining the river dry, and it concerns a mystical battle against the Sultan of Brunei. The stories begin with the Sultan demanding tribute. The community in question shows its contempt for this demand by sending him the severed head of a pig. The Sultan responds by bewitching all the wild boar in the region and making them attack the longhouse. The significance of this is that Upriver People claim no expertise at magic; on the contrary, it is coastal Moslem people who are the origin of *ilmu*, "knowledge," taken as synonymous with secret knowledge. In the 1970s, it was Kedayan who had the greatest reputation for magic, so that longhouse people occasionally went to Kedayan villages to purchase spells. In previous epochs, it was the Sultan himself who monopolized magic, so that he appears in upriver stories as a kind of grand wizard. Made frenzied by his spells, the boars attack the pilings of the longhouse and have almost succeeded in pushing it over when they in turn are attacked and driven off by snakes – or sometimes by one huge supernatural snake, or an alliance of snakes and crocodiles. This episode is best understood in connection with a whole genre of myths concerning animals, but for present purposes suffice it to say that this battle manifests a balance in nature echoing that in society. By an inverse logic, the Sultan can control pigs because they are taboo to him, but he can not control other wild animals, who take the side of Upriver People. As a corollary, the story explains the origin of blow-dart poison, which is prepared from the sap of a tree, *Antiaris toxicaria* (Hose and McDougall 1912:I:218). Supposedly, the snake(s) bit the posts of the longhouse by mistake, which then sprouted into trees that ever after contained the snake's venom.

What is of note here, however, is the social balance expressed in the story between the power of the Sultan, projected upriver beyond his physical control, and the ability of upriver communities to maintain their autonomy. Of course, the Sultan's magic is the charm of commodities, through which he manipulates the activities even of people outside his "fence." The reaction of the latter is passive; they are saved, as it were, by the jungle itself. What could more neatly express the nature of fortuitous commodities?

In practical terms, the socioeconomic balance lay between exploitation and reward, and not only between upriver communities and Brunei traders. Within communities, the profits of trade were not shared equally. On the contrary, the only durable imports – brassware, beads, and ceramics – were monopolized by elites, and indeed served to define those elites. That others were induced to contribute their gleanings of jungle produce, and to join laborious and dangerous down river expeditions, for marginal gain, attests to the attraction of manufactured goods.

Slavery and Assimilation: The Limits on Exploitation

Upriver leaders were not uniformly successful in dominating trade, however. Even Kayan chiefs like Tama Wan, who had many slaves, could not produce fortuitous commodities on command. Slave labour could not be applied in the manner of plantation owners in the American South. Certainly, slaves enabled a Kayan chief to live, as St. John remarks, without working himself. But he had no way of feeding them, apart from a few domestic slaves, other than to set them up as farmers in their own right. Undoubtedly, he would relieve them promptly of anything valuable they happened to find in the jungle, but he could not exploit them directly. There was no Borneo equivalent of the brutal regimes that Michael Taussig (1987) describes in the South American jungle. Forced labour could be set to work there finding rubber because wild rubber trees all produce latex, even though they are spaced far apart in the jungle. The same was not true of the jungle products basic to the trading system of Brunei. Consequently, a Kayan leader had nothing to gain from brutality toward his war prisoners, and captives had every incentive to forget their ancestry and integrate themselves as rapidly as possible into their new communities. In other words, slavery led to assimilation, and the coverage of ethnic labels expanded and contracted accordingly.

Although limited, the exploitation possible for Kayan chiefs exceeded what other leaders could manage. In comparison, Aban Jau had only patchy success in browbeating his Sebop and Berawan followers into paying "taxes" on their independent trade, whatever claims to "exercising authority over the country of Tinjar" were advertised on the door to his room. Meanwhile, the circumstances of Kenyah chiefs in the upper Baram, such as Tama Bulan Wang, were different again: having had no part in raiding down river, he lacked slaves, or at least any large number of slaves. Moreover, the defensive location of his community in the remote and rocky Akah River meant long journeys to the nearest source of trade, but these circumstances only honed the organisational skills that he later put to such good use, simultaneously aiding Charles Hose's project of "pacification" and making his community paramount among the Lepo Umbo in the upper Baram.

Assimilation without Conquest

That slavery should act to create ethnic unity rather than bitter division is a paradox for anyone familiar with the history of the United States, but it was not the only process of assimilation evident in the hinterland of Brunei. A good example is provided by the Lelak – one of those groups of "lowlanders" described in Chapter 8 who had stayed in the same locality since time immemorial.

Even though the Lelak escaped the attentions of their Kayan neighbours in the late nineteenth century, their leaders were quite aware of their vulnerability. Consequently, they were quick to throw in their lot with the Brooke Raj and hastened to assist successive district officers in their efforts at "pacification." The key man in this diplomacy was Orang Kaya Luwak, who played a role in Tinjar resembling Tama Bulan Wang's in the upper Baram. During the tense period when Aban Jau was announcing that he was "the Rajah who exercises authority over the country of Tinjar," Orang Kaya Luwak avoided confrontation. He kept channels of communication open, and when a punitive expedition against Aban Jau was discussed, he urged moderation. Undoubtedly, he found the prospect of a Kayan war party in the Tinjar thoroughly alarming. Even if they were supposedly under Brooke control, the Kayan just might conclude that the Lelak were followers of Aban Jau, with disastrous results. Instead, Orang Kaya Luwak promoted diplomacy and, on several occasions, escorted district officers in their trips upriver.

Orang Kaya Luwak's willingness to aid the Raj led the Lelak people to move for the first time away from the banks of their treasured lake. At Hose's request, they moved their longhouse down to the banks of the Tinjar, to the mouth of a small stream that connected with the lake, the Teru. Hose's goal was to have a place to stop on his way up the Tinjar and, more important, a chance to change his crew of paddlers, letting the first return to Marudi. Consequently, the Long Teru people maintained their cosmopolitan sophistication, in touch with communities both upriver and down. A half century later, Luwak's successor Lawai became Penghulu (government-appointed chief) with authority over the people of Tinjar – so achieving what for Aban Jau had been a mere boast (Metcalf 2002:71–6).

This triumph came too late, however, to save the Lelak community. In comparison with others in the Baram watershed, it had always been small and declined further in the 1920s. Just why this was so is not clear, although it also occurred in other small ethnic groups at the same time. There were rumours of the abuse of abortifacients, used to save the parents of unmarried daughters from the embarrassment of an unwanted pregnancy, but no one could explain why this had occurred during the 1920s and not before. Whatever the reason, in the 1970s, old people remembered a time when the longhouse was oddly quiet and lacking life, and genealogies show many childless women. Ironically, the Lelak survived the genocidal warfare of the nineteenth century, only to succumb to barrenness in the twentieth.

In the face of impending extinction, Lelak leaders took drastic measures. They invited settlers to come from a Berawan community in the lower Tutoh where an internal rivalry was already causing a split. The tactic was effective in reviving the fortunes of Long Teru, but at the cost of assimilation. Lelak was spoken only at Long Teru, whereas Berawan could be used all along the Tinjar and Tutoh. Consequently, Lelak gradually lost ground to Berawan, until by the 1970s it had virtually disappeared. Only in some ritual contexts did the Lelak heritage remain important. In practical terms, Long Teru became a Berawan community. Intermarriage soon made it impossible to isolate any "pure" Lelak population, and as an ethnicity it became an empty category, a name only.

Missing Pieces of the Network: The Lemeting and Pelutan

The Lelak case is intriguing because it closes a circle. In Chapter 2, we see an ethnonym come into existence. After Aban Jau put together his alliance, the name Long Batan stopped being the name of a place and became the name of a people, a people who were both Berawan and Sebop, and neither Berawan nor Sebop. The reverse process went on at Long Teru: an ethnicity fading away by degrees like the Cheshire cat.

Other ethnicities disappeared more suddenly. For instance, we simply do not know what people it was that were destroyed in the Kayan attack described in Chapter 5. St. John's account (1862:I:90–2) came from the Brunei nobleman Makota, and he paints a graphic picture: the stockade breached by treachery, the longhouse set alight, and people cut down as they fled or dragged off into slavery. Makota refers to these people as "Murut," his catch-all category for non-Moslem subjects of Brunei, but there were no Lun Bawang in what St. John calls "the Blait country."

The Belait is a small river, flowing directly into the sea just to the east of the Baram River mouth. Being relatively isolated, it repeatedly provided a refuge for people fleeing violence in the lower reaches of the Baram itself. The population is now Moslem, but they have stories of upriver origin. For example, a remnant of the once numerous Lemeting arrived there sometime in the eighteenth century. At Long Teru, the ethnonym survived only as the Berawan name for the Tinjar, and I was assured that the people themselves had died out long before in the face of Berawan military superiority – a case of "highlanders" destroying "lowlanders," to use the terms coined in Chapter 8. So hazy were the Lemeting that I took them to be as mythic as the race of charcoal eaters described in Lelak legend, and I was surprised to learn years later that there are still people in the Belait calling themselves Lemeting (Martin 1990). Consequently, Lemeting persists as an autonym, even if seldom used, and that marginal persistence points to the possibility that there were other communities speaking Lower Baram languages that disappeared entirely during the nineteenth century. If so, there may once have been a series of small communities similar to the Lelak comprising links in the Brunei trading network throughout the lower reaches of the Baram, Tinjar, and Tutoh. That is, it may once have been a more elaborate and coherent network than it appears in retrospect.

From the opposite end of the Baram, the Pelutan provide another example of the same phenomenon. They are nowhere mentioned in the ethnographic literature, for the good reason that they disappeared long ago. They figure only in the migration stories of one branch of the Berawan, but the river from which they took their name is still on the map. They are described as simple folk, relying mostly on wild sago and plentiful game for a living. Lingering in the neighbourhood for a generation or two, the Berawan intermarried with them, so the story goes, and assimilated them in much the same way as the Lelak at Long Teru. Like the Lelak, the Pelutan lacked traditions of previous residence in the Usun Apau, but they were not geographically far from it because the Pelutan stream flows into the Baram well above the first rapids. Consequently, the former existence of the Pelutan people suggests that there may have been more continuity between the populations of "highlanders" and "lowlanders" than now appears, and less distinction between agricultural and foraging adaptations. There may have been communities speaking Lower Baram languages along the entire length of the river, facilitating trade connections from the coast to the mountains.

Dispersal and Assimilation: The Tring and Tabun

Lelak and Pelutan persist as names, at least. About the different communities that together constituted the Tring, we know next to nothing. Reports from Brunei, colonial records, and Berawan oral histories all agree that the Tring were once numerous and occupied multiple sites throughout the watershed of the Tutoh. It is a safe assumption that these communities generated ethnonyms in a fashion similar to Aban Jau's Long Batan, but those names disappeared along with the Tring themselves. Their Berawan and Kayan enemies certainly had no reason to remember them.

The only partial exception is the Tabun. St. John (1862:II:53–4) reports that they were the first people in the Limbang watershed attacked by Kayan raiders, which is what we would expect given that they lived in the Medalam, directly in the path of war parties coming from the Baram via Tutoh and Melinau. Previously, they themselves had raided into Brunei territory, indicating that they lived outside "the Sultan's fence." After the Kayan attacks, however, they had reason to regret hostile relations with their Lun Bawang cousins. St. John tells of an incident near his house in Brunei, while he was serving as British consul, when his servants saw two hapless Tabun running away from a party of "Muruts" evidently intent on murdering them (St. John 1862:II:173). He took it as yet another sign of the collapse of all civil order, even at the capital itself. In addition to all this violence, Benedict Sandin (1980:189) reports that they were badly hit by the cholera epidemic of 1888. By the 1980s, there were only a handful of people claiming Tabun descent, in a longhouse in Medalam dominated by Iban immigrants (Abdul 1984).

In Sarawak, I have been asked by government officers whether the Tabun were part of the Tring or a separate "tribe," but there is no answer to that question. We simply do not know how the ethnonym was used prior to the holocaust of the nineteenth century. Nor can linguistic taxonomy shed any light on the issue. Blust (1984) shows plainly enough that Tring fits within his "Kelabit–Lun Bawang–Saban" subfamily of North Sarawak languages, but we do not know what dialect variation previously occurred within Tring isolects or how Tabun related to them. For present purposes, the point is that we have instances of ethnonyms becoming defunct, by degrees losing relevance and fading out of memory.

What became of the Tring/Tabun population is clear enough, however. Those who survived the Kayan raids became slaves; were assimilated to the language, culture, and society of their masters; and so increased the population of Kayan. Because that in turn enabled yet bigger Kayan war parties, we have a positive feedback effect that caused demographic shifts on the same scale as epidemics.

Persistence under New Names: The Bitokala, Lakipo, Kapita, and Belubo'

In addition to outright extinction, ethnonyms change in response to changing external political circumstances. That is, they are modified so that they sound like proper names to other people. Examples are provided by the ethnonyms used of and by the "highlanders" among the Lower Baram speakers.

In the 1970s, there was a Berawan community at a place in the lower Tutoh called *Batu Belah*, and so labelled on many maps. The name looks innocuous enough, meaning something like "split rocks" in Malay. When I asked where the rocks were, however, I was told that they were far away in the upper Baram and that, properly speaking, they were not "split" but red.

Making any sense of this required a full recitation of their migrations, from which I learned that their ancestors lived at one point in the turbulent Akah River, near a place where a deep red mineral pigment was to be found. They used this to colour everything from the posts of their house to their shields, and so they acquired the name Bitokala, *bito* meaning stone, and *kala*, red. After many adventures, including the wars with the Tring, the Red Stone people settled in the Tutoh. After the breakup of the megacommunity at Long Kelejeo, the Bitokala built a separate longhouse nearby. There the name became corrupted into a Malay form that has a similar sound but not quite identical meaning. Given that Malay was the *lingua franca* of trade in the Tutoh, the mutation is not surprising, but the repeated changes in format of the ethnonym are worth noting. First, the name of a place became the name of a people. That much is familiar; at Aban Jau's Long Batan, for instance, the Sebop component called themselves Long Taballau because they had previously lived there. The only difference in this case is that the place name is not constructed by specifying the confluence of rivers using the prefix *long*. The process is reversed, however, when the ethnonym gets rendered into Malay so that it sounds like a place: the Batu Belah people are those who live at the Split Rocks, even though no one has seen any split rocks. Consequently, it becomes a place name and is so marked on maps. This shows just how slippery even autonyms can be: when talking Malay, Bitokala people are perfectly content to call themselves Batu Belah. There are in effect two autonyms, and the choice between them depends on who is being spoken to, not who is speaking. We might contrast them as internal and external autonyms.

The derivation of other lower Baram ethnonyms is equally idiosyncratic. The branch of the Berawan who moved far up the Tutoh in the mid-nineteenth century under the leadership of Orang Kaya Temenggong Lawai are usually called *Long Pata* in the colonial records, as if, following the familiar pattern, they had previously lived near the mouth of the Pata River, which flows into the Baram some distance above the first rapids. Indeed, they may have done so because they migrated down the Baram like the Bitokala. Nevertheless, the Kenyah form of the external autonym is spurious; the name used by Berawan speakers among themselves is Kapita. There were good reasons for the Kapita to manufacture a Kenyah-style name. First, Lawai liked to emphasize his dynastic connections with the Lepo Umbo, particularly with the prestigious family of Tama Bulan Wang. Second, it was what the officers of the Raj expected, having grasped the Kenyah system of naming places.

The name Long Kiput adds another twist: it is not only a Kenyah-cized version of the internal autonym Lakipo', it is also used to name the place where the Lakipo' now live. The ethnonym has been converted to a place name in the same manner as Batu Belah. There is, however, no more a Kiput River at Long Kiput than there are split rocks at Batu Belah. We are once again confronted by a hall of mirrors, and that is the nature of ethnic names and place names in the Brunei hinterland.

Finally, the name Berawan is itself a name manufactured for external consumption. By mere coincidence, the internal autonym Melawan happens in Malay to look like a verbal form of the noun *lawan*, "antagonist, opponent," consequently meaning something like "to go against." In the Berawan account of it, the external autonym was devised in the distant past to avoid embarrassment for both parties when dealing with Malay traders. Given how delicate a matter trade was outside "the Sultan's fence," one can see why unintended references to violence might be avoided. The usage evidently influenced Sebop usage; their usual name for the Berawan is Belau'un. Meanwhile, the Berawan of Tinjar, having shared a common history – whether united in one longhouse or dispersed in several – mark their difference from other Berawan simply by calling themselves Melawan Tu'o, the "Real Berawan." Summarising:

Internal Autonym	External Autonym	Change of Idiom to
Bitokala	Batu Belah	Malay
Kapita	Long Pata	Kenyah
Lakipo	Long Kiput	Kenyah
Melawan	Berawan	Malay

Even these multiple autonyms do not exhaust the complexities of naming in the Lower Baram, however, because there are also the echoes of assimilated communities. It was the Bitokala Berawan who intermarried with the Pelutan people, as described previously. The encounter was not, however, recounted in terms of conquest and annexation. On the contrary, as late as the 1970s, the elite families of Batu Belah made a point of emphasizing their Pelutan descent. Putting the case in stronger terms, they claimed at times to be Pelutan, but this claim in no way invalidated their ethnicity as Bitokala, and also as Berawan. This is only puzzling if one takes an essentialist view of ethnicity. The situation was similar at Long Teru, where it was understood that the most elite people in a Berawan community were Lelak, or at least had the best claims to the Lelak heritage. But at Long Teru, the ancestors – those who "owned" the land and were most often mentioned in prayers – were clearly Lelak. What was surprising at Batu Belah was that the leading families continued to prize their indigenous ancestry even after they had migrated far away from the Pelutan River.

The names of assimilated peoples did not always imply superior status, however. Their great leader of the Lakipo/Long Pata gained his Brunei title of Temenggong for constantly harassing the Tring and destroying their communities. Consequently, it is ironic that the final remnant of the Tring wound up sharing a longhouse with the Long Pata at Long Terawan in the middle Tutoh, where they were until recent times stigmatized as a conquered people rather than respected as autochthones. Nevertheless, it is tempting to see in the word "Terawan" a fusing of Tring and Berawan. No one at Long Terawan offered this etymology, and, in contrast to Long Kiput, there is a Terawan River. But after all the refractions of place and ethnicity that we have already observed, one can only wonder whether the river was named after the community or vice versa.

This account, complex as it may seem, oversimplifies the dynamics of ethnicity in the Tutoh in the past century and a half. Survivors of the Kayan raids persisted in several places and even managed to briefly re-establish separate communities.

Elements were present at the metropolis of Long Kelejeo, where, according to Berawan accounts, they even mixed with Kayan. Supposedly, a small group of Kayan, arriving in advance of the main body, lived with, and became assimilated by, the Long Kiput. In the Lakipo' and Bitokala languages, they are called *Belubo'*, presumably a Berawanization of the Kayan ethnonym Uma Beluvu.

The Invisibility of Assimilated Slaves

As noted previously, slavery in effect constituted a form of cultural assimilation. In the nineteenth century, Kayan raiders digested entire communities, turning them with surprising promptness into part of the Kayan body politic, even if at the lowest status level. It is, of course, the winners who write history, but even in the accounts of Westerners like Hose there is no hint of slaves nursing their subjugated ethnicities. Instead, the majority seem to have adopted Kayan ethnicity as rapidly as they learned the Kayan language. One effect of this was to make it difficult in the 1970s to find out about assimilated ex-slaves. The longhouse communities of the lower Baram claimed to formerly have had slaves, but since colonial times it had been prohibited to call someone a slave, and such an insult was a fineable offense. By the 1970s, slave origins were a matter of whispered gossip, too inflammatory to speak out loud. Elite people in Kayan and Kenyah houses sometimes implied that their ex-slaves still "knew their place," and showed great deference, but I saw little evidence of it.

Only with long familiarity was it possible to pick up echoes of former slavery. At Batu Belah, I met an old man who was Tagal by origin – that is, he was born in a longhouse far away in the Lawas watershed, belonging to a small offshoot of the Visaya (Rutter 1929:6). Enslaved as a child by their enemies the Lun Bawang (Sandin 1980:190), he had changed hands several times by purchase, until he arrived at Batu Belah as a youth. By his account of it, he had known no other home, spoke no other languages than those spoken at Batu Belah, and had lived a life not much different than his fellow villagers. His life story revealed, however, that he had remained a dependent of the leading family; a status that Stephen Morris (1980:305) glosses as an "inside" slave. Berawan claimed that their slavery had been "less cruel" than that of the Kayan, and that elite Tring captives even intermarried with their leading families. Far from denying that assimilation was the result of enslavement, they boasted about it.

Entering Malaydom

Another form of assimilation was of even greater historical significance, the process described as *masok Melayu*, "entering Malaydom." Its effect was to remove people from the category Orang Ulu because it implied not only conversion to Islam, but also the adoption of Malay life ways incompatible with those of the longhouse. It would be a mistake, however, to exaggerate the abruptness of this cleavage. In the introduction, the contrast Malay/Upriver was compared to that of Shan/Kachin that Leach so neatly deconstructed. Much of the previous description of the trading network of Brunei shows just how subtle were the connections between upriver and down. Certainly, those speakers of Lower Baram languages who fled to the coast to avoid Kayan depredations did, by degrees, enter Malaydom. They intermarried with Brunei Malays and adopted a wide range of Malay attributes. But even a century and a half later, the memory of their upriver origins persisted, and had a bearing on their interactions with other "Malays." Clifford Sather (1979) demonstrates this in connection with the Miri people, who number upward of 2,000 people living in various locations around the coastal town of the same name. They cannot be called a "community" in the restricted sense in which I use the term here, but even so they preserve autonyms relating to previous communities and splits between communities. Much the same is evidently true of the people calling themselves Belait, living near the town of Kuala Belait (Martin 1990).

Outside these urban areas, communities that converted to Islam preserved greater cohesion. Adjacent to the bazaar at Marudi, the administrative centre from which Charles Hose and his colleagues extended Brooke rule in the

Baram watershed, there is a large village called Kampong Narom. It was here that the Narom people settled after their wars with other lower Baram peoples and the dangerous years of the Kayan raids. As they became active in the trade that circulated through Marudi, so they were drawn into the Malay world and converted to Islam. But that did not mean that links with upriver communities were severed. On the contrary, the Narom were more interested than ever in maintaining them, so as to profit from trade. Even after migrant Chinese traders gained the upper hand in this trade (Goldman 1968), the social and economic links persisted. An example concerns the technique that Long Teru people developed for bringing the surplus catch of their lake to market. They built large bamboo cylinders, as much as ten feet in diameter and twenty feet long, in which they stored live fish. When the cages were full, they drifted them down to Marudi, a slow and risky process, but remarkably effective. Once at Marudi, the live fish could be sold off at leisure, and this was essential if the fishermen were not to be at the mercy of Chinese traders working together to maintain rock bottom prices. In the interim, they stayed in Kampong Narom, where they were received as cousins.

It must also be noted that these alliances were maintained through marriage. A daughter married to a man at Kampong Narom certainly ensured her father's reception there. Whether she formally converted to Islam does not seem to have been a matter of any great weight. Often in-marrying women preferred not to, on the grounds that they could then go home again if they wanted. Indeed, in the 1970s, there was a senior member of the local Malay community, whose name I do not give, who had two wives from upriver communities. Both insisted firmly on their status as Upriver People, and cheerfully entertained upriver guests, male and female, with distilled liquor. The husband had throughout his life maintained close links with several longhouse communities and was well respected throughout the lower Baram. He joined in on these noisy and convivial occasions with gusto – a remarkable example of cross-cultural adeptness and tolerance now unfortunately almost impossible. It must be added that this man had been born a Moslem and was active in a mosque that also served the needs of Brunei Malays settled at Marudi.

In addition, there had been for several generations Malays who had married into upriver communities. Because marriage in these communities had nothing of the sacramental quality that it has in Christianity – no union before God – temporary marriages were not frowned on. Indeed, they could have elite connotations related to alliances. As noted in Chapter 3, Aban Jau's famously beautiful daughter did not restrict herself to any single alliance. Trading connections sometimes operated in a similar way. For example, one leading family among the Berawan living in the Tinjar boasted about its descent from a Brunei nobleman. They were only too happy to repeat the aristocratic claims the man had made when he arrived among them, several generations prior.

A final example of the permeability of the barrier between Moslem and non-Moslem in the Brunei hinterland concerns a community in the watershed of the Bakong. As noted in Chapter 8, the Bakong was the ancient home of some of the peoples I refer to as "lowlanders." The Bakong is a small river, running through extensive swamps, so it provided a refuge against Kayan raids similar to the Belait, but Bakong people did not put their faith in inaccessibility alone. In addition, they sought the protection of Malay leaders in those same coastal villages that had neatly deflected Aban Jau's attacks. In this way, they came within the orbit of Brunei society and so came to *masok Melayu*. However, according to their headman, interviewed in the 1990s, for decades after their conversion they continued to seek omens from the flight of birds in the traditional manner (Metcalf 1976) and to practice secondary burial. Most remarkable of all, they continued to live in a longhouse – the only instance of which I am aware of a Moslem longhouse. The persistence of this one longhouse community did not, however, prevent the dispersal of other fragments of the Bakong. Benedict Sandin (1958) found a heterogeneous collection of people living in Malay-style houses, even including some Penan, and styling themselves "Bakong," as if that name were an ethnicity – which means of course that it was. The uniqueness of the Moslem longhouse is that becoming Moslem generally removes people from the kind of ritual life that characterised upriver society, and that brings us to the next section.

Long Teru's Eight Ethnonyms

On my first visit to Long Teru, where I based my fieldwork, I asked people who they were, and I went on asking it because I got confusing responses. I elicited eight different ethnonyms, but no one was trying to confuse or deceive me. On the contrary, they were trying to provide me with an answer that I could understand, that is, matched to my level of understanding.

There were three names that formed a kind of food chain, each larger one gobbling up the lesser. By the 1970s, it was really only the ancestors that were Lelak, the living community was Berawan, and that had come about by peaceful assimilation. Meanwhile, Long Teru people were content to be classified by government officials as Kenyah. There was no threat of assimilation by "real" Kenyah, however, because none lived in the neighbourhood. Nor did the Berawan express any kind of inferiority about not being "real" Kenyah; on the contrary, they held themselves superior to all other Upriver Peoples. The only person confused by the label was me because I had been given a bad impression of the Long Teru people by missionaries. They were, I was told, decadent and drunken, and, although refusing Christianity, had lost their traditional culture. As evidence, it was pointed out that the grand naming ceremonies so important to the Kenyah no longer occurred at Long Teru. It took me some months to discover that such ceremonies had never occurred at Long Teru and that it was different rites of passage that were crucial to the ritual life of the community. Moreover, they had certainly served rice wine whenever missionaries had come to visit and, indeed, forced their guests to drink it, in the traditional fashion of muscular Berawan hospitality. No one was allowed to sit out a Berawan party.

It must be emphasized that what is going on here has to do with historical processes, not with taxonomic hierarchies. Superficially, the proliferation of proper names at Long Teru resembles the situation that Edward Evans-Pritchard encountered among the Nuer. His frustrations are summed up in his famous pun, to the effect that he was victim of a "neurosis," but he nevertheless manages to lay out an elegantly clear model of Nuer political organisation (Evans-Pritchard 1940:23, 139–58). The key insight was that varying answers to questions about group allegiance were simply the result of different contexts. In one situation, a man called on his fellow clansmen in the same tertiary tribal section to oppose those in another, but the former enemies would become his allies when his quarrel was with someone in a different secondary section, and so on. Processes of fission and fusion were predictable because tribal segments fit neatly into a taxonomic hierarchy. The situation at Long Teru was fundamentally different. Lelak people were not one of several kinds of Berawan people, and Berawan people were not one of several kinds of Kenyah people. This is true despite the misleading implications of two other ethnonyms with which I was presented – in all good faith. As I learned enough to deconstruct for myself the Kenyah label, I was supplied with hyphenated labels. Long Teru was special, I was told, because it was inhabited by Kenyah–Lelak people, or alternatively, by Berawan–Lelak.

The Berawan-Lelak label became redundant once my hosts perceived that I had grasped something of the varieties of Berawan. With some relief, my informants were able finally to affirm that Long Teru people were really just Bitokala who had moved there from Batu Belah. However, they reminded me, because it was some of the best people who had moved, that they were really Pelutan. As proof of this deeper truth, they pointed to tombs in the elite graveyard on an island in the middle of the lake. They had, curling along their shingled roofs, the design of a river dragon, in memory of the founding ancestor of the Pelutan, who had been born from a river dragon's egg. However, the Lelak have a similar legend and a similar motif on their tombs, so that the elite claims of long abandoned communities jostle with each other across the generations.

These multiple ethnonyms were not so much social categories as encapsulated narratives. They existed only because the community of Long Teru existed. Had its diverse inhabitants never come to Long Teru, there would have been other stories, not these. Like other longhouse people, those at Long Teru were inclined to boast about the pedigree of their community. Indeed, such showing away is a feature of longhouse life. Finally, there were the more embracing terms "Lepo Pu'un" (People who Own, expressed in a Kenyah idiom) and "Orang Ulu" (Upriver People, in a Malay phrase), for a total of eight autonyms, none false, each telling a different part of the history of Long Teru.

Part V

Longhouses and Ritual

Chapter 10

The Ritual Consensus

To understand the dynamics of longhouse communities, it is necessary to take into account the historical circumstances that shaped them. When I asked why a particular community existed, I was given, not rules of residence governed by kinship, but a narrative.

Meanings versus Survivals

Such historicism was not my preference. What I wanted to study was religion, and in anthropology, that means studying ritual. W. Robertson Smith (1889) was the first to make the strikingly counterintuitive argument that ritual – that is, religious action – historically and logically precedes belief, or religious thought. This proposition was naturally unattractive to theologians, but the great majority of the world's religions lack theologians anyway. Such religions teach people what to do, not what to think. A century later, Victor Turner developed this approach, showing that through the observation and interpretation of ritual we might learn about other peoples' most profound understandings of a range of things, from what Westerners call the "natural" to the "supernatural," including the proper relations between people, the origins of the afflictions that bedevil us, what is worth striving for, and much else besides – in short, the whole meaning of what it is to live and to die. Forty years after the publication of *The Forest of Symbols*, I still find its vision breathtaking. Falteringly to be sure, and taking only small steps at a time, we may find our way into experiences of existence utterly different from our own.

Consequently, I was frustrated to find that my enquiries about the meanings of ritual were constantly answered by narratives reaching back into a hazy past. The fundamental principle of upriver religions was "when in Rome, do as the Romans do." Because every longhouse community was its own Rome, discussions of ritual became discussions of what the ancestors had done, and so who the ancestors were, and so to migration stories. That is one reason why ethnicity is an inescapable aspect of longhouse life, however confusing its details may be to an outsider. Indeed, there are no words for "ritual" or "religion." Instead, ritual is part of *aded*, to use the Berawan version of a term found widely across island Southeast Asia. *Aded* constitutes the correct way to do things that is peculiar to each community. As Smith (1889) foretold, no one was interested in meaning – that was my obsession. Religion was about what needed to be done, not what needed to be believed.

My understanding of longhouse religion rapidly took on a nineteenth-century complexion. It began to seem like a kind of attic where odds and ends of ritual had accumulated over generations. This phantasm evoked those "survivals" that in *The Golden Bough* supposedly provide evidence of previous stages of human mental evolution. Looking to the past to explain ritual usages summoned the ghost of Sir James Frazer and all the hocus-pocus of nineteenth-century evolutionism that I had learned so thoroughly to distrust. It only made my dilemma sharper that my hosts were perfectly willing to invoke "custom" as justification and claim simply to be following the ways of the ancestors. For a while, it seemed that I had sought Claude Levi-Strauss' (1966) primitive philosophers, only to find Edward Burnett Tylor's (1871) ritual automatons.

Things came to a head when I was struggling to get a full grasp of the complex death rites of Long Jegan, the large Berawan community in the middle Tinjar that was the lifetime achievement of the leader Tama Lire, and his heir Tama Tiri, as recounted in Chapter 4. The nature of the crisis was that I had thought I understood the underlying meaning of the rites, that is, the premises that underlay them concerning what it was to live and to die, based on my existing research at Long Teru. But at Long Jegan I was told things that contradicted my understanding. Having spent some months at Long Teru, participated in several funerals, and discussed details of ritual with several informants, I was expecting to find at Long Jegan variations on a theme. Instead, I found usages that were flatly inconsistent. Either the account I had assembled was wrong, or there were no shared premises about life and death, and consequently, no Berawan religion. Either option threatened *my* premises, on which my interest in religion was based in the first place.

God in the Details, Once Again

To make clear just what was inconsistent with what, I must again launch into a mass of detail. Ethnographies of religion always face this problem because the rites that have most to teach are often the most complex. Anyone who has read the chapter on Ndembu initiation in *The Forest of Symbols* (1967:151–280) will certainly have noticed this. The essay begins with thirty pages introducing the players involved in the drama, and then launches into seventy pages of breathless narrative, interspersed with exegesis by Turner's famous informant Muchona. The essay is, in that familiar phrase, "rich in data," but it is not easy to follow. Because I am comparing *two* elaborate ritual sequences, there is a serious danger of losing the thread. Nevertheless, the detail cannot be avoided; they are exactly the point, providing the whole texture of upriver religion. The only salvation lies in applying a strict criterion of need-to-know.

By the 1970s, Long Jegan was split between converts to Roman Catholicism and adherents of a revivalist cult called *Bungan*, but both factions were new. People older than forty had spent most of their lives following the indigenous practices. Older people talked nostalgically about former longhouse festivals, and I had no lack of informants. So, I sat with them, going through the rites step by step, carefully checking over details. It was not the same as experiencing the rituals first hand, as I did at Long Teru, but the freshness of peoples' memories made it a good second best. So I was told, *inter alia*, that jars had not been used at Long Jegan for storing corpses. This was curious because jar burial was common among many of the communities of the Brunei hinterland. In the Tutoh and Apoh river valleys, massive jars, cut at the shoulder to allow insertion of the corpse, were the most conspicuous evidence of ancient Tring graveyards. I had seen them used at Long Teru, but they were indeed absent from the graveyards that I had visited in the middle and upper Tinjar. There were massive and beautifully carved hardwood tombs still to be seen, but they contained only coffins, not jars. Moreover, as I pushed on with my check list of ritual details, I found that jars were also prohibited for secondary disposal, that is, to store bones recovered after a corpse had decomposed. Berawan mausoleums elsewhere often contained small brightly coloured jars containing disarticulated bones, but those in the middle Tinjar revealed none.

The Significance of Secondary Treatment

There were more prohibitions peculiar to Long Jegan. A corpse, I was told, could not be taken away from the longhouse for primary storage in the graveyard and then brought back again later for rites of secondary treatment. This rule seemed to contradict the whole logic of the mortuary ritual sequence, and why that is so will require a word of explanation. I keep it as brief as possible because I have discussed the significance of these rites in detail elsewhere (Metcalf 1982). The key feature is that there is not just one ceremony – a "funeral" – but two, separated by months or years. The second is what Robert Hertz (1960 [1907]) called the "great feast," and it is noticeable that wherever it is practiced in Borneo it constitutes the grandest of all longhouse festivals, in terms of duration, resources employed, and number of people participating. So striking was the expenditure on these occasions that the Western observers often assumed that the whole point of delaying the funeral was to allow time to assemble resources (Miles 1965; Wilken 1884:77).

To explain the rites in economic terms is, however, to ignore their content (Metcalf 1981). For that, Hertz's famous essay, "A Contribution to the Study of the Collective Representation of Death" (1960 [1907]), is a better guide. Hertz's argument has several interwoven strands (Metcalf and Huntington 1991:79–85), but the most original posits a slow decomposition of the connection between corpse and soul that existed in life. Death did not occur, "in one instant"; instead, it was a gradual transition of the soul of the dying person into a spirit ready to take its place in the company of the ancestors. Moreover, there was "a kind of symmetry or parallelism between the condition of the body . . . and the condition of the soul" (Hertz 1960 [1907]:28, 45). As the corpse fell into corruption, so the soul sank into a miserable condition, excluded from the worlds of both the living and the dead. In its misery, it became vindictive, so that one death might lead to others. The urgent goal of the primary rites, or funeral, was to contain death, and consequently, they had a fearful quality. As the bones became dry, the danger ebbed, and the "great feast" was a joyful celebration, even at the same time that it was charged with the awful power as the ancestors, who were invited en masse to come and collect their new recruit. This concept of dying is radically different from the contemporary Western understandings of death as the failure of the body as machine. Consequently, to grasp it was to realize the vision of *The Forest of Symbols* – literally, to see the meaning of what it was for others to live and to die.

The Long Jegan Anomaly

Meanwhile, back at Long Jegan, to prohibit the re-entry of mortal remains into the longhouse sat oddly with this schema: the very name of the "great feast" in Berawan, *nulang*, is a verbal inflection of the noun *tulang*, "bones." It is literally the rite of "boning," or perhaps "doing the bones." My informants hastened to reassure me that *nulang* was of course held at Long Jegan, it was only that the corpse was kept inside the longhouse during the period between funeral and *nulang*. They described the little lean-to shed that was built on the veranda to accommodate the coffin, consisting of walls and a roof of rough planks set against the front of the dead person's room. It might sit there for months or even years, gathering dust. Their description of the little shed precisely matched a sketch made by Charles Hose in the 1890s (Hose and McDougall 1912:I:82, plate 54).

There were comparable procedures elsewhere. At Long Teru, it had been common to keep corpses on the veranda, sealed up inside massive jars. All openings in the jars were tightly sealed with damar gum, and a bamboo drain tube allowed the products of decomposition to drain into a sump under the house. The coffins used at Long Jegan could be sealed equally effectively, being cut out of massive hardwood logs. The lid was a section split from the same log so that it fit neatly, and burnt earth and charcoal were put inside the coffin to absorb fluids. The labour and time involved in making such a coffin was considerable, and that was one reason given at Long Teru for the popularity of jars (Metcalf 1987). In addition, the option also existed in other Berawan communities of returning jars and coffins unopened from the cemetery to the longhouse for rites of secondary treatment. That is the bones were not taken out, cleaned, and put in a smaller jar.

What was surprising at Long Jegan was that so many ritual options available elsewhere were prohibited. Worse was to follow, however, a real anomaly, laid out for me by my most valued informant at Long Jegan, the headman Sadi Pejong. He was a respected religious leader, and the emphasis that he laid on his statements made it clear that he saw their significance, in terms of both the distinctiveness of his community and the logic of the rites. In Long Jegan practice, he asserted, it was permissible to commence a *nulang* immediately after the conclusion of the funeral. Ten days for the funeral, ten more for the *nulang*, and the entire ritual sequence was wrapped up. Sadi Pejong watched me with a broad grin, waiting to see if I understood enough to be properly amazed. Surely, it makes no sense to do the ritual of the bones when there is still a rotting corpse. You cannot send the soul of the dead person to meet the ancestors before it has completed the transition to pure spirit. It contradicted everything I believed that I had learned.

Having achieved the desired effect, Sadi Pejong was ready to come to my assistance. It was not, he said, that anyone would have actually done the funeral and *nulang* back to back, only that it was theoretically possible. He was not sure that it had ever happened, if only for practical reasons. The all-night vigils of a funeral were exhausting; thus, who would choose to go immediately to those of the *nulang*? Seeing me still crestfallen, he pointed out that, as I well knew, even at Long Teru not everyone merited the full mortuary sequence. Less wealthy people were satisfied to entomb their dead directly after the week or so of the initial funeral, and that did not mean that those persons never got to the land of the dead. It was only that their arrival there was not celebrated by a magnificent feast, temporarily reuniting the living and the dead. Moreover, I had already noticed that the sacred songs that convey the deceased to the land of the dead could be sung at the end of a funeral (Metcalf 1982:190–206). For this, I had already been provided with a neat logical rationale: what was imparted by the songs during the funeral would be made use of *later*, I was told, when the soul had finally shaken off its mortal coils and was ready to travel to the land of the dead. The songs were, in effect, a briefing, provided a little too soon perhaps to be immediately useful, but better than no instructions at all. Why should it not be the same for the somewhat rushed *nulang* of Long Jegan?

These rationales were of course made up for my benefit, in answer to questions that almost nobody but Sadi Pejong had ever bothered asking themselves. Nevertheless, they made clear an important point that I might not otherwise have noted. Berawan death rites are celebratory, not instrumental. *Nulang* no more brings about the freeing of the soul from the body than a debutante ball brings about sexual maturation.

Echoes of Long Batan

Sadi Pejong was pleased with his explanation, but I was left with much to ponder. Why were there all these anomalous practices? Why was Long Jegan so different from other Berawan communities? There was only one possible answer, and I was once again drawn into historical narratives. The exceptional features of Long Jegan death rites had the combined effect of disguising the most conspicuous aspects of secondary treatment of the dead, namely, the two distinct festivals and the repackaging of the bones. Jars, large ones for corpses or small ones for bones, were nowhere to be seen.

Coffins were not taken out of the house between funeral and *nulang*, as if the funeral went on for months at a time. Finally, there was no occasion for opening the coffin and cleaning the bones. It would have inconceivable for that to occur inside the longhouse. Such a confusion of graveyard and longhouse was unthinkable.

If we now ask why the Jong Jegan Berawan should have disguised the nature of their death rites, the answer is not far to seek. The Sebop had no rites of secondary treatment, and even in the 1970s, most expressed an aversion to them. Sebop religion was focussed on the ancestors just as was Berawan religion, but it did not allow for the intimate contact with them that was involved in *nulang*.

Parallel Eccentricities of the Long Taballau

Ritual innovation was not, however, a one-way street. When I began to examine the other party to the Long Batan community, I found interesting modifications in the death rites of the descendents of those particular Sebop. If the Long Taballau Sebop did not adopt rites of secondary treatment, they did extend the duration of their funerals beyond the tens days allowed else-where. This was confirmed in the 1970s by their descendents living at Long Sobeng, even though they had become Catholic some years earlier. In addi-tion, a neat confirmation is provided in a chatty account of an expedition of Oxford University students to the region in 1932. The interests of the participants were mainly in botany and entomology, and they spent most of their time in uninhabited places beyond the Dulit range, but they visited the homes of their Sebop guides. Very properly, they introduced themselves to the Penghulu, Tingang Sa'ong:

> A few days later the news came that he was dead. Over six weeks passed before we heard the day of the burial. One morning, exactly fifty days from the day the old chief died, Shackleton, Banks, and Hobby, armed with a camera, and I, went to Long Miwah. There was not a little speculation as to the greeting we should get from a fifty-day old corpse, but Banks assured us that the aborigine knew his job, and that there would be a spout attached to the coffin. (Ford 1938:77–8)

It is evident that Tingang Sa'ong's funeral did not continue at the same intensity for nearly two months. Instead, there had been rites lasting some days, and then a period of minimal activity, followed by a ritual climax. For the final phase, visitors were summoned from far and wide, including the members of the Oxford Expedition. The result was that the extended funerals of these Sebop could hardly be distinguished in practical terms from the funerals and *nulang* of their former Berawan allies. The "spout" attached to the coffin provides another link to Berawan practice.

Further details about Tingang Sa'ong are provided in the *Sarawak Gazette*. The notice of his appointment as Penghulu (*Sarawak Gazette* 665: December 1914) describes him as chief of the "Leppu Poun Sebop." What that implies, as we see in Chapter 8, was that he belonged to the first wave of Sebop immigrants. In other words, Tingang Sa'ong was a successor of Aban Jau.

The evidence that these ritual innovations, both Berawan and Sebop, occurred at Long Batan is circumstantial, but no less strong for that. Obviously, there are no eyewitness accounts. The most direct evidence is from graveyards. In the far headwaters of the Tinjar, I was shown the remains of two very old mausoleums that, according to the local Penan, dated back to the time when Berawan lived there, shortly after their migration out of the central plateau. One tomb consisted of a single massive ironwood column with a niche in the top to house a small jar. That there was no extant jar was not surprising given the age of the monument. The niche itself attests to the recovery and restorage of bones, at a time predating the Long Batan confederation. Meanwhile, the Long Taballau graveyards contained mausoleums too massive and elaborately decorated to have been erected in ten days, keeping in mind that it is taboo to begin work on a tomb before its intended occupant has "lost breath." Tingang Sa'ong's tomb provides a good example, as shown in the photographs taken by the Oxford Expedition (Ford 1938:83). Nevertheless, it is the circumstantial evidence that is most convincing. It is inconceivable that so neat a convergence of ritual practice occurred by accident, and if it did not occur at Long Batan, then where?

Ritual Consensus

What the Long Batan case shows is that longhouse communities cannot function without a ritual consensus. It is instructive because it is extreme: those brought together there by historical circumstances differed sharply in a key aspect. The need to paper over their differences makes a strong statement about the nature of longhouse communities as ritual communities.

It is also striking that cultural differences were bridged by means of ritual, not belief. No philosophical debates were necessary concerning the nature of life and death. Nor was there any "clash of values" in the manner we take as inherent in achieving "multiculturalism." Instead, both parties arranged their death rites so that there was a superficial similarity. In some ways, the Sebop contributed more to the compromise because they had to bend rules, whereas the Berawan merely abandoned some ritual options. The result was that the Berawan and Sebop could cheerfully participate in each other's rites without ever confronting the issue of whether what was going on constituted secondary treatment. The creativity of the arrangement is remarkable, and it neatly conforms to Robertson Smith's argument that "in ancient religion there was no authoritative interpretation of ritual. It was imperative that certain things should be done, but every man was free to put his own meaning on what was done" (Smith 1889:399).

An intriguing mystery is what part Aban Jau himself played in bringing about Long Batan's unique ritual consensus. As we see in Chapter 3, the Long Taballau Sebop were certainly aware of their new neighbours when they migrated into the Tinjar. Because marriage alliances had already existed, they may well have attended each others' grandest funerals. We can be sure that there was a period of negotiation before the founding of Long Batan, made urgent by the threat of attack by Kayan war parties. Were the ritual compromises worked out in advance by some assembly of elders, or did they evolve a step at a time as situations required? We may be sure that discussions went on about what was appropriate at every funeral, and Aban Jau had a stake in their outcome. How fascinating it would have been to be a fly on the wall while his process of "nation building" was under way.

Ritual as Archive

In addition to consensus, another feature made plain by this case is the persistence of ritual innovations once in place. Not only did the Long Taballau extend their funerals effectively into two stages when they encountered the Berawan, but they also kept the extended rites after they again moved upriver, away from Long Batan, to Tingang Sa'ong's house at Long Miwah, and then to Long Sobeng. Moving away in the opposite direction, the Berawan of Tinjar similarly maintained their unique combination of rites.

The conservatism of ritual is important to my argument because I relate data from two epochs. A large part of previous sections had to do with events in the nineteenth century, whereas my observations were made in the 1970s. For a historian, it would undoubtedly seem unprofessional to juxtapose data from such different periods. Even for an anthropologist dabbling in history, it requires justification; luckily, the evidence of ritual continuity is everywhere at hand. In addition to the contents of old graveyards, the accounts of St. John and Low contain many references to recognisable ritual practices. For instance, the murder recounted at the beginning of Chapter 5 is immediately comprehensible because in the 1970s, corpses were displayed in exactly the manner St. John describes (see Metcalf 1982:36–7, for details of these displays). In his role as amateur ethnographer, Hose provides the richest data. One of his photographs (Hose and McDougall 1912:II:plate 145) shows a Berawan prayer site (*tapo*) identical to those I saw almost a century later (Metcalf 1989:73–9). Examples could be multiplied indefinitely.

Continuity does not imply immutability, however. Instead, the proposition is that rites are liable to change in response to community dynamics and that such innovations accumulate. Consequently, the ritual peculiarities of each community provide an archive of sorts, a historical record that can be read only in comparison with other longhouses.

Moreover, this pattern of change and retention parallels the genesis of ethnonyms in new communities, and their persistence long after the disappearance of those communities. Even when ethnonyms fade into social irrelevance, they leave behind ghostly traces in ritual. At Long Teru, what was left of the Lelak heritage in the 1970s was a few death songs known only to a handful of old people.

In a nutshell, ethnicities arise from the communality of longhouses, which are in turn manifested in ritual.

Function versus History

At this point, it might seem that my account of ritual manages to combine the most reviled elements of both nineteenth- and twentieth-century anthropology. On the one hand, I imply that religion is a kind of attic or junk room in which are stored things made long ago for purposes long since forgotten, just as in *The Golden Bough*. On the other hand, the notion of ritual consensus brings to mind Bronislaw Malinowski's functionalism, in which the purpose of religion is to satisfy "integrative needs."

In fact, neither of these viewpoints is implied. What is missing from both are historical processes – not grand evolutionary schema, but the histories of particular communities. Ritual peculiarities may have their origins in the past, but that does not mean they lack significance in the present. For one thing, they connote ethnicity. Meanwhile, whatever minimal consensus is required to allow communities to function, it certainly does not guarantee their permanence. The paradox is that the solidarity of longhouse communities did not match the solidarity of the buildings themselves. On the contrary, their stories were full of movement and change. Consequently, ritual was not the final capstone on a finished social structure, but rather the material from which that structure was built and rebuilt. Just how that was accomplished is the subject of Chapter 11.

Chapter 11

The Ritual Operator

Having argued in Chapter 10 that longhouse communities require a ritual consensus, I shall now appear perversely to argue the opposite. The paradox is neatly illustrated by Aban Jau's confederacy in the 1880s. At Long Batan, people who had radically different ways of manufacturing ancestors – one component forbidding secondary treatment, the other promoting it – came together in a single community. The result was not religious strife, like Protestants versus Catholics, but instead an elaborate ritual accommodation. This was necessary because the essential basis of longhouse community was that everyone be able to participate in everyone else's rituals. That is, they comprised a "congregation" in the sense in which Durkheim (1965 [1912]) used the term. What was not required was a consensus of belief. No one had to recite a credo. Moreover, ritual eccentricities were only to be expected. The funerals of the Berawan at Long Batan were not identical to those of their Sebop neighbours, even after the ritual accommodation had been worked out. Moreover, the Berawan had minor differences among themselves, reflecting a history of previous communal divisions.

Consensus did not imply uniformity. If I argued that it did, I would fall back into the old fallacy, often attributed to Durkheim, that the sociological function of religion was to glue collectivities together. In fact, longhouse ritual subverted solidarities as often as it supported them. This chapter is designed to show the constant shifting of attention among different levels of inclusiveness, from the whole community to the individual. To demonstrate how that worked, I must again go beyond generalities and examine particular rites in a particular community. There can be no question of "average" rites somehow "representative" of all longhouses.

A Small Window

My choice of which community's rituals to describe is predetermined by the circumstances of fieldwork. When I lived at Long Teru for two years in the mid-1970s, it was the last community of Upriver People in the whole Baram watershed, and as far as I know, in all of central Borneo, that could make the claim of having continuously maintained its indigenous rites. What that in practice meant was that its conservative leaders had persuaded the majority of people at Long Teru neither to convert to Christianity nor dabble in revivalist cults.

The first missionary efforts among Upriver People began in the early twentieth century, when a Catholic priest was based at Marudi. He made slow progress. The first large-scale conversions occurred only in the 1940s, when fundamentalist Protestants from Australia, organised into the Borneo Evangelical Mission (BEM), converted almost the entire Lun Bawang population of the Trusan watershed. After World War II, the influence of the BEM spread south and west, but not before large numbers of Kenyah in the upper Baram had joined the Catholic Church. The subsequent struggle for converts was further complicated by the appearance of an indigenous revivalist cult – to use the established if unsatisfactory anthropological term – centred on a female deity called *Bungan*. The appeal of Bungan was that it reduced the demands of the traditional religions by standardising and radically simplifying ritual, while requiring no basic changes in worldview. For a while, Bungan spread rapidly among the Kayan of the middle Baram, and even among recent Christian converts. By the 1960s, however, Bungan was losing ground. The details of this process are fascinating, but they take us too far afield for present purposes.

By the mid-1970s, Long Teru was an island in a sea of apostasy, but no one there gave any sign of feeling beleaguered. To a surprising degree, everyday life, with its small rituals, went on with serene disregard for what was happening elsewhere. This was possible precisely because of the community-based nature of indigenous religions, each sufficient to itself. If taxed with their eccentricity, Long Teru people reacted with a pride bordering on chauvinism, taking it as an example of their independent spirit. A Catholic priest once remarked to me that Long Teru people no doubt thought they would get better service, now that their old gods had so few people to care for. His quip missed the mark; the point is that every community had its own company of ancestors.

There was sometimes friction when visitors came to longhouse festivals, but that was true even in houses that had nominally converted. Religion was on everyone's mind at the time, as people tried to work out the implications of the changes. The only serious problems concerned marriages, since missionaries insisted that the non-Christian spouse converted before they would administer the sacraments. This one-way road created a Christian fifth column inside communities that could be surprisingly disruptive. Longhouse festivals demanded everyone's participation. To have a few people guiltily hanging back could sour the entire event, especially when the priests made a point of turning up at just the most awkward moments for their conflicted flock.

Moreover, it would be absurd to imagine that change had not occurred even before conversion to what became known as *Aded Luna*, which I gloss as "the old way of doing things," or simply, the "Old Way." To take only the most obvious example, the suppression of headhunting had been a key element in the process of colonial "pacification." In many communities in the Brunei hinterland, headhunting had been the focus of grand festivals lasting a week or more. In the twentieth century, head-less head rites only survived tacked on to the end of funerals (Metcalf 1996).

In the second half of the twentieth century, the pace of change accelerated. Consequently, it is reasonable to ask what might be learned about indigenous religions from my experiences at Long Teru in the 1970s. In the manner of ethnographers before me, I answer this question by turning it on its head. The rites of the Old Way at Long Teru provided an invaluable window into a rapidly vanishing world. Moreover, even a small window may afford a surprisingly wide view. The conversion to Christianity was sufficiently recent that it was possible nearly everywhere to find older people who were only too glad to give detailed descriptions of rituals they had known for most of their lives, up to the past ten or twenty years. Their enthusiasm partly had to do with pride in the uniqueness of their community, but they also enjoyed reminiscing about the excitement of longhouse festivals, compared to which Christian holidays lacked drama. There was, of course, the possibility of exaggeration, the nostalgia of older people for their youth, but the crucial thing from my point of view was that the details of ritual so profusely provided could be compared from one community to another. In this, there was no chance of collusion between informants to tell me lies because they had never conferred with one another.

Mutatis Mutandis

This feature bears directly on what the Long Teru rites might reveal about other communities. Having seen something at Long Teru, I could ask about similar things elsewhere. When I described Long Teru rituals to informants at Long Jegan, I elicited a flood of recollections, not only of what they had seen, but also of what they had heard from their parents and grandparents. In these discussions, there was often a competitive edge. My informants found fault with the Long Teru way of doing things and explained the proper way, meaning, of course, the Long Jegan way. Far from colluding, the experts were keen to disagree, throwing into relief even minor differences. This reaction was not confined to ritual experts; longhouse residents tended to exaggerate the uniqueness of their own communities.

A nice example is provided by prayer. When I played elsewhere the tape-recordings I had made at Long Teru, they were immediately recognized for what they were, even in places where Berawan was not spoken. What people recognized was the staccato style of prayer, which involved short lines uniformly voiced so as to suppress the intonations of ordinary speech. Typically, a few lines were spoken slowly, then a few fast, first loud, then soft. In addition, there was a free use of parallelism, involving pairs of words that showed rhyming or alliteration – both features that can be heard without understanding the meaning of what was said (Metcalf 1989). The standard reaction to hearing the prayers was amazement – but that sounds exactly like our prayers! – and before long an old man would be found to produce snippets in their own language. In addition, it is possible to recognize the same stylistic features in the descriptions of travellers and colonial officers, even though no prayers had been transcribed and published before my study. Consequently, there is good evidence that a similar form of prayer existed in indigenous religions across the whole of central Borneo (see Figure 11-01).

This example supports the proposition that the indigenous religions of Upriver People shared an underlying similarity of form. Certainly, rites varied from community to community. There were even whole festivals that occurred in some places and not others. For example, the people of Long Teru, not being "real" Kenyah, had no naming ceremonies. The Sebop had no *nulang*, even if a minority of them had amazingly long funerals.

The point I want to emphasize is that everywhere there was a range of rituals running the gamut from those mobilizing entire communities, through smaller ones involving only the residents of one or two rooms, to others that were focused on individuals. It is that range that concerns me, and the great advantage of the data from Long Teru is that it allows me to describe one example in detail. Beyond that, I appeal to the principle of *mutatis mutandis*, of variation within a pattern.

There are, of course, many things that we will never know. The ethnographic record is frustratingly patchy, but it does contain invaluable resources, including the memoirs of Charles Hose, organised into a comprehensive two-volume account by the Cambridge scholar Charles McDougall (Hose and McDougall 1912). Jerome Rousseau's (1998) important work on the Kayan of Belaga includes an account of their religious practices in the 1970s, which involved rejection of Christianity in favour of Bungan. He shows that the effect of conversion was to simplify rituals and abandon many of the old taboos, but that a full range of rites continued to be practiced and to be as much implicated in communal politics as before. In addition, Rousseau (1990) has assembled an overview of the societies of central Borneo, drawing on the impressive corpus of material written by Dutch explorers and administrators in the late nineteenth and early twentieth centuries.

Prayers of the House

The ethnographic record is sufficient to show that communal festivals were everywhere a feature of longhouse life. Often, there was an annual festival of some kind held after the harvest, when people moved back from their farms. At Long Teru, it was called *papi lameng*, or "prayers of the house," and it had a simple format. It lasted only one day, although it might take several days to prepare for – and recover from. During *papi lameng*, the main activity was wandering up and down the veranda from early morning until late at night, entering first one room and then another, in random order. Supposedly, everyone should visit every room, and at each stop on the circuit, the hosts would serve rice wine, which was prepared in vast quantities for the occasion. Around meal times, food was also brought out, including pork, fish soup, salt, and mountains of rice.

It can well be imagined that these visits rapidly became disorderly, in exactly the manner that Berawan people associated with rituals, or at least successful rituals. Soon, there were knots of men heading down the veranda to their next destination, calling out for friends to join them. The raucous noise they made when they arrived and settled down to drink would attract people from neighbouring rooms, which would suddenly be left abandoned. Women and children ran around just as vigorously as the men, sometimes joining them, sometimes making their own circuit. All day, half a dozen parties moved up and down the veranda, sometime picking up new followers, sometimes fragmenting. Meanwhile, everyone was not only a guest, but also a host, and had to keep a wary eye out in case people came to their rooms. Husbands and wives took turns staying "home," and tried to anticipate matters by collecting groups of their peers and steering them into their rooms. People who had overdone things early in the day dropped out to take naps in whatever quiet spots they could find, but were soon roused to renewed effort by passing revellers at a more active stage. Men expected to go through this cycle several times before the night was out. Women were more cautious, but certainly did not abstain.

No one napped during the rite that occurred around midday. A large crowd collected on the down river end of the veranda carrying rice pestles, or pots and pans. Then they marched slowly along the veranda, pounding the pestles on the floor, which acted as a massive sounding board, or banging the pots with a stick. At each door, a contingent veered off to make a circuit through the room before rejoining the crowd on the veranda. The appalling din was supposed to scare away evil spirits, but people made a game out of it, competing to see who could make the most noise. By the time they reached the other end of the house, everyone was too deafened to hear anything less than a shout, and that seemed to be the main goal. People grinned at each other, satisfied with the success of the rite.

What I have described so far sounds like a properly Durkheimian celebration, an outpouring of good feeling, and an affirmation of social solidarity, and so it was on the occasions I witnessed. But there is nothing automatic in this; there was always something edgy about the drunken hilarity of men. Although banter usually remained good humoured, there were occasions when tempers suddenly flared. Any move toward violence was rapidly restrained, and verbal abuse was strongly censured. Onlookers, particularly authoritative older women, muttered *paloi* – "stupid" – and the miscreant was usually shamed into silence. Nevertheless, everyone knew that there was a risk of old quarrels breaking out at longhouse festivals, a tendency that, to say the least of it, ran counter to social solidarity.

Another interesting aspect of the festival is the nature of the hospitality extended. We could imagine a feast at which everyone sat down together on the veranda to eat and drink fare prepared collectively, as was done at grand weddings and funerals. Instead, at *papi lameng* every room offered hospitality to the others, so emphasizing the status of each as an independent unit of production. Putting it another way, feasts laid out on the veranda were provided for visitors from other communities, in the face of whom the hosts became a uniform body, a united front. When feasting themselves, the mutual relations between different rooms were emphasized, and once again, this opened the door, so to speak, for antagonisms to be made obvious. What if one room received few guests, or the occupants failed to provide adequate hospitality?

Moreover, exactly what solidarities were being emphasized became more complex when we come to what was nominally the point of the whole festival, the prayers of the house. They were made in the morning, before it was too hot and while everyone was still active, in the space outside the front of the longhouse. There was no notion of private prayer, as provided for in Judaism, Christianity, and Islam. Instead, prayers were always made in public, by men, and on behalf of everyone attending the ritual. Consequently, the prayers of *papi lameng* were for the welfare of the entire community.

Nevertheless, they had to be made by someone. In theory, every adult man could pray if the occasion arose, for instance, at a small gathering for the coresidents of a single room, and all were at least minimally competent. In addition, the residents of every room had the option to construct a prayer site (*tapo*) for themselves. No great expense was involved. All that was needed was four eggs, some sticks to hold them, and a chicken to sacrifice (Metcalf 1989:73–80). But not all rooms did make *tapo*. Usually, there were only five or six prayer sites for the whole longhouse, often set up next to the clumps of cordyline that marked places where prayers had been said many times before.

Consequently, the sites of the "prayers of the house" were conspicuously tagged to the rooms of leading men in the community. Rivalries were not overt, and people came from all over the longhouse to hear the prayers at every site; however, there was a clear understanding of who should be heard. An elegant performance was felt to be natural in leading men because they had more opportunities to pray than others – a neat chicken-and-egg proposition. Several well-respected men might take turns saying prayers at the same site, so that in total a dozen or more prayers were offered. However, a man of little standing who pushed himself forward would be laughed at behind his back.

Finally, the climax of the sequence came at the prayer site associated with the most respected leader, set in a veritable sacred grove of codyline bushes. The grandest *tapo* was erected behind a hardwood rack holding several large stones, worn smooth in the river bed. Each "house stone" (*bito tiloi*) had been found as the result of a dream, and together they were associated with the welfare of the community. They were said to grow as a result of the blood poured on them, and it was at the house stones that the largest sacrifices were made, consisting of at least one large male pig. The house stones were tangible evidence of the continuity of the community from one site to another. Prayers at the house stones invariably began with the ancestors, as in this example:

> Oooooooooooo . . . . . (noise to attract the attention)
> Where are you all,
> > spirits of grandparents, spirits of ancestors,
> > spirits of the forebears, spirits of old ones,

229

who rule over everything,
who rule over this land.
Grandfather Ajan Tama Langet,
grandfather Tama Julan Tinggang,
grandfather Lawai,
who rule around this lake,
who rule along this river.
Spirit of grandfather Orang Kaya Luwak,
who supports the whole of this watershed,
supports this land,
supports this plain.
Come all of you,
eat these eggs,
eat this food,
eat these offerings.
Give us at this community of Long Teru,
a good life, a cool life,
a slow life, a calm life,
a deep life, a thick life,
a happy life, a laughing life,
grant us this.
Let us have money, let us have rice,
Let us have dollars, let us have cash,
luck, luck,
luck, luck,
you push, push to us.
(Metcalf 1989:104–7)

Note that the speaker begins with the ancestors in general, using a set formula of two matched couplets that occur in almost every prayer, but continues to a list of specific personages. They constitute great leaders of the past, the famous ancestors whose names live down the generations, but they do not comprise all famous ancestors. Instead, the speaker invokes those to whom he is closely related and omits those related to his rivals.

Ritual in Operation

It would be hard to imagine a festival more squarely centred on the community than "prayers of the house"; yet, even here we find a shifting reference, not to one collectivity, but to several, and not only to the longhouse as a unit, but also to its constituent rooms. Having noticed that, it is difficult not to think of Claude Levi-Strauss' (1966) famous "totemic operator" as set out in his *The Savage Mind*.

Figure 11-01. A site for making prayers in front of the longhouse at Long Teru. This picture was taken by Charles Hose at the end of the nineteenth century, but exactly the same ritual apparatus was made in the 1970's. (From Hose and McDougall 1912, Vol II, plate 145.)

What is appealing about Levi-Strauss' model is that it neatly evades the ambiguities of the term "identity" and the circular debates they have provoked. The problem with the notion of identity is that it involves two contradictory things: what makes me the same as other people, and what makes me different from them. I gain my identity from belonging to social groups and categories, as well as from not doing so, and ultimately by being uniquely myself. The last is often called "the individual," and that concept must be sharply distinguished from the "person," a term that was given clear meaning in the English structuralist jargon. The social person is simply the sum total of the social statuses that he or she possesses, each conferred by performing a role vis–à–vis another person. The person is the individual stripped of hopes, fears, fantasies, neuroses, and other things difficult to observe by means of the classic British methods of participant observation. To study the subtler aspects of individuals is indeed remarkably like studying the abstract ideas of religion, and there is surely a huge overlap between the two.

Levi-Strauss (1966) arrived at his model as part of a deconstructive strategy: the exposure of the "totemic illusion." This famous demonstration neatly reveals the continuity between structuralism and poststructuralism because Levi-Strauss' point was that the things that seemed so bizarre about totemism were a product of the category itself. In his famous phrase, nature was "good to think," and totemism became simply one element in broader systems of classification. However, the term "totemism" has seldom been applied to the religions of Borneo, and so there is nothing to deconstruct in that regard.

Instead, what interests me about the totemic operator is that it shows how the individual and the collectivity are *simultaneously* produced by the same process. The operator comprises "a sort of conceptual apparatus which filters unity through multiplicity, multiplicity through unity, diversity through identity, and identity through diversity" (Levi-Strauss 1966:153). This neatly captures the essence of longhouse ritual as well, so I borrow the model and relabel it the "ritual operator." Figure 11-02 shows the same diagram as the one that appears in *The Savage Mind*, with the totemic categories supplemented by ones relevant to life in the longhouse. Fitting the festival of "prayers of the house" into the model, we can see the same rites mobilizing different collectivities from moment to moment. When people wander up and down the veranda sampling the wine in one room after another, the contrast between host and guest is constantly reshuffled, so that everyone represents in turn their membership both in the community and in one of its constituent rooms. During the prayers, the anonymous company of the ancestors in invoked time after time, a source of power and protection to which everyone feels equally attached. At the next moment, however, the mention of a particular leader causes each person to bring to mind the paths by which he or she is related to the great man, as well as the closeness of the connection. Consequently, the constituent elements of the community are thrown into relief.

Annual festivals like "prayers of the house" are only the beginning, however. There are many other rites, and I review a variety of them to show how each repeatedly mobilizes different levels of inclusion and exclusion.

Agricultural Rites and Units of Production

Rituals related to the agricultural cycle were not elaborate at Long Teru, reflecting a heavier reliance on sago than people further upriver. Prayers were made at the farms, but the most instructive of rice rituals occurred at the longhouse, after the harvest. Coresidents of a room assembled to eat the first of the new rice, and everyone not belonging to the room was excluded. It was one of the few occasions when the door of a room in the longhouse would be closed, and no one would open it again. It was neither a boisterous occasion nor a furtive one, and it was the job of the head of household to pray to the ancestors of that room for "small stomachs" – that

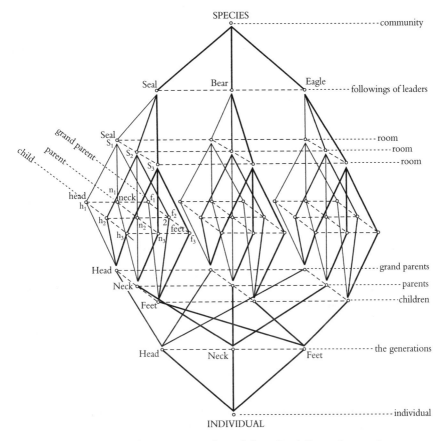

Figure 11-02. The ritual operator as adapted from Levi-Strauss' totemic operator. Labels attached to the diagram are those used in the original, those connected by dotted lines are the ones substituted here.

is to say that the residents would not have such large appetites that their common store of rice would run out before the next harvest, This was also one of the few occasions when a woman might make prayers, if there were no senior man in the room.

The emphatic exclusion of nonresidents from tasting the new rice is an inversion of the hospitality offered during "prayers of the house," but with the same underlying message. It is individual rooms that are the units of agricultural production, not the longhouse community. There was no hint of "primitive communism," and a room that still had a stock of rice when their neighbours had run out felt no obligation to share. This was less harsh than it sounds because rooms that had been idle or unlucky in their farming simply ate more sago.

There was in longhouse society no equivalent of the Polynesian chief's role in the redistribution of food. As summarised by Patrick Kirch (1984:39), tribute presented to chiefs provided a kind of welfare system, so that no one was left destitute. In addition, coastal villages that offered fish as tribute might receive root crops in return, and villages further inland the reverse. Marshal Sahlins (1968) even makes this process a defining feature of the chiefdom level of society. In contrast, longhouse leaders look more like capitalists, busy accumulating beads and brassware for themselves, and this reflects the ancient involvement in commodity production and exchange.

There are, however, contexts in which food must be shared. If someone entered a room and found people eating, he or she would be immediately and repeatedly summoned to eat with them. Etiquette – and indeed more than etiquette, as we will see – required that the inadvertent guest do so. The invitation was sincere, and neighbours often took a seat on the mat and helped themselves. Someone who had blundered in unaware might simply take a pinch of rice before discreetly leaving, but there was a firm insistence on the offering and acceptance of food. It was this ethic that was flaunted at the tasting of the new rice, and that was why doors needed to be firmly closed beforehand.

The Person and States of Ritual Danger

Meanwhile, to refuse food that had been offered could have grave consequences. Anyone who was invited to eat but left without at least touching a plate immediately fell into a condition called *sijang*. The same applied to tobacco, which was regarded as an essential adjunct to conversation. The effect of being *sijang* was to make the individual vulnerable to attack by wild animals. The most feared were crocodiles, which sometimes appeared near the longhouse. One of the few things for which children were scolded was swimming and diving along the riverbank outside the areas encircled with bamboos stuck into the riverbed. These barriers were too frail to keep crocodiles out, but a sudden thrashing of the poles alerted swimmers to their approach. Snakes were also a danger to those who had become *sijang*, and the only way to remove its effect was to make prayers to the Creator Spirit. *Sijang* involved no spirits of any kind; its operation was considered purely physical, much as we regard gravity. Consequently, only the Creator could suspend its otherwise automatic effects. In terms of the ritual operator, *sijang* related to the level, not of the community or of the room, but of the person. That is, membership in the community involved the familiar Maussian obligations to give and to receive. To refuse such social bonds laid the offender open to natural hazards.

Sijang is one of several states of ritual danger resulting from failure to observe a status relationship. Another, *tulah*, afflicts children who do not pay attention to the instructions of their elders. If a boy were to continue climbing a tree after his uncle had told him he had gone far enough, the child risked a fall as a result of being *tulah*. If, however, the uncle so forgot himself as to add "or you'll fall," then he provoked a condition called *padju*. If the child were then to fall and hurt himself, it would be the uncle's fault. *Padju* implies wariness about referring to outcomes. One could never say "good hunting" to a man leaving the longhouse with hunting dogs and a spear; he would wince and turn back, his chances of success having evaporated. The only proper reaction was a studied indifference. Similarly, no preparation could be made for the funeral of even a very sick person. To do so would bring about the death.

Teknonymy and Torsion

Naming practices also emphasize the person, rather than the individual. Each man or woman has a "body name" (*ngaran usa*), but it is often hidden by a teknonym, that is, a title constructed by reference to someone else. There is a considerable literature on the varieties of teknonymy found in Borneo (Needham 1954b; Pollard and Banks 1937), but the most commonly used are simple enough. For example, a husband and wife who have a child called Lawai are addressed as Tama Lawai and Tina Lawai, respectively, that is, Father of Lawai and Mother of Lawai. A grandparent would be called Sadi Lawai, meaning either Grandmother or Grandfather of Lawai. Two-thirds of the adults at Long Teru in the 1970s had names beginning with Tama, Tina, or Sadi.

As a result, the thing most frequently indicated by naming is generation. In my revision of the totemic operator, that is the element that provides what Levi-Strauss (1966) calls "torsion." What that means is that one mode of "filtering unity through diversity" is transformed into another. In the top half of Levi-Strauss' diagram, a society is divided into the Seal clan, the Bear clan, and the Eagle clan, each of which is divided into subclans associated with different species of seals, bears, and eagles. These subclans are then further differentiated internally by apportioning people among different body parts of the totemic animal. In this theoretical schema, everyone has a role to play in ritual according to their association with their totemic animal. Indeed, it requires no less than $3 \times 3 \times 3$ different roles, for a total of 27, which is more than in any of his ethnographic examples. Here is where the interesting move occurs, however. People divided by their totemic associations, seal versus bear, seal species 1 versus seal species 2, and so on, are united by their association with the body parts of their totems, the head people with other head people, the neck people together, and so on, and then again whole individuals can be assembled out of heads and necks, etc. The power of the totemic operator is that twisted in one direction it assembles whole societies; twisted the other way, it creates the individual (Figure 11-02).

My proposition is that, in communities focussed on the ancestors, the equivalent move is the specification of generations, which is an important social status and an individuating feature. Putting it another way, every community is divided into rooms, and every room is divided into generations. When the rooms are assembled, they constitute the community. Within each room, however, grandmother and grandfather are special people, revered for themselves, as individuals. Their generational status makes them not members of a category, but possessors of unique characteristics and experiences. This feature is neatly incorporated in prayer, where the ancestors appear both unnamed — the spiritual counterpart of the community as a whole — and named — individuals who had memorable abilities and careers. My argument is that all longhouse ritual operates in the same way, assembling community at one moment and creating individuality the next.

Individuation: Dreams and Augury

Teknonymy provides the torsion in the ritual operator because it faces both ways, as it were, articulating the collectivity on one side and the individual on the other. Moving now to the lower half of the diagram, there are practices that are exclusively individuating. The importance attached to dreams provides endless examples. For example, each "house stone" (*bito tiloi*) honoured in the "prayers of the house" resulted from the idiosyncratic and interior experiences of one individual. That is, someone was told in a dream where to find it. Moreover, dreams could be "owned." If someone had a vivid dream that seemed to contain portents, he or she made prayers and offerings, with the explicit goal of ratifying favourable portents and averting evil ones. These prayers were public acts, however, allowing the dreamer to lay claim special inspiration. I was, of course, intrigued to know what Berawan dreamed about and ready to look for deep symbolism, but I was usually disappointed. Dreams as reported seldom came to more than a stereotyped image, such as a full fishing net (good omen) or broken teeth (bad omen). How anyone but an overworked dentist could dream about broken teeth, I never understood.

The same kind of autonomy of interpretation also applied to many types of augury. There are a dozen creatures whose appearance or cries might be taken as having meaning. Most are birds, but there are also species of snakes and deer. When new farm sites were being chosen, an older man would often sit alone in the forest trying to work out whether a particular location will produce a good crop. No doubt all manner of technical knowledge is involved in this, concerning such things as drainage and soil type and how long it has been since the last farm was made there. However, what farmers most often report as crucial in their choice was the call of birds, audible even in dense secondary forest. Their interpretations were idiosyncratic, or even contradictory. For instance, one farmer told me that the *tek-tek-tek* cry of *pengape* (the oriental pygmy pied woodpecker, *Dendrocopus canicapillus aurantiventris*) was a good omen because it predicted the creaking of a rice barn filled to capacity. His neighbour's opinion, in contrast, was that it sounded like nails being hammered into a coffin. Snake sightings are positive for some, negative for others, and so on (Metcalf 1976a). If the omen creatures communicate with humans, they apparently use different codes for each.

The key point here is that none of these interpretations of dreams or omens had any correspondence with status and role relationships. Everyone was free to try, and in that way, intuition and inner experience received social recognition.

Shamanism as Ultimate Individuation

The process of inspiration reached its extreme expression with shamans. In the 1970s, there were half a dozen active at Long Teru, and when the house was full, there were sessions on many evenings, and occasionally, two or three going on simultaneously. When I first arrived, I was kept away from these sessions because it was known that missionaries of all stripes strongly disapproved of shamans. Fundamentalists, in particular, condemned them as devil worshipers. Moreover, people worried that I might react in some unexpected way and endanger the life of the shaman. Had I for instance decided to take a photograph, the flash might have startled the spirit inhabiting the body of the shaman, causing it to leave so suddenly that the shaman would fall dead. Shamans provided protection for everyone, and in return, everyone was solicitous of their welfare. Keeping me away from them was increasingly cumbrous, however, and by degrees I was admitted to their sessions.

In total, I probably spent as much time at shamanic sessions as at all ritual occasions combined – life crisis rites, annual festivals, and so on. Consequently, much of the lower half of the ritual operator as I have drawn it concerns shamanism. Properly speaking, I should call it the ritual-shamanism operator. Shamanism should get as much attention as ritual, but it will not because it lends itself even less readily to generalisation than does longhouse ritual. More important, my interests at present are in the politics and economics of longhouse communities, for which the upper half of the ritual operator is more relevant. If my focus were on the construction of individuals, including their hopes and fears, dreams and neuroses, and other things excluded from the British structuralist notion of the person, then shamanism would be a key element. It would be necessary to examine in detail particular interactions between shaman and those they tried to help, so as to draw out the nuances of their interactions.

For now, I restrict myself to a general sketch and two examples. For the most part, shamans in central Borneo were pyschopomps in the sense established by Mircea Eliade (1964). That is, they had the ability to transport their own souls into other spirit realms, where they attempted to recover the souls of people ensnared by malign spirits. In pursuit of errant souls, the shamans typically went into trances, during which their bodies were occupied by their spirit familiars. At Long Teru in the 1970s, the adepts of this kind were women, and each had her own range of special equipment as taught by her spirits. Each had an assistant, usually her husband, whose job it was to interpret as best he could what was revealed by the spirits inhabiting his wife's body, to prevent her from injuring herself, and often to play tunes on the *sape* (a three-stringed instrument) when the spirits wanted to dance. Each shaman had her own way of becoming inspired — by chanting, sprinkling mystically charged water, or dancing to a slow tune — and would then suddenly change demeanour. Everyone then paid close attention to determine what spirit had arrived because experienced shamans might have dozens of spirit familiars. Once inside the body of the shaman, spirits behaved in an erratic manner, dancing or singing, and making all kinds of pronouncements, comprehensible and otherwise. Every once in a while they demanded something to drink, or a cigarette, and it was said that the spirits "came to play" in the body of their human host. This process might go on for hours, and there was no orderly process of healing. Occasionally, one spirit or another would sit down on a large gong, seeming willing to listen, and then the assistant began explaining problems and asking questions, to which he might or might not get answers.

In the 1970s, the most impressive exponent of this style was Sadi Miri of Long Jegan. She was a woman of about sixty, with a long career as a shaman and innumerable spirits. As each arrived, one after another, Sadi Miri's whole body posture would change, along with her voice, so that she was sometimes female, sometimes male, first young and vigorous, then old and frail. The effect was startling, and for me completely uncanny. Soon I began to see not Sadi Miri, but a succession of different persona. She had one spirit that was particularly popular, a boy who had died through neglect many generations ago. His story was sad, but his spirit was cheerful and mischievous, and he ran around the veranda playing tricks on the audience. When he arrived, people who had already gone to bed called out from their rooms to greet him or rushed outside to see what he would do. Then, in an instant, he was gone, replaced by another, and then another, sometimes so rapidly that no one could keep up with what was going on, and Sadi Miri's body seemed buffeted about by the spirits struggling to gain access. These spirits spoke all kinds of languages, including some that the waking Sadi Miri did not speak at all, and some unrecognizable to anyone there. Despite all this turmoil, however, the bodily restraints of Upriver People remained in place: no shrieking or collapsing to the floor or anything of that kind. Instead, every once in a while, one could see the tiny, dignified figure of Sadi Miri through all the comings and goings. Her sessions lasted many hours, until she was finally released and sat back down again on her gong, shuddered, and then looked up, her face drained by exhaustion. After wiping her face wearily, she would turn to her husband and ask how it had gone.

The most common impetus for one of Sadi Miri's sessions was the illness of a child, but anyone could ask for help from her spirits. If in a cooperative mood, they could capture souls on the blade of a knife, using its brightly polished cutting edge as a kind of telescope. When they caught sight of the overdue soul, they would draw it back to its reflection, and then slap the flat of the blade firmly down on top of the afflicted person's head. Once the soul had re-entered through the fontanel, the blade was carefully withdrawn with a wiping motion. The technique was not unique to Sadi Miri. Charles Hose saw it used nearly a century before (Hose and McDougall 1912:II:30). In fact, healing was not Sadi Miri's only motive for holding sessions. Like shamans elsewhere, she was prone to chronic illness, including headaches and nausea, and she took this as a sign that her spirits wanted to "play." In part, Sadi Miri performed in order to heal herself, but her skills were nevertheless highly valued by people at Long Jegan.

At Long Teru, the foremost shaman was a man who had originated a unique style. He was not a psychopomp, and he did not go into trance. He did heal, and so was classified as *daiyung*, literally "singer," even though he neither sang nor danced. Tama Ukat Sageng's special power was that his spirit helpers came to him wherever he happened to be, just as his human friends might do. His sessions were markedly unspectacular compared to Sadi Miri's. He simply sat beside a tray of offerings prepared for the occasion and chatted away, sometimes in everyday Berawan to people sitting nearby, and sometimes to the spirit companions at his side in their languages. Sometimes people paid attention to what he was doing, but at other times the general hubbub of conversation drew peoples' attention elsewhere. He made no attempt to "perform" at all, but asked questions back and forth between his visible and invisible friends. The effect was homely, and all the more uncanny for that. In effect, Tama Ukat Sageng was permanently in trance, and from moment to moment, one never knew whether he was alone or surrounded by spirit beings.

The origin of Tama Ukat Sageng's powers was equally idiosyncratic. Far from being ill frequently, like Sadi Miri, he was physically strong even in old age. While still in his twenties, he disappeared one day from the log rafts in front of the longhouse and was not seen again for some hours. People were worried that he had been taken by a crocodile, as indeed he had, and he had deep wounds on his leg to show where the crocodile had grabbed him. When I met him decades later, the crocked scars were still plainly visible. The crocodiles intended him no harm, however. Instead, they took him down to their inverted world under the water, entertained him, and taught him the secrets of communicating with spirits. Then they deposited him on a sandbar some distance downriver from the longhouse, where he was duly found. There are many stories about the deeds of Tama Ukat Sageng, but the point is made: the powers and activities of shaman are highly individualistic.

However, it is not only the shaman herself who is individuated, but also those she helps. The central issue in curing is the spiritual state of the patient, and again, this has no connection to status and role relationships. On the contrary, it comes very close to what we might call the psyche. Moreover, just as someone's psychic health may have to do with family relations, so may an individual's travails in distant spirit worlds, in complex ways only understood by the specialists, whether shaman or psychiatrist. Some people seemed to always be in need of the shaman, whereas others managed to lead untroubled lives. Sooner or later, however, everyone in the longhouse needed help – if not for themselves, then for a child. Shamanism constantly drew attention to a spirit world beyond the community, a world with which each individual's relations were unique and changeable. The cures that shaman prescribe often left a trace of this idiosyncrasy in such things as special food prohibitions. The only way to refuse rice wine at a party and get away with it was to claim a shaman's prohibition – as I did while recovering from hepatitis.

Changing Gear: The Operator in Reverse

Sometimes, however, a shaman referred patients to other specialists. For instance, if she discovered that the underlying problem has to do with the breach of a taboo, then the appropriate response was prayers. Her spirits could do nothing to reverse the automatic action of conditions like *sijang*, and only the intervention of the Creator Spirit would help. For prayers what was required was a senior man, and so the ritual operator went into reverse, moving the focus of attention away from the needs of the individual and back to the resources of the community.

In this way, shamans might prompt elaborate rituals, scheduled and catered like miniature versions of "prayers of the house." On one occasion, the parents of an ailing child, following the advice of a shaman, made a promise to offer a feast to the spirits if their child recovered. Some months later, when the child was better, they redeemed the promise with food and drink for their neighbours and elaborately decorated trays of offerings for the spirits. The rite was described as *kumaan selamat*, roughly "feasting the recovery" (*kumaan*, "to eat," *selamat*, "safe"). After an hour or so of socializing, a series of prayers was made by senior men for the continued safety of the child (Metcalf 1989:136–53). The shamans were given seats of honour, especially Tama Ukat Sageng, presumably accompanied by his spirit helpers. There was no element of competition between shamans and leaders; instead, they worked as a team, smoothly engaging the mechanisms of the ritual operator.

Another example of an event part ritual, part shamanic session involved the construction of a mystical barrier around the longhouse to keep out evil influences. The barrier (*reng*) was made of spiky vines cut from the jungle, producing much the same effect as barbed wire. A gathering to celebrate its completion included shared food and drink, but the critical step making the barrier effective was performed by a whole company of shamans, each calling down his or her own spirit helpers. Novice shamans often made their first attempts at such gatherings, when there were experienced adepts at hand to help them. No visitors could enter a longhouse after such a barrier had been erected, and *reng* served to quarantine the community when epidemics were sweeping through the area.

Even augury, that idiosyncratic pursuit of signs, had an aspect that was powerfully engaged in the affairs of the entire community. There was one augural animal, the Malaysian black eagle *plake* (*Ictinaetus malayensis*) that was not simply observed in its flight, but actively summoned to give council by ritual specialists who were said to "hold the omen creatures" (*dukep aman*). *Plake* could only be called for the most serious reasons, involving the welfare of the whole house. Previously, that often meant warfare. In the 1970s, the most frequent context was the culmination of a cycle of mortuary rituals, when the augur asked whether everything necessary had been done or whether death still threatened the community. The adept sat by the riverside so that he had a good view of the sky and then made his appeal for the eagle to appear, using the same staccato form as in prayer.

Then he would relax and chat with whoever came by to watch his progress. Every half hour, he would renew his prayer. When an eagle finally appeared, he would renew his *piat* with greater urgency, and everyone would rush to the spot to watch the tiny speck far off in the sky. The interpretation of the bird's flight was standardized so that most onlookers could recognize good and bad omens without being told (Metcalf 1989:184–213). The augur could continue his efforts all day for up to three days, after which it was concluded that the omens were very bad. At other times eagles turned up with remarkable promptness, given that they are rare. I once saw positive omens obtained within ten minutes of starting. The augur could barely contain his delight, despite his modest attempts to disguise it.

I close with an example that demonstrates the entire range of the ritual operator engaged in the same context: an entire longhouse festival based on the dream inspiration of one man. In the 1970s, a unique monument stood in front of the longhouse at Long Jegan. It was a post about twenty feet tall, neatly squared and carved with elegant designs, with two short cross-bars near the top and an large inverted jar above them. It was described as *kaju unong*, a phrase that means nothing more than "standing wood." It had originally been erected in the 1900s at the instigation of man whose ancestors had appeared to him in a dream and instructed him to make it, and its completion was marked with a longhouse festival paid for by the dreamer. It had subsequently been renewed at one longhouse site after another, accompanied on each occasion by another festival, subsidized by the heirs. Needless to say, these events – although supposedly the result of some unaccountable interior experience – had major political impact and were obviously designed to do so. They were ploys in that long-lasting struggle for leadership among the ancestors of the Long Jegan community described in Chapter 5.

The most intriguing feature of the idiosyncratic edifice was the inverted jar on top of it. The pole – innocently described only as a piece of wood – resembled a raised tomb of the type found throughout the Tutoh watershed, and the jar evoked the containers used for storing bones after a *nulang* or rite of secondary treatment of a corpse. As we saw in Chapter 10, however, both jar burial and restorage of bones had been abandoned by the Berawan of Tinjar in order to preserve the appearance of a ritual consensus with the Sebop, when they all lived together at Aban Jau's community at Long Batan. The invented rite of *kaju unong* slyly commented on what had been given up, simultaneously invoking the prestigious ancestors who led the Berawan before Aban Jau ever appeared on the scene. As a final stroke of genius, the festival could not be co-opted or copied by political rivals because it was not part of a general cultural heritage, but rather originated in a dream – a virtuoso manipulation of the ritual operator.

Chapter 12

The Impresarios of the Ancestors

At the outset, I justified my use of the term "community" by saying that it referred to clearly delineated populations – the residents of those spectacular buildings that so impressed travellers in the nineteenth and twentieth centuries. However, this formulation leaves out something that was important to longhouse dwellers. For them, the community was comprised not only of the living, but also of the ancestors. For Upriver People, their community stretched out in time like a meteor crossing the sky – a moving point of light trailing a long, luminous tail.

The Nulang Arc

Consequently, it is not surprising that funerals were important events. Needless to say, that does not imply that death rituals were the same everywhere. In particular, there was a marked division between communities that do and do not practice secondary treatment of the dead. In Chapter 10, we saw what devices were necessary to paper over the divide between Sebop and Berawan rites.

The peoples practicing secondary treatment were distributed in a broad arc from the Kelabit plateau, through the Trusan and Limbang watershed, across the lower Baram region (including the Tutoh and Tinjar), and south along to coast to the mouth of the Rejang. In terms of the main linguistic components reviewed in Chapter 8, this constitutes the speakers of Blust's North Sarawak languages, with the exception of those he classifies as "Kenyah" – using that term in his sense, and not as an ethnonym. In terms of the migration of populations, the distribution suggests the rim of a wheel, for which the hub is the Usun Apau. The main rivers are the spokes, along which people migrated. In other words, we might hypothesize that the people practicing secondary treatment were some centuries ago spread more evenly across a contiguous region of northwestern Borneo. If we further hypothesize that the Kenyah-speaking peoples abandoned secondary treatment as a result of their contact with the Kayan, who lack the practice, we have a reasonable account of how the "nulang arc" came into existence (Metcalf 1976c).

These hypotheticals are relevant only because the people who inhabited the hinterland of Brunei during the time when that city-state's trading system was at its height, for the most part, did practice secondary treatment. This must be emphasized because the literature on central Borneo is dominated by the Kayan and Kenyah – not surprisingly, given how numerous and widely distributed they are on the far side of the mountain chain from Brunei, in Indonesian Kalimantan. The result, however, is to create a "culture area" in which speakers of Lower Baram and Lun Bawang languages are marginalized. In the hinterland, they were central, and the mortuary rites of Long Teru provide a valuable vantage point from which to observe their communal dynamics.

The Communal Response to a Death

All deaths mobilized the community into an elaborately choreographed response. There was no more serious obligation for a member of a community than to return to the longhouse immediately on hearing of a death. In eschatological terms, this was because every death threatened the entire community. Only a co-ordinated response had any chance of averting further deaths. For many people, notification came by means of a massive gong that hung on the veranda and was beaten only to announce a death or an attack. In still air, the deep boom of the gong echoing through the forest could be heard at farms some miles distant from the longhouse. In addition, messengers were sent to outlying farms, and by nightfall, the longhouse was full. There was, to be sure, some variation in the urgency of the response. If a person of no importance was known to have been at death's door, people might dawdle back to the house over a few days, or send only a representative. But ignoring the summons was not an option. People who did so even once or twice ceased to be members of the community.

The only exception I ever heard of to this was a man who had decided to settle in his farmhouse and cut himself off from longhouse society. He later became a Moslem, which was logical because by his residence alone he had already *masok Malayu*, or "entered Malaydom." In addition, cases of "bad death" provoked no response at all. The most common was a woman dying in childbirth, and the malevolence of her soul was considered so irredeemable that no mortuary rites were capable of containing it. Instead, the corpse was dragged off as far as possible into the jungle by the failed midwives and abandoned. Meanwhile, the men hid in the rafters because their manhoods were at risk (Metcalf 1982:254–6). One reason often given for moving a longhouse to a new site was the accumulation of such threats – a kind of spiritual trash.

Frantic activity followed the announcement of a death. The appearance was one of chaos, with women wailing, men running around aimlessly, and confused children looking for reassurance, the gong pounding away all the while. After the initial shock wore off, however, people began to assume responsibilities. Since no acknowledgment of an imminent death could be made until "loss of breath" was announced, there were no contingency plans. So, unless the deceased had been saving a jar for his or her own use, a coffin was needed. Some vigorous middle-aged man not closely related to the deceased was needed to take the lead in this. He immediately rounded up a group of young men and headed off into old jungle to begin the arduous work of chopping down a large tree, cutting off a segment, hollowing it out, and hauling it back to the longhouse, all before the corpse had time to become *melarak*, "drippy." Meanwhile, other men had to prepare the seat on which the corpse would be displayed for a couple of nights, and others had to get down the heavy heirloom boxes from the attic so that the women could find clothes and jewellery to hang around the seat. Others had to chop a hole in the wall because the corpse could not leave the room through the normal door. While all this was going on, there was the steady keening of women, who scolded the deceased for leaving them.

Next, the corpse had to be washed and dressed, and then manoeuvred through a series of rites in which it became in effect a kind of puppet. It was sat up in bed, so that the spouse, if any, could share a cigarette with it. He or she took a puff on the cigarette, and then held it to the lips of the corpse. It was then marched into the kitchen, where it was force fed with newly cooked rice from the store of the room, then marched again around the room, all the while being instructed to continue to love its family and bring them only good luck. All this, plus installation on the death throne, had to be completed before rigor mortis set in, so the whole series of rites was done with an incongruous urgency, as if the corpse were in some kind of race.

For a Westerner, these rites are extraordinary, but they were only the beginning. In subsequent days, the corpse was stored in a coffin or jar, elaborately feted, and then moved to the graveyard. Mourning continued for months, and was especially severe for the surviving spouse and children. In effect, they were immobilized by the necessity to remain by the corpse day and night. Consequently, the funeral rites could not proceed unless the entire community went to work collecting and preparing food and drink, and building the tomb. However, the entire community was in mourning, and the normal activities of festive social gatherings, such as music and dancing, were prohibited. Any weddings that had been planned had to be cancelled. At the same time, there were activities that could *only* occur at funerals, such as playing with tops. The whirring noise they made was said to resemble the voices of the ancestors, whose awesome presence was not to be lightly invoked, but whose presence was necessary at funerals.

Every night for four, six, or eight days, according to the status of the deceased, there was a gathering that everyone in the community was required to attend, excusing only pregnant women, children, and the sick. Nominally, everyone was supposed to stay awake all night, drinking, talking, and whiling away the time with little games reserved for death rites. Those who nodded off were subject to cruel practical jokes, despite the fact that many had been working hard all day. A crucial element of the evening gatherings was the singing of the all-important death songs, whose formidable sacredness came from their power to summon the ancestors to the longhouse, and then to conduct them away again with their new recruit when the festival was over. Properly executed, the songs had the power to reinvigorate the entire community. Incorrectly done, they only provoked yet more death.

The funeral was, however, only the first in a series of rites potentially extending for years, climaxing in an entire second funeral, what Robert Hertz called "the Great Feast," the festival of *nulang*, or "doing the bones." Since the sophisticated eschatology that underlies these rites has been the topic of a previous monograph (Metcalf 1982, also Metcalf and Huntington 1991:79–86), I do not pursue that topic further here. Suffice it to say that souls journey through a desolate stage of dissolution and exile before they are finally admitted into the glorious land of the dead and transformed into spirit. It was in the death rites that life itself came into focus, and that was a consequence of the centrality of the ancestors in their ontology. What I have not previously described was the political and economic implications of the death rites.

In material terms, what was most needed was rice – and lots of it – because it provided not only the staple food, but also the means to make the rice wine consumed in large quantities at major events. Since no one productive unit could possibly accumulate such stocks alone, the community was called on to help. Rice represented farm labour, but labour was also needed to pound rice, to fish and to hunt for game, and to build whatever mausoleum was needed – altogether a formidable communal effort. Other material needs were marginal: a sacrificial animal or two, sugar and coffee, paint for the tomb, and the like. Heirloom property was not consumed, but only put on display. As for political capital, we come to that later in this chapter.

Debating Ritual Formats

After the first frantic half hour, when the corpse was finally seated on the veranda, appropriately washed and dressed and surrounded by valuables, it was time to discuss arrangements for the funeral. This involved a meeting, usually in the room of a neighbour, that anyone might attend. A series of decisions needed to be made in rapid order, but discussions were seldom orderly. People seized on different issues as the most pressing, and there was no one to play the role of chairperson. Leading men hung back at the outset because they did not want to announce a decision that they would later have to reverse in the face of an emerging consensus to the contrary. The wishes of close relatives were important, but not determinative. Since everyone had to assist, everyone could have their say, and there was no way to control busybodies and meddlers. Even the dead person's wishes might not be observed – he or she had as much trouble being heard as anyone else. Older women often saved the day because their experience was respected, and their organisational skills were necessary to arrange the mass catering.

The most immediate questions concerned ritual format. At Long Teru, there were multiple options because both Berawan or Lelak practices were available. It was only in a minority of cases that the full sequence of mortuary rites was an option. People important in the community were candidates for *nulang*, but that begs the question of who it was who was important. At this point, eschatology – the fate of the soul of the deceased – gave way to politics. The same was true concerning the number of days that the funeral would last, that is, the number of nights the corpse would remain on the veranda of the longhouse before being transported to the graveyard. The choice of four, six, or eight nights constituted a public referendum on the standing of the deceased and of the room from which he or she came. Clearly, it was a delicate matter, but people were seldom offended; those with low prestige knew their places well enough. For them, a leading man would solicitously express concern that the bereaved room should not go to too much expense entertaining their neighbours.

Less delicate was the choice of container for the corpse. Jars were commonly used at Long Teru, and some old people made provision for themselves years in advance. They simply turned a jar upside down and said to their children: this is for me when the time comes. At the postmortem debate, relatives might sometimes offer a suitable jar, which would allow the deceased to go into a mausoleum already containing jars. If instead a coffin was going to be needed, the work party needed to move off as soon as possible.

Which graveyard to use and what kind of mausoleum to build were issues of the same kind as length of funeral. In the 1970s, Long Teru had several cemeteries in use, the most ancient and prestigious being on a small island in the middle of the lake that had played so large a part in Lelak history. It was an impressive location, with open views to the mountains beyond – a rare opportunity in jungle-covered terrain. Graveyards could only be cleared of brush and vines when a funeral had already begun, and then they were decorated with brightly coloured flags on long bamboo poles. The effect of the flags snapping in the breeze was uncanny when viewed from the lake, as if some army were camped there. There was a variety of mausoleums on the island, some so old that no one knew who they belonged to. Most contained jars, both large and small. The lake was difficult to access from the longhouse, however, especially for the funeral barges, which were made of two canoes lashed together. Consequently, there was another graveyard across river from the longhouse, which had the advantage that prestigious tombs built there were visible to passersby on the main river. In addition, there were smaller graveyards on side streams associated with people who repeatedly made farms there.

These choices were often more complex for men than women – deceased men and women, that is. Since husbands usually moved into the rooms of their wives, they were mobile, not only up and down the veranda, but also between communities. Only rarely were in-marrying men taken home when they died, but the wishes of their natal kin would be taken into account, if there was time to consult them. More subtly, his affinal relations would not want to impose rites foreign to his home community. Jar burial would not be considered, for instance, for a man from Long Jegan. Phrasing that positively, they would choose for him rites that resembled those in his home community. In addition, there were women who had married into the community, often as a result of political alliances between leaders. Choices for them were every bit as nuanced as for any man.

Meanwhile, there was room for individual eccentricities. On one famous occasion at Long Jegan in the 1960s, a dead man simply refused to go into the tomb prepared for him. At that time, massive concrete vaults were coming into fashion, looking for all the world like World War II gun emplacements.

It was thought that these "modern" tombs would last forever, but the poorly made concrete actually crumbled in a few years, while the elegant and lofty wooden structures remained as impervious as ever to the jungle conditions. Whether he guessed this or not, the old man in question made it plain before his death that he wanted to be in the same airy house as his ancestors. At the discussion concerning funeral arrangements, however, he was overruled by his progressive son who wanted a "modern" tomb. However, when the coffin was brought to the vault after the eight-day funeral, it was a few inches too long to fit. This was odd because everything had been measured beforehand. Nevertheless the coffin was taken back to the longhouse and a slice carefully sawed off each end. Then back to the graveyard, where everyone was amazed to find that the coffin was still too long. At this point, the son capitulated. The father was returned to the longhouse and kept there until an existing wooden mausoleum could be readied to receive another coffin. Both empty vault and mausoleum were pointed out to me in the 1970s. It was a nice theological question as to whether the second period in the longhouse constituted an immediate *nulang*, as was in theory permitted at Long Jegan, but the headman Sadi Pejong ruled against it. No one, he said, can have an accidental *nulang*.

Matters of style and taste were everywhere manifest in the death rites. Wooden mausoleums of the old type, with elaborately carved supporting posts, delicately incised planks, and all kinds of filigree work were the most spectacular works produced by longhouse artists (Metcalf 1977). The carvers of Long Jegan were particularly skilled, and leading men became patrons of the arts when they commissioned new mausoleums (*salong*). Even in the details, however, there was room for creativity. At a grand funeral or *nulang*, red and white cloths, draped over the rafters, formed a bright canopy running the length of the veranda. The colours symbolised the lightning and heavy rains expected at such events, as the charisma of important people dissipated into the sky. Decorations of other kinds were hung along the veranda, in addition to the show of valuables, cloths, and jewellery displayed first around the corpse, and then around the jar or coffin. Large banners were prepared to decorate the funeral barge, with bold curlicue designs in black and red on white. In short, many people had the opportunity to exercise their sense of design and taste, and there was something of the atmosphere of a fashionable wedding in the West, with the endless fussing over a thousand small decisions.

Catering was also a major concern, not because of selection of dishes, which remained the familiar fare of rice, fish, and game, but because of the sheer amount of food and drink required. This is not to suggest that three meals a day were served to everyone. Until the final day, residents mostly continued to eat in their own rooms and entertain their own visitors there.

But there was still the effort required to organise the feasts of the last day, the feeding of visitors throughout, and the preparation of rice wine for each night's vigil. Often the flimsy walls separating the cooking spaces in several apartments would be knocked down to provide one huge kitchen. The largest available ironware cooking pots and kettles were assembled from throughout the longhouse. The cooking was in addition, of course, to the daily pounding of rice. At that first meeting after the corpse was settled decently on the veranda, it gradually emerged who was going to take the lead in all this, directing the labour of dozens of women and girls, and it could not be a close relative of the deceased.

What all this decision making adds up to is the ritual operator at work. There was nothing abstract or unconscious about the process. On the contrary, the debate was explicitly about who the deceased person was, as well as his or her individual eccentricities, and exactly what communal reaction was appropriate. In the process, the ritual operator could be seen shifting gears, focussing first on some matter of intracommunity politics, then moving to something as idiosyncratic as an omen received in a dream, then shifting back again to the connection to an important person of the past, and so on, repeatedly. On these occasions, the operator was made explicit in a literal discourse, for everyone to hear, including the ethnographer.

Legitimation

Lurking behind these discussions were political ambitions and manoeuvres, but they no more implied solemnity than did the serious ritual function of sending the dead soul on its way.

Soon after beginning fieldwork at Long Teru, I was startled to be told that we were all rushing off to join a funeral already under way at Long Jegan. What seemed odd to me was the air of excited expectation among the young people. No one seemed downcast; no mournful faces, no hauling out of dark suits. On the contrary, women chose their most elegant sarongs, and young men unwrapped precious shirts of bright-coloured batik, carefully preserved for such an occasion. There were sombre undertones to be sure: the possible malice of the deceased, the threat of more death. But visitors from other communities were least at risk. They honoured their hosts by attending, and they could expect to be entertained. For the adults, there would be the chance to catch up with old friends, and for the young, an opportunity to meet eligible partners in another community. Such opportunities were rare. Parties in one's own house were certainly fun, and a huge contrast to lonely times at the farms, but there was no chance of meeting someone new. Moreover, at funerals, there was a frank encouragement of sexuality, as if to offset the presence of death. Boys and girls played roughhouse games involving body contact that would have been scandalous at any other time. Meanwhile, old people looked on indulgently, remarking that the energy of the youngsters was the community's hope for the future. Parents took note and discussed the possibilities of match making.

A similar balance of risk and attraction was noticeable in connection with graveyards. Outside mortuary rites, no one wanted to go into a cemetery. A hunt would be abandoned if the chase headed toward a graveyard, old or new. Yet, whenever I announced a desire to visit graveyards, there was never any lack of volunteers to show them to me. Longhouse elders wanted me to see the magnificent mausoleums of their ancestors, and young men grabbed at the chance to look at them up close. Usually, I needed to provide a chicken, so that a sacrifice could be made, with prayers, before entering. This was particularly necessary if I wanted to chop away enough jungle creepers to get decent photographs of the most splendid structures. If disturbed, the ancestors just might decide to add someone new to their company.

These preliminaries made one aware of approaching sacred places, but they were themselves impressive enough. The undergrowth in old rainforest is not dense because the canopy cuts out most of the light. But there are always entangling vines, so one must cut one's way through with broad strokes of a bush knife. I remember one occasion when we were moving along in this way, looking for a cemetery associated with the successful community at Long Tisam (see Chapter 5), when the man in front let out a gasp. We looked around and found ourselves surrounded by columns, some intricately carved, reaching up into the canopy – a veritable enchanted forest. I felt as if I had stumbled onto a lost civilisation. We eventually made out several massive vaults, one mounted on six columns, another on nine. In addition, there were loftier ones, on single posts carved out of the largest trees. On that expedition, we went as far as the headwaters of the Tinjar, and everyone came back to Long Jegan delighted with the glories we had discovered.

When we got back to Long Jegan – the current residence of the descendents of the Long Tisam community – I set about comparing notes with the oldest residents. Each cemetery we had seen corresponded to a former longhouse. My guides often identified the specific site by locating fruit trees along the bank. There was usually nothing to be found behind the trees because the valuable ironwood planks and posts had all been shipped off elsewhere, and the rest had rotted away. Further upriver from Long Tisam, there was always the possibility that the fruit trees marked the site of a former Sebop longhouse rather than a Berawan one, so there were many geographical details to be untangled. Having done that, it was sometimes possible to discover the names of people associated with the monument. The *salong* we had seen were mostly intended for multiple use, and in some, we found a dozen or more coffins, often fallen to the ground (see Figure 12-01).

When I was collecting these details, I took it for granted that that first occupant of a mausoleum had been the most important and that those who joined later mere hangers-on. Indeed, there was sometimes a kind of miniature second storey, with its own raised roof, reserved for the first occupant. Moreover, the time needed to prepare the mausoleum meant that the individual must have received the full rites of secondary treatment, and so been someone of importance. However, the details I collected did not fit this assumption. The names of the initial occupants of large mausoleums, when they were remembered, were not those of great leaders of the past. Some were downright obscure. Berawan did not keep long genealogies, and the most that anyone could offer was that they had somehow been related to the leaders of the time.

Why would a leader build a mausoleum for a 'nobody'? The answer is that he could not build a mausoleum for himself. A Pharaoh of Fourth Dynasty Egypt set about building his pyramid as soon as he was crowned. This was not an option for Berawan leaders because no preparation for his demise was allowed, any more than for anyone else's. The 'nobody' for whom he built the grand mausoleum that would demonstrate his power was simply a relative who happened to die at the right time, that is, the moment in the career of a leader when he was ready to consolidate his position.

In Chapter 5, we followed the story of the Berawan people in the Tinjar after the collapse of Aban Jau's megacommunity at Long Batan. At the end of that account, I pointed out the tendency for longhouses to undergo a kind of life cycle, growing in size and vigour as an energetic new leader emerged, reaching maturity, and then often sinking into leaderless dispersion. In this model, it was the longhouse itself that was the crowning achievement of a memorable leader, but longhouses are not built overnight. An enormous amount of work needed to be done to prepare stocks of timber and shingles. Some planks and pilings could be salvaged from former longhouses, but that also required labour. Meanwhile, everyone had to go on working at their farms, and their farmhouses may have been more solid than the shacks they occupied at the construction site. Inevitably, some people would hang back, fighting a rearguard action for some other site perhaps, so that the longhouse had gaps like missing teeth. Even though the senior men in every room must by this stage have reached a working consensus, the rising leader's effort at cajoling and motivating must have been endless. Even in the face of immediate threats from Kayan or Iban raiders, I was told, there were always those who dawdled.

Moreover, the process of longhouse construction was uneven, so that there was no moment when the project might be declared finished. By the time the last sections of the veranda were in place, the first-built rooms might be in need of repair. Consequently, there was no clear moment when the leader's task of community renewal was finished, nor any grand festival to celebrate it. The only leader who literally made his longhouse his monument was Aban Jau, but his eccentric instruction to leave him in his room and abandon the longhouse was an admission of defeat rather than a claim to glory.

The great advantage of the death rites, from the emergent leader's point of view, was that they constituted a dramatic climax, in which he was, if not the hero, then at least the producer. For full effect, the extended sequence was required, allowing plenty of time to prepare the guest list and accumulate stocks of rice. The delay also enabled the commissioning of a suitably impressive mausoleum, involving a lot of heavy hauling, and the efforts of all the carvers who could be found. This edifice would be placed near a major watercourse, so that passersby might admire it. Finally, the *nulang* festival began with the summoning of the ancestors en masse. If everything went well, their awe-inspiring presence provided the ultimate legitimation of the event and of the leader. He had managed to make himself impresario of the ancestors.

In sociological terms, his achievement consisted of mobilizing the community to support the festival, seeing it as reflecting glory on them collectively. That is, they had come to see his reputation as their own. However, this possibility required only a slight shift in a ritual paradigm that applied to all funerals, large and small. Most important, every longhouse member had to participate in every funeral, meaning both attending the rites and helping to stage them. Moreover, responsibility for the rites devolved onto the community because the close kin of the deceased were immobilised by mourning. They could do nothing more than sit by the coffin, but by doing so they deflected the malice of the hovering soul, and so helped to protect everyone else. The same reciprocal logic applied to the grandest rites. Paradoxically, at the climactic moment of his power play, the leader became passive. By then, however, he knew whether his followers had been willing to work hard over many months in order to put on a good show for the visitors.

Subversion

What constituted failure for a leader is plain enough. Any kind of foot dragging imperilled the effort. A bad harvest was also a risk, but things could always be postponed for another year. The *nulang* for Tama Tiri (see Chapter 5) was delayed for five years because Japanese soldiers requisitioned Long Jegan's rice supplies. Such delays were no disaster; the real threat was weak support, During the emergence of an important leader, there were always rivals. If the community had been fragmented into smaller longhouses, each had inevitably become associated with its own leaders. They might also have absorbed new members, immigrants or refugees from elsewhere, and as a result, slightly modified their language and ritual. Such minor differences would persist in the newly reunified house, providing a basis for political rivalry. The longhouse I saw at Long Jegan in the 1970s appeared to be single building, but its inhabitants insisted that it was four houses, and there were small spaces between some rooms, crossed by little bridges.

There was a much more important aspect to such rivalry than merely obstructing the efforts of an emerging leader to stage impressive mortuary festivals. It was crucial that no leader, however firmly established, could *monopolize* the rites of secondary treatment. That is, the same route to legitimacy that he had taken lay open to his rivals. The logic of communal responsibility still applied, and there was no reason why a thriving community might not back a series of mausoleum building projects over several years. It was in this way that the magnificent collection of mausoleums at Long Tisam was accumulated by one vigorous community in only a few decades. Many were associated with Tama Lire, but others housed relatives of his old nemesis, Aban Avit.

This example makes clear the interaction of religious concepts and political empowerment. In contrast to functionalist ideas, it was not the case that festivals like *nulang* served simply to promote solidarity. Instead, they were a doubled-edged weapon, and they could not be used to establish any kind of hegemonic power. Putting that another way, no one could prevent the ritual operator from shifting gears and bringing attention to bear not on the whole community, but on one of its factions. Aban Jau, despite all his posturing, never did make himself Rajah.

Charismatic Confusion

In Section III, we saw how the ancient trading network of Brunei was disrupted in the mid-nineteenth century, bringing war to the hinterland and enslavement to those who failed to get themselves installed behind large stockades with numerous allies. Even with such pressure toward cooperation, however, there were certainly struggles for leadership within each of these megacommunities. The evidence was still visible in the 1970s, in the form of mausoleums and tomb posts in the graveyards associated with each community.

There were, however, a couple of intriguing anomalies. Both at Long Batan and at Long Kelejeo, I was shown impressively tall mausoleums, richly decorated with carved designs, that had stood directly in front of the longhouses, inside the stockades that had surrounded them. Such an extraordinary breach of custom implied nothing less than the confusion of the living and the dead. Graveyards must be separated from living sites by water, at a minimum by the width of the river. In these two cases, leaders had taken it on themselves to make the longhouse itself into a graveyard. It was, of course, Aban Jau who did this at Long Batan. At Long Kelejeo I could not identify the leader who had resorted to this expedient, but his goal was plain enough. It had been to associate himself so closely with the charisma of the ancestors as to make his position as leader unassailable. Had the strategy succeeded, it would have constituted a revolution, and perhaps the founding of an indigenous state. That it failed showed the strength of indigenous political institutions to resist self-appointed autocrats.

The Gift in Borneo

The communal support of longhouse festivals constitutes an especially Bornean variation on the concept of the gift, as famously framed in the essay of Marcel Mauss (1950). It corresponds to a notion of leadership that is equally original, as contrasted with those of the Melanesian "big man" and the Polynesian chief described by Marshall Sahlins (1963). Critics have since argued that the "political types" that he describes are oversimplified, but they continue to circulate as ideal types. What the types have in common is that they stand at the centre of elaborate rites of prestation. The wealth of a "big man" lay not in what he possessed, but in the debts that were owed to him. Having acquired things – pigs, shells, whatever – the immediate object-ive was to give them away again. By themselves, such understandings of the value of things pose a severe critique of Western materialism (Gregory 1982). So do those of the Polynesian chief, but in a different way. The pur-pose of the great prestations over which he presided was to bring together in one place large amounts of relatively imperishable food, mainly tubers. The amount of food is a measure of the number of a chief's followers and, hence, his prestige. Once it has been displayed, this wealth is redistributed.

Among Upriver People, there are no rites of prestation in this manner. Grand funerals and *nulang* do not reach their climax in the handing over of wealth. Indeed, in terms of those elite commodities traded upriver in exchange for jungle produce, wealth was not given away at all, but jealously

Figure 12-01. One of the last grand mausoleums to be constructed at Long Miri, in a cemetery associated with the Berawan leader Tama Tiri. The jungle around it had been cleared at my request, after appropriate offerings and prayers had been made. The central post is carved in the design called "great spirit," and the roof is topped with a valuable jar, significantly, upside down. By the 1970's the original paintwork had faded. (Photograph by the author.)

hoarded. Heirloom property was hidden away out of sight in trunks, except during the grandest of occasions. It was passed between people almost exclusively by inheritance.

Nevertheless, there was a flow of wealth occurring within the longhouse, principally in the form of rice and labour. There was a distinctly egalitarian ethic behind this distribution. All funerals conformed to the same ritual format, and all brought the entire community together to help the bereaved, regardless of who the dead person was. There is in this a neat inversion of the festival of "prayers of the house." On those occasions, each room offered food and drink to everyone else in the community. At a funeral, the whole house provided food and drink for the members of the deceased's room, as they sat by the coffin or jar. In both cases, the ritual operator brought attention to bear on the relationship between the elements of a longhouse and the whole.

In theory, exactly the same communal values applied to the mortuary rituals organised by leading men, the only difference being one of scale. The quantitative difference amounted to a qualitative one, however, because rice and labour flowed disproportionately to leaders. Since it was then eaten by the community, there is an element of the redistribution of food that Sahlins associates with Polynesian chiefs, but with the catch that the subsidies that ordinary longhouse people provided to their leaders could be withheld or transferred to a rival. A leader's job was never done. Throughout a career in which he hoped to build and maintain a community, his persuasive skills were constantly required, and in this, he resembled a Melanesian "big man."

Another comparison might be with the khans of Swat described by Frederick Barth (1959), who placed on their followers heavy taxes in agricultural produce and then gave some of it back in the form of hospitality in the men's house. The rest they invested in lavish entertainment for other khans, in a never-ending struggle for prestige. This parallel suggests that the rivalry of longhouse leaders is amenable to a transactional analysis of the investment of political "capital" in mortuary ritual. But that would hardly do justice to the drama of the rites, made awful by the hovering presence of the ancestors.

Part VI

Longhouses and the State

Chapter 13

Longhouses during the Raj

In Chapter 12, I liken a longhouse community to a meteor, streaking across the heavens, its path marked by a luminous trail of ancestors. But it is the fate of meteors to burn themselves up in the process, and longhouse communities were indeed defunct in the hinterland by the end of the twentieth century. That is why my discussion of them has been phrased throughout in the past tense. What is amazing is not that they are gone, however, but how long they lasted. This chapter reviews the historical circumstances that allowed or encouraged this to occur. I make no attempt at a history of Sarawak or Brunei, however brief. The point is to consider the impact of external circumstances on longhouse society.

The Golden Age of the Raj

In the first four decades of the twentieth century, longhouse communities not only survived, they enjoyed a cultural florescence. Even in the 1970s, Upriver People still looked back on that time as a Golden Age when they enjoyed both independence and peace, so that trade flourished. As we saw in Chapter 7, new products such as gutta-percha were in high demand, and old ones such as birds' nests could be exported in larger quantities. Many communities, especially those nearer the coast, became wealthier than ever before. The nature of the wealth, however, remained largely what it had always been: beads, brassware, elite fabrics, and ceramics. The expression of wealth also remained the same. When old people in the 1970s reminisced about those days, they invariably spoke of lavish longhouse festivals lasting days or weeks, with guests from far and wide, and of the fabulous bride wealth exchanged between leading families – war canoes loaded to the gunnels with brassware, so that the least ripple threatened to swamp them! That these were not empty boasts was made clear by the amounts of valuables still tucked away in longhouses in the 1970s.

The grand rituals also left their record in the form of those airy tombs. Having been taken to old graveyards throughout the Tinjar and Tutoh watersheds, it was not difficult to identify regional styles. In the Tutoh, the popular style for the grandest tombs was a single massive post, with the re-mains of the deceased in a jar tucked into a niche near the top. In the Tinjar, chambers were built atop one, two, four, five, and even nine posts, allowing for the storage of multiple coffins (Metcalf 1977). Everywhere there were variants reflecting personal taste, but the point for the present is that the most impressive date from *after* the establishment of the Raj in Baram. They show a delicacy and elegance of carving not seen before and constitute major artistic achievements of Upriver People.

The Light Hand of Government

It was under the second Rajah, Charles, that Sarawak achieved its final boundaries and a cohesive administrative structure. The first Rajah had been largely an adventurer. His Borneo years, the 1840s and 1850s, he spent in acts of derring-do, fighting pirates along the West coast of the island. He had his hands full holding onto a small fief, some three hundred miles away from Brunei along the coast to the southwest, to which he had been appointed by the Sultan in return for military services. Charles was a very different sort of man, exceptional in the annals of colonialism. He came to Sarawak in his early twenties, and spent much of his early years in and around Iban longhouses, to the point that he was more comfortable there than in English drawing rooms. His familiarity with the Iban was what allowed him to channel their warlike propensities in directions that suited his interests. The results were sometimes messy, as in the Great Kayan Raid of 1863, but they were effective. Charles steadily expanded his Raj until he had reduced the Sultanate to a mere remnant, surrounded on all sides by Sarawak (Cresswell 1978). The details of his manoeuvring, alternately supported and opposed by the British government, are complex (Baring-Gould and Bampfylde 1909; Runciman 1960), and we need only note that the Baram watershed was ceded to Charles in 1882, the Trusan in 1884, and the Limbang in 1890.

Charles' struggles were not only political, but also financial. A certain amount of revenue came from taxing trade, notably the export of sago from the Rejang region to Singapore, but they were always inadequate (Morris 1991:213–28; Runciman 1960:215–16). To some extent, this suited the Rajah's policies because he distrusted nineteenth-century dogmas of Progress. He thought his subjects materially and spiritually better off than the working classes of industrial Europe. As Robert Pringle describes his attitude:

> Charles Brooke appreciated Sarawak as he had found it, and for that reason neither education nor economic development came high on his list of priorities. He offered only limited inducements to attract European planters, tending to regard them as a class of unscrupulous speculators who deprived gullible stockholders in England of their savings and natives in Asia of their lands. (1970:138)

Tight budgets hampered district administration, however, forcing an ad hoc reaction to particular situations, rather than uniform policies. This left a lot of room for a District Officer (DO) to extemporize and imprint his own mark on his district. Not only was the Rajah's rule highly personalised, being in theory an absolute monarchy, but so was that of his local appointees.

In the heroic early days of the Raj in Baram, there were constant alarms and excursions, and officers like de Crespigny had to move decisively to recruit allies from one region in order to discourage trouble makers in another. This required an intimate knowledge of the leaders of Upriver communities, and constant river voyaging, trips often lasting weeks or months at a time. At the edges of areas where a tenuous order had been established, there were always regions waiting to be explored. The climax of this period was the great peace meetings that drew contingents from all over the Baram, and eventually even from the other side of the mountains in what was officially Dutch territory. It is Hose's name that is most associated with that time, largely because he proved so effective at self-promotion, sometimes to the irritation of his more "stiff upper lip" fellow officers. But there is no doubting Hose's contribution. He organised peace makings, cultivated allies, and led expeditions into uncontrolled parts of the country.

As an example of such activities, in 1898, Hose organised an expedition to what he called "the Madang country." He left the administrative headquarters at Marudi in the lower Baram aboard a small steam launch, towing canoes for use above the first rapids. His force comprised just half a dozen rangers, regulars from the Rajah's small corpse of trained Iban soldiers. As he went upriver, he collected followers from the large Kayan houses of the middle Baram, and then from the Kenyah communities long resident in the upper Baram, the Lepo Pu'un, led by his indefatigable ally Tama Bulan Wan. "As usual," Hose writes, "there was no lack of enterprise and 'go' among the Kenyahs, and they were all keen to make the venture; while the Kayans on the other hand were, as always, more cautious, more inclined to dwell on the possibilities of failure, and slower to take up the plan and make it their own" (Hose and McDougall 1912:II:285). Given the fearsome reputation of the Kayan, it is surprising to hear them described as cautious. But their attacks into the Tutoh and Limbang watersheds a generation before had usually been made in overwhelming numbers, and they certainly possessed no monopoly of warlike spirit.

Hose's progress upriver was delayed by endless palavers and by rivers in spate from heavy rain in the mountains. Finally, his flotilla of canoes entered the Silat, the last major tributary of the Baram, where they were met by emissaries from the Madang. Just who the Madang were remains something of a mystery. Since they were clearly not Kayan, by the dualistic logic of the Raj, Hose had no hesitation in classifying them as Kenyah. But they were certainly not the same as the Lepo Pu'un Kenyah, nor later immigrants such as the Lepo Aga and the Lepo Tau. Indeed, they managed to have hostile relations with all their neighbours and seem to have moved about repeatedly in search of an isolated valley. Iban depredations had only recently caused them to move from the headwaters of the Rejang, to the east of the Usun Apau, and so into the remote upper Silat River (Hose and McDougall 1912:II:281–92).

At this point most of the Kayan turned back, claiming bad omens, but perhaps intimidated by the presence of so many Kenyah. Hose went ahead with the Madang emissaries, and received a friendly, not to say relieved, reception. They were gathered in one large community with several long-houses. Hose then shuttled back and forth between his new and old friends negotiating compensation for killings on both sides. The final meeting was not without tension, beginning with a mock battle in which shrewd blows were given and received, but without serious bloodshed. A feast followed, during which everyone expressed their goodwill – altogether a most satis-fying display of the policies of the second Rajah and totally at variance from the mayhem of the Great Kayan Raid not long before.

There is another aspect to this happy scene, however. While Hose was away on this lengthy expedition, the whole of the rest of the Baram water-shed was left to its own devices. Back in Marudi, there was at most an English junior officer and a number of Malay clerks. Moreover, after Hose's expedi-tion, it would be a long time before anyone in Silat, or indeed the whole of

Figure 13-01. Tama Avit Belalang Sigeh at the bi-annual Baram Regatta in Marudi In 1974. He wears the uniform of an Upriver Agent during the Raj, when he served in the upper Tinjar. He is also wearing medals that he earned by helping allied airmen escape the Japanese during World War Two. He was originally from the Long Jegan community, but later married the widow of the former Penghulu at Long Teru. He traced his descent from Aban Avit, the great rival of Tama Lire at the end of the nineteenth century. (Photograph by the author.)

the upper Baram, saw the DO again. Personalised administration could not be everywhere at once. Later, there evolved a system of Upriver Agents – as they were called – usually respected people from longhouse communities, who represented the Raj locally, collecting taxes, issuing licenses to traders, and keeping Marudi informed of what was going on. But these men, loyal and dutiful as they often were, had little power to take independent action.

The result was that for all practical purposes, longhouse communities remained as independent as they had always been. Only if there had been serious violence, especially involving an outsider, would the DO hear about it. Annual reports from the various districts were often published in the *Sarawak Gazette*, in abbreviated form, and those from Baram often had murders to report. Sometimes the victims were lone Chinese traders, robbed and killed while travelling between longhouses. More often, parties of Iban youths, nominally searching for jungle produce, would cause trouble. There was always the threat that their ventures would turn into headhunting expeditions, and sometimes Upriver People would guard against this possibility by murdering them pre-emptively. Even where Iban youths intended nothing more than gathering forest produce, Upriver People resented their presence because they rapidly exhausted local supplies of the valuable gutta-percha. Moreover, Iban often mixed other gums into the product to make it weigh more, pushing the price down for everyone. DOs agonized over whether to issue collecting licences to Iban. On the one hand, it promoted economic activity; on the other hand, it was a constant source of friction.

Apart from such cases, everything else had to be handled within longhouse communities: disputes over marriages, inheritance of heirloom valuables, ownership of fruit trees, and all manner of affrays and assaults. Just what mix of public opinion and leader's fiat this involved varied from community to community, but it is probably fair to say that, even in the most hierarchical, leaders did not care to be too often at odds with the majority. Upriver Agents no doubt kept in touch with the gossip from at least some communities, but they seldom had any reason to interfere. That such independence should exist in remote longhouses, such as those in the headwaters of the Silat, is perhaps not surprising. But it was virtually the same situation even in more downriver longhouses. For example, the Long Teru longhouse had far more than its share of visits from DOs because it was the only community in a long stretch of the lower Tinjar. It was convenient to stop there to pick up a new crew of paddlers, allowing the first to head back down to Marudi. Even so, it was a world largely closed to outsiders. For example, one infamously unstable leader in the 1930s killed several people in fits of rage, including his sister. No news of the murders ever reached the DO.

The Third Rajah and Economic Development

Charles Brooke died in 1917, thirty-five years after the cession of Baram to Sarawak. His heir, Vyner Brooke, was not a man of the same stature.

Personalised rule continued, but the personality at the head of it was less familiar with Sarawak and less comfortable there. His wife positively disliked it, preferring to use her title as Ranee Sylvia to confer on herself a certain *eclat* in London society. Vyner was often absent from Sarawak for long periods, leaving his younger brother as caretaker (Runciman 1960:232). Judging by the reports in the *Sarawak Gazette*, outstation life seems to have become more languid and office bound. There are more stories than previously about social events in the main centres, and less about patrols into the interior.

What this meant for Upriver People was that the hand of government rested even more lightly on them. The Brooke Raj took on the distant, mythic air that had surrounded Brunei a half century before. This is not to say that nothing had changed. Most obviously, and especially by comparison with the ever restless Iban to the south, Upriver People readily embraced the peace promoted by the Raj. The virtual end of warfare and headhunting among themselves had far-reaching consequences. For instance, the great festivals devoted to headhunting and warrior status gradually faded away (Metcalf 1996). Meanwhile, those peace-making events organised by Hose and others created opportunities for alliances on a new scale, expressed in terms of those marriages that old people in the 1970s associated with the Golden Age. This in turn may have had the effect of increasing the social distance between elites and the bulk of longhouse residents.

Moreover, the expansion of trade included not only forest products, but also new cultigens, notably rubber. During the rubber boom of the 1910s, vast European-run plantations in the Malay Peninsula were making huge profits, employing coolies from India housed in bleak "labour lines." This was just what Charles Brooke wanted to avoid. Instead, he promoted planting by local small holders. He maintained experimental agricultural stations, at government expense, from which seedlings could be bought at subsidised prices. He also protected small holders by prohibiting the sale of their gardens to nonnatives (Pringle 1970:138, 202–4). Missionaries also played their part. In Baram, there was a lone Roman Catholic priest established at Marudi, and he took a positive attitude to economic development. He made small loans available to several longhouse communities for establishing rubber gardens. Ironically, one or two did well enough to maintain labour lines of their own, a kind of parallel longhouse behind the main one. The workers were mostly impoverished Chinese peasants fleeing the chaos in their homeland, some of whom would later set themselves up as traders. Using loans from established Chinese merchants, they lived rough in their little boats, and worked hard for small margins of profit. Within a generation, they had virtually driven the Malay traders of the old sort out of business (Goldman 1968).

Even with such wealth, however, there was not much money circulating within longhouses. Most rubber producers had arrangements with particular Chinese traders, and they simply took what they wanted from his shop house, until they had used up their credit. In other colonial regimes during the same time period in India, for example, peasants were vulnerable to exploitation by money lenders, to the point were they effectively became serfs on their own land. But merchants had little leverage on longhouse people because longhouse people had nothing to offer as collateral. Land and rubber gardens were off limits, and traders hardly wanted to repossess the elite goods that were the wealth of distinguished families, even if they could conceivably have forced their way into a longhouse to seize them. The balance of physical force remained with Upriver People, and that was another important aspect of their independence.

There were several consequences. First, loans taken by Upriver People from Chinese traders tended to be small, often just enough to cover the expenses of a longhouse ritual. For these events, rice was the essential resource, both for feeding guests and making rice wine. Everything else, such as biscuits, coffee, and sugar, were luxuries. It is true that loans were sometimes taken out even to buy rice, allowing a sequence of death rites to be completed in months rather than the years it might otherwise take to accumulate a sufficient surplus (Metcalf 1981). But these loans could only be repaid by future rice or rubber production, for which the trader could only wait. Some devised a way to circumvent the problem of acquiring rubber gardens themselves. For example, at Lepu Leju in the remote upper Tinjar, there was a "bazaar" consisting of one shop, plus the "office" of an Upriver Agent. The shop owner encouraged his sons to marry into a neighbouring longhouse and to acquire land in their wives' names. In this way, he became an important local figure, founder of veritable dynasty of part-Chinese traders. However, by assimilating in this way, his family gradually distanced itself from the urban Chinese merchants, and so from his sources of credit.

A second result of the separation of longhouse and Chinese economies was that most trade consisted of tiny purchases – a box of matches, a sarong – either from the nomadic boat traders, or from one of the dozen or so tiny bazaars established upriver from Marudi. According to reports in the *Sarawak Gazette*, Upriver People were often the victims of price gouging and false measure. Major shopping expeditions were rare events, requiring travel down to the much larger bazaar at Marudi, which had upward of thirty shop houses and a far greater range of goods. To accommodate visitors, a substantial guest house was built, and it became a social centre, where news circulated from all over the Baram watershed.

A sense of solidarity among Upriver People was enhanced by re-enactments of the great peace making at Marudi in 1899. On that occasion, Hose had tried to displace old hostilities into sporting competition in the proper English fashion. Lacking cricket pitches, he had organised races between the great war canoes, crewed by sixty or more paddlers (Hose and McDougall 1912:II:293–300). As late as the 1970s, massive canoes continued to be constructed for these events, which came to be called the Baram "Regatta." In this way, the old pattern of trading expeditions was preserved, except that they were no longer armed forays. Even so, according to the missionary Hudson Southwell (personal communication), as late as the 1930s, people did not care to stop at the longhouses of their former enemies. Instead, they would halt a little way upriver and drift past in the dead of night. Coming back, they paddled quietly by, hugging the opposite bank. As in previous epochs, canoes went downriver laden with jungle produce and came back with manufactured luxury goods – that is, luxurious by the spartan standards of Upriver life. No large amounts of cash travelled either upriver or down, so that there was little to circulate upriver.

The marginality of money to the internal economies of longhouse communities produced a third consequence: it was possible to be both powerful and penniless. Putting that another way, the relative wealth of the Golden Age was not such as to undermine the social order established during the heyday of the Brunei trading network. There were as yet no *nouveaux riches* to offer a competing model of social standing. Upriver People were not oppressed by capitalism. They did not feel themselves impoverished when they could not afford the commodities circulating through the cash economy. The members of a longhouse room could feed themselves perfectly well as they had always done with the produce of their farms and rainforests, and experienced no personal sense of inadequacy. This was the true basis of their cheerful independence, and it lasted into the 1970s. I remember once stopping at a longhouse in my canoe, which was driven by a new twenty-horsepower Johnson outboard motor. At the informal dock, made out of floating tree trunks, there was a family preparing to go off to their farms. Their canoe had an ancient three-horsepower English motor on the back, as simple a motor as could be imagined. The brand name was Seagull, and one or two were found in every longhouse throughout the interior. Even children could pull them apart and make rough-and-ready repairs. In this case, the owner was patiently wrapping a piece of string around his motor's flywheel and pulling hard to start it, but without success. Another man in the canoe grinned broadly at me and explained with a nod, "*miskin, lah*." In Malay, *miskin* means poor, but upriver it meant simply having no money. If the family had cash, maybe they would buy a new one. In the meantime, life went on as normal, and there was no shame in not having money.

The Impact of the Great Depression

The lack of dependence on a cash economy softened the blow of the Great Depression of the 1930s. For the most part, longhouse people made do with less trade store clothes, biscuits, and coffee. The principle effect was to reduce the already modest financial resources of the Raj. Between 1929 and 1932, there was a 37% drop in revenues. This forced a reduction in already skimpy social services. The Education Department, which had only recently been formed, was abolished, and the Medical and Health departments were merged, with reduced staff. The salaries of government officials across the board were cut (Reece 1988:47). Little of this had any impact at all on Upriver People, because no schooling had been available to them anyway, and there were no medical facilities closer than Marudi.

Moreover, there were still pockets of wealth upriver, provided most notably by the valuable birds' nest caves in the hills south of the middle Baram. Demand for the high-quality white nests remained strong, until the Japanese invasion of China in 1932 disrupted trade across the South China Sea. Evidence of their value is provided by the famous "Dollar Princess," Balu Ulau, who managed to consolidate in her own hands ownership of almost all of them. Her obituary in the *Sarawak Gazette* (656:February 1912) reveals that she was none other than that daughter of Aban Jau, whose marriage had been a key element in his policy of alliance with the expansionary Kayan. She had nearly ruined this policy by her multiple infidelities, but she nevertheless managed to be married successively to the first, second, and third Kayan Penghulus (government-appointed chiefs) in Baram, as well as a Brunei aristocrat, whom she soon turned out of doors. When the third Penghulu died, his subjects had no hesitation in nominating her as his replacement. The English DO was more sexist than they, however, and insisted on a male successor. Her nephew was appointed, but he candidly confessed that she retained real power, adjudicating major disputes and universally respected for her sagacity. Whether wealth brought her power, or the other way around, what is clear is that she accumulated a fortune beyond anything that was needed for beads and brassware. Had the infrastructure existed for profitable local investment, she and her heirs might have initiated indigenous economic development in time to profit from the much faster pace of change after 1946. The lack of preparedness for such development was a major failure of Brooke rule and left Upriver People unprepared for the sudden arrival of "development" in the late twentieth century.

Enterprise was not lacking. The rapidity with which people in the hinterland seized the opportunity to grow rubber is evidence enough of that. In many corners of the British Empire, in East Africa and New Guinea, for example, colonial administrators had to exert pressure to get indigenous people to plant cash crops, such as copra palms. In comparison, Upriver People were only too willing to experiment with pepper and coffee, and this reflects their experience over centuries with the notion of commodities produced locally for consumption far away. The fact that their trade relied on direct barter without the intermediary of money is neither here nor there. What they could not understand was the apparently random ups and downs of international markets. Although birds' nests held their price, the payoff for the new crops went up and down alarmingly. A visiting DO would talk up the profits to be made from, say, pepper, but by the time the new gardens came into production their owners would find the price to be a fraction of what had been promised. Sometimes they would make losses on the whole venture, even without taking into account their own labour. This was discouraging to say the least, and Upriver People could only believe that they were being cheated, probably by the Chinese, perhaps by the government, or even by the poor Catholic priest who had tried to help them with small loans.

Profits were more reliable in commodities that were in local demand. An example of upriver enterprise is provided by the ingenious technology developed at Long Teru to exploit their resources of fish. These came from the large, shallow lake that had been the homeland of Lelak people since time immemorial. The level of the lake rose and fell in a complex relationship with the height of the Tinjar River, and there were seasons when large catches of fish could be made, far more than could be consumed in the longhouse. Long Teru people devised not only huge dip nets for catching fish, but also cylindrical bamboo cages some twenty feet long and six feet in diameter in which to keep them live. In the tropic heat, fish pulled out of the water would go off long before they could be brought to Marudi, but the cages could be allowed to drift downriver on the current, and so arrive with their contents in marketable condition. To keep oxygen levels high enough inside the crowded cages and to flush away waste products, it was necessary either to tow them gently forward or to anchor them with a line ashore every once in a while to let the current flow through. Arriving in Marudi, the cages could be moored, and deals made with Chinese traders and local Malays at leisure. When the cages were empty, they could be rolled up and returned to Long Teru by canoe, ready for the next harvest

(Metcalf 1976b). The *Sarawak Gazette* reports this system in operation by 1915 (June 758), and it was still going strong in the 1970s.

Timber, particularly the rot and termite-proof *bilian* so useful for house posts, could be moved down river in the same way. As we saw in Chapter 1, *bilian* is difficult to work and too dense to float, so that it required rafts to move it. But there was always a good price for it in Marudi, from where it would be shipped to the coast in steam-driven launches. In contrast to pepper gardens, returns on the labour of cutting and moving *bilian* were modest, but they were secure and prompt.

Whether Charles Brooke would have found ways to channel upriver enterprise into any kind of steady economic growth is uncertain. What was needed was some kind of savings arrangements available in longhouse communities, or at least in Marudi. Lacking that, communal efforts were constantly frustrated by crooked headmen, who simply embezzled the profits. Despite the experience that Upriver People had with commodities, nothing in the trading system of Brunei had encouraged institutions that resembled joint stock companies or cooperatives. Elite families had always taken the lion's share of trade goods for themselves, and men put in leadership roles saw no reason not to do the same. One headman at Batu Belah in the 1920s stole the entire profits of a communal rubber-growing scheme. When his neighbours objected, he coolly set himself up in a single residence, Malay-style, some distance away. They had no recourse short of murdering him, a course of action that they certainly considered. It was in situations of this kind that a more intrusive, or even attentive, administration might have worked wonders for economic growth.

As it was, the opportunity was lost. When the price of rubber collapsed during the depression, the daily chores of cutting the trees and collecting the sap became a matter of pocket money, mainly attractive to children and old people. Meanwhile, efforts to draw remote longhouses into the polity grew even less frequent. A 1936 report in the *Sarawak Gazette* July (997) pointed out that no government personnel of any kind had visited the Kelabit highlands in many years. This was not light-handed administration, this was no administration at all. In effect, most of the Kelabit lived "outside the Rajah's fence," as did many of the later Kenyah arrivals. The ancient pattern of differential inclusion in a trading sphere had not so much disappeared as moved upriver.

By the 1930s, there was criticism in British colonial circles in Malaya of the quality of Vyner Brooke's administration. Bob Reece (1993:51) quotes Mr. Peter Scott, who resigned the Sarawak Service in 1930; he describes his former colleagues as "narrow-minded, pig-headed, ignorant and ill-mannered." They kept their jobs only because Vyner Brooke was so gullible, and most were mere "time-servers." Scott may have had some grudges to settle, but his sentiments echo the biting satire of Somerset Maugham's (1926) account of his time in Sarawak.

Brooke Policy on Longhouse Residence

A relatively static economy allowed longhouse life to persist into the mid-twentieth century, not unchanged to be sure, but recognisably the same. This was in accordance with Charles Brooke's willingness to "appreciate Sarawak as he had found it." That policy in turn provided a perfect example of the tendency of British colonial regimes to produce what Julian Huxley (1936) sarcastically described as "a human zoo, an Anthropological Garden." But there was more going on here than sentimentality or apathy. On the contrary, it was very much in the interests of the Brooke administration to positively promote longhouse residence.

This is neatly demonstrated by a comparison with colonial situations elsewhere in the same period. C.D. Rowley begins his account of *The New Guinea Villager* (1965) by confessing that he uses the term "village" for the sake of convenience only. The directory of the Department of District Administration listed over a thousand "villages," but they turn out to be a mixed bunch. Some were "dancing grounds" to which administrative officers summoned people from the surrounding areas. There were often no houses at these places. Others were names of clans – that is, people claiming common descent, but living in isolated farmhouses across a vaguely defined area. Some had multiple names. This was a major headache where "government must be taken by patrol to the people." In such inconvenient circumstances, people were "forced or encouraged to establish villages beside a road which they had to maintain" (Rowley 1965:32–4). Such "line villages" and the tracks between them were intended to produce a colonial infrastructure, but many such villages merely stood empty whenever the administrative officers were not around.

In comparison, DOs in the Baram watershed were lucky indeed. There was no need to press labour to clear roads because all travel was by river, and all longhouses were located beside rivers. Nor was there any need to force Upriver People into villages because all of them – apart from the foraging Penan – already lived in longhouses, whose straight lines could hardly be improved on. Consequently, it is no surprise to find DOs doing everything they could to promote community stability. As we saw in Chapter 5, after the collapse of Aban Jau's megacommunity at Long Batan, Hose tried to pull the scattered elements back together again. He scolded the rival Berawan leaders Tama Lire and Aban Avit, and he urged all the Sebop – old followers of Aban Jau, plus the recent arrivals in the Tinjar – to muster in one large community (*Sarawak Gazette* 530 February 1909). In neither case was he successful, and he had no choice but to let indigenous political processes run their course.

Similar circumstances applied in the Tutoh, after the breakup of the large, heavily fortified community gathered at Long Kelejeo, for protection against Kayan war parties headed into the Limbang. The Long Kiput (Lakipo') had been a major element in the confederacy, but by 1914, we find them living at their farms, without longhouse or leadership (*Sarawak Gazette* 656 June 1914). The then DO, Mr. Adams, assembled all the petty leaders and harangued them about the necessity to build a new longhouse at their old site at Long Tutoh. There was, however, a complication of which Adams was not aware. Long Kiput oral history tells of a series of leaders who all came to rapid and unpleasant ends. Omens were taken and repeatedly predicted more of the same, causing a stalemate. After much discussion, it was eventually decided to recruit from outside. Elite families were consulted in nearby Kenyah communities, all of which had been in the first wave of immigrants into the Baram watershed and, consequently, neighbours of the Long Kiput for generations. Remarkably, the candidate they offered became a leader in a renewed longhouse community whose language he did not speak. Moreover, the graft took, and all subsequent leaders came from his stock. This arrangement was not unique. In his ethnographic survey, Leach (1950) reports the case of three brothers who had been installed as leaders of three neighbouring but ethnically distinct longhouse communities.

There were many other occasions when DOs exerted what pressure they could to get decaying or abandoned longhouses rebuilt by communities that were going through a phase of dispersal in that cycle described at the end of Chapter 5. It is evident that by the 1920s, official anxiety about the vitality of particular communities had gone beyond administrative convenience and become a premise of the entire, overarching ethnic classification. Upriver People were *supposed* to live in longhouses, and that was that. Consequently, acknowledged longhouse leaders were empowered to fine people who moved away from the community or failed to maintain their part of the longhouse. This was a radical departure from custom because it tried to freeze communities and suppress mobility. In theory, no new longhouses could be formed by factions splitting away from moribund communities. Not surprisingly, practice was very different to theory, but the ossifying colonial reflex is clear.

Another reason for pressuring Upriver People not to leave longhouse communities was to prevent them from building single family houses in the Malay fashion, but that also occurred. Along the true right-hand bank of the Baram between the mouth of the Tutoh River and the government station at Marudi, there was a whole string of isolated houses belonging to people who originally came from Batu Belah, the Berawan longhouse some distance up the Tutoh. They had not, however, converted to Islam, and so became impossible to classify. The administrative response was, of course, to ignore them. Meanwhile, Malays (i.e., Moslems) were forbidden to live in longhouses, where it was said that they "caused trouble" (*Sarawak Gazette* 775:April 1919). This ignored the fact that there had always been close links between Malay villagers and longhouse dwellers in the hinterland of Brunei, as noted in Section III. DOs felt the same way about Iban men who married into Upriver communities, and it decreed that families of "mixed marriages" must go to live in a longhouse community reserved only for them. It was situated in the previously uninhabited watershed of the Peking, a small tributary of the Tinjar. In the 1970s, I can report that it was a thriving Iban community, active in traditional Iban festivals (*gawai*), but showing no trace of its Upriver heritage.

Brooke Policy on the Recognition of Leaders

It has often been remarked (Cohn 1996; Dirks 1992) that tidiness is a compulsion of the colonial mind, but that attempting to freeze existing social arrangements removes their ability to respond to changing political and demographic circumstances. Despite the reputation of the British functionalist ethnographers of the 1940s and 1950s for complicity in this rigidity of mind, they did in fact provide many cautionary examples, if anyone had been paying attention. For instance, Max Gluckman – that arch-functionalist – was asked to report on the proper way that the role of Citimukulu among the Bemba of Zambia should pass from one incumbent to another. There were rules of descent for British monarchy, so why not for the role they took to be the "kingship" of the Bemba? Gluckman's report is a model of legalistic exegesis, complete with genealogies, but he concludes that the rules could only apply for a few generations before becoming unworkable. Then what had occurred was in effect a *coup d'état* by one leading family or another (Gluckman 1963:84–108). The administration of Northern Rhodesia, as it then was, had the choice of imposing its own rules or abolishing the entire system of chiefly titles. So much for "indirect rule."

No such difficult adjudications were required of the officers of the Brooke Raj because it had limited power to interfere in indigenous politics anyway. There was the ghost of a bureaucratic administration, represented locally by the "headman" (Tua Kampong in Malay) appointed in each longhouse. But DOs had little choice but to follow communal opinion because there was no point in selecting an unpopular or marginal man. Officially, the headman's job was to represent government to the community, explaining government policies and collecting taxes. Such taxes were small and never covered the costs of even the minimalist Brooke administration. All three Rajahs insisted on them, however, mainly as an inducement for longhouse people to get involved in some way or another in the cash economy. We have already seen how poorly that worked, and taxes often arrived months late, or never showed up at all, simply because there was no money to be had.

Meanwhile, headmen preferred to see their function in the reverse way, as representing the community to the government. This put the true leaders of longhouse communities in a dilemma. If they chose to accept the title of Tua Kampong and collect taxes themselves, they risked being seen as tools of the government, but if they put a lesser man in the role they had no direct link to the district administration, and so risked being marginalised. This situation resembles one from Africa during the same epoch, as reported by Lloyd Fallers. The colonial administration of Uganda offered to pay small salaries to village headmen, in return for their labour on behalf of the government. After much debate, however, the assembled headmen decided to refuse pay on the grounds that "if someone pays me to clean my table, it becomes his table" (Fallers 1965:174). In that way, they made clear who they were representing, and to whom. In Sarawak the ambiguity remained.

For a well-connected leader, the best solution to the dilemma was to be installed in the much more prestigious role of Penghulu, of which there were always a half dozen in the Brunei hinterland. They could then present themselves as councillors to the DO, advising him in an avuncular way about longhouse affairs. This was not far off the mark, at least for DOs smart enough to take advantage of their Penghulu's local knowledge. Meanwhile, the Penghulu could bustle around the dozen or so longhouses under their nominal supervision, advancing their own standing at the expense of other community leaders.

The conferring of chiefly titles was familiar to Upriver People because it followed Brunei practice. For Brunei, it had been a way to draw longhouse people into a theoretical polity that extended further upriver than the "Sultan's fence," and the success of the strategy is shown by the enthusiasm with which such titles were received. One might have imagined that the unruly Kayan of the middle Baram would have scorned titles conferred by a failing state that they had come close to overthrowing. That the reverse was true, that the titles served to bolster the standing of Upriver leaders in the eyes of their own followers, shows that there was indeed a political system that stretched far upriver, even amidst the instability of the mid-nineteenth century. The polity might have been weakened, like the Roman Empire in its last century, but there was no anarchy. On the contrary, Brunei and Upriver leaders were still struggling for the same prizes as always. There was nothing in this of bureaucratic organisation, but the same was true of the Brooke Raj; that is, titles comprised recognition of achieved status rather than recruitment of civil servants.

Brunei was, however, more prolific in its titles than the Brooke Raj. The most common was Orang Kaya, simply "rich man," an appropriate form of recognition for an empire built on trade. Then there was Penghulu, and on one occasion they appointed a Temonggong, or paramount chief. The Orang Kaya Temonggong Lawai was leader of the large Berawan community in the middle Tutoh region, and his aid against the enemies of Brunei was crucial for the Sultan. In the years immediately before and after the cession of Baram to the Raj, the Orang Kaya Temonggong was the most influential leader in the hinterland. His only rival was the infamous Aban Jau, whose hostility earned him no titles other than those he conferred on himself. At the same time that the Sultan was granting a few titles upriver, however, he was handing out far more grandiose ones right and left within Brunei. This served to remind those Upriver People who had been drawn into the Brunei's orbit of the infinitely greater dignity of the royal court itself.

Brooke Policy on Land

In addition to having their neatly linear villages provided with no effort on their part, DOs in Sarawak were seldom drawn into disputes over land. Contrast this with the situation in many parts of East Africa, for example, where harassed administrators spent a major part of their time trying to resolve endless disputes over land, involving convoluted family feuds going back generations. The litigants argued in local dialects often incomprehensible to the DO, so that he was forced to rely on court translators who may or may not have been interested parties or the targets of bribery. Meanwhile, across central Borneo, land disputes were rare. The obvious reason for this was that population density was very low. Maps in a survey of development in Sarawak show all of the Baram and Limbang watersheds with a density of less than 5 persons per square mile (Cramb and Reece 1988:7).

This statistic fails to take note, however, of the distribution of people within the region. Large upland areas had never seen human habitation, and the ancient rainforest remained undisturbed. Apart from hunting expeditions, the economy of Upriver People restricted them to the valleys, where there were pockets of alluvial soils that provided the opportunity for a reasonably productive agriculture. As we saw in Chapter 5, such niches might be exploited for several generations, regardless of changes in location of the longhouse, but then the community might move en masse to another valley or segment of the same valley. In the lowlands, reasonable land not prone to constant flooding was even harder to find. Consequently, there was the possibility of competition. The fact that it seldom arose was a function of longhouse residence because the niches in a given stretch of river would be occupied by members of one community, even if that community was in decline. If the community migrated, the niches would simply be abandoned. What did not occur was a few settlers from another community becoming interlopers on currently occupied land, and that is why there were few disputes that came to the DO's attention.

This state of affairs continued until the arrival of the Iban, starting in the late nineteenth century, and gathering momentum during the twentieth. The problem was precisely that Iban *did* move in dribs and drabs, a few families at a time. When Upriver People took legal action against the settlers, they often won, but gained nothing because another band of Iban would appear, and the whole process would begin again. This situation grew worse in the postcolonial period.

Upriver People often claimed to "own" vast tracks of land. The Berawan coolly announced that the whole Tinjar Valley belonged to them, and everyone else was there merely on sufferance. They pointed out that fruit trees planted by them, at longhouse sites long abandoned, extended into the far headwaters. In practice, there was little substance to this boast because no Upriver community really expected to retain control over land that it was not occupying. None of the first settlers in the middle Baram (the Lepo Umbo' or Roots People) continued to claim land there in the 1970s because they had abandoned it long ago. No one saw fit to contest the subsequent Kayan appropriation of the region.

Meanwhile, within Upriver communities, there were seldom any serious conflicts over land. The study of indigenous land tenure has become entrenched in the literature of Borneo, largely as a reflection of its importance to British anthropology in the 1950s and 1960s. In practice, the only rule I ever heard cited was that primary rights to land belonged to the man who first cut down the virgin forest there – no small task, given the size of the trees that had to be cleared. His rights passed down within the economic unit of which he was a member, his "room." Such rights seldom occasioned disputes, however. People farming near one another were invariably friends and relatives who cooperated in the labour of planting and harvesting. Having chosen a farm site, the correct thing to do was check that the "owners" were not planning to use it themselves, and that everyone thought that it had been lying fallow long enough.

A Cool Life, a Slow Life

This review of Brooke policy indicates that, for the most part, the Raj did not interfere in the internal affairs of longhouse communities because it did not need to. Given that it lacked the financial or administrative resources to do so anyway, this was a convenient relationship for both parties. What resulted was the colonial stasis. For better or worse, longhouse life persisted through a long Indian summer.

This was the period of the Golden Age, but it is characteristic of such mythic times that nothing much happens. In comparison, the oral histories of the previous epoch are filled with swaggering heroes and desperate encounters. It is not, of course, true that strife suddenly came to a halt. Even if the time of the *volkerwanderung* was past, communities still migrated en masse, usually down river. Rivalries continued between aspirants to leadership, if indeed they did not intensify after the breakdown of the large confederations such as Long Kelejeo and Long Batan. However, in the recollections of older people in the 1970s, their narratives tended to become bland. What people wanted to emphasize was the grand scale of social occasions. In this, there is a bizarre mirror image of the languid inactivity of the officers of the Raj, as reported in the *Sarawak Gazette*, who seem during the 1920s and 1930s to become increasingly preoccupied by social events at the administrative centres. Perhaps there is a moral here somewhere.

That this state of affairs was what Upriver People desired is neatly illustrated in the snippet of prayer quoted in Chapter 11, which asked for "a good life, a cool life, a slow life, a calm life." The paradox is that many Upriver People prize a personality that is "fast," meaning swift of movement, energetic and vigorous, even impetuous. In Berawan, the term used to describe these attributes is *sagem*, and there are equivalent terms in Kenyah languages. In comparison, the Kayan are said to be cautious and restrained. The quality of *sagem* was often brought to my attention because I was apparently the very embodiment of its opposite. I was so *maport* that by the time I got ready to do something, everyone else had lost interest. By way of consolation, people assured me that "slow" people were the best at making fishing nets – perhaps a book is like a fishing net.

The structuring of time in ritual provides one solution to the paradox. It was noticeable that during any rite that lasted more than an hour or so, the pace varied between relaxed and frenzied. Always, I was told, the next phase of the ritual would begin in a while, after so and so had found something or had his bath. Meanwhile, everyone took their ease on the veranda, talking and drinking the rice wine that accompanied all ritual.

Then, all of a sudden, people would jump up and throw themselves into the task, as if everything depended on the speed with which it was finished. Ritual climaxes were manufactured, so allowing participants to demonstrate *sagem* in the context of a collective effort.

This ability to structure time was characteristic of longhouse society and provided another perceived advantage to that mode of residence. Upriver People looked to the longhouse for activity and excitement, in vivid contrast to the lonely, uneventful weeks at the farm. This temperament also reflects a warrior tradition that was still much in evidence in the 1970s. In one of his military memoirs, George McDonald Frazer describes army life as "ninety nine percent boredom, and one per cent poetry." The poetry of longhouse life was most obvious in the sagas of famous leaders of the past, whose daring in tight situations was nothing short of reckless. Upriver men would boast "we don't care," meaning that they were prepared to suffer whatever fate served up to them, as soldiers must, and I did indeed witness remarkable acts of stoicism in the face of pain. It was surprising how many adult men, even as late as the 1970s, could still provide themselves with the full panoply of war: animal skin cloak, rattan helmet, spear, and short sword (see Figure 01–03).

As another example of the transformation of time, I was once asking an old man about life in the 1920s and 1930s. He described how men from the longhouse would work together in the jungle, chopping down the huge trees with axes, cutting the trunks into sections, and manhandling the logs to the river bank. When they had enough logs in the water to assemble a raft, they would build a little shack on it, lay in some food, and set out to drift the logs down to the bazaar at Marudi, where they could be sold. In the midst of this story, I realized I had been drawn into the pace of longhouse life because I could share the narrator's sense of adventure. On the face of it, it would be hard to imagine anything much more boring than drifting down river, day after day, on a clumsy raft. But I could imagine the excitement when everyone aboard had to struggle furiously to keep the raft off a sandbar, and the camaraderie of evenings spent on the moored raft. Moreover, there was at the end a golden prize – money in hand and the delights of the Marudi bazaar to sample.

Low Birth Rates

There was, however, a disquieting aspect of the slow life of the 1920s and 1930s. For reasons I cannot explain, birth rates plummeted. In Chapter 9, factors making for high death rates were noted, particularly warfare and disease, but that is not the same as low birth rates. L.W. Jones (1966:71) suggests that it may have had to do with malaria, but offers no evidence that the incidence of malaria was any higher in the twentieth century than in the nineteenth. Yet, the populations of the hinterland of Brunei declined steadily, if the estimates of DOs are to be believed. They measured the size of communities in terms of "doors." This was easiest thing to count in a longhouse community, but it takes no account of how many people there were in the "rooms" behind the doors. It may have disguised population loss because longhouse residents tried to maintain the continuity of "rooms," even if that meant spreading people out more thinly. Conversely, it may not have taken into account crowded rooms in old longhouses.

In the 1970s, longhouses were filled with the noise of children. Older people never tired of pointing this out and contrasting it with the unnatural quietness of the 1930s. It was whispered that in those days young women made altogether too much use of an abortifacient whose composition was a secret known only to the old women. Having abused the drug before marriage, they found afterward that they were barren. This account is supported in the genealogies I collected, which contain many childless women. Moreover, I knew of the cases where an abortion was procured. A teenager became pregnant immediately after a late-term miscarriage had left her very weak. The mother of her equally young husband was furious at her son's irresponsibility at so endangering her life and announced that she would take care of the situation. Nothing more was heard of the pregnancy.

Techniques of abortion cannot provide the whole answer, however. Why were they not used in previous epochs, with similar effects? There is no reason to believe that illegitimate birth became more of a stigma during the Raj than beforehand, nor that sexual activity increased. Moreover, the phenomenon was found among other colonised peoples. The Maori of New Zealand, for instance, suffered such drastic population decline in the early nineteenth century that missionaries spoke of "smoothing the pillow" of a dying race. But the trend reversed itself in the mid-twentieth century, and the Maori population is now growing rapidly. It appears that this is a phenomenon for which demographers have as yet no explanation. For the Maori, as for indigenous peoples elsewhere, it might be possible to associate population declines with a kind of existential despair, a historical moment when traditional culture became unworkable or irrelevant. There was perhaps something of this among the Lun Bawang people of the Trusan, who were infamous drunkards. DOs complained that their diet suffered, and children were not properly cared for (*Sarawak Gazette* 1003:April 1937). The majority of Upriver People, however, experienced a time of cultural florescence, the Golden Age with which we started, and no traveller of the time found them in a state of despair. On the contrary, what visitors remarked on was their exuberant zest for life.

Continuing Threats of Violence

There is a final factor in the persistence of longhouse residence that should not be underestimated: the threat of Iban attacks did not disappear. As already noted, Upriver People took readily to the *pax Brookinensis*, and warfare between them effectively ceased after 1882. There were occasional accusations of murder and the taking of heads, but they were rare. Meanwhile, to the south, the second Rajah had his hands full containing Iban "rebels," especially the "revolt" led by Bantin (Pringle 1970:210–37). Rumours of this warfare percolated into the Brunei hinterland, and there was nothing unreasonable about the anxiety they provoked. What Charles Brooke saw was resistance to his government, a refusal to be "pacified." Most of the violence, however, was directed at the neighbours of the Iban – the more harmless, the better. Small affrays, involving deceit and sneak attacks, were continuous. In 1912, for instance, seven Penan were killed in the Dapoi, a tributary of the Tinjar, by Iban who came from as far away as the Rejang watershed (*Sarawak Gazette* 606:June 1912). In 1916, fourteen Penan heads were taken by Iban raiding into the Belaga watershed, a tributary of the Rejang to the south of the Brunei hinterland. News of that attack alerted the DO to the presence of a raiding party, but he was far away at Sibu on the coast. He hastily assembled a scratch force of fifty Malays armed with modern bolt-action rifles, plus eighty Kayan, and managed to head off the raiding party before it entered the Belaga. The Iban decided to fight it out, attacking the DO and his party. As a result, 200 Iban were shot down. In his report in the May *Sarawak Gazette*, Gifford expresses the hope that this defeat would send a message into the interior and across the border into Dutch Borneo.

As Gifford makes plain, these Iban raiders came from a remote area probably no more closely administered than the far headwaters of the Baram. But in 1905, an equally large incursion was mounted directly into the Brunei hinterland by Iban, not from the far interior, but from the coastal region of Mukah and Bintulu, an area supposedly "pacified" for decades. As described in Chapter 5, a war party 1,000 strong got as far as Long Tisam in the middle Tinjar, close to the Berawan house of Tama Lire, before they were confronted by a small contingent of rangers. In this case, the Iban did not attack, but they brazenly argued that they had a perfect right to go out looking for jungle produce. Meanwhile, the DO reports, all the longhouses in Tinjar were armed to the teeth for war, and some had repaired their stockades (*Sarawak Gazette* 480:January 1906).

Such violence presented a dilemma to the Brooke administration because it had always relied on Iban levies to fight its wars. Indeed, Iban from

Bintulu and Mukah had assisted in the horrendously destructive punitive raids launched by the Rajah himself into the Belaga region, attacks that for the most part failed to reach those who had roused his anger, but nearly annihilated smaller and unoffending communities. Once the genie was out of the bottle, it was difficult to control, and Upriver People continued to distrust Iban motives even in the late twentieth century, and not without reason.

Chapter 14

Longhouses after the Raj

The centenary of the Brooke Raj was celebrated in September 1941 with processions and loyal speeches in Kuching and outstations all over Sarawak. Only three months later, it came to an abrupt end. Some 5,000 Japanese troops landed unopposed on the coast near the mouth of the Baram River. Their immediate strategic objective was the oil wells around Miri. There was little resistance, and within weeks, the invaders were in full control of Sarawak. The long Indian summer of Brooke rule was over.

Four years later, as the Pacific war drew to close, the situation had hardly changed. There were in the final months some guerrilla actions, organised by a handful of Australian commandos airdropped into the interior. The Berawan longhouse at Long Beruang (later rebuilt at Long Terawan) was burned down by way of reprisal, but Upriver People sustained no combat casualties. Borneo was one of the islands bypassed by the American advance across the western Pacific, and consequently, there were no marines storming ashore from landing craft. Instead, the Japanese troops surrendered in situ in September 1945, following the orders of their Emperor (Reece n.d.). What is most remarkable about the war years in Sarawak is just how *little* happened, especially as compared to the devastation elsewhere.

The Vacuum of Japanese Rule

The direct impact of the Japanese occupation on Upriver communities was slight. Having secured the coast, Japanese commanders had little interest in projecting any kind of presence into the interior. In the first few months, patrols were sent upriver to capture a handful of Europeans who tried to hide out in the mountains. In the case of the popular District Officer (DO) of Baram District, A. J. Haddon, their work was done for them by a couple of Iban who pretended to be friends, and then murdered him. After that, Japanese occasionally arrived at the relatively more accessible longhouses to collect food for their soldiers. In all the cases I heard about, Upriver People had no time to hide their rice stocks, and surrendered them entire, at gunpoint. This caused deprivation, but not famine, because people in the hinterland had a familiar staple that could be substituted. Sago palms grow wild in the forest, and when Upriver People cut them down, they always plant a few new shoots so as to preserve the resource. Even in the 1970s, it was common for people in the Tinjar and Tutoh watersheds to run out of rice before the new harvest and to be forced to revert to sago. Boiled into a sticky gruel, it is neither appetizing nor nourishing. It does, however, provide virtually inexhaustible quantities of carbohydrates. Other dietary requirements were met as they always had been, by hunting wild boar and deer, by fishing, and by collecting fruit and green stuff from the forest. In contrast to so many other places during the war, malnutrition was not a problem upriver.

Consequently, when old people in the 1970s talked about the deprivations of the "Japanese war" (in Upriver Malay *Prang Jepon*), they spoke about nonessential items, things that had clearly been great luxuries just a few decades earlier. For instance, they spoke with passion about the lack of refined sugar, despite the fact that store-purchased sugar had always been in short supply. Moreover, there was an indigenous substitute in the form of sugar cane. It was still grown in the 1970s, and sections were routinely handed out at work parties, to be chewed on the spot. The problem was that Upriver People had no mills to crush the cane, and that meant there was nothing to sweeten coffee.

On the face of it, this seems utterly trivial in a time of war, but there is something more going on. Sweetened coffee was something that, under the Raj, Upriver People had grown accustomed to offering their guests at longhouse festivals. To fail to do so seemed to demean the event. Consequently, the lack of sugar was emblematic of what was by all accounts an almost total cessation of longhouse festivals. When the famous Berawan leader Tama Tiri died at Long Jegan in 1942, his final death rituals (*nulang*) had to be postponed year after year because of lack of not only rice, but also everything else that was judged necessary: paint for the mausoleum, kerosene for the lamps that lit the veranda at night, store-bought biscuits, and coffee itself. He was not finally entombed until 1947. Evidently, what Upriver People were not able or willing to do was revert to longhouse ritual as it had been practiced in the nineteenth century. The dispensations of the Raj had become the norm for them, the basis by which they calibrated their own "traditions." Lacking those facilities, an important aspect of social life simply came to a halt.

The other "deprivation" commonly mentioned was lack of cloth. In Chapter 7, it is noted that the availability of cheap cotton cloth was one of the wonders of industrial society that most impressed Upriver People at the beginning of the colonial era. Its sudden unavailability produced a corresponding sense of loss. Old people spoke of wearing sarongs until they fell apart and of being forced to recover the lost art of making bark cloth. The "primitive" connotations of this state of affairs were made plain. They were, they complained, only one step away from living in the jungle like the Penan.

By their own account of it, Upriver People experienced the years of Japanese control on the coast as a time simply of waiting, a sort of historical vacuum. There is a paradox in this that should not escape us. During the Raj, communities had been largely left to take care of their own affairs. After the light hand of Brooke rule was lifted, they should have been well prepared to deal with the absence of administration. Why indeed was this not a time of cultural fluorescence, when old political patterns of alliance were renewed as a defence against possible Iban aggression? The main necessity for such festivals had never been coffee, but rice wine, and its production required nothing from the trade store. Why was no effort made to disperse farms and keep stocks of rice hidden there, so evading Japanese seizures? Why were lookouts not posted to prevent being taken by surprise?

The neglect of practical responses during the "Japanese war" suggests that Upriver People were confused as to how to react to what was occurring. What disoriented them most was that they had no idea who the Japanese were, or what they were doing in Sarawak. The Chinese press in the coastal cities had been reporting for several years on the Japanese invasion of Manchuria, and money had been collected to send back to the homeland. Upriver People heard nothing of this, nor did they have any historical context in which to make sense of it. In early encounters, the Japanese, lacking Malay, got their message across with bayonets. After that, they simply disappeared. Rumours circulated. When the Japanese started rounding up forced labourers to build an airport at Miri, it was rumoured that they planned to enslave and kill everyone upriver. The airplanes that used the airstrips

286

became mystical vehicles. Increasingly, the Japanese became phantoms, all the more frightening because they were not to be seen.

British Colonial Progressivism

Immediately after the war, Sarawak came under direct British administration. The circumstances were complicated, with a range of vested interests, both colonial and local. The British government had always been deeply involved in Sarawak affairs. Without the help of the Navy, the first Rajah would not have achieved his objective of controlling piracy along the coast. Under the second Rajah, however, further expansion of Sarawak was opposed by a British government seeking to prop up an enfeebled Brunei Sultanate. During the 1930s, colonial officers in Malaya had often criticised the third Rajah's administration and advocated a British buyout. This opinion was seconded by reformers after the war, who saw their duty as preparing the colonies for independence by helping them develop economically and politically. The deciding factor was, however, Vyner Brooke himself, who clearly had no desire to resume his role. In a message to his people, he said bluntly that he was the sole authority in the land, and he had decided to cede Sarawak to the King, whose acceptance had "consummated the hopes of the first Rajah" (Reece 1982:203–4).

These events moved so rapidly that most Sarawakians had no time to respond. The Malay population was the only one sufficiently well organised and politically sophisticated to make any organised protest, in the form of marches and rallies. Their leaders argued, reasonably, that they had not survived a world war just to become a British colony. They saw no reason why Sarawak could not continue as an independent nation. The Chinese were more divided in their reactions. Some anticipated a period of rapid economic growth, whereas others looked to the victorious Republic of China for new leadership in Southeast Asia. Most people in the interior hoped simply for a restoration of the status quo ante, but they were given little chance to express their opinions. Some were invited to meet with a visiting mission of British Members of Parliament, but no transport was made available to bring them down river. Some leaders signed documents they could not read, only to find out later that they had agreed to cession (Reece 1982:207–40. Sutlive 1992).

In the memories of Upriver People in the 1970s, however, the passing of the Raj led naturally to British rule. What was important to them was that the familiar pattern of district administration was restored, complete with sunburned and generally jovial Englishmen who took a personal interest in each Upriver community. The new DOs were, however, younger and

287

more idealistic than those they replaced Morrison 1993). They travelled more, and everywhere talked about the benefits of progress: better health standards, access to education, improved agriculture, and economic growth. Funds were made available for these projects on a scale unimaginable under the Raj, but even so they had to be rationed carefully because Britain's war-ravaged economy was in no position to shower resources on a new colony. Nevertheless, and by degrees, a lot was accomplished.

For longhouse dwellers, the most obvious aspect of British rule was improved access to medicine. Under the Raj, the health facilities available to Upriver People had been virtually nonexistent. Now the government set about tackling the two main killers, tuberculosis (TB) and malaria. Effective drugs for treating TB were developed in the 1950s, and the administration responded by opening treatment centres in Kuching and at Miri, near the mouth of the Baram. TB remained common upriver, but it became routine for sufferers to be posted down to Miri and to return a few months later fully cured. About the same time, it was established that the most effective way to interrupt the life cycle of the malaria vectors was to spray insecticides on the inner walls of houses. An efficient system of Malaria Eradication teams was set up in the Baram region, so that every longhouse apartment and outbuilding was regularly sprayed with DDT. The dusty white residue was a familiar feature of Upriver interiors. In addition, basic health facilities were brought to longhouse communities by "floating dispensaries," in the form of large canoes crewed by male nurses. They treated infected wounds – the common and often dangerous "tropical ulcers" – with antibiotics, cured the endemic pink eye with ointments, and took serious cases down river. Their services were much appreciated by longhouse dwellers. Extension workers also travelled about, promoting hygiene and better natal and child care (Porritt 1997:345–64). Whether as an effect of these measure or not, the populations of longhouses rose rapidly, mostly as a result of higher birth rates and lowered infant mortality. Unnaturally quiet longhouses were a thing of the past, and it became commonplace for half of the population of a community to be comprised of children and adolescents.

Of equal significance for the future was access to education. The Raj had provided no educational opportunities to Upriver People, so the British administration had to begin from scratch (Ooi 1992). Primary schools were established in many Upriver communities, drawing students from the immediate area. After a few years, it became possible to staff these schools with Upriver teachers who graduated from the training college established at Batu Lintang, near Miri. Progress, however, was slow. An Education Department survey in 1960 found that many parents took their children to the farms during busy times in the agricultural cycle, that candidates for teacher training were few, that standards were low, and that schools were not well maintained by their communities. Literacy rates hovered in the low single digits (Porritt 1997:293–343). The crucial point, however, was that a door had been opened, if only a crack. A secondary school was opened in Marudi, and students were collected from all over the Baram and Limbang watersheds. Since transportation was irregular and expensive, this inevitably meant boarding in spartan dormitories, at least during the school year. Many students arrived carrying nothing but a sack of rice as a contribution to the school kitchen. Nevertheless a remarkable camaraderie grew up between the students, as I discovered in the many hours that I spent talking to them. They were valuable informants because they could report on all manner of details concerning Upriver communities, and they were always the first to know about canoes arriving or leaving Marudi. It was among these young people that a sense of solidarity as Upriver People first emerged, and eventually, a professional class of Upriver People. I might add that interactions were also relaxed with and between Chinese, Iban, and Malay students. It was an environment delightfully free of the interethnic hostility that was so conspicuous a feature of life in the Malay Peninsula.

In the area of economic development, the impact of postwar British progressivism was less significant (Morrison 1988). As a cash crop, rubber was already past its prime. Experiments with cocoa, pepper, and coffee were conducted by the Agriculture Department, and many Upriver farmers, mostly in the Limbang and lower Baram, invested their labour in setting up small plantations. Many developing countries were introducing the same crops at the same time, however, and overproduction soon forced prices down. Explaining this to longhouse people was not easy, and many felt cheated. Meanwhile, extension workers tried to promote better farming techniques, but with marginal results. They discovered what their peers elsewhere in the Third World were learning – that local people often knew best what suited their environment. For example, Upriver People were encouraged to improve their diet by growing vegetables in gardens adjacent to their longhouses, but the patches of soil in which they were planted were swept away whenever the rivers flooded. More ominously, the attempts of Upriver People to obtain timber cutting licenses were denied, on the grounds they could only be issued to "those having the necessary capital, knowledge, and experience to work them efficiently" – in effect the Chinese industrialists who already dominated the business (Porritt 1997:182–91, 223).

The Postwar Persistence of Longhouses

The result of low population densities and lack of economic opportunities was that even after World War II, living circumstances upriver did

289

not change substantially. When I began my first fieldwork in the 1970s, I entered a world that still revolved entirely around longhouse communities. At that time, there were sixty-two of them in the Baram watershed, not counting houses intermittently occupied by groups of the hunting and gathering Penan. Over the first three months, I visited about half of them, including most of the largest ones. Since there was no regularly scheduled transportation above Marudi, this meant hitching rides wherever I could. To go far upriver required canoes slim enough to weave through the rapids, their sixty-horsepower outboard motors racing, but large enough to transport worthwhile amounts of cargo, including their own petrol supplies in forty-four-gallon drums. Some behemoths had three or four wide planks built up along the sides of dugouts carved from the most massive trees. Sixty feet or more long, they were driven by two inline motors, each with its own driver and in its own well. Large canoes had corrugated iron roofs, to provide both shade for the passengers and cover from the inevitable late afternoon downpours. Clearly, such longboats were owned only by men of substance, and used only when there was sufficient cargo to make the sometimes long and laborious trips worthwhile. In this way, an ancient pattern of trading expeditions was perpetuated. Other longboats were owned by the RC mission to maintain links to its upriver stations, and the DO had several for official use. Finally, the Malaria Eradication teams not only visited every community on a regular basis, but also kept updated sketch maps of them, showing every residential unit − a veritable treasure trove of information. Later, when I had a canoe of my own with a twenty-horsepower motor, I was able to visit many of the smaller longhouses that I had previously bypassed.

Of the dozens of longhouses I visited, I found a half dozen where people were listless and their house tumble down. About the same number were going through a phase of bitter internal factionalism. But this was as it had always been, as migration myths testify, and such cases could not be taken as evidence of any general malaise. Indeed, in most places I found vital communities, proud of their own special traditions and origins. This was true even where people were occupying rickety temporary housing along a riverbank, while a new longhouse was under construction.

It was in these communities that I began to absorb that sense of metropolis that I tryied to convey in Chapter 1. The longer I stayed in longhouse communities, the more irrelevant the outside world seemed to be. This is no doubt a common feature of village life everywhere, a kind of medieval parochialism. But there was an intensity to this feeling in longhouses unlike anything I have experienced elsewhere. When American soldiers returned from World War I, they were greeted with "how you gonna keep 'em down on the farm, now that they've seen Paree?" Longhouse people did not lust after the cultural delights of cities, and they had no sense of cultural inferiority. On the contrary, they were already in their own Paris, and it was everyone else that was marginal.

Reflecting this view of things, longhouse people consistently exaggerated the uniqueness of their own ways of doing things. It came as no surprise to me that there were myths that could be found in different versions in many communities. But when I asked about them in communities I had not visited before, people were amazed that I knew about them. With details of ritual practice, I got the same response. For example, it is universally the case that corpses cannot exit a house by the normal route; instead, a hole must be made in the wall, and a temporary staircase erected. I had imagined that everyone knew this from attending funerals in neighbouring communities, yet they still reacted with surprise.

Some Statistics from the 1970s

From my ethnographic survey and the data provided by the Malaria Eradication teams, I was able to inventory the longhouse communities in the Baram watershed (excluding Iban houses and those in the far headwaters identifying themselves as Kelabit). The Appendix gives details and a map showing the location of communities. Figure 14-01 summarizes the data in terms of the distribution of communities according to size, as measured by the number of "doors" or residential units – the "rooms" described in the introduction. There is a wide range, from five to ninety-nine, with an average of 32.8.

The findings conform well with the historical events described in Section IV. In the centre of the region that I am calling the hinterland of Brunei, in the Apoh and middle Baram, there were half a dozen very large Kayan houses. At ninety-five doors and almost a thousand people, Long Bemang was huge. Meanwhile, Long Laput had shrunk to a mere seventy-two doors, from a high of ninety-eight in the early 1950s (MacDonald 1958:270). It had extended for almost half a mile along a relatively flat area on the left bank of the Baram – a truly imposing sight. These megacommunities are the legacy of the Kayan incursion of the mid-nineteenth century, and a result of Kayan success in integrating large numbers of prisoners or slaves taken from the Lower Baram peoples. This is confirmed by a comparison with the Belaga and Baluy watersheds, to the south of the Brunei hinterland, where there were no comparable political circumstances. Kayan longhouses in that region have apparently always been small or midrange (Rousseau 1978). Returning to the Baram, it is also significant that the only comparably large Kenyah community in the hinterland, at Long Moh in the upper Baram, was

Figure 14-01. Kayan and Non-Kayan
Communities Compared in Terms
of Number of Rooms

Rooms	Kayan	Non-I
90–9	1	
80–9	2	
70–9	2	1
60–9	1	
50–9	1	3
40–9	3	4
30–9	1	6
20–9	3	10
10–9	3	5
5–9	2	8
	19	37

comprised of immigrants from across the mountains who arrived only during the colonial period. Consequently, the community's history is unrelated to the patterns characteristic of the Brunei hinterland.

In the large (forty to fifty-nine doors) and midrange (twenty to thirty-nine doors) categories, non-Kayan longhouses (i.e., Kenyah, Sebop, Berawan) outnumbered Kayan ones, seven to four and sixteen to four, respectively. In tune with their diverse ethnicities and origins, they were scattered across the region (Figure 14-01).

There were just five small Kayan houses (five to nineteen doors), or a little more than one-fourth (28.6%) of the Kayan total. In terms of population, they are insignificant, but they do display a tendency for groups of commoners to escape into pioneer communities. Two small Kayan longhouses, at Long Ikang and Long Teran Batu, existed as minorities in a Kenyah community and a Berawan community, respectively. Small houses were more numerous among non-Kayan, thirteen in all, comprising one-third (35%) of the total. We must remind ourselves that even these "small" houses would constitute large structures in any other part of Southeast Asia (Waterson 1990). Nevertheless, they clearly represent different circumstances to the massive Kayan houses. Some constituted remnants of formerly more numerous people. The thirteen-door house at Long Nuah, for example, was all that was left of the once-powerful Lirong, decimated by cholera in the early twentieth century. Others were fragments that somehow got left behind during long-distance migrations. The people at Long Tuyut called themselves Long Suku, that being the site of one of their previous longhouses, but they were culturally indistinguishable from the more numerous Long Wat, who had migrated some decades previously into the Apoh watershed. Both were elements of the Sebop diaspora.

What was interesting about the Long Suku people was their robust self-regard. One might imagine that being so few would make them timorous, but their oral history was phrased in exactly the same terms as those described in Chapter 2. Their leaders also strutted on a grand stage, like the kings of medieval Europe. Indeed, it would be a mistake to assume that the communities with the largest populations have always been the most powerful or prestigious. It is not so among nations. In the statistics of the Malaria Eradication teams, Long San is a mere twenty-four doors. Yet, it was home to the most influential man in the Baram watershed, the Temonggong (paramount chief) Oyong Lawai Jau. His grand-uncle had secured the primacy of the Long Tikan people (as they called themselves), not by military exploits, but by a sophisticated policy of creating alliances and aiding the Raj.

In terms of population, as opposed to numbers of doors, the statistics provided Malaria Eradication teams probably underestimate community size. This was my conclusion from comparing their counts with returns from the State census, which I was able to obtain for Long Teru and Long Jegan. The concern of the teams was to ensure that all living spaces were accounted for, rather than all residents. Moreover, in the 1970s, a baby boom was under way, which meant that many old longhouses were overcrowded. The longhouse at Long Jegan, for instance – which the inhabitants claimed was actually four longhouses in a row, as explained in Chapter 5 – had been built before the Japanese occupation. When it was rebuilt on the same site in the late 1970s, it nearly doubled in number of "doors," from thirty-four to more than sixty. The statistics at hand, however, have the advantage of being organised by community, which the published census does not, so it is not possible to show which communities were overcrowded relative to others. For present purposes, it is sufficient to notice that the average number of occupants per apartment is 8.6. Moreover, the averages do not vary much between Kayan and non-Kayan longhouses, being 8.7 and 8.5, respectively.

Aggregating the figures provided by the Malaria Eradication teams, the total Orang Ulu population of the Baram watershed comes to 15, 676, of which 7,234 were Kayan and 8,442 were non-Kayan.

Finally, it must be noted that there is a glaring gap in these data. The statistics apply to the Baram watershed, and I have nothing remotely comparable for the Limbang because longhouses had effectively disappeared from the Limbang by 1970. In 1973, the Curator of the Sarawak Museum, Benedict Sandin, made an ethnographic survey of the region. He includes a map showing just three communities that are "Murut" in whole or part. As discussed in Chapter 6, the label Murut, although widely used in colonial times, is misleading. The preferred term is "Lun Bawang," but for present purposes the point is that these indigenous people once comprised the majority of the population of the valleys of the Limbang and its tributaries, with dozens of longhouse communities. This much we know from the accounts of European travellers in the nineteenth century, as discussed in Chapter 6. But these communities were devastated by Kayan war parties arriving from the middle Baram. People were enslaved, or fled eastward into the remote headwaters of the Limbang or across the mountains into the Trusan region, and so out of the Brunei hinterland. Remnants of the Bisaya and Tagal communities moved down river to gain an uncertain protection from Brunei. Their last longhouse was abandoned in 1964 (Sandin 1973:50). Subsequently, the vacuum left by these indigenous peoples was filled with Iban settlers, as Sandin's map shows.

What then can we say about longhouses in the Limbang prior to the Kayan raids? The first thing to emphasize is the key location they occupied in the trading system of the Brunei hinterland, whether inside the "Sultan's fence" or otherwise. Second, all indications are that the longhouses in the middle and upper Limbang were relatively small. In part, this was due to "continuous internecine strife and raiding" (Deegan 1973:177), which hampered their ability to resist Kayan raiding parties. All early travellers in the Limbang remarked on the tendency, and Berawan oral history reports the same thing about the once numerous Tring in the Tutoh region. They shared the same tendency and suffered the same fate.

Some indication of the previous state of affairs in Limbang can be gained from studies of the Lun Bawang conducted in recent years in the Lawas Valley, across the mountain divide from Limbang. James Deegan (1974) begins by noting that in this area "the valleys tend to be narrow and the sides steep" compared with the broad basin of the Baram. This limited the size of communities to a maximum of about thirty rooms because pockets of usable land are small and dispersed. Nevertheless, the number of rooms in a longhouse was seldom less than twelve because of the need for shared labour in swidden agriculture. The middle reaches of the Limbang are in between these extremes, being neither as enclosed as the one nor as open as the other, perhaps allowing somewhat larger communities. Longhouses also provided protection against Kayan raiders, who penetrated even as far north as Lawas. However, the massive war parties that swept through the Limbang, and threatened Brunei itself, were not seen in the Trusan or Lawas valleys. In the 1920s and 1930s, the Lun Bawang fell into what Deegan calls a "cultural malaise," and community fragmentation began. Whereas prior to the coming of the Brooke Raj, there were no single dwellings or isolated households, such houses became increasingly common. Jay Crain, working just across the border from Lawas in Sabah, reports that by 1970 longhouses were not being rebuilt. He gives figures for eight communities in Sipitang District, which had between six and seventeen doors, with an average of nine and a half doors.

When the Baram Flowed Backward

Even in the Baram watershed, however, where large and vigorous longhouse communities persisted in the 1970s, great changes had occurred. Perhaps the most significant was conversion to Christianity. Here, as elsewhere, conversion is a mysterious process. Clearly, no one can know the motives of individual converts. Nevertheless, I was able to collect dozens of personal accounts of the process, and the order of events at least is plain.

Throughout the long Indian summer of the Brooke Raj, longhouse people in the Baram region showed no interest in conversion. It is true that missionary activity was modest, in accordance with Charles Brooke's policy of discouraging it. Even so, there was a Roman Catholic priest, Father Jensen, based in Marudi from 1907 onward (*Sarawak Gazette* 501:1907). He made many trips upriver, despite the slow pace of travel before outboard motors. A particular focus of his attention was the Kenyah leader Tama Bulan Wan, who had played a major part in helping establish Brooke control. But Tama Bulan explained to Jensen that the ancestors would be angry if they were not honoured as they always had been, and that would bring disaster to the community. Arriving a couple of decades later, the protestant missionary Hudson Southwell (1999) received the same response. When the Japanese arrived, both missionaries were interned.

Then, in 1947, there was a sudden change of heart among people in the upper Baram. They sent requests down river for a missionary to come and convert them to the *Adat Sebayang*, as they called it – the Pray Way (*Adat* meaning in the Malay *lingua franca* "the way of doing things," *sebayang* meaning "to pray"). Sick and weak as they were, both missionaries heard the call and hastened upriver to finally complete their life's work. From indigenous accounts, it is clear that Upriver People understood little of Christianity and nothing of the various denominations. That is born out by the pattern of religious allegiance. To this day, Roman Catholic (RC) communities are the ones that Jensen reached first during their hectic race upriver, and vice versa. This unforeseen complication undermined the goals of the man who had issued the summons in the first place, the future Temonggong (paramount chief) Oyong Lawai Jau, grand nephew of Tama Bulan, who wanted Upriver People to share the same religion.

For the moment, however, the question is what happened between Tama Bulan's polite but firm refusal and his grandnephew's summons, and the most obvious answer is the Japanese occupation. The paradox is that many communities in the far interior never saw a single Japanese soldier, whereas those further down river continued to be indifferent to Christianity. This situation persisted long after conversion in the far interior was well advanced. As old people remarked to me, it was the time when "the Baram flowed backward." What they meant was that outside influences had previously percolated upriver, along with manufactured goods such as beads and brassware. In contrast, Christianity made its way down river.

What changed to allow the spread Christianity did not constitute a presence, but an absence. It is helpful in this context to compare the offstage presence of the Japanese with that of the Raj, and of Brunei before that. As we saw in Chapter 6, Brunei control of its hinterland had been minimal, but that did not prevent Brunei from being a crucial point of reference in Upriver life for centuries. The regime that replaced Brunei became even more integrated into longhouse society, however lightly the hand of the Brooke Raj rested on it. When that order was without warning swept away, it came as a complete shock – incomprehensible and traumatic. The result was a loss of confidence in old certainties, including the protection of the ancestors. Upriver People turned to a religion of global reach and influence. Islam was not an option because to become Malay was by definition to cease being Upriver People. In addition, Christianity was associated with the progressive message of British colonialism, so prompting a fateful alliance with Western ideology.

The association of Christianity and modernity was neatly illustrated by the large RC mission station established on land given by the Temonggong adjacent to his longhouse at Long San. The site was far upriver from the coast, but the resources of the Church provided for the importation of the necessary building materials, such as concrete and roofing. The rainforest provided timber, cut and squared by work parties from all the Kenyah communities in the upper Baram. Long San became a hive of activity, an Upriver metropolis of a new kind. A solid church was built, clearly designed to last for generations. Around a large sports field were grouped school buildings, a dispensary, and accommodation for a staff of priests, nuns, and lay brothers. The mission was served by regular transportation, carrying both freight and passengers.

The People Upriver Become the Upriver People

Oyong Lawai Jau led the way in conversion, but that was only one aspect of his plans. His underlying goal was to draw longhouse people together, regardless of ethnicity. He was far sighted enough to realise that they would have no say in their own future unless they could present a united front (Galvin 1982). Displacing the ancestors as the focus of community life was only the first step in reaching that goal. The next was to create a positive sense of solidarity, particularly among the emerging educated elite. In the 1970s and 1980s, I met many former students of the secondary schools in Marudi and Miri, and they had fond memories of the corpulent and convivial Temonggong, bustling through their dormitories and lecturing them at length. His messages were that they must not forget who they were and must work for the welfare of their people. In delivering this message, he displayed formidable linguistic agility. He devised a kind of personal lingua franca to talk to the Kenyah students, exploiting linguistic similarities so as to make himself understood in something approaching their mother tongues. As a leader with widespread family connections, he also spoke Kayan, and failing everything else he could resort to Malay. He had no English, however, and could not use what was then the medium of instruction in the schools.

To promote his goals of unification, Oyong Lawai Jau set about creating a new ethnicity. Before the 1960s, it had been common to speak of "people upriver," a phrase found in some form or another all over Borneo. From the descriptive term, the Temonggong forged an ethnicity. Initially, when he spoke of the Upriver People (Orang Ulu), he meant the Kenyah of the upper Baram and the Kayan of the middle Baram, people who had been allied since the nineteenth century and were the basis of his influence. He had been disappointed that he could not cajole them all to back the same church. Moreover, Kayan and Kenyah leaders in the watershed of the Belaga to the south did not always welcome his interference in their affairs. Nevertheless, the awareness of a shared ethnicity steadily expanded. It soon included all those other peoples in Baram who had been classified by the DOs of the Brooke Raj, rightly or wrongly, as Kenyah. The status of the foraging Penan remained for some time ambiguous, but by the 1970s they were generally included.

The last and most difficult extension, given the animosities of the nineteenth century, was to embrace all the Lun Bawang speaking peoples (see Chapter 8) in the Limbang, Lawas, and Trusan watersheds, and in the Kelabit highlands. Once that was accomplished, the Upriver People in effect comprised everyone in northern Sarawak who was not Malay, Chinese, or Iban (Chin, Jawan 1993). It was a remarkable feat of enlightened leadership, and it gained concrete expression in the foundation of an Orang Ulu Progress Association, headed by members of the small educated elite. The political aims of the organisation were modest, but it did succeed in drawing the attention of the colonial administration to the existence of Upriver People, their aspirations, and their presence in urban areas. By the

1970s, there were Orang Ulu community centres in several cities on the coast, including Kuching, the state capital.

Finally, that ethnicity with which I began – those people marked ORANG ULU on Figure 01-01 – had been assembled. Note, however, that the proposition cannot be reversed. Not all Kayan, Kenyah, and Lun Bawang were Orang Ulu because many of them lived across the border in Indonesian Kalimantan, where the term is not used in the sense that it is in Sarawak. Once again, we find that ethnicities in central Borneo do not consist of the sum of some list of constituent subethnicities.

From Colonialism to Neocolonialism

Barely was this sense of Upriver solidarity achieved before the entire political landscape was transformed yet again. In September 1963, Sarawak was absorbed into the newly created nation of Malaysia (Milne 1967). The impetus for federation came from the British Colonial Office, whose bureaucrats evidently saw it as a convenient way to divest themselves of their responsibilities. They were convinced that small countries could not find the resources to administer and defend themselves. In the Caribbean, all manner of combinations were proposed, none of which survived. The logical conclusion of this process was reached when tiny Anguilla, population 7,019, refused be "ruled" from nearby St. Kitts-Nevis, population 45,000. Despite British efforts to cajole them back, they stubbornly insisted on "independence." In Borneo, what the Rajahs had left of Brunei refused to join the Malaysian federation and is now an oil-rich Sultanate that affords its population of about 200,000 a comfortable lifestyle with free medicine and education, and negative taxation. The grandest postcolonial fantasy was the Central African Federation, which was to include what were then Northern and Southern Rhodesia, plus Nyasaland. African leaders denounced it as a conspiracy by white settlers to retain power, and the project died a natural death (James 1994:611).

In Sarawak, however, Malaysia was forced down the throats of interior people, whose opinions were barely considered. Upriver People were particularly hostile to it (Leigh 1974:40), but opinion among the coastal populations of Malays and Chinese was, to say the least, divided. An Iban, Stephen Kalong Ningkan, was elected Chief Minister in the British-supervised elections of June 1963. He had made enemies in Kuala Lumpur, however, by championing English as the medium of education in Sarawak's schools. The federal government insisted on switching to Malay in order to assert the political primacy of the Malays. Ningkan argued that English offered better chances for indigenous people to continue their education overseas, furnishing Sarawak with its future professionals and administrators. In presenting this view, he implied that Sarawak retained the right to secede from Malaysia. The Prime Minister of Malaysia, Tunku Abdul Rahman, accused Ningkan of being the tool of British imperialism and insisted on the imposition of the "national language" (Leigh 1974:89–94). Stephen Yong, a Chinese politician whose party had achieved considerable support among Iban, advocated a referendum to find out whether Sarawakians preferred full independence, with the possibility of a union of Borneo states in the future. To this, the Tunku replied flatly that such a referendum was "a dream" and that Sarawak and Sabah would remain in Malaysia "until doomsday" (Porritt 2004:132).

Three years later, Kuala Lumpur engineered a political crisis as a pretext for the removal of Ningkan from office. Refusing to resign, Ningkan made this challenge: "if the Prime Minister thinks he will, with the help of his puppets, succeed in making Sarawak a Colony of Malaysia, the Tunku is suffering from a terrible illusion" (Leigh 1974:105). But Ningkan was unable to prevent it. In his place, a Malay, Penghulu Tawi Sli, was appointed, and power passed into the hands of a clique that has controlled it ever since.

A few statistics will demonstrate the neocolonial situation. Sarawak is by far the largest state in Malaysia. Indeed, at 48,235 square miles, it is almost as big as all the states of the Malay Peninsula put together (50.790 square miles). Its population, however, is only about one-tenth that of the peninsula (1,233,000 compared to 11,427,000, using data from the first reliable national census in 1980). Meanwhile, Sarawak is rich in raw resources, notably oil and timber. The profits from the offshore oil fields go directly to Kuala Lumpur, and little finds its way back. At the same time, images of the rainforest stretching across mountains and valleys, seemingly endlessly, convinced everyone in West Malaysia that Sarawak was virgin territory, ripe for exploitation, and inhabited only by a few scattered natives in dire need of civilisation. This mind-set is evident in newspaper reports and even scholarly writing from West Malaysia. "Malaysia" turns out almost invariably to be just West Malaysia, and the existence of the colonies in Borneo is totally marginalized. Sarawak has become Malaysia's 'Wild West.'

The forced entry into Malaysia effectively disenfranchised indigenous peoples. Head counts of different ethnic groups are suspect, for reasons that should by now be familiar. Nevertheless, relying on the categories used in the 1980 census, Evelyn Hong (1987) finds that some 44% of Sarawak's population were "Dayak," that is, non-Chinese, non-Malay. This is probably an underestimate because whole ethnic groups, such as the Melanau, are classified as "Malay" when they actually may not be entirely Moslem. The largest categories within the "Dayak" population were Iban (368,208) and Bidayuh (104,885). (The Bidayuh have not previously been mentioned because they are mainly found in southern Sarawak and have not migrated like the Iban into the Brunei hinterland.) In comparison, the Malays (including the Melanau) comprise only 26% of the population of the state, and the Chinese (of all ethnicities or language groups, including Hokkien, Cantonese, Hakka, Henghua, and others) constitute 29%. The Iban alone outnumber the Malays and equal the number of Chinese. One might then imagine that Dayak people, especially the Iban, would dominate state politics. But this is not the case.

That Dayak people are politically marginalised is a direct result of politics in West Malaysia – what used to be Malaya – in at least two ways. First, in terms of brute numbers, they are swamped. Altogether they comprise 3.8% of the population of Malaysia, too few to have any impact on national politics. They have been reduced to Fourth World people in their own country, powerless to influence policy in any significant way. As for the Orang Ulu, their position is hopeless. Adding together all those in the 1980 census classified as Kenyah, Kayan, Murut, Punan, and Kelabit gives a total of 47, 070, or 3.8% of the Sarawak population. In Malaysia as a whole, that amounts to 0.34%.

Second, the enflamed ethnic politics of West Malaysia have overflowed into Sarawak. As independence for Malaya drew near, the British administration looked for ways to safeguard the rights of the indigenous Malay people against the overwhelming Chinese control of the economy. This involved enshrining special political and educational privileges for Malays, perhaps with the belief that this balance would allow a slow integration. But neither party trusted the other, and each guarded its powers jealously (Comber 1983). In this way, the politics of the peninsula became rigidly dualistic. Other minorities, notably people of Indian descent, had no place in the equation. With the creation of Malaysia, this dualistic model was imposed on Sarawak, although it made no sense there at all. The most obvious example of this is the restriction of *bumiputera* status, which allows, among other things, preferred access to government employment and educational opportunities. In the constantly repeated formula, *bumiputera* are "sons of the soil," as opposed to people of foreign origin. But in Sarawak only "Malays" are classified as *bumiputera*, even though they are no more or less indigenous than their neighbours who do not happen to have *masok Melayu*, "entered Malaydom." The ridiculous result is that 44% of the population is treated as foreigners in the land that had been their home for millennia.

Finally, Kuala Lumpur has maintained for decades a large military presence in Sarawak. This came about because there had been a small-scale communist insurgency in Sarawak since the end of World War II. Given the political situation in Southeast Asia in the early 1960s, it is not surprising that the colonial administration took the threat seriously. British troops were brought in to contain the insurgency, using the tactics successfully employed in Malaya. The dispersed population of Chinese farmers around the major cities of Kuching and Sibu were collected into fortified villages so as to isolate them from the armed groups operating in the jungles. This early stage of the war is well documented by Vernon Porritt (2004), who participated in its planning. The troops stayed on for some years after the formation of Malaysia. Had Sarawak remained independent, such troops could have been assisted by the largely Iban force of Sarawak Rangers initially raised by Charles Brooke. Instead, British troops were replaced by regiments raised in West Malaysia.

What happened in the war after "Malayanization" is murkier, and the full story may never be known. It is obscured by the propaganda use that the neocolonial government made of the threat of communism, a familiar tactic throughout the world during the Cold War. I can do little to disperse the shadows, other than to report what I heard in the mid-1970s from junior officials in the administration, including Upriver People who had profited from the educational opportunities that opened up in the 1950s and 1960s. From them, I gathered that the insurgency was no longer limited to Maoist Chinese youth. Instead, it had become, at least in part, another expression of that Iban restlessness that had kept the Rajahs busy. Unlike the Rajah, however, the government no longer needed Iban supporters to help them suppress Iban rebels. The presence of West Malaysian soldiers was a constant irritant. The stock complaint was that army units would camp just upriver from Iban longhouses, and then defecate in the river. Regardless of whether this actually occurred, it neatly captures Iban attitudes. Those of my informants who had served in parts of the Third Division, in the watershed of the Rejang River, told me that there were "no-go" areas for the armed forces. Only the unarmed representatives of the District Office were able to move about freely. At that stage, it was unclear whether the Malaysian army was controlling the resistance or causing it.

The Destruction of the Rainforest

This military activity was for most Upriver People nothing but a distant rumour. There was to my knowledge no fighting against insurgents in the Baram or Limbang watersheds, and Malaysian soldiers were seldom seen upriver. What was apparent was the activity of timber companies. Sitting on the verandas of longhouses in the lower Baram region, it was a familiar sight to see huge rafts of logs, hitched together with wire cables, slowly drifting by. Each raft was headed by a diesel tug, whose power was just sufficient to give the ungainly mass enough steerage way to avoid drifting onto sandbars. A swarm of speedboats buzzed about, trying to nudge logs away from obstacles. Meanwhile, crew members ate, slept, and hung out their washing on top of the rafts, so that there was a strange sense of alien worlds drifting past each other, with no sign of recognition from either.

In addition, there were always men from the longhouses working in the logging camps. In the 1970s, it was virtually the only way to get money. The price of rubber was by then so low that only children and old people bothered collecting it, and the extensive rubber gardens that had been so productive in the 1920s were abandoned. The prices paid for pepper and coffee had collapsed. Not surprisingly, wages in the camps were low, and the most dangerous jobs were reserved for Upriver People. Men who suffered injuries, sometimes appalling injuries, received trivial compensation. Living conditions in the logging camps were bad. Amidst a sea of mud churned up by the logs bulldozed into the river, the workers lived in low hovels roofed in corrugated iron. Life there was rough, and few men chose to take their families with them. In this manner, the lumber industry coexisted with longhouse life throughout the 1960s and 1970s.

Beginning in the 1970s, however, and gathering momentum through the 1980s and 1990s, new technologies were introduced that rapidly increased the pace of rainforest destruction (Brookfield and Byron 1995). Rough roads were cut directly through the rainforest, pushing ever deeper into the interior. Along them passed trucks hauling out the trunks of the tallest trees, as much as a hundred feet long and weighing many tons. The scale of the machinery was massive, dwarfing the people that operated it. The ecological destruction it produced is well known, having been exposed by environmental organisations despite the efforts of the Malaysian and Sarawak governments to deny them access. Going beyond the statistics – which are horrifying enough – William Bevis gives a moving account of the process as seen up close. He describes in detail a single forest tree, which supports an amazing variety of life forms – vines of a dozen different species, lichens, flowers, parasites, and epiphytes, all full of insects and birds. Watching it cut down, he says, was like witnessing the destruction of an entire world. As he wanders around the lumber camps, he finds waste everywhere – logs thirty foot long and six feet in diameter abandoned to rot because larger and more valuable ones were already piling up to await transportation (Bevis 1995:68–78).

It is hard to imagine a more apt symbol of the long-delayed arrival of modernity in central Borneo than the bulldozer (Anonymous 1994). Indigenous land rights were ignored, and community leaders were either bribed or intimidated into signing "agreements" with timber companies that were enforced by company goons, police, and soldiers. There was more resistance by local people than is generally known because government efforts to enforce a media blackout were largely successful. The local press was entirely subservient and co-operated in portraying green activists – both local and foreign – as communists. By the mid-1990s, paranoia ran high, and I was amazed to find Upriver People who did no care to be seen talking to me, even though I had research clearance and no attachment to green organisations. Consequently, it is unlikely that the full story of the resistance of Upriver People to the destruction of their environment will ever be told, especially as it tended to occur piecemeal. Communities only understood the danger when the bulldozers were at their gates, and they were powerless to resist the concentrated force of the state. Peter Brosius (2007) offers an account of the remarkable resistance put up by some Penan. Regarding the abuse of land rights, the details have been documented in a remarkable piece of research by Evelyn Hong (1987).

The reason for the unseemly haste of rainforest destruction in the 1980s and 1990s was the greed of timber barons and the crooked politicians in their pay. The prize was timber-cutting licences, which were nominally granted by a government department in charge of forest resources. In the 1970s, one of its experts, a man trained overseas in forestry, showed me how individual trees could be identified from aerial photographs, and a selection made of those to be harvested. When I next saw him a decade later, he had taken early retirement, unable to watch as licences were handed out with no oversight. They went mostly to relatives and cronies of the ruling clique. The recipients were not planning to start businesses themselves, however. Instead, they simply sold the licences on to established timber companies, becoming in the process wealthy overnight. Such people could naturally be relied on to contribute to the election campaigns of progovernment politicians. These shenanigans became public knowledge during a political fracas in 1987, when two factions in the ruling clique fell out, and each accused the other of handing out 50% of all timber licences to their immediate supporters (Ritchie 1987). If both accusations were correct, there was evidently little left over for anyone else. As was once explained to me by a self-identified political insider, timber licences could also be used to silence any local leader whose popularity posed a threat to the government. Such people were given small tracts to exploit in their home districts – insufficient to make them really wealthy, but enough to arouse jealousy among their followers.

The pity of all this greed and waste was that resources were squandered that could have funded steady development in Sarawak for decades to come. By the late 1990s, the timber roads had reached the Indonesian border, and the companies that had reaped so rich a harvest began to look elsewhere. In a special edition of *The Contemporary Pacific* on logging in the southwest Pacific, the editors note that Malaysian companies were rapidly becoming the most aggressive, overtaking those from Japan, Korea, Singapore, and China. One Sarawak company, in particular, Rimbunan Hijau, controlled about 50% of all logging in Papua New Guinea. The degree of consolidation was even greater than that, however, because Rimbunan Hijau was only one of several subsidiaries of Tiong Toh Siong Holdings. Datu Tiong (Datu is a Malay title, roughly equivalent to "Sir") was busy establishing multiple corporate fronts on the Kuala Lumpur stock exchange (Barlow and Winduo 1997:6).

The Longhouses Empty Out

The dirt roads bulldozed through the rainforests by the timber companies were not meant to last, but their effect on longhouse communities was permanent. During rainy seasons, the roads needed constant maintenance. Such was the pace of exploitation that there was no time to build bridges over every small watercourse, or even over midsize ones, and soil was simply bulldozed into the streambeds, sometimes over a pile of logs. After any serious rain, the lakes that built up behind these dams would burst through, sweeping mud down river. Fish could not survive in the silt-laden water, and longhouse communities lost a major source of protein, one on which many had relied. At the same time, game such as deer and wild pigs became scarce.

The overall effect of logging on traditional swidden agriculture is not clear. On the one hand, farmers made use of the roads to gain access to places that had never been accessible before. As noted in Chapter 5, only land near rivers was exploited by Upriver People, and even then only in niches between the hills where enough topsoil had accumulated to make farming worthwhile. Many mountainous areas had never seen agriculture or long-term human habitation. For those enterprising farmers who could somehow gain access to a four-wheel drive vehicle, there was the possibility of finding land never before used. On the other hand, the erosion caused by logging threatened not only the newly exposed patches of usable land, but also those that had been exploited repeatedly in the past. On balance, it seems likely that the practicality and productivity of traditional agricultural practices declined as a result of the timber boom.

It was not primarily the impossibility of continuing in the old ways, however, that caused the longhouses to empty out during the last decades of the twentieth century. Instead, it was the seemingly irresistible attractions of the cash economy. As job opportunities in the lumber camps expanded, not only did young men leave to work elsewhere, they stopped thinking of making farms. Living as their parents had done was not an option they would consider. When they were unemployed – which was frequently, given the speed with which timber concessions were worked out – they simply hung around the longhouses, looking bored. For the first time, a "generation gap" appeared in the manner familiar in the West. For older people, it came as a bitter realization that everything they knew about how to make a living, not to mention communal lore, was suddenly judged worthless.

Longhouses themselves reflected the new cash economy. Corrugated iron roofing was already common enough, although it was noticeably hotter than traditional materials. By the mid-1980s, it became inescapable because the wood needed to make the shingles was no longer available, nor was there anyone willing to spend time splitting the wood. Glass louvered windows became popular, installed in the front walls of apartments facing onto the veranda, but they did little to improve ventilation or lighting inside the rooms, especially as they were usually closed with curtains. Manufactured materials were imported for internal walls, notably sheets of formica, and their shiny surfaces gave the interiors of longhouses the air of seedy motels. New designs were tried, involving two-storey longhouses. That is, what was once storage space under the longhouse became its "ground floor," a change made possible by the widespread construction of poured concrete floors stretching the length of the house. The "upstairs" became sleeping spaces, while the veranda shrivelled to a covered walkway. Architecturally, such "modern" longhouses resembled army barracks. Domestic interiors were furnished as never before, often with upholstered chairs or sofas, although most people still preferred to sit cross-legged on mats.

The first things purchased, however, when a little money became available, were invariably television sets. The impact of TV on longhouse life is worth a monograph on its own, and I restrict myself here to only its most obvious features. Clearly, TV opened up to the view of Upriver People to worlds they had never known existed. By the same token, it forced on them a realisation of their own insignificance. That sense of cultural self-reliance – not to say chauvinism – that had characterised longhouse communities withered away. This does not imply that Upriver People were passive recipients of whatever they were served up by the mediascape – to use Arjun Appadurai's (1990:35) term. On the contrary, their tastes developed rapidly. Broadcast television did not interest them because the only station they could receive was in Brunei, and its slow pace and heavily Moslem content bored them. Consequently, each room needed not only a TV, but also a video player. Tapes were bought in the bazaars, and then passed from hand to hand around the longhouse, or to other longhouses. Chinese traders soon learned to cater to the market, which favoured "action" movies. The most popular of all videos, however, showed professional wrestling. During the 1980s, Hulk Hogan was the great Upriver hero, replacing all those swaggering, impetuous figures who had inhabited Upriver folklore, climbing to the skies and picking fights with spirits. It was noticeable that the blonde Hogan rapidly replaced Bruce Lee (an American of Chinese descent) in the affections of Upriver People, matching the Western orientation that they chose in converting to Christianity. As I have argued at length elsewhere (Metcalf 2001a), what endeared Hogan to Upriver People was his ability to absorb punishment. Unlike Bruce Lee, with his black belt and fancy moves, Hogan was knocked down again and again, only to stand up and face his tormentors. He displayed that ultimate virtue of the warrior, stoicism.

TVs require electricity, but there were no longhouses connected to the national grid. To meet this need, many communities were supplied with diesel generators by the timber companies working in their areas. Evidently, the company managers calculated that television would provide an effective opium of the masses. The generators created a whole new temporal dimension to longhouse life. Usually they were started up at sundown, and for a couple of hours verandas sparkled with light bulbs strung along them, although there were few people sitting there or passing to and fro. Instead, a walk up and down revealed the residents of each apartment huddled in front of their own TV. At the longhouses I knew best, the generators were turned off at 10 pm sharp, and everybody scrambled for their flashlights, to find their way to their newly built bedrooms. Ten minutes later, the house was silent – a far cry from the late-night gatherings that had been so familiar a feature of longhouse life in the 1970s. Electric generators need maintenance, however, and when the timber companies moved on, communities often lacked the resources to keep them in repair. Even raising cash to buy fuel caused problems. People argued about how much electricity they had used vis-à-vis their neighbours – a novel type of negotiation in the longhouse context. Those out of work had no money to give, and those with work were absent. Some individualists bought their own small generators, and the high-pitched whine of two-stroke motors became the regular accompaniment of evenings in the longhouse.

Meanwhile, even as luxuries like electricity were arriving in the longhouses, their populations were dispersing. The same roads that carried the felled trees to the coast also carried the young men there, in search of continuing work and urban lifestyles. An informal transportation system rapidly grew up to serve the needs of Upriver People, using four-wheel

drive vehicles that carried half a dozen people. These were mostly operated by Upriver People themselves, and even though fares were cheap,
several enterprising young men had made themselves relatively wealthy. A
few owned several passenger vehicles, or even trucks large enough to haul
building materials. Nothing moved according to fixed time tables, however.
As in the days of river transport, it was necessary to ask around about who
was travelling where and when. One obvious place to enquire was at the
taxi stands in downtown Miri, next to the bus station. Regular bus services existed along the coastal roads south to Bintulu and north to Brunei,
but travel inland along the logging roads was a much more hit-or-miss
affair.

The migration of workers to the coast soon made Miri the metropolis
of the Upriver People. By the mid-1980s, there were half a dozen squatter
settlements around town. One of them occupied a hill overlooking the old
downtown area, with its Chinese shops and colonial era public buildings,
and the extensive settlement there had almost the air of a village. Some
houses were solidly built and shaded by large trees. The steep gradient
meant that any moderately heavy rain would sweep out the ditches that
provided the only sewage disposal. Canada Hill, as it was called, had no
regular water supply, there was trash everywhere, and some houses were
flimsy. Even so, it had a certain vitality, and it was possible to find there
people from all over the Baram watershed. In the early 1990s, a few evenings
spent on Canada Hill would provide me with news from far and wide. It
was obvious, however, that so desirable a piece of real estate would not
for long continue to be occupied by squatters, and by the mid-1990s, the
bulldozers were already circling. This was hardly surprising because the
"developers" were those who had grown rich from the timber boom and
who were already in control of the political apparatus. Those displaced
moved to squatter settlements in less desirable locations further from town,
some passable, others squalid.

Not all urbanised Upriver People were squatters, however. There were
those who had profited from education and taken white-collar jobs in
the administrative headquarters of the international corporations that were
working the offshore oil fields. These were the plum jobs because they
paid well, had security, and gave access to such facilities as the luxurious
waterfront club. There were also positions in less prestigious enterprises and
in the civil service, and they allowed the growth of a distinct middle class of
Upriver People, who lived in the suburbs springing up around Miri. Some
of these suburbs comprised tiny cinder-block houses, crowded together
on a bleakly rectangular grid of roads. Low and shadeless, I found them
much less habitable than the longhouses had been. There were more elite

suburbs, however, that catered to a small professional and managerial class, with brick houses that would pass unnoticed in the suburbs of an American or European city, each with a car in the driveway.

The overall demographic picture is of the draining of population from the interior, with a dispersed residue left behind. The process was already far advanced among the Lun Bawang by the 1970s because the relatively placid Limbang River had made logging along its banks easy. It was less so in the more remote Kelabit highlands, although people there had been quick to grasp educational opportunities. The young Kelabit men who were sent away to school in the 1950s and 1960s were well placed to take the jobs that became available in the 1970s, when the oil companies rapidly expanded their offshore operations. They in turn could steer lucrative manual labour on the rigs themselves toward friends and relatives. By degrees, longhouses in the Kelabit highlands were abandoned to the old and infirm. In the Baram watershed, the process of emptying out longhouses was slower to take hold and proceeded at varying rates in different communities. For example, those along the middle Tinjar increased their involvement in the cash economy in several stages. As early as the 1960s, they often had men away working in the lumber camps, but not so many as to destabilize longhouse society. Then, during the massive expansion of logging in the 1980s, the new roads skirted the region because of the extensive swamps between the river and the coast. For communities further inland, however, the sudden arrival of roads in the 1980s caused severe dislocation.

As a result of outmigration, each longhouse community in the Brunei hinterland underwent its own diaspora, a kind of twentieth-century echo of the *volkerwanderung* of the nineteenth century (Metcalf 2001b). There was an important difference, however. The earlier migrations caused the formation of longhouse communities – including such megacommunities as Long Batan and Long Kelejeo – within which the complexities of Up-river ethnicity were negotiated. The modern migrations promoted homo-geneity. Urbanised people with roots in longhouse communities began to think of themselves primarily as Upriver People, rather than Kenyah or Berawan, or any of the endless other ethnic labels available. In the process, the detailed histories of migration that could be collected in every long-house in the 1970s, usually in multiple versions, became radically truncated. I was told by young and old alike that the Upriver People had come from the Usun Apau – the plateau at the headwaters of the Baram and the Tinjar (Figure 02-02) – and that was all. In fact, I was told more than once by elderly people that it was best now to forget those old stories, full of warfare. Everyone was the same now, they said, simply Upriver People. With that claim, we arrive back where I started in the introduction, with the ethnic entity ORANG ULU on Figure Int-01.

The Future of Longhouses

At the end of the twentieth century, the longhouse society that I knew in the 1970s was finished. Never again would the lives of Upriver People revolve around their longhouse communities, such that the outside world seemed distant if not irrelevant. The longhouses were still standing, but they no longer had that self-contained air that had made each one its own metropolis. Instead, they were at best sleeper suburbs of Miri – with only poor transportation services for getting into town. Money had been invested in "modernising" longhouses during the timber boom of the 1980s and 1990s, but no one could say exactly who would repair the roof when it started to leak. For longhouses to fall into disrepair was nothing new, but not for all of them to do so at once. It was hard to imagine how the impetus to renew them would arise.

The first generation of emigrants maintained strong emotional connections with their home communities, and there were still occasions when longhouses were a bustle. The communal festivals that most reliably drew people home was Christmas, especially as the school holidays gave time enough for young people to make it home. Moreover, there was no problem distributing visitors among "rooms" – even those who had been born and raised in Miri. The concept of "room of origin" (in Berawan *ukuk asan*) allowed any descendent of a resident or former resident to claim membership, not only in the community as a whole, but also in a specific room. Gradually, however, even elite marriages tended to be celebrated in town, and old people came down to them, rather than their children coming back to the house. Moreover, the school year, established during the Raj, was changed at the insistence of Malay politicians who objected to holidays following the Christian calendar. With this change, there was no regular event that drew people home, and the decrease in communal vitality was noticeable.

To some degree, church congregations filled the gap left by the dissolution of the longhouse communities, but they did nothing to preserve the old communal loyalties. There is nothing surprising in that, given that joining a global ecumene had been a major motivation in the first place for "throwing away the Old Way." It had been the goal of Temonggong Oyong Lawai Jau to unite Upriver People in one religion, and he had succeeded in that they had not "entered Malaydom," but instead become Christian. It was not his fault that the missionaries had divided people, as well as uniting them. Moreover, few congregations in Miri were exclusively composed of Upriver People. They were usually outnumbered in Catholic and Anglican churches, which drew substantial numbers of Chinese and Iban adherents. Those most responsive to the needs of Upriver People were congregations of Sidang Injil Borneo, the indigenous church organised among converts of the Borneo Evangelical Mission.

In theory, former longhouse residents and their descendents retained rights to land held in customary title. In practice, it was nearly impossible to gain government recognition for any such rights (Hong 1987:37–72). Nevertheless, I sometimes met people in Miri who planned to go back to their longhouse communities to begin farming one or another cash crop. In a few cases, they were former civil servants, who had retired at fifty. These enterprising men held up the prospect of communal revival in the future, similar perhaps to the Maori of New Zealand. Even while the migration of Maori to the cities was in full flood, the sites of ancient *pa* – villages and strongholds – were marked with ceremonial gathering places. Abandoned for months at a time apart from a few old people, the *marae* would spring to life for festivals that drew visitors by the busload, not only those belonging to the place, but also their guests from other *marae*. Elaborate formal speeches and dances of welcome gave substance to what it was to be a Maori (Salmond 1975). In the twenty-first century, Maoridom is undergoing a remarkable revival, grounded in the ongoing existence of *marae*.

Upriver People are faced with formidable problems in achieving the same end. Longhouse sites do not possess the sacred quality of *marae*. It was the community itself that was the embodiment of the ancestors, not any place or structure, and it is the communities that have evaporated. Their unique character can hardly survive intermarriage on the current scale, not only with Upriver People from other communities, but also with Iban. Language death is occurring on a large scale. Children born in the city are not learning the languages of either parent, so that one generation will suffice to eliminate many of the languages with relatively few speakers. A couple that I knew in Miri both came from distinguished families, one Kayan, one Sebop. At home, they and their children spoke English.

During the 1990s, the educated elite of Upriver People for the most part remained faithful to the command of the Temonggong and had not forgotten their origins. Many worked hard to stay in contact with the scattered members of their communities, despite the increasingly obvious class differences. They organised events that would draw people together, and they tried self-consciously to promote their "cultural heritage." These earnest young men and women would often quiz me – What is our culture? What is it we need to preserve? Needless to say, they found my responses disappointing. I would always end up with the same conclusion, that what was special about Upriver People had to do with living in longhouses. But that was no longer an option. It will require all their inventiveness and ingenuity to remake themselves as a people without longhouses.

Conclusion

The General in the Particular

From the point of view of historians and sociologists, ethnographers are often seen as making generalisations based on skimpy data – little more than a few personal experiences. During his *enfant terrible* phase, Edmund Leach made the same charge against the pioneers of modern fieldwork:

> When we read Malinowski we get the impression that he is stating something which is of general importance. Yet how can this be? He is simply writing about the Trobriand Islanders. Somehow he has so assimilated himself into the Trobriand situation that he is able to make the Trobriands a microcosm of the whole primitive world. And the same is true of his successors: for Firth, Primitive Man is a Tikopian, for Fortes, he is a citizen of Ghana. (1961:1)

I avoid the charge by denying that I am saying anything generalisable, that is, anything about the essential nature of cultural difference. On the contrary, my goal is to show how ethnicity was constructed in a specific region and under specific historical circumstances.

My method is unabashedly analytic; it makes no concessions to postmodernism. Its premise is that nothing about the process of ethnification can be taken for granted. On the contrary, working out how ethnicity works in different places is part of the business of ethnography, what, for want of a better word, we might call "ethnology." Locating ethnic groups – "naming the tribes" – is a goal of research, not a preliminary.

Constructing Cultural Difference

To say that cultural difference is, in the fashionable phrase, "socially constructed" is stating the obvious (Hacking 1999). The point is to show how it is constructed. In the hinterland of Brunei, three basic processes were at work.

New labels made up because of new communities. My example concerned the community led by Aban Jau, which was made up of peoples who had not previously lived together. What was merely a map reference – Long Batan, the place where the Batan stream debouched into the Tinjar – became the name of a community, and so the name of an ethnicity. The name "Long Batan" was used as if it was an ethnonym, and consequently, it was an ethnonym.

Labels derived from previous communities. Meanwhile, when people at Long Batan wanted to say what kind of Long Batan people they were, they named communities that their ancestors had lived in before settling at Long Batan. Some came from Long Taballau, which had evidently been a vigorous, enduring community, or its name would not have lasted. Someone who claimed to "be" Long Taballau might have ancestors from other communities, however – a grandfather who had married in, perhaps. Consequently, there was no subtext of "ethnic purity." Indeed, those closely related to leaders of the past were more likely than others to have ancestors whose marriages had been part of a political alliance between communities.

Labels that have lost their place reference. As oral histories stretch out, the location of places become hazy, especially if in the interim there have been migrations into whole new river systems. In the 1970s, no one could tell me exactly where Long Taballau had been because they were no longer familiar with the geography of that region. But even in Hose's time, he had informants at Long Batan who called themselves simply Tebalo'. In effect, Long Taballau had ceased to be a place at all. Ethnonyms with broad coverage – that is, used by people in several different communities – such as Sebop and Melawan may have arisen in the same way.

The political system of Brunei made no demands on ethnic identity. A trader was content to know that there were potential customers at Long Batan, and for an aristocrat back in Brunei, they were all simply Murut anyway. It was of course British colonialists, dutifully followed by anthropologists, who set out to construct taxonomies that showed "genuine" ethnic relations, that is, ethnicity defined in essentialist, genetic terms. It is noticeable that Hose preferred "Long Taballau" to "Long Batan" as an ethnic label because it was older, and antiquity connoted authenticity. He preferred "Sebop" to either because it looked like an ethnic name, pure and simple.

What confounds taxonomy is that new ethnicities arose not only by fragmentation, but also agglutination. Whatever categories colonialists thought
they had discovered, longhouse communities were founded, grew, went
into decline, and dispersed, in a process of formation and reformation that
paid no attention to ethnic "boundaries." Linguistic diversity was produced
in the same way as ethnic diversity, and in both cases, longhouse communities were the sites of production. Longhouse religion was intensely
communal, requiring innovation to create an operating ritual consensus
and simultaneously preserving the innovations of communities long since
defunct.

The paradoxical conclusion is that the hinterland of Brunei manifested ethnic, linguistic, and religious diversity, but no bounded ethnicities,
languages, or religions, in sum, no "cultures."

Numberless Tribes

Apparently, much the same could be said about the Kachin Hills. In the
conclusion of his ethnography, Leach states flatly:

> it is futile to attempt to record all the stereotyped ethnographic variations
> for they are almost numberless. The assiduous ethnographer can find just as
> many different "tribes" as he cares to look for. (1964:291)

His reaction was to ignore cultural diversity, and that is how he achieved
the theoretical reach that has given *Political Systems of Highland Burma* such
perennial appeal. There was a price to be paid, however. Privileging the
negotiation of social status to the exclusion of all else drew him back into the
functionalism that he criticized in his famous essay, *Rethinking Anthropology*
(Leach 1961). In a series of sharp exchanges with Claude Levi-Strauss about
the consequences of Kachin marriage rules, he moves steadily away from his
earlier experiments with structuralism toward a very British pragmatism:

> In Levi-Strauss's view the circulation of women in a system of *echange generalise*
> is a system in itself; the circulation of prestations in the other direction is
> another system in itself: the two should not be confused. But certainly that
> is not how the Kachin themselves think about it. They are not, of course,
> specialists in the theory of structuralism but they know very well how their
> marriage system really works. They know that political power consists of the
> control of material assets and that women are pawns in the game of politics.
> Levi-Strauss, as always, has everything back to front. (Leach 1968:284)

This is the position that came to be called "transactionalism" (Bailey 1969;
Barth 1959). What makes that plain is Leach's invocation of "power" as a

Conclusion

universally applicable concept, but his ethnography shows that "thigh-eating chiefs" have virtually no economic or legal functions, no power in terms of the classic formulation: command-obedience (Clastres 1977:4). What we have instead is an elaborate system of snobbery, an intense competition for advantage that is utterly mysterious to anyone outside the system. The parallels with the English class system are too tempting to resist. Perhaps that is why it is an American, Thomas Kirsch (1973), who comes closest to offering a cultural account of what is at stake in his little-known essay *Feasting and Social Oscillation: Religion and Society in Upland Southeast Asia*. Kirsch surveys an area even larger than Leach's Kachin Hills, looking for recurring patterns in ritual. What he finds is "religious conceptions regarding rewards for activities in this life which are meted out in an afterlife" (Kirsch 1973:5). These ideas are very different from those described in Section V, and this underlines the cultural nature of Kirsch's account. He is describing concepts specific to a region, rather than invoking a supposedly universal drive, like Leach. Instead he provides an ontological framework within which Kachin status competition makes sense.

Disposing of the Facts

Leach's problem with cultural variation was that he did not know what to do with a mass of "ethnographic" minutiae. He had the same problem with historical details. As he says at the beginning of his chapter, "The Evidence from Kachin History":

> I suppose that the main difficulty that every anthropologist has to face is what to do with the facts. When I read a book by one of my anthropological colleagues, I am, I confess, frequently bored by the facts. I see no prospect of visiting either Tikopia or the Northern Territories of the Gold Coast and I cannot arouse in myself any real interest in the cultural peculiarities of either the Tikopia or the Tallensi. I read the works of professors Firth and Fortes not from an interest in the facts but so as to learn something about the principles behind the facts. I take it for granted that the vast majority of those who read this book will be in a similar position with regard to the Kachins. How then should I dispose of the facts, the detailed evidence? (Leach 1964:227)

His solution was to put the "facts" in a separate section at the end of the book, segregated from the "principles behind the facts," so that the common reader need not be bothered by them.

Once again, one is forced to admire Leach's daring; having at one stroke severed cultural variation from his account, he then pares off the superfluous evidence. Lacking his bravura, I have retained all manner of details, down to

314

the slight differences in ritual between neighbouring communities described in Chapter 10. Rather than abstracting "principles," I follow the maxim that God (or the Devil, if you prefer) is in the details. The modus operandi of an ethnographer is in my view a kind of sleuthing, a search for key pieces of evidence that carry conviction, that substantiate an entire plot. Certainly, the reader must be protected from an avalanche of irrelevant facts, but that does not mean that details are unimportant. Instead, it is the job of the ethnographer to pick his or her among them so as to make a case.

History and Process

Leach marshals his historical evidence, as he explicitly says, in order to document his account of "historical process" in highland Burma. In fact, the nature of this process was his principal bone of contention with Levi-Strauss. In *The Elementary Structures of Kinship* (1969), Levi-Strauss theorized that systems of generalised exchange were inherently unstable. Sooner or later, he argued, the cycle of reciprocity that they required would be broken by a self-interested few, who would then accumulate both women and goods at the expense of their neighbours. This grand drama he called the "feudal crisis," and, like Adam's fall, it marked the end of an epoch of innocence, specifically elementary kinship systems. Leach rejected all this as mythic history. In its place, he proposed a model of regular movement back and forth between relatively hierarchical (*gumsa*) and relatively egalitarian (*gumlao*) forms of Kachin society. In the 1950s, this model seemed radical as compared to the static, not to say frozen, accounts that British functionalists of the era were producing. The appearance of change is superficial, however. As Leach says, both *gumsa* and *gumlao* forms were equally Kachin, and consequently, the movement between them constituted a variety of social reproduction. The model that I offer at the end of Chapter 5 is of the same kind: longhouse communities changing over time in a characteristic manner, passing through a kind of life cycle. It is, however, a model of social process, not historical change.

To account for the latter requires us to consider external factors, the most ancient being trade. The most obvious difference between Burma and Borneo in this regard was the absence infrastructure. Trade flowed through the Kachin Hills on caravans, providing a steady profit in tolls to suitably located Kachin chiefs. Longhouse leaders in the Brunei hinterland had no such source of income. The particulars of the commodities traded are also significant, however. Leach gives a list of products mentioned by early Chinese sources, comprising "rhinoceros, elephant, tortoiseshell, jade, amber, cowries, gold, silver, salt-wells, cinnamon and cotton trees, hill paddy and pannicled rice." It is an odd assortment, but Leach gives no further details. Were rhinoceros hunted in the Kachin hills? Did cotton grow there? Elsewhere, Leach mentions the production of tea, but says nothing about tea plantations (Leach 1964:235, 237–9).

From Farmhouse to Longhouse

Meanwhile, it is my argument that the specific nature of the commodities produced from the Borneo rainforest, their mode of accumulation, and the way they made their way down river were formative of longhouse society.

It is characteristic of the most ancient long-distance trade routes that the commodities that moved along them were of small volume and high value. Beads – the most significant item going upriver – provide a perfect example. Those going down river were equally compact, but they were not manufactured. In fact, they were not produced at all, in the sense of being the result of the application of labour. Instead, they were just found; they were fortuitous commodities. Monkeys were easy to hunt, and the bezoar stones that were occasionally found in their intestines were valuable, but that did not mean that it was profitable or practicable for swidden farmers in the interior to spend their time slaughtering monkeys. Moreover, the stones had no value unless a market could be found for them.

For the precolonial trading system in the hinterland of Brunei to exist at all required social arrangements that allowed for the accumulation of fortuitous commodities and their transportation to market. Needless to say, the longhouse communities that the first European visitors found there in the nineteenth century were not the only imaginable institutions that could have fulfilled these requirements. They were, however, plausible ones. Houses with raised floors are found throughout the Austronesian-speaking world. They have the advantage of being well ventilated, raised above muddy ground, and protected from flooding or high tide. Washing water and kitchen waste can be simply dumped through the floor, especially if there are pigs to clean it up. Not the least of their advantages in the Borneo rainforest is that there are less flying insects six or more feet above ground, most notably mosquitoes. One has only to spend a night or two camping in the jungle to be convinced of that, and to understand why people asserted that to lack longhouses was to live in the forest. Moreover, as is argued in Chapter 5, the nature of swidden agriculture is not that farmers work their way across the landscape, a slice at a time. On the contrary, suitable niches are relatively rare, especially ones accessible by river. Consequently, there is often a cluster of farms in one place, then none for some distance upriver or down, and then another cluster. For neighbours to share a common structure has efficiencies of scale. Cutting timber and squaring planks is heavy work for one farming group to manage alone. A team of men working together can build a more solid structure raised on sturdy posts.

The crucial leap in scale comes when people build houses that are removed from their farm sites, with people who are not their neighbours there, and for this there is no ecological imperative or practical advantage. We should pause, however, to notice that community as a social value in and of itself is already implicit in joint farmhouses. Indeed, as the example of the Berawan diaspora after the collapse of Aban Jau's megacommunity shows, there was always a tension between longhouse and farmhouse, if not indeed an ambiguity. When a group of neighbours invested a lot of effort on building a row of tenement farmhouses, raised high on heavy pilings, with a roof made of hardwood shingles, they were in effect building a long-house. All it needed was a place name, which was not hard to devise, to become a nascent ethnicity. Moreover, if and when a more encompassing community arose, that ethnicity would not be forgotten. So it was that the Berawan people living at Long Jegan in the 1970s insisted that there were four longhouses there, belonging to the Long Sijoi, the Long Ugeng, Long Lamat, and Long Penuwan. The persistence of such solidarities indicates that intensity of communal feeling is not proportional to the size of the longhouse. As I noticed in the 1970s, tiny communities often manifested as much pride in their shared history and traditions as larger ones. Like faded aristocrats, they boasted of a time when they had been more powerful than the parvenus who now outnumbered them.

The Leader as CEO

The genius of longhouse leaders was to mobilize the values of community to assemble larger communities. They did not have to create those values, however. Their most important resource was the collective memory of previous longhouse communities. They had to hold up the promise of cultural resources that outweighed practical considerations.

The material expression of those resources was the wealth that came from trade. In all longhouse narratives, exemplary communities of the past had thriving populations, rice supplies adequate to host major festivals, and large amounts of heirloom property. In contrast to Kachin chiefs, however, a longhouse leader could not simply wait for passing caravans to tax. Instead, he had to actively promote trade. Indeed, he had to take a leading part in it, if he wanted to profit himself. The nature of fortuitous commodities was that they accumulated in small caches here and there, in farm houses or rooms in the longhouse. So the first task was to assemble enough produce to make it worth making an expedition down river. He then needed to build canoes of the largest kind, and assemble supplies of rice to provision the entire trip. What he could not do was tax the trade that others organised – Aban Jau tried to do that and failed. A reasonable hypothesis would be that the greater the distance down river to the coast, the larger the expeditions, and the less frequently they occurred. Unfortunately, the evidence to test it is lacking.

Even when Malays came upriver to trade, the same pattern repeated itself. The account given by Spenser St. John and quoted in Chapter 7 makes clear the central role played by "the chief." He "settled the terms" of trade and took first choice. He did not, however, exercise a monopoly on trade any more than he did on leadership. He could not buy everything, and after making his selection, he was followed by "the next in rank in rotation" (St. John 1862:I:124). Even the humblest might close a deal before trading was over. Moreover, even if no expedition had to be fitted out, there were expenses in playing host to a party of Malay traders. Rounding up the necessary forest products took months, and all that time the traders had to be fed and entertained. This could become burdensome, as shown in the incident recounted at the beginning of Chapter 6, when the "Burong Pingai" were violently expelled from the Tutoh River.

Reciprocity and Charisma

The economic role of longhouse leaders makes an interesting contrast to that of Polynesian chiefs, as portrayed by Marshall Sahlins (1963). Chiefs acted as redistributors of subsistence products – root crops and pigs – previously offered to them as tribute. In the process, they gained prestige, but there was no way that they could accumulate material wealth. The situation in Borneo was different because exchange involved commodities, and those received in trade – beads and brassware – certainly could be accumulated. I might say that longhouse leaders had more room for "free enterprise," provided it is understood that beads are "capital" only in a metaphorical, not technical, sense (Wallerstein 1983:13–46).

Longhouse leaders received no tribute in the Polynesian manner, but subsistence products did accrue to them. The interesting feature is that this occurred in an ideological framework of egalitarianism. Any death called forth a communal response. The bereaved "room" (i.e., coresidents of a room) were immobilized by mourning, and provision for the funeral had to be made by the rest of the community, providing a kind of ritual welfare state. Meanwhile, the results were, of course, anything but egalitarian. Since the majority of members of the community ended up giving more than they received, the question arises of what they gained in return. The answer is that they shared in the prestige that the community as a whole received from the grand funerals and elaborate tombs of their leaders.

This was the peculiar nature of "the gift" in Borneo, and it has an intriguing echo of generalised exchange. For Levi-Strauss, its egalitarianism followed from its nature as an elementary structure of kinship, as a transformation of the thoroughly egalitarian restricted exchange. Leach showed that in practice the reverse was the case. An ideology of marriage among equals remained in place, available equally to endogamous aristocratic elites and democratically inclined founders of *gumlao* communities, but for everyone else marriage created inequality.

The trick for a longhouse leader was to mobilize the community, not only to engage in communal activity – the building of a shared longhouse – but also to support the grand rituals that he sponsored – the death rites of close relatives who died at convenient moments. In contrast to Polynesian chiefs, he could not invoke principles of descent to justify his priority. Since all connections to leading men of the past were equally valid, including those through marriage, there were always other men able to claim their mantles.

That death rituals provided an important arena in which competition for leadership occurred was a consequence of the conception of the community as comprising more than those who currently lived in the longhouse. It included the ancestors, whose presence was almost palpable. They were invoked in the prayers that accompanied every ritual large and small, and their influence was entirely benevolent. The ancestors did not punish the living for moral infractions, nor did they demand constant offerings or sacrifices. In that sense, longhouse religion was not a stereotypic "ancestor cult" of the variety described by Edward Burnett Tylor (1871). Prayers implored the attention of the only spirit agency whose attention and goodwill could be entirely relied on (Metcalf 1989:59–71). There was no notion of anything resembling witchcraft or black magic, no way that one longhouse member could direct supernatural malice against another. Other than the automatic, mechanical results of incurring a state of ritual danger, all evil influences came from outside the community. The ancestors and the living stood together, surrounded by the unknown.

Nothing outside the death rituals had the same quality of sacredness. If, during the festival of "prayers of the house," a drunken man staggered into the display of offerings carefully arranged on a row of sticks, knocking them all askew, everyone simply laughed. But the songs that began the death rites were truly awesome; even to hum their tunes at any other time would cause someone to die. As the ancestors arrived en masse, everyone shivered – including me. The contact with them was massively invigorating;

it was they that brought rice and wealth and good luck to the community, in short, "a good life, a cool life." When the funeral or *nulang* was over, however, it was necessary to recall the soul of every single living member of the community, to make sure that none departed with the ancestors.

The threat of liminal confusion required that the death rituals be carefully managed, and in this, leaders played the central role. Regarding the procedural details, they had to invoke, or perhaps negotiate, a ritual consensus. Having done so, they had to utilise the ritual operator so as to identify themselves with their communities. In the process, they became producers of a great show, the impresario of ancestors.

Defence Becomes Primary

In the second half of the nineteenth century, the trading system that had supported longhouse society was convulsed by historical forces that came from beyond the ancient Asian world economy. British and Dutch ships largely bypassed Brunei, even as they were making available new commodities. At roughly the same time, a wave of immigrants from the interior arrived in the Brunei hinterland, presumably in an attempt to replace old trading opportunities and take advantage of new ones. Having moved a considerable distance, from across the central mountain range in what is now Indonesian Borneo, they came in force. This is as we would expect because trading expeditions were generally larger the further they had to travel. Having established themselves in the middle Baram, they found themselves in a niche that they could exploit in novel ways.

The Kayan depredations of the epoch annihilated many small communities in a fourth process of "constructing cultural difference," in addition to the three listed previously. In effect, it was a process of de-ethnification, but we should not assume that the extinction of ethnic labels always involved violence. The Berawan of Batu Belah do not speak of warfare with the Pelutan people they met long ago in the river of the same name. On the contrary, it was by all accounts an entirely amicable encounter, but the result was the same as for many of those subjugated by the Kayan: assimilation.

As Kayan communities grew in population and power, others had to respond in kind if they were not to suffer the same fate. Consequently, we find megacommunities appearing in the lower Baram, larger than anything that had existed previously – or at least within the time depth of anyone's oral history. At Long Kelejeo in the lower Tutoh were assembled not only people who had been allies and neighbours for decades, the Lakipo' and Bito Kala, but also some of their recent enemies, the Tring. There were three longhouses, surrounded by a massive stockade. Malay traders maintained a permanent residence there, even having their own single-dwelling houses within the stockade. There was also something else inside the stockade: mausoleums. Their presence – still visible in the 1970s – was evidence of the intensity of competition among the leaders at Long Kelejeo for the charisma of the ancestors. None triumphed, however. There was in the 1970s no single leader acknowledged in the oral history of both Lakipo' and Bito Kala people as having been supreme at Long Kelejeo.

At Long Batan, it was a different story. The megacommunity there was, in both its rise and fall, closely associated with Aban Jau. His pretensions as Rajah Ulu – the king upriver – were ridiculed by the officers of the Brooke Raj, but they may not have been so absurd. To again draw an analogy with the Maori of New Zealand, formerly hostile Maori groups managed to organise a new level of political integration in response to growing European settlement (King 2003:211–24). The Waikato chief Te Wherowhero was formally installed in 1856 as the first Maori king, with his "capital" at Ngaruwahia, despite the fact that the chiefs who appointed him had only a short time before been engaged in savage warfare among themselves (Crosby 1999). The Maori king movement did not succeed in founding a modern nation-state, but it did provide a focus for Maori political aspirations. It is not beyond the bounds of possibility that, given more time, some leader could have achieved the same result in the hinterland of Brunei. As it was, a sense of unity did not emerge among Upriver People until late in the colonial period.

Modernity Delayed

The Brooke Raj was such as to allow the continuity of longhouse society. The proposition cannot be phrased in stronger terms because the main contribution of the Raj was a lack of interference, rather than any positive support. Things might have been otherwise, however. The Dutch administration in Flores, for examples, demolished the multifamily houses of the Manggarai on grounds of "hygiene" (Waterson 1990:36–8). The postwar period of direct British rule brought improvements to health care and access to education, but little economic development. The changes were sufficient, however, to set in motion yet a fifth process of ethnification that did not make use of the place names of communities, whether old or new. Instead, it involved lumping together multiple communities. As Immanuel Wallerstein predicted, the labels Orang Ulu (Upriver People) and Lun Bawang (People from Around Here) arose in a context of global capitalism. They do not, however, match his notion of ethnic groups as "sizeable groups of people to whom were reserved certain occupational/economic roles in relation to

Conclusion

other such groups in geographical proximity" (Wallerstein 1983). Until the 1980s, the cash economy of the hinterland of Brunei remained small and continued to rely on products that had been traded for centuries. Only after modernity arrived in the form of massive machinery eating up the forest did the majority of Upriver People find a place in the national economy – as a lumpen proletariat in the coastal cities. Modernity came, not as liberation from oppressive tradition, as the modernists imagined, but as cultural and economic impoverishment. But the final collapse of longhouse society must not be allowed to obscure its remarkable longevity and vitality.

Appendix: Longhouse Communities in the Baram Watershed, 1972

Population figures are estimates made by the Malaria Eradication Program survey. Some had grown considerably by the late 1970s, and this was reflected in additional "doors" or rooms added when rebuilding occurred. Long Jegan, for instance, jumped from thirty-four to fifty-six. Kayan communities are listed separately. Iban communities and those in the highlands identifying themselves as Kelabit are not listed.

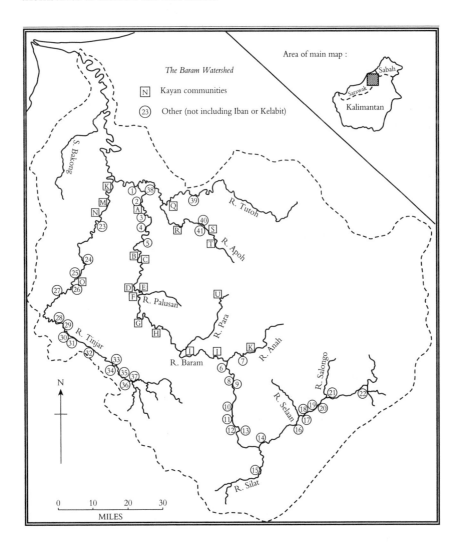

Communities in the Baram District classified as "Kenyah"

River	Number	Place Name	Doors	Population	Language/Ethnic Group Name	Related Groups	Present Religion
Baram	1	Long Tutoh	43	234	Long Kiput	Lepo Pu'un	RC
	2	Loagan Sibong	6	61	Long Belukun	Lepo Umbo'	RC
	3	Long Ikang	40	281	Long Sebatu, Long Ulai	Lepo Umbo*	RC
	4	Long Banio	55	410	Murik	Long Simiang	RC
	5	Long Puak	26	190	Uma Akeh	(in Belaga)	RC
	6	Long San	24	179	Long Tikan	Lepo Umbo'	RC
	7	Long Tap	23	185	Long Tap	Lepo Umbo*	RC
	8	Long Selatong (ilir)	10	121	Likan, Leppo Ga	Lepo Tau	RC
	9	Long Selatong (ulu'i)	12	110	Likan, Leppo Ga	Lepo Tau	RC
	10	Long Apu	37	327	Uma Pawa	Lepo Dunin	RC
	11	Long Julan	14	110	Lepo Abong	Lepo Tau	RC
	12	Long Anap	32	242	Lepo Sawa	?	RC
	13	Long Palai	3	310	Lepo La'ang	Lepo Tau	RC
	14	Long Jeeh	53	570	Lepo Aga	Lio Matu	SIB
	15	Long Menkaba	23	186	Lepo Tau	Lepo Tau	RC
	16	Long Moh	73	189	Lepo Tau, Lepo Jingan, Lepo Ke'	Lepo Tau	emMostly Bungan some RC
	17	Long Sela'an	22	211	Long Belukun, Tepuan	Lepo Umbo'	RC
	18	Long Simiang	12	119	Murik	Long Banio	RC
	19	Long Mesigau	11	81	Lepo Ke'	Long Moh	SIB
	20	Long Tungan	24	383	Leppo Nyamok	Lio Matu	RC

	21	Lip Matu	38	Badang	Long Jeeh	SIB
	22	Long Balang	8	Lepo Ke'	Long Mesigau	?
Tinjar	23	Long Teru	31	Berawan	Berawan	Old religion, some RC
	24	Long Tuyut	5	Long Suku	Sebop, Long Wat	RC
	25	Long Taveng	22	Berawan + Maloh	Berawan	Various
	26	Long Teran Batu	8	Berawan	Berawan	Old religion
	27	Long Jegan	34y	Berawan	Berawan	$\frac{1}{2}$ Bungan, $\frac{1}{2}$ RC
	28	Long Batan	6	Sebop	Sebop	RC
	29	Long Loyang	48	Long Pokun Sebop	Sebop	RC
	30	Apaugun	14	Berawan, Sebop, Kejaman		RC
	31	Long Aya	8	Sebop + other	–	RC
	32	Long Dunin	15	Uma Pawa	Long Apu	RC
	33	Long Pejawai	9	Seping	(Belaga)	RC
	34	Long Sobeng	25	Long Taballai Sebop	Sebop	RC
	35	Long Atun	19	Lepo Anan	Lepo Tau	RC
	36	Long Nuah	13	Lirong	Sebop	RC
	37	Long Selapon	9	Sebop	Sebop	RC
Tutoh	38	Batu Belah	18	Berawan		Most SIB, some RC
	39	Long Terawan	54	Berawan	Berawan	
Apoh	40	Long Wat (Ilir)	19	Long Wat	Sebop	RC
	41-	Long Wat (ulu)	13	Long Wat	Sebop	SIB

River	Letter	Name	Doors	Population	Religion
Baram	A	Long Ilcang (Ilir)	19	182	RC
	B	Long Laput	72	686	Mostly Bungan, some SIB, few RC
	C	Sungai Dua	42	362	Mostly RC, few SIB
	D	Uma Bawang (Ilir)	13	127	Bungan
	E	Uma Bawang (ulu)	38	273	RC
	F	Long Miri	60	526	RC
	G	Long Pila	81	726	Mostly RC, few Bungan
	H	Long Kasih	23	222	SIB
	I	Long Na'ah	43	390	SIB
	J	Long Liam	48	413	SIB
Akah	K	Long Tebanggan	19	147	SIB
Tinjar	L	Long Maro	8	–	SIB
	M	Lubok Kulat	6	–	SIB
	N	Long Sepeling	25	150	SIB
	O	Long Teran Batu	10	88	SIB
	P	Long Teran	26	193	SIB
TutohApoh	Q	Long Panai	32	310	Mostly RC, few Bungan
	R	Long Bemang	95	890	SIB
	S	Long Atip	73	740	SIB
	T	Long Bedian	82	620	SIB
Pata	U	Long Anyat	21	189	SIB

Bibliography

Abdul Ghafur, Sharif. 1984. "The Tabun of Limbang." *Sarawak Gazette* 1485:15–20.

Abu-Lughod, Janet. 1989. *Before European Hegemony: The World System A.D. 1250–1350.* New York: Oxford University Press.

Alexander, Jennifer. 1992. "The Cultural Construction of Hierarchy among the Kenyah Badang." *Oceania* 26:194–206.

Alexander, Jennifer. 1993. "The Lahanan Longhouse." In James Fox (ed.), *Inside Austronesian Houses*, pp. 3–43. Canberra: Australian National University.

Anderson, Benedict. 1972. "The Idea of Power in Javanese Culture." In Claire Holt (ed.), *Culture and Politics in Indonesia*, pp. 1–69. Ithaca, NY: Cornell University Press.

Anonymous. 1984. *Beads.* Kuching: Sarawak Museum.

Anonymous. 1994. *Logging against the Natives of Sarawak.* Kuala Lumpur, Malaysia: Institute of Social Analysis.

Appadurai, Arjun. 1990. "Disjuncture and Difference in the Global Cultural Economy." *Public Culture* 2:1–24.

Arnold, Guy. 1955. "Prehistory of Usun Apau." *Sarawak Museum Journal* V:166–81.

Arnold, Guy. 1959. *Longhouse and Jungle: An Expedition to Sarawak.* London: Chatto and Windus.

Bailey, F.G. 1969. *Stratagems and Spoils: A Social Anthropology of Politics.* New York: Schocken.

Baring-Gould, S., and Bampfylde, C. 1909. *A History of Sarawak under Its Two White Rajahs 1839–1908.* London: Henry Sotheran.

Barlow, Kathleen, and Winduo, Steven. 1997. "Introduction." *The Contemporary Pacific* 9:1–24.

Barth, Frederick. 1959. *Political Leadership among the Swat Pathan.* London: Athlone Press.

Belawing, Tingang. 1974. "The Story of the Long Kiput Kenyah." *Sarawak Museum Journal* 22:349–52.

Bellwood, Peter. 1979. *Man's Conquest of the Pacific: The Prehistory of Southeast Asia and Oceania.* New York: Oxford University Press.

Bellwood, Peter. 1985. *Prehistory of the Indo-Malaysian Archipelago.* Sydney: Academic Press.

Bibliography

Bellwood, Peter, and Matussin bin Omar. 1980. "Trade Patterns and Political, Developments in Brunei and Adjacent Areas, A.D. 700–1500." *Brunei Museum Journal* 4:155–69.

Bernstein, Jay. 1997. "The Deculturation of the Brunei Dusun." In Robert Winzeler (ed.), *Indigenous Peoples and the State: Politics, Land, and Ethnicity in the Malayan Peninsular and Borneo*. New Haven, CT: Yale University, Southeast Asia Studies.

Bevis, William. 1995. *Borneo Log: The Struggle for Sarawak's Forests*. Seattle: University of Washington Press.

Bewsher, Robert. 1959. "The Bisaya Group." In Tom Harrisson (ed.), *The Peoples of Sarawak*, pp. 95–102. Kuching: Borneo Literature Bureau.

Blusse, Leonard. 1991. "In Praise of Commodities: An Essay on the Cross-cultural Trade in Edible Bird's Nests." In Roderich Ptak and Brothermund Dietmar (eds.), *Emporia, Commodities and Entrepreneurs in Asian Maritime Trade, c. 1400–1750*. Stuttgart: Franz Steiner.

Blust, Robert. 1972. "Report of Linguistic Fieldwork Undertaken in Sarawak." *Borneo Research Bulletin* 4:12–14.

Blust, Robert. 1974. "The Proto-North Sarawak Vowel Deletion Hypothesis." Unpublished Ph.D. dissertation, University of Hawaii, Honolulu.

Blust, Robert. 1984. "The Tring Dialect of Long Terawan." *Sarawak Museum Journal* XXXIII:101–35.

Blust, Robert. 1992. "The Long Consonants of Long Terawan." *Bijdragen tot de Taal-, Land- en Vokenkunde* 148:409–27.

Braghin, Cecilia. 1998. "An Archaeological Investigation into Ancient Chinese Beads." In Lidia Sciama and Joanne Eicher (eds.), *Beads and Bead Makers: Gender, Material Culture and Meaning*, pp. 273–94. New York: Berg.

Braudel, Fernand. 1968. *Capital and Material Life*. London: Macmillan.

Brightman, Robert. 1995. "Forget Culture: Replacement, Transcendence, Relexification." *Cultural Anthropology* 10:509–46.

Brookfield, Harold, Potter, Lesley, and Yvonne, Byron. 1995. *In Place of the Forest: Environmental and Socio-economic Transformation in Borneo and the Malay Peninsular*. Tokyo: United Nations University Press.

Brosius, Peter. 2007. "Prior Transcripts, Divergent Paths: Resistance and Acquiescence to Logging in Sarawak." In Peter Sercombe and Bernard Sellato (eds.), *Beyond the Green Myth: Borneo's Hunter-Gatherers in the Twenty-First Century*, pp. 289–333. Copenhagen: NIAS Press.

Brown, Donald. 1970. *Brunei: The Structure and History of a Bornean Malay Sultanate*. Monograph of the Brunei Museum Journal, vol. 2, no. 2.

Brown, Donald. 1984. "Patterns in Brunei History and Culture." *Borneo Research Bulletin* 16:28–33.

Brumann, Christoph. 1999. "Writing for Culture: Why a Successful Concept Should Not Be Discarded." *Current Anthropology* 40(Suppl):1–27.

Carsten, Janet, and Hugh-Jones, Stephen. (eds.). 1995. *About the House: Levi-Strauss and Beyond*. Cambridge: Cambridge University Press.

Cense, A.A., and Uhlenbeck, E.M. 1958. *Critical Survey of Studies on the Languages of Borneo*. s-Gravenhage: Martinus Nijhoff.

Chang, Pin-tsun. 1991. "The First Chinese Diaspora in Southeast Asia in the Fifteenth Century." In Roderich Ptak and Dietmar Rothermund (eds.), *Emporia, Commodities, and Entrepreneurs in Asian Maritime Trade, c. 1400–1750*, pp. 13–28. Stuttgart: Franz Steiner.

Chauduri, K.N. 1990. *Asia before Europe: Economy and Civilisation of the Indian Ocean from the Rise of Islam to 1750*. Cambridge: Cambridge University Press.

Chew, Daniel. 1990. *Chinese Pioneers on the Sarawak Frontier 1841–1941*. Singapore: Oxford University Press.

Chin, John. 1981. *The Sarawak Chinese*. Kuala Lumpur, Malaysia: Oxford University Press.

Chin, Lucas. 1988. *Ceramics in the Sarawak Museum*. Kuching: Sarawak Museum.

Chin, Lucas, and Datan, Ipoi. 1991. "Prehistory and History." In Lucas Chin and Valerie Mashman (eds.), *Sarawak Cultural Legacy*. Kuching: Atelier.

Clastres, Pierre. 1977. *Society against the State*. New York: Zone.

Clayre, Beatrice. 1972. "A Preliminary Comparative Study of the Lun Bawang (Murut) and Sa'ban Languages of Sarawak." *Sarawak Museum Journal* 40:145–72.

Cleary, Mark. 1997. "From Hornbills to Oil? Patterns of Indigenous and European Trade in Colonial Borneo." *Journal of Historical Geography* 23:29–45.

Coedes, G. 1948. *Les Etats Hinduises d'Indochine et d'Indonesie*. Paris: Boccard.

Coedes, G. 1968. *The Indianized States of Southeast Asia*. Honolulu: University of Hawaii Press.

Cohn, Bernard. 1996. *Colonialism and Its Forms of Knowledge: The British in India*. Princeton, NJ: Princeton University Press.

Colfer, Carol, and Juk, Along Pelibut. 2001. "Beadlore of the Uma' Jalan Kenyah." *Sarawak Museum Journal* 77:29–36.

Comber, Leon. 1983. *13 May 1969: A Historical Survey of Sino–Malay Relations*. Singapore: Graham Brash.

Condominas, Georges. 1977. *We Have Eaten the Forest: The Story of a Montagnard Village in the Central Highlands of Vietnam*. New York: Hill and Wang.

Crain, Jay. 1970. *The Lun Dayeh of Sabah, East Malaysia: Aspects of Marriage and Social Exchange*. Unpublished Ph.D. dissertation, Cornell University.

Cramb, R., and Dixon, Gale. 1988. "Development in Sarawak: An Overview." In R. Cramb and Robert Reece (eds.), *Development in Sarawak: Historical and Contemporary Perspectives*, pp. 1–20. Monash Papers on Southeast Asia No. 17. Melbourne: Monash University.

Cresswell, Colin. 1978. *Rajah Charles Brooke: Monarch of All He Surveyed*. Kuala Lumpur, Malaysia: Oxford University Press.

Crosby, R.O. 1999. *The Musket Wars: A History of Inter-Iwi Conflict, 1806–45*. Auckland: Reed.

Cushman, Jennifer. 1993. *Fields from the Sea: Chinese Junk Trade with Siam During the Late Eighteenth and Early Nineteenth Century*. Ithaca, NY: Cornell University Press.

Deegan, James. 1973. *Change among the Lun Bawang, a Borneo People.* Unpublished Ph.D. dissertation, University of Washington.

Deegan, James. 1974. "Community Fragmentation among the Lun Bawang." *Sarawak Museum Journal* XXII:229–47.

Dening, Greg. 1988. *History's Anthropology.* Lanham, MD: University Press of America.

Dirks, Nicholas. 1992. *Colonialism and Culture.* Ann Arbor: University of Michigan Press.

Dunn, F.L. 1975. *Rain-Forest Collectors and Traders: A Study of Resource Utilization in Modern and Ancient Malaya.* Monograph No. 5. Kuala Lumpur: Malaysian Branch of the Royal Asiatic Society.

Durkheim, Emile. 1965 [original 1912]. *The Elementary Forms of the Religious Life.* New York: Free Press.

Dyen, Isidor. 1965. "The Lexicostatistical classification of the Austronesian Languages." *International Journal of Linguistics.* Memoir 19.

Eliade, Mircea. 1964. *Shamanism: Archaic Techniques of Ecstasy.* Princeton, NJ: Princeton University Press.

Everett, Harold. 1908. "History of Santubong of Sarawak." *Journal of the Straits Branch of the Royal Asiatic Society* 51:1–6.

Fallers, Lloyd. 1965. *Bantu Bureaucracy: A Century of Political Evolution among the Basoga of Uganda.* Chicago: The University of Chicago Press.

Fitzgerald, Charles. 1973. *The Tower of Five Glories.* Westport, CT: Hyperion.

Ford, John. 1938. "Borak and Belles." In Tom Harrisson (ed.), *Borneo Jungle: An Account of the Oxford University Expedition of 1932,* pp. 63–120. London: Drummond.

Forrest, Thomas. 1779. *A Voyage to New Guinea and the Moluccas Islands from Balambangan: Including an Account of Magindano, Sooloo and Other Islands.* London: G. Scott.

Fortes, Meyer. 1949. *The Web of Kinship among the Tallensi.* Oxford: Oxford University Press.

Fortune, Reo. 1935. *Manus Religion.* Lincoln: University of Nebraska Press.

Fox, James. (ed.). 1993. *Inside Austronesian Houses: Perspectives on Domestic Designs for Living.* Canberra: Australian National University.

Fox, James. 2000. "Maritime Communities in the Timur and Arafura Region." In Sue O'Connor and Peter Veth (eds.), *East of the Wallace Line: Studies of Past and Present Maritime Cultures of the Indo-Pacific Region,* pp. 337–56. Rotterdam: Balkema.

Francis, Peter. 1986. *Chinese Glass Beads: A Review of the Evidence.* Contributions of the Center for Bead Research, Bulletin No. 2. Lake Placid, NY: Lapis Route Books.

Francis, Peter. 1989a. *Beads and the Bead Trade in Southeast Asia.* Contributions of the Center for Bead Research, Bulletin No. 4. Lake Placid, NY: Lapis Route Books.

Francis, Peter. 1989b. *Heirloom and Ethnographic Beads in Southeast Asia.* Contributions of the Center for Bead Research, Bulletin No. 6. Lake Placid, NY: Lapis Route Books.

Francis, Peter. 2002. *Asia's Maritime Bead Trade, 300 B.C. to the Present*. Honolulu: University of Hawaii Press.

Frazer, James. 1963 [1890]. The Golden Bough. New York: Macmillan.

Freeman, Derek. 1970 [original 1955]. *Report on the Iban*. London: Athlone.

Freeman, Derek. 1981. *Some Reflections on the Nature of Iban Society*. Canberra: Research School of Pacific Studies.

Friedman, Jonathan. 1974. "Marxism, Structuralism, and Vulgar Materialism." *Man* 9:444–69.

Furness, William. 1902. *The Home-Life of Borneo Headhunters*. Philadelphia: Lippincott.

Galvin, A.D. 1972. "A Sebop Dirge." *Brunei Museum Journal* 2:1–75.

Galvin, A.D. 1982. "The Passing of a Kenyah, Chief: The Honourable, Senator Dato, Temmenggong Aban, Lawai Jau. *Sarawak Museum Journal* XXX:83–90.

Geddes, William. 1957. *Nine Dayak Nights*. Oxford: Oxford University Press.

Gibson, Thomas. 1990. *On Predatory States in Island Southeast Asia*. Canberra: Research School of Pacific Studies.

Gladney, Dru. 1991. *Muslim Chinese: Ethnic Nationalism in the Peoples' Republic*. Cambridge, MA: Harvard University Press.

Gluckman, Max. 1963. *Order and Rebellion in Tribal Africa*. London: Cohen and West.

Gockel, Guido. 1974. "The Long Pokun Sebop." *Sarawak Museum Journal* 22: 325–9.

Goldman, Richard. 1968. "The Beginnings of Commercial Development in the Baram and Marudi Following the Cession of 1882." *Sarawak Gazette* 94:54–66.

Gregory, Chris. 1982. *Gifts and Commodities*. London: Academic Press.

Groeneveldt, W.P. 1880. "Notes on the Malay Archipelago and Malacca Compiled from Chinese Sources." *Verhandelingen van het Bataviaasch Genootschap van Kusten En Wetenschappen* XXXIX:1–87.

Hacking, Ian. 1999. *The Social Construction of What?* Cambridge, MA: Harvard University Press.

Haddon, Alfred. 1901. *Headhunters Black, White and Brown*. London: Methuen.

Hall, D.G.E. 1981 [1955]. *A History of Southeast Asia*, 4th ed. New York: St. Martin's Press.

Hall, Kenneth. 1985. *Maritime Trade and State Development in Early Southeast Asia*. Honolulu: University of Hawaii Press.

Handler, Richard. 1988. *Nationalism and the Politics of Culture in Quebec*. Madison: University of Wisconsin Press.

Hansen, Eric. 1988. *Stranger in the Forest: On Foot Across Borneo*. London: Century.

Hardt, Michael, and Negri, Antonio. 2000. *Empire*. Cambridge, MA: Harvard University Press.

Harrisson, Tom. (ed.). 1939. *Borneo Jungle: An Account of the Oxford University Expedition of 1832*. London: Lindsay Drummond.

Harrisson, Tom. 1950. "Kelabit, land Dayak and Related Glass Beads in Sarawak." *Sarawak Museum Journal* 5:201–20.

Bibliography

Harrisson, Tom. 1956. "Origins and Attitudes of Brunei Tutong – Belait – Bukit – Dusun and Sarawak 'Bisayan,' Meting and Other Peoples." *Sarawak Gazette* 80: 293–321.

Harrisson, Tom. 1959. *World Within: A Borneo Story*. London: Cresset.

Harrisson, Tom. 1970. *The Malays of South-West Sarawak before Malaysia: A Socio-Ecological Survey*. London: Macmillan.

Harrisson, Tom, and O'Connor, Stanley. 1968. "The Pre-Historic Iron Industry in the Sarawak River Delta." *Sarawak Museum Journal* 16:1–54.

Helliwell, Christine. 1993. "Good Walls Make Bad Neighbours: The Dayak Long-house as a Community of Voices." In James Fox (ed.), *Inside Austronesian Houses*, pp. 44–63. Canberra: Australian National University.

Herbert, Patricia, and Milner, Anthony. (eds.). 1989. *Southeast Asia: Languages and Literature*. Honolulu: University of Hawaii Press.

Hertz, Robert. 1960 [1907]. *Death and the Right Hand*. New York: Free Press.

Hobsbawm, Eric. 1968. *Industry and Empire*. London: Pelican.

Hong, Evelyne. 1987. *Natives of Sarawak: Survival in Borneo's Vanishing Forests*. Penang: Institut Masyarakat.

Horton, A.V. 1995. *A New Sketch of the History of Brunei*. Bordesley, UK: A.V. Horton.

Hose, Charles. 1927. *Fifty Years of Romance and Research, or, a Jungle Wallah at Large*. London: Hutchinson.

Hose, Charles, and McDougall, William. 1912. *The Pagan Tribes of Borneo*. Volumes I and II. London: Macmillan.

Hoskins, Janet. (ed.). 1996. *Headhunting and the Social Imagination in Southeast Asia*. Stanford, CA: Stanford University Press.

Howell, Signe, and Sparkes, Stephen. (eds.). 1999. *The House in Southeast Asia*. Honolulu: Curzon.

Hudson, Alfred. 1978. "Linguistic Relations among Bornean Peoples with Special Reference to Sarawak." *Studies in Third World Societies* 3:1–44.

Hughes-Hallett, H.R. 1940. "A Sketch of the History of Brunei." *Journal of the Malayan Branch of the Royal Asiatic Society* 18:10–52.

Hutterer, Karl. 1974. "The Evolution of Philippines Lowland Societies." *Mankind* 9:287–99.

Hymes, Dell. 1968. "Linguistic Problems in Defining the Concept of 'Tribe.'" In June Helm (ed.), *Essays on the Problem of the Tribe: Proceedings of the 1967 Annual Spring Meeting of the American Ethnological Society*, pp. 46–68. Seattle: University of Washington Press.

James, Lawrence. 1994. *The Rise and Fall of the British Empire*. New York: St. Martin's.

Janowski, Monica. 1998. "Beads, Prestige and Life among the Kelabit of Sarawak, East Malaysia." In Lidia Sciama and Joanne Eicher (eds.), *Beads and Beadmakers: Gender, Material Culture, and Meaning*, pp. 213–46. New York: Berg.

Jawan, Jayum. 1993. *The Iban Factor in Sarawak Politics*. Serdang: Universiti Pertanian Malaysia.

Jones, L.W. 1966. *The Population of Borneo: A Study of the Peoples of Sarawak, Sabah, and Brunei*. London: Athlone Press.

Kathirithamby-Wells, J., and Villiers, John. (eds.). 1990. *The Southeast Asian Port and Polity*. Singapore: Singapore University Press.

Kaur, Amarjit. 1993. "Transport and the Sarawak, Economy, 1841–1983." *Borneo Research Bulletin* 25:76–100.

King, Michael. 2003. *The Penguin History of New Zealand*. Auckland: Penguin.

King, Victor. (ed.). 1978. *Essays on Borneo Societies*. Oxford: Oxford University Press.

King, Victor. 1991. "Brassware and Sarawak Cultures." In Lucas Chin and Valerie Mashman (eds.), *Sarawak Cultural Legacy: A Living Traditio*, pp. 155–64. Kuching: Atelier.

King, Victor. 1995. (ed.). *Explorers of South-East Asia: Six Lives*. Kuala Lumpur, Malaysia: Oxford University Press.

Kirch, Patrick. 1984. *The Evolution of the Polynesian Chiefdoms*. Cambridge: Cambridge University Press.

Kirsch, Thomas. 1973. *Feasting and Social Oscillation: Religion and Society in Upland Southeast Asia*. Ithaca, NY: Southeast Asia Program, Cornell University.

Lah Jau, Uyoh, and Munan, Heidi. 2001. "A Kayan Bead Song." *Sarawak Museum Journal* 77:19–28.

Lamb, Alastair. 1965. "Some Observations on Stone and Glass Beads in Early Southeast Asia." *Journal of the Malayan Branch of the Royal Asiatic Society* 38:87–124.

Langub, Jayl. 1991. "Orang Ulu Carving." In Lucas Chin and Valerie Mashman (eds.), *Sarawak Cultural Legacy*. Kuching: Atelier.

Langub, Jayl. 1992, July. "My Early Life in the Adang: Excerpts of an Interview with Datuk Racha Umong." *Sarawak Gazette* 1520:18–21.

Leach, Edmund. 1950. *Social Science Research in Sarawak*. London: His Majesty's Stationary Office.

Leach, Edmund. 1961. *Rethinking Anthropology*. London: Athlone Press.

Leach, Edmund. 1962. *Pul Eliya: A Village in Ceylon*. Cambridge: Cambridge University Press.

Leach, Edmund. 1964 [1954]. *Political Systems of Highland Burma*, 2nd ed. Boston: Beacon Press.

Leach, Edmund. 1968. "'Kachin' and 'Haka Chin': A Rejoinder to Levi-Strauss." *Man* 3:277–85.

Leh, Charles. 1993. *A Guide to Birds' Nest Caves and Birds' Nests of Sarawak*. Kuching: Sarawak Museum.

Leigh, Michael. 1974. *The Rising Moon: Political Change in Sarawak*. Sydney: Sydney University Press.

Leur, J.C. van. 1955. *Indonesian Trade and Society: Essays in Asian Social and Economic History*. The, Hague: Nijhoff.

Levi-Strauss, Claude. 1963. *Structural Anthropology*. New York: Basic Books.

Levi-Strauss, Claude. 1966. *The Savage Mind*. Chicago: University of Chicago Press.

Bibliography

Levi-Strauss, Claude. 1967. *Structural Anthropology*. New York: Anchor Books.

Levi-Strauss, Claude. 1969. *The Elementary Structures of Kinship*. Boston: Beacon Press.

Levi-Strauss, Claude. 1983. *The Way of the Masks*. London: Jonathan Capes.

Lim, J.S., and Shariffuddin, P.M. 1976. "Brunei Brass: The Traditional Method of Casting." *Brunei Museum Journal* 3:142–66.

Logan, J.R. 1848a. "Traces of the Origin of the Malay Kingdom of Borneo, with Notices of Its Condition When First Discovered by Europeans and at Later Periods." *Journal of the Indian Archipelago and Eastern Asia* 2:513–27.

Logan, J.R. 1848b. "Notices of European Intercourse with Borneo Proper Prior to the Establishment of Singapore in 1819." *Journal of the Indian Archipelago and Eastern Asia* 2:611–15.

Low, Hugh. 1848. *Sarawak: Its Inhabitants and Productions: Being Notes during a Residency in the Country with H.H. the Rajah Brooke*. London: Richard Bentley.

MacDonald, Malcolm. 1958. *Borneo People*. New York: Knopf.

Martin, Peter. 1990. "The Orang Belait of Brunei: Linguistic Affinities with the Lemeting (Meting)." *Borneo Research Bulletin* 22:130–8.

Maugham, Somerset. 1926. *The Casuarina Tree*. London: Allen and Unwin.

Mauss, Marcel. 1950. *Essai sur le Don*. Paris: Presses Universitaires.

Maxwell, Allen. 1996. "Headtaking and the Consolidation of Political Power in the Early Brunei State." In Janet Hoskins (ed.), *Headhunting and the Social Imagination in Southeast Asia*, pp. 90–126. Stanford, CA: Stanford University Press.

Maxwell, Allen. 1997. "The Ethnicity and Ethnohistory of the Kayan." In Robert Winzeler (ed.), *Indigenous People and the State: Politics, Land, and Ethnicity in the Malayan Peninsular and Borneo*. New Haven, CT: Yale University Press.

McDonald, Terrence. (ed.). 1996. *The Historic Turn in the Human Sciences*. Ann Arbor: University of Michigan Press.

McKinley, Robert. 1976. "Human and Proud of It! A Structural Treatment of Headhunting Rites and the Social Definition of Enemies." In George Appell (ed.), *Studies in Borneo Societies: Social Process and Anthropological Explanation*, pp. 92–126. De Kalb, IL: Center for Southeast Asian Studies.

Metcalf, Peter, and Huntington, Richard. 1991. *Celebrations of Death: The Anthropology of Mortuary Ritual*. Cambridge: Cambridge University Press.

Metcalf, Peter. 1974a. "The Baram District: A Survey of Kenyah, Kayan, and Penan Peoples." *Sarawak Museum Journal* XXII:29–40.

Metcalf, Peter. 1974b. "Berawan Adoption Practices." *Sarawak Museum Journal* XXII:275–86.

Metcalf, Peter. 1976a. "Birds and Deities in Borneo." *Bijdragen tot de Taal-, Land-, en Volkenkunde* 132:96–123.

Metcalf, Peter. 1976b. "Fishing in Sarawak's Biggest Lake." *Sarawak Gazette* 1193.

Metcalf, Peter. 1976c. "Who Are the Berawan? Ethnic Classification and the Distribution of Secondary Treatment of the Dead in Central North Borneo." *Oceania* XLVII:85–105.

Metcalf, Peter. 1977. "Berawan Mausoleums." *Sarawak Museum Journal* 24:121–38.

Metcalf, Peter. 1981. "Meaning and Materialism: The Ritual Economy of Death." *Man* 16:563–78.

Metcalf, Peter. 1982. *A Borneo Journey into Death: Berawan Eschatology from Its Rituals.* Philadelphia: University of Pennsylvania Press.

Metcalf, Peter. 1987. "Wine of the Corpse: Endocannibalism and the Great Feast of the Dead in Borneo." *Representations* 17:96–109.

Metcalf, Peter. 1989. *Where Are You, Spirits: Style and Theme in Berawan Prayer.* Washington, DC: Smithsonian Institution Press.

Metcalf, Peter. 1992. "Aban Jau's Boast." *Representation* 37:136–50.

Metcalf, Peter. 1996. "Images of Headhunting." In Janet Hoskins (ed.), *Headhunting and the Social Imagination in Southeast Asia*, pp. 249–90. Stanford, CA: Stanford University Press.

Metcalf, Peter. 2001a. "Global 'disjuncture' and the 'sites' of anthropology." *Cultural Anthropology* 16:1–18.

Metcalf, Peter. 2001b. "Diaspora vs. Volkerwanderung: The Orang Ulu Apparition." In Jukka Siikala (ed.), *Departures: How Societies Distribute Their People*, pp. 46–66. Helsinki: Finish Anthropological Society.

Metcalf, Peter. 2002a. *They Lie, We Lie: Getting on with Anthropology.* London: Routledge.

Metcalf, Peter. 2002b. "Hulk Hogan in the Rainforest." In Timothy Craig and Richard King (eds.), *Global Goes Local: Popular Culture in Asia*. Vancouver: University of British Columbia Press.

Metcalf, Peter. 2008. "Islands without Horizons: Rivers, Rainforests, and Mariners." In Clifford Sather and Timo Kaartinen (eds.), *Beyond the Horizon: Essays in Myth, History and Travel*, pp. 37–50. Helsinki: Finish Literature Society.

Miles, Douglas. 1965. "Socio-economic Aspects of Secondary Burial." *Oceania* 35:161–74.

Mills, J.V. 1974. "Arab and Chinese Navigators in Malaysian Waters in about A.D. 1500." *Journal of the Malaysian Branch of the Royal Asiatic Society* 97:1–82.

Milne, R.S. 1967. *Government and Politics in Malaysia.* Boston: Houghton Mifflin.

Morgan, Lewis Henry. 1965 [1881]. *Houses and House-Life of the American Aborigines.* Chicago: The University of Chicago Press.

Morgan, Lewis Henry. 1870. *Systems of Consanguinity and Affinity of the Human Family.* Washington, D.C.: Smithsonian Institution Press.

Morris, Stephen. 1953. *Report on a Melanau Sago Producing Community in Sarawak.* London: Stationary Office.

Morris, Stephen. 1980. "Slaves, Aristocrats, and Export of Sago in Sarawak." In James Watson (ed.), *Asian and African Systems of Slavery*, pp. 293–308. Oxford: Blackwell.

Morris, Stephen. 1991. *The Oya Melanau.* Kuching: Malaysian Historical Society.

Morrison, Alastair. 1988. "Development in Sarawak in the Colonial Period: A Personal Memoir." In R. Cramb and R. Reece (eds.), *Development in Sarawak*, pp. 35–48. Melbourne: Monash University Press.

Bibliography

Morrison, Alastair. 1993. *Fair Land Sarawak: Some Recollections of an Expatriate Official*. Ithaca, NY: Cornell University Press.

Munan, Heidi. 1988. "The Southwell Collection of Kayan Beads." *Sarawak Museum Journal* 34:105–9.

Munan, Heidi. 1991. "Beads." In Lucas Chin and Valerie Mashman (eds.), *Sarawak Cultural Legacy: A Living Tradition*, pp. 177–90. Kuching: Atelier.

Munan, Heidi. 1995. "Lun Bawang Beads." *Sarawak Museum Journal* 48:49–64.

Needham, Rodney. 1954a. "Penan and Punan." *Journal of the Malayan Branch of the Royal Asiatic Society* VVVII:75–83.

Needham, Rodney. 1954b. "The System of Teknonyms and Death-Names of the Penan." *Southwestern Journal of Anthropology* 10:1–22.

Needham, Rodney. 1955. "A Note on Ethnic Classification in Borneo." *Journal of the Malayan Branch of the Royal Asiatic Society* XXVIII:167–71.

Needham, Rodney. 1958. "Punan Ba." *Journal of the Malayan Branch of the Royal Asiatic Society* XXVII:24–36.

Needham, Rodney. 1964. "Blood, Thunder, and the Mockery of Animals." *Sociologus* 14:136–49.

Nicholls, Robert. (ed.). 1975. *European Sources for the History of the Sultanate of Brunei in the Sixteenth Century*. Brunei: Brunei Museum.

Nieuwenhuis, Anton W. 1901. "Mededelingen over het Vervolg der Commissiereis naar Centraal-Borneo." *Tijdschrift van het Koninklijk Nederlandsch Aardrijkskundig Genootschap* 18:1013–73.

Nieuwenhuis, Anton W. 1904. *Quer durch Borneo: Ergebnisse seiner Reisen in den Jahren 1896–7 und 1898–1900*. Leiden, The Netherlands: Brill.

Nooteboom, C. 1939. "Versieringen van Manggarische, Huizen." *Tijdschrift voor Indische Taal-, Land-, en Volkenkude* 79:221–38.

Nyipa, Hang. 1956. "Migrations of the Kayan People." *Sarawak Museum Journal* 7:82–9.

Ooi, Keat Gin. 1992. "Education in Sarawak, 1841–1963." *Borneo Research Bulletin* 24:62–7.

Pelzer, Karl. 1945. *Pioneer Settlement in the Asiatic Tropics*. New York: American Geographical Society.

Peranio, Roger. 1972. "Bisaya." In Frank Lebar (ed.), *Ethnic Groups of Insular Southeast Asia*, Volume I, pp. 163–66. New Haven, CT: Human Relations Area Files Press.

Pigafetti, Antonio. (1525?). "Primo Viaggio intorno el Mondo." In Emma Blai and James Robertson (eds.), 1903–9 *The Philippine Islands 1493–1803: Explorations by Early Navigators, Descriptions of the Islands and Their Peoples, Their History and Records of the Catholic, Mission, as Related in Contemporaneous, Books and Manuscripts, Showing the Political, Economic, Commercial and Religious, Conditions of Those Islands from the Earliest, Times to the Beginning of the Nineteenth Century*. XXXIII: 25–267, XXXIV:38–180. Cleveland: A.H. Clarke.

Pollard, F.H. 1933. "The Muruts." *Sarawak Museum Journal* 4:139–55.

Pollard, F.H. 1935. "Some Comparative Notes on Muruts and Kelabits." *Sarawak Museum Journal* 4:223–7.

Pollard, F.H., and Banks, E. 1937. "Teknonymy and Other Customs among the Kayans, Kenyahs and Klemantans and Others." *Sarawak Museum Journal* 4:395–409.

Porritt, Vernon. 1997. *British Colonial Rule in Sawak 1946–63*. Kuala Lumpur, Malaysia: Oxford University Press.

Porritt, Vernon. 2004. *The Rise and Fall of Communism in Sarawak 1940–1990*. Clayton: Monash Papers on Southeast Asia.

Prentice, David. 1970. "The Linguistic Situation in North Borneo." In S.A. Wurm and D.S. Laycock (eds.), *Pacific Linguistic Studies in Honour of Arthur Capell*, pp. 369–408. Canberra: Research School of Pacific Studies.

Pringle, Robert. 1970. *Rajahs and Rebels: The Ibans of Sarawak under Brooke Rule, 1841–1941*. Ithaca: Cornell university Press.

Reece, Robert. (n.d.). *Masa Jepun: Sarawak Under the Japanese 1941–1945*. Kuching: Sarawak Literary Society.

Reece, Robert. 1982. *The Name of Brooke: The End of White Rajah Rule in Sarawak*. Kuala Lumpur, Malaysia: Oxford University Press.

Reece, Robert. 1988. "Economic Development under the Brookes." In R. Cramb and R. Reece (eds.), *Development in Sarawak*, pp. 21–34. Melbourne: Monash University.

Reid, Anthony. 1989. "The Organisation of Production in the Pre-colonial Southeast Asian Port City." In Frank Broeze (ed.), *Brides of the Sea: Port Cities of Asia from 16th–20th Centuries*. Honolulu: University of Hawaii Press.

Revel, Nicole. 1988. *Le Riz en Asie du Sud-est: Atlas du Vocabulaire de la Plante*. Paris: Ecole des Hautes, Etudes en Sciences Sociales.

Ritchie, James. 1987. *A Gentleman's Victory for Taib Mahmud*. Kuala Lumpur, Malaysia: Pelanduk.

Rosaldo, Renato. 1980. *Ilongot Headhunting, 1883–1974*. Stanford, CA: Stanford University Press.

Roseberry, William. 1991. *Anthropologies and Histories: Essays in Culture, History, and Political Economy*. New Brunswick, NJ: Rutgers University Press.

Rousseau, Jerome. 1978. "The Kayan." In Victor King (ed.), *Essays on Borneo Societies*, pp. 78–92. Oxford: Oxford University Press.

Rousseau, Jerome. 1979. "Kayan Stratification." *Man* 14:215–36.

Rousseau, Jerome. 1980. "Iban Inequality." *Bijdragen tot de Taal-, Land- en Volkenkunde* 136:52–63.

Rousseau, Jerome. 1990. *Central Borneo: Ethnic Identity and Social Life in a Stratified Society*. Oxford: Clarendon Press.

Rousseau, Jerome. 1998. *Kayan Religion: Ritual Life and Religious Reform in Central Borneo*. Leiden, The Netherlands: KITLV Press.

Rowley, C.D. 1965. *The New Guinea Villager*. Melbourne: Chesire.

Runciman, Steven. 1960. *The White Rajahs: A History of Sarawak from 1841 to 1946*. Cambridge: Cambridge University Press.

Rutter, Owen. 1929. *The Pagans of North Borneo*. London: Hutchinson.

Sabang, Clement Langat. 1991. "Lg. Pekun Chebup and their Migration." *Sarawak Gazette* 1518:21–9.

Sahlins, Marshall D. 1963. "Poor Man, Rich Man, Big Man, Chief: Political Types of Melanesia and Polynesia." *Comparative Studies in Society and History* 5:285–303.

Sahlins, Marshall D. 1968. *Tribesmen*. Englewood Cliffs, NJ: Prentice-Hall.

Sahlins, Marshall D. 1998. "Two or Three Things That I Know about Culture." *Journal of the Royal Anthropological Institute* 5:399–421.

Salemink, Oscar. 1991. "The Invention and Appropriation of Vietnam's Montagnards from Sabatier to the CIA." In George Stocking (ed.), *Colonial Situations*, pp. 243–84. Madison: University of Wisconsin Press.

Salmond, Anne. 1975. *Hui: A Study of Maori Ceremonial Gatherings*. Wellington, New Zealand: A.H. & A.W. Reed.

Sandin, Benedict. 1958. "Some Niah Folklore and Origins." *Sarawak Museum Journal* 8:646–62.

Sandin, Benedict. 1967. *The Sea Dayaks of Borneo before White Rajah Rule*. Glasgow: Maclehose.

Sandin, Benedict. 1973. "The Bisayah and Indigenous People of Limbang." *Sarawak Museum Journal* 21:41–51.

Sandin, Benedict. 1980. *The Living Legends: Borneans Telling Their Tales*. Kuala Lumpur, Malaysia: Dewan Bahasa dan Pustaka.

Sather, Clifford. 1979. "Recent Studies of the Orang Miri." *Borneo Research Bulletin* 11:42–6.

Schafer, Edward. 1963. *The Golden Peaches of Samarkand: A Study of T'ang Exotics*. Berkeley: University of California Press.

Schafer, Edward. 1967. *The Vermillion Bird: T'ang Images of the South*. Berkeley: University of California Press.

Schneider, David. 1977. "Kinship, Nationality, and Religion in American Culture: Towards a Definition of Kinship." In J. Dolgin, D. Kemnitzer, and D. Schneider (eds.), *Symbolic Anthropology: A Reader*. New York: Columbia University Press.

Schneider, David. 1984 (original 1968). *A Critique of the Study of Kinship*. Second Edition. Ann Arbor: University of Michigan Press.

Schneider, William. 1977. "Longhouse and Descent Group among the Selako Dayak." In William Wood (ed.), *Cultural-Ecological Perspectives on Southeast Asia*, pp. 83–101. Athens: Southeast Asia Program, Ohio University.

Seling, Sawing. 1974. "The Flight from the Usun Apau to the Headwaters of the Tinjar." *Sarawak Museum Journal* 22:331–9.

Shariffudin, P.M. 1969. "Brunei Cannon." *Brunei Museum Journal* 1:72–93.

Singh, Ranjit. 1984. *Brunei 1839–83: The Problems of Political Survival*. Singapore: Oxford University Press.

Siti Zaharah and Abang Haji Husaini. 1991. "Kain Songket and Salayah." In Lucas Chin and Valerie Mashman (eds.), *Sarawak Cultural Legacy: A Living Tradition*, pp. 91–106. Kuching: Atelier.

Sleen, van der. 1964. *A Handbook on Beads*. New York: Shumway.

Smith, W. Robertson. 1889. *Lectures on the Religion of the Semites: First Series. The Fundamental Institutions*. Edinburgh: Black.

Southwell, Hudson. 1999. *Uncharted Waters*. Calgary, Alberta, Canada: Astana.

St. John, Spenser. 1862. *Life in the Forests of the Far East, Volumes I and II*. London: Smith Elder.

Sutlive, Vinson. 1992. *Tun Jugah of Sarawak*. Kuala Lumpur, Malaysia: Penerbit Fajar Bakti.

Sweeney, P.L. Amin. 1968. "Silsilah Raja-raja Berunei." *Journal of the Malaysian Branch of the Royal Asiatic Society* XLI:1–82.

Tambiah, S.J. 1976. *World Conqueror and World Renouncer: A Study of Buddhism and Polity in Thailand*. Cambridge: Cambridge University Press.

Taussig, Michael. 1987. *Shamanism, Colonialism, and the Wild Man: A Study in Terror and Healing*. Chicago: The University of Chicago Press.

Teeter, K.V. 1963. "Lexicostatistics and Genetic Relationships." *Language* 39:638–48.

Tien, Ju-K'ang. 1953. *The Chinese of Sarawak*. London: London School of Economics.

Troulliot, Michel-Rolph. 1995. *Silencing the Past: Power and the Production of History*. Boston: Beacon Press.

Tsing, Anna. 1993. *In the Realm of the Diamond Queen*. Princeton, NJ: Princeton University Press.

Turner, Victor. 1967. *The Forest of Symbols*. Ithaca: Cornell University Press.

Tylor, Edward Burnett. 1871. *Primitive Culture*. London: John Murray.

Urquhart, I.A.N. 1959. "Nomadic Punans and Pennans." In Tom Harrison (ed.), *The Peoples of Sarawak*, pp. 73–89. Kuching: Sarawak Museum.

Wagner, Roy. 1967. *The Curse of Souw: Principles of Daribi Clan Formation and Alliance in New Guinea*. Chicago: The University of Chicago Press.

Wallerstein, Immanuel. 1976. *The Modern World System*, Volumes I and II. New York: Academic Press.

Wallerstein, Immanuel. 1983. *Historical Capitalism*. London: Verso.

Warren, James. 1981. *The Sulu Zone 1768–1898: The Dynamics of External Trade, Slavery and Ethnicity in the Transformation of a Southeast Asian Maritime State*. Singapore: Singapore University Press.

Waterson, Roxana. 1990. *The Living House: An Anthropology of Architecture in South-East Asia*. New York: Watson-Guptill.

Watts, Sheldon. 1997. *Epidemics and History: Disease, Power and Imperialism*. New Haven, CT: Yale University Press.

Wheatley, Paul. 1961. "Geographical Notes on Some Commodities Involved in Sung Maritime Trade." *Journal of the Malayan Branch of the Royal Asiatic Society* 186(32):5–140.

Whittier, Herbert. 1973. *Social Organisation and Symbols of Social Differentiation: An Ethnographic Study of the Kenyah Dayak of East Kalimantan*. Unpublished Ph.D. dissertation, Michigan State University.

Whittier, Herb. 1978. "The Kenyah." In Victor King (ed.), *Essays on Borneo Societies*, pp. 92–122. Oxford: Oxford University Press.

Wilken, G.A. 1884. "Het Animisme bij de Volken van den Indischen Archipel." *Indische Gids* IV(1):925–1000, IV(2):191–42.

Bibliography

Winters, Clyde-Ahmad. 1979. *Mao or Mohammad: Islam in the Peoples' Republic of China*. Hong Kong: Asian Research Service.

Winzeler, Robert L. (ed.). 1997. *Indigenous Peoples and the State: Politics, Land, and Ethnicity in the Malayan Peninsula and Borneo (Southeast Asia Studies Monograph Series)*. Monograph 46. New Haven, CT: Yale University Southeast Asian Studies.

Wolf, Eric. 1982. *Europe and the People without History*. Berkeley: University of California Press.

Wolters, O.W. 1967. *Early Indonesian Commerce: A Study of the Origins of Srivijaya*. Ithaca, NY: Cornell University Press.

Wong, Lin Ken. 1960. "The Trade of Singapore, 1819–69." *Journal of the Malayan Branch of the Royal Asiatic Society*. Special Issue No. 192 XXXIII:1–315.

Zainah, Ibrahim. 1982. "The Mirek: Islamized Indigenes of Northwestern Sarawak." *Contributions to Southeast Asian Ethnography* 1:3–18.

Index of Ethnonyms

Index of Ethnonyms

Malay, 59–60, 82, 131, 195, 264, 267, 271, 275, 282, 289–90, 309, 320
  as ethnonym in Sarawak, 16, 131, 206, 245, 296
  language, 73, 203–4, 269, 297–8
Maloh, 106
Melanau, 56–7, 160–61, 166
Melawan, *see* Berawan
Miri, 185
Murut, 130, 134–5, 160, 187–8

Narom, 184–5, 207

Orang Ulu, 15, 17, 298,
  see also Upriver People

Pelutan, 201, 204, 206, 209, 320
Penan, 76, 150, 185, 286, 290, 297

Sebop, 66–8, 72–4, 116, 192, 198, 200, 203–4, 251, 273
  migrations, 74–77, 80, 84–5, 90, 109, 176, 185, 293, 312
  ritual, 219020, 223, 226, 243

Tabun, 201–2
Tagal, 206, 294
Tring, 126, 128–9, 134, 186, 201, 215, 294, 296, 320

Upriver People *passim*, 15–18, 38, 52, 61, 73, 76, 119, 197, 239, 255, 261–2, 267–72
  as ethnonym, 20, 187, 189, 296–7, 321–2
  longhouse residence, 45–6, 62, 65, 243, 274, 309–10

Visaya, 189, 206, 294, 308

342

Index of Authors and Subjects